Good and Evil
After Auschwitz:
Ethical Implications for Today

Good and Evil After Auschwitz:

Ethical Implications for Today

edited by

Jack Bemporad, John T. Pawlikowski,
and Joseph Sievers

KTAV Publishing House, Inc.
Hoboken, New Jersey

Library of Congress Cataloging-in-Publication Data

Good and evil after Auschwitz : ethical implications for today / edited by Jack
Bemporad, John T. Pawlikowski, and Joseph Sievers.
    p. cm.
Includes bibliographical references.
ISBN 0-88125-692-7
    1. Auschwitz (Concentration camp)--Congresses. 2. Holocaust, Jewish
(1939-1945)--Moral and ethical aspects--Congresses. 3. Genocide--Moral and ethical
aspects--Congresses. I. Bemporad, Jack. II Pawlikowski, John. III Sievers, Joseph.

D804.3 .G662 2000
296.3'1174--dc21

                            00-061548

Distributed by
Ktav Publishing House, Inc.
900 Jefferson Street
Hoboken, NJ 07030
201-963-9524 FAX 201-963-0102
Email ktav@compuserve.com

Table of Contents

Part I. Thinking About God After Auschwitz

Part II. An Ethical Challenge

Part III: Philosophy Faced with the Shoah

Part IV: Within the Shoah

Part V: Proposals

Part VI: By Way of Conclusion

Dedication

God of our fathers,

you chose Abraham and his descendants

to bring your Name to the Nations:

we are deeply saddened

by the behaviour of those

who in the course of history

have caused these children of yours to suffer,

and asking your forgiveness

we wish to commit ourselves

to genuine brotherhood

with the people of the Covenant.

Jerusalem, 26 March 2000

Joannes Paulus II

Jerusalem, Israel (March 26, 2000):- A copy of the letter placed by Pope John Paul into a crevice of the Western Wall. The letter is to go on permanent display at Jerusalem's Yad Vashem Memorial of the Holocaust.

Acknowledgments

An international symposium and the publication of its proceedings require much energy and the cooperation of many people and institutions with diverse areas of expertise. We would therefore like to thank all those who in different ways have contributed to make this book possible.

The symposium was co-sponsored by SIDIC (Service International de Documentation Judéo-Chrétienne), by the Pontifical Gregorian University, and by the University of Rome "Tor Vergata." Our thanks go to his Excellency Archbishop Giuseppe Pittau, S.J., who as rector of the Pontifical Gregorian University enthusiastically endorsed and supported the idea of the symposium and agreed to host it in his institution. With him we would like to thank the staff and faculty of the Gregorian University who contributed to making the symposium a success. To the rector of the University of Rome "Tor Vergata," Prof. Alessandro Finazzi Agrò, our gratitude for making possible this cooperative venture between religious and public institutions in such a sensitive and important area.

We would like to thank Sr. Lucy Thorson, N.D.S., directress of the SIDIC Center, who has been in many ways the moving force that brought together people, institutions, and resources to make it all possible. Together with her, our thanks go to the dedicated staff of the SIDIC Center, as well as to the many volunteers, for the secretarial support and many other services they rendered.

A special thanks goes to Prof. Emilio Baccarini. In spite of his numerous other commitments, he selflessly served on the organizing committee from its very inception. To him we owe in particular the idea of the theme of the symposium and the structure of the present volume. Together with Lucy Thorson he co-edited the Italian version of the conference proceedings (*Il bene e il male dopo Auschwitz: Implicazioni etico-teologiche per l'oggi*, Milan: Paoline, 1998). We wish to thank also the other members of the organizing committee, namely Prof. Irene Kajon, Bro. William J. Martyn, S.A., Prof. Paul McNellis, S.J., and Prof. Arij Roest Crollius, S.J. Centro "Incontri Romani" generously provided much logistical support. Sr. Fernanda Di Monte, Directress of the Press Office of the Daughters of St. Paul in Milan, worked very hard and did a superb job in keeping relations with the media.

The symposium included speakers from Australia, Belgium, Canada, France, Germany, Israel, Italy, the Netherlands, Switzerland, the U.S., and the Vatican. They spoke in English, French, or Italian. To all of them our thanks for making the symposium and this volume possible. The impossible but necessary task of translating the Italian and French contributions by Baccarini, Carucci Viterbi, Dalmasso, Dupuy, Giuliani, Kajon, Meghnagi, and Rigobello into English was expertly handled by Ms. Leslie Wearne. Dr. Massimo Giuliani checked the notes, quotations, and bibliographic information.

An enterprise such as this would have been impossible without financial support from a variety of individuals and institutions. We would like to express sincere thanks to all those who generously contributed in one way or other, among whom we would like to name at least the following: Vitale Borghese & C., S.p.A., for a most generous grant; the Konrad Adenauer Foundation for the initial and continued support that gave the organizers the courage to go ahead with this project; the Congregation of Our Lady of Sion which gave much more than a financial contribution. Additional support came from The Franciscan Friars of the Atonement; The Society of Jesus; The Center for Christian-Jewish Understanding of Sacred Heart University, Fairfield, Connecticut; Banca di Roma; the English-language Catholic Parish of Geneva, Switzerland. We would further like to recognize the assistance received from Mr. Rolf Bloch, Dr. Victor Goldbloom, Dr. Frank Henderson, Mr. Edward Kossoy, Baron Edmond de Rothschild, Rev. Thomas Trepanier, and Mr. Boris Zalcman. The Marc Tanenbaum Foundation and Sir Sigmund Sternberg made grants specifically in support of the publication of this volume.

We are grateful to Mr. Bernard Scharfstein for having accepted to publish this volume through KTAV. The staff at KTAV was most helpful in making stylistic improvements, especially in the contributions of non-native English speakers.

Last not least we would like to thank the publishers who kindly gave permission to use selections from the following copyrighted material:

Moshe Flinker, "Young Moshe's Diary: The Spiritual Torment of a Jewish Boy in Nazi Europe". Jerusalem: Yad Vashem, 1965.

Etty Hillesum, Publisher: New York: Metropolitan Books; Henry Holt & Co., 1996

Dietrich Bonhoeffer, Ethics (NY: Simon & Schuster)

Preface

For each human being the question of *good* and *evil* represents a continuous challenge. We ask ourselves what is good and what is evil, why is this good and that, on the other hand, evil. We wish to understand what is the relationship between the Creator, who found all that He had made "*was indeed good*" (Gen. 1:31), and evil, which is so much part of our lives. How does a God who is goodness itself permit such abuse of the beauty that He himself has made, such defiance of the laws that He has given, such intolerance and violence between the children that He has made in His own image and likeness (Gen. 1:27)? These questions illustrate the paradox of our own existence: the presence of evil is the consequence of that very freedom that God has given to us and thanks to which we are able to reject evil and choose good.

Each of us is confronted by the alternatives that God, through the prophet Moses, placed before His people: "See. I have set before you today life and prosperity, death and adversity... choose life so that you and your descendants may live, loving the Lord your God, obeying Him, and holding fast to Him" (Deut. 30:15, 19).

And yet, the sons and daughters of this very people were destined for total extermination by nazism; they were condemned to death. According to Pope John Paul II's words, the terrible fate of European Jews during the time of Auschwitz has become a "symbol of the aberration of which man is capable when he turns against God."[1]

While describing that period as "one of the darkest and most tragic moments in history," the Pope made the following reference to the *Shoah*: "It was a darkening of reason, conscience, and the heart. Recalling the triumph of evil cannot fail to fill us with deep sorrow, in fraternal solidarity with all who bear the indelible scars of those tragedies.Unfortunately, however, our days continue to be marked by great violence. God forbid that tomorrow we will have to weep over other Auschwitzes of our time. Let us pray and work that this may not happen."[2] For this reason, the interventions made by the participants to the International Symposium "Good and Evil After Auschwitz, Ethical Implications for Today" have been so important. The Pope, in one of his addresses to the Diplomatic Corps at the Holy See, asserted: "Glancing at the world today, we can only state with deep regret that too many human beings are still their brother's victims."[3]

The theme of the Symposium led us to examine these questions and to learn from our joint reflection, in order to prevent evil from prevailing over good in the future, as happened at Auschwitz. The *Shoah* and Auschwitz (together with the names of all extermination camps that recall for us the unspeakable crimes committed by nazism during the Second World War), are still a symbol of how evil triumphs when society loses its respect for God and its respect for humankind. Those tragedies have forced us to seek new philosophical, anthropological, ethical and theological orientations. It is sad to have to admit that this search has come "after Auschwitz" and because of Auschwitz. This is also true for the progress in Catholic-Jewish relations. And yet, this progress has enabled us to rediscover that "Christians and Jews together have a great deal to offer to a world struggling to distinguish good from evil, a world called by the Creator to defend and protect life but so vulnerable to voices which propagate values that only bring death and destruction."[4]

This is my heartfelt wish: may our various joint initiatives, such as the Symposium, the acts of which are contained in this volume, help humanity to progress without delay or any turning back along the path that leads to the creation of a global family, in which good will prevail over evil!

Cardinal Edward I. Cassidy

[4th June 1998]

NOTES

1. Pope John Pall II, Encyclical Letter *Centeslmus Annnus* (1991).
2. Pope John Paul II, on the occasion of the fiftieth anniversary of the release of prisoners from the concentration camp of Auschwitz, before praying the *Angelus* on Sunday, January 29th, 1995.
3. 15th January 1994.
4. Pope John Paul II, on the occasion of the Concert at the Vatican commemorating the *Shoah*, 7th April 1994.

Foreword

In September 1997 some thirty scholars gathered at the Pontifical Gregorian University in Rome under the sponsorship of S.I.D.C. (International Service of Jewish Christian Documentation), the Gregorian University and the University of Rome "Tor Vergata" for a three-day conference focused on issues of good and evil in light of the Shoah. They were joined by several hundred additional participants in an in-depth probe of human meaning in the face of the monstrous evil unveiled during the Nazi era. What can we assert about ethics and theology when confronted by the Shoah? The question was examined from a variety of perspectives, some looking back to religious and secular perspectives that have been part and parcel of Western History for centuries while others turned their attention primarily to what might be an adequate post-Shoah morality. This volume presents a selection of the papers presented during this important symposium. Its authors represent several disciplines and geographic regions. They are not in total agreement as to how to understand ethical commitment after the Shoah. But they are all convinced that we cannot speak about ethics after the Shoah in the same manner as we did prior to this cataclysmic event in human history.

Professor Steven Katz of Boston University has argued that there is simply no way we can "fit" the evil at the heart of the Shoah within existing moral categories. The Shoah has transformed the way we need to think about fundamental theological understandings both within Christianity and Judaism. For both communities, issues such as the continuing presence of God, covenant, power, human responsibility, etc. are on the table in a new way. And for Christians Christology and the self-understanding of the Church call out for restatement as well in light of the Shoah.

The volume begins with the keynote papers by two of the foremost thinkers on theology after the Shoah, Professors Emil Fackenheim and Johann Baptist Metz. Fackenheim was one of the earliest Jewish scholars to think through the significance of the Holocaust for Jewish faith. He is well-known for his conviction, that the image of God was destroyed during the Holocaust and that the task facing the human community stated forcefully in his volume *The Jewish Return Into History* today, especially the survivors of the Shoah, is to restore the divine image, but in a way that conveys a sense of a new curtailment of divine power in comparisons with past images. Professor Metz has been unquestionably the foremost proponent within the international Catholic scholarly community of the necessity of taking the Shoah as a fundamental "datum" for all theological expressions in our day. He has underlined that the post-Shoah Christian theology cannot be done apart from a relationship to Jews and their religious tradition. After the Shoah the Christian churches are summoned not only to revise the theology of their relationship to the Jewish people, but to revise their theology as such since all Christian theology in the past has been premised on the notion that Christians replaced Jews in the covenantal relationship with God.

In their contributions to this symposium Professors Fackenheim and Metz continue their pursuit of themes that have been the hallmark of their writings. Fackenheim insists once more that the Shoah represents the most challenging assault on the Abrahamic covenant that human history has witnessed. It therefore demands a response from Jews, Christians and Muslims. The responses will not follow an entirely parallel path because, in the case of Christianity, there is need to expunge the tradition of theological anti-Judaism, which continued to play a role in concrete decisions to rescue or not rescue Jews during the Third Reich. Metz's contribution extends his previous critique of the whole of Christian theology to the prevailing postmodernist cultural scene that dominates much of Europe and beyond in our time. He speaks of the Shoah as a basic challenge to cultural amnesia. The current cultural scene demonstrates a lost ability to "remember." Recapturing the memory of those who perished under the Nazis is one way human society today can break through our current cultural malaise.

Three scholars, Rabbi Jack Bemporad, Rabbi Benedetto Carucci Viterbi, and John T. Pawlikowski, wrestle with the implications of the Shoah for imaging God in our time. Rabbi Carucci's response is rooted primarily in a classical perspective "God's hiding of himself" while Bemporad and Pawlikowksi are less inclined to accept retrieval as the basis for God-perception today. An underplayed notion in Lurianic Kabbalah developed in the twentieth century by the great master of Jewish tradition Rabbi Joseph Soloveitchik serves as the focal point of Carucci's essay. This notion describes God as having withdrawn to a degree from direct involvement in human affairs and left humanity with a high degree of human autonomy which, in the end, can be exercised responsibly only within a framework of human solidarity and direct experience of "ain" or the "nothing" in the Jewish mystical tradition.

Bemporad is not quite as sanguine as Carucci that a mere retrieval of the Jewish mystical tradition's sense of God's hidden face will suffice after the Shoah. He does agree with Carucci that the Shoah has exposed us to "a kind of drastic limitation of God's activity in the world," though he stresses that this does not leave God powerless or impotent in human affairs. For

Bemporad the confrontation with the Shoah found in the writings of Emil Fackenheim, Henry Slonimsky and particularly Hans Jonas show a way of taking the traditional notion of divine limitation into a modern, post-Shoah context.

For Pawlikowski the Shoah requires a major reformulation of our understanding of human and divine agency. We need to rediscover a sense of a "compelling God" if we are to have a moral foundation for human activity. Such a "compelling God" cannot be recovered from tradition alone, whether biblical or post-biblical but must involve a forging of biblical perspectives with modern consciousness' understanding of human liberation. Pawlikowski feels that Irving Greenberg has moved us in significant direction in this regard, though he has exaggerated the transformation of divine and human responsibility in the face of the Shoah.

Professor Maureena Fritz picks up on Pawlikowski's call for Christological reformulation. She does so in a more limited context, however, not relating such reformulation directly to the effort to re-image God after the Shoah. Her approach involves recognition of changing paradigm shifts throughout Christian history, including most recently at the Vatican Council. We require another paradigm shift in her perspective in response to the Shoah. That shift involves a move from emphasizing a Christ-centered" Christology which is exclusivist and often triumphal to stress on a God-centered" Christology which paves the way for greater recognition of, and solidarity with, the Jewish people.

In the final essay in Section I, Dr. Dirk Ansorge, who lectures at the Catholic Academy of Essen, Germany, carries on the God-theme after the Shoah, specifically relating it to the question of universal reconciliation. What role can God play in such a process of reconciliation? Is God to be the one who forgives? No, not alone, says Ansorge. Rather God must honor the decision of the victims regarding such reconciliation even if it is a refusal at this moment to forgive. But Ansorge, following the line of thought advanced by Emananuel Levinas, maintains that God retains the capacity to "woo" such reconciliation while respecting human autonomy, especially among the victims.

Dr. Ansorge's discussion of reconciliation in light of the Shoah serves as a transition to the second part of this volume, which centers on specific ethical questions raised by the event. Professor Emilio Baccarini begins this section with an in-depth discussion of how we can speak of the human person after the Shoah. Elie Wiesel put this issue in the forefront of post-Shoah discussion when, in responding to the question of a young Jew at a conference at Northwestern University some years ago as to how Wiesel could maintain any semblance of God-belief after the Shoah, he said to the questioner that the real issue was not whether he could believe in God any longer but whether he could still believe in the human person. Baccarini surveys a group of philosophers such as Karl Jaspers, Emmanuel Mournier, and Emmanuel Levinas, as well as thinkers such as Elie Wiesel and Primo Levi, for possible answers to the restoration of human dignity after the Shoah. Baccarini does believe it is possible to work through the challenge to human integrity created by the Shoah, but only with difficulty. It will be necessary to affirm a certain continuing human fragility which in fact in the end becomes an ethical imperative against killing and which, as a result establishes sociality as the "mutual recognition of the other's need."

Professor Peter Haas, who has written on the topic of ethics after the Shoah in his volume *Morality After Auschwitz,* repeats the basic thesis advanced in that work and then builds on it in his contributions to the present volume. In *Morality After Auschwitz* Haas argued that the Shoah did not result from random acts of violence. It was rather a systematically thought-through "ethic" of a sort. That is the reason it was able to generate support from some scientists and thinkers of the period. The question Haas now probes in greater depth is how could intelligent people regard genocide as a morally acceptable moral option? His response in part is that Social Darwinism represented a significantly coherent moral alternative to classical ethics to override the older ethic in the mind of many cultured people. The lesson to be drawn from this, according to Haas, is that people are prone to accept any moral system that appears to them internally consistent and, more importantly, corresponds to their current worldview, whatever the actual content of that ethical system. Haas then asks whether the possibility exists of creating a "meta-mortality" that would allow for a more conscious evaluation of an ethical system such as that offered by the Nazis. Haas has no easy answer to this dilemma. But he insists that part of this effort must be the restoration of personal human consciousness in the development of an ethical stance. The destructive dimension of the Nazi ethic was that it "freed" people from the obligation to think through their personal moral posture because of the compelling nature of its all-embracing consistency.

Didier Pollefeyt, a younger scholar in ethics from the Catholic University of Leuven Belgium presents a response to the writings of Peter Haas on the morality of the Holocaust. Haas and Pollefeyt both have participated on an ongoing basis in an international group of scholars focusing on ethics after the Shoah. Pollefeyt surveys Haas' general line of argumentation regarding a "Nazi ethic" and indicates initially that such a term troubles him as it does Emil Fackenheim as well. He believes that the characteristics Haas puts forth for an ethic (coherence, non-contradiction and intuitive rightness) are insufficient. To assert that an ethical point of view can be asserted only within a contingent ethical framework, as Haas seems to argue, is for Pollefeyt both unwarranted and dangerous. Such a posture leaves us, according to Pollefeyt, with no basis for protesting crimes against people who fall outside the system. There needs to be a transnarrative foundation for judging the criminal actions of Nazis and similar other groups. Nazism should not be described as an "ethic," but rather as a comprehensive perversion of morality. Nazism in fact represents the supremacy of politics over ethics. For Pollefeyt the powerlessness and bankruptcies of objective morality during the Nazi era need not, in fact should not, lead to an embrace of ethical relativism and power positivism. We should not confuse fact and norm.

This section concludes with an essay by Etienne Lepicard, M.D., from the Hebrew University in Jerusalem and the Hadassah Hospital Medical School. As a practicing physician Dr. Lepicard addresses the contemporary implications of the Nazi medical experiments. He provides an overview of the Nazi program of sterilization and euthanasia as a background of the Nuremberg Code. The ten major points that comprise this code remain an important barometer for medical practice in our day. For Lepicard medicine during the period of the Third Reich reveals the disappearance and then a reintroduction of the patient as subject of medical practice. But the Shoah has also shown in unprecedented fashion medicine's inherent capacity for aggression. As medicine continues to gain increased power over life itself, the Code may no longer be totally viable. But it does continue to signify a profound change in the very nature of medicine that we can build on in our approach to medicine today.

In section three we move into a series of philosophical reflections on the Shoah. This was in the main the Italian contribution to the original conference. Four leading Italian thinkers, Armando Rigobello, Gianfranco Dalmasso, Stefano Levi Della Torre and Irene Kajon, are joined by Bernard Dupuy, O.P., of Paris in a search for meaningful philosophical foundations after the Shoah. Rigobello feels such foundations require a shift from a focus on human nature to an emphasis on the human condition. Methodologically we need to begin such a quest by employing a phenomenological method and then eventually shift into a hermeneutical framework. For Rigobello the Shoah represents a phenomenon of rationality overturned. While the roots of Nazism were certainly pagan, elements of the Enlightenment also contributed to the growth of Nazism. Christian ideals have become so disconnected for Rigobello from Christian faith. We can be helped in our recovery of morality today by studying the example of the victims. The Shoah uncovers the challenge to humanity to remain moral under extreme social conditions. Continued reflection on the Shoah will not easily resolve all our questions about God and evil. But it can help us understand better the roots of human wretchedness and how we might respond to them in a better way.

Dalmasso focuses his reflection on the significance of human judgment in the midst of a catastrophe such as the Shoah. As for several others in this volume, a principal mentor for him in such a reflection is Emmanuel Levinas. For Dalmasso, as for Ansorge, the principal Shoah issue is far more the human person rather than God. The human community needs to reformulate the way it speaks about God, especially the way it understands human responsibility in the face of divine power. The experience of the Shoah requires a radical redefinition of what it means to be human away from an ideal of self-mastery towards a sense of the person as "one who does not posses himself." Such a definition will open the possibility to the kind of moral judgment that was often lacking during the period of the Shoah.

Levi Della Torre examines central aspects of Nazi ideology such as racism, mythology, technological development and totalitarianism. He rejects the interpretation advanced by Zigmunt Bauman and others that the "Final Solution" was the result of a chain of subsequent decisions made within a "problem-solving framework. His critique here is reminiscent of Pollefeyt's critique of Haas. He rejects a functionalist approach to understanding the Shoah. For Levi Della Torre it resulted from ethical fragmentation in the use of technical power. Nazism failed to measure its activities against a more comprehensive moral picture.

Fr. Bernard Dupuy looks at the issues of evil through the lens of the writings of Hannah Arendt and Hans Jonas. Their reflections, he believes, take us beyond classical categories of evil as Professor Katz has urged. As Dupuy sees it, Arendt and Jonas are much closer than we may imagine at first, given their diverse language and tonality. Both point out in the end that the dark experience of the Shoah should give rise to a new summons to human responsibility. Both seem to think that a response to such a summons is a real possibility. Despite the evil that was the Shoah the human community is capable of genuine moral renewal.

Professor Irene Kajon takes us through the thought of André Neher and once again Emmanuel Levinas on the issue of good and evil after the Shoah. She is especially taken by the notion of the "Lord's suffering servant" in the Book of Isaiah. She believes that confronting the evil inherent in the Shoah requires that philosophers take seriously the testimony of its victims. Such confrontation cannot take place in an abstract vacuum. Neher and Levinas have taken philosophy beyond its previous parameters. They use a language drawn from Scripture as well as philosophy, but understand as well that language ultimately must give way to silence when speaking of the Shoah. For her this is the appropriate direction for philosophy after the Shoah.

The fourth section finds five scholars taking up diverse aspects of the Shoah. Eve Fleischner begins with a reflection based on her extensive research into rescuers during the Shoah, particularly French rescuers. While it is difficult to generalize about the character of those who risked their lives to save Jews during the Nazi era, she does find some commonalties. They see themselves as "ordinary people"; they are prone to non-violence; a fair number saw rescue as demanded by their Christian faith. Fleischner's question is why so few saw the link between faith and rescue? Her moral lesson for today is that we cannot allow the lives of many victims to be so dependent on a few. We need to create societies in which the human rights of all will be protected by social, political and legal structures.

The newly appointed rector of the Ecumenical Institute at Tantur near Jerusalem, Fr. Michael McGarry, C.S.P., explores the meaning of courage in the face of the Shoah. His essay complements Fleischner. While she highlights what she has gained from interviews with rescuers, McGarry surveys the ever-growing body of literature on the subject and looks for some threads of consistency among rescuers. He underscores some of the same characteristics of rescuers uncovered by Fleischner. He then examines the notion of courage in the writings of St. Thomas Aquinas and how this notion relates to the witness of the rescuers.

Massimo Giuliani understands the Shoah in a way that echoes several other chapters in this volume. He calls it the "apotheosis of an asserted knowledge of good and evil" which became possible in part through the bureaucracy of suspending or even eliminating any ethical doubt and autonomous judgment. He seems here close to the thinking of Peter Haas. The Shoah for him also represents the "star of irredemption" and the "broken bridge" of contemporary religious conscience. Judaism and Christianity are not totally submerged in its abyss. But to become genuine religions of redemption in the post-Shoah age both religious traditions will need to redefine their basic understanding of God and humanity.

David Meghnagi introduces us to two pieces from Marek Edelman, Second-in-Command of the Warsaw Ghetto Uprising. The first is a political report composed right after the end of World War II; the other an interview some thirty years later by Hanna Krall, a Polish Jewish writer, who was a young child during the time of the Shoah. Meghnagi analyzes Edelman's report and interview as a case study as it were of working through bereavement. He sees unresolved tension in Edelman regarding his relationship with other Jewish leaders of the period such as Mordecai Anielewicz. Meghnagi's account provides us with a personal portrait of how one Jewish leader had dealt with the face of evil that appeared during the Shoah.

Professor James Bernauer's contribution which rounds off section four takes us into an area that has been little explored thus far in studies on the Shoah. In a way he poses the same question that other authors in the volume such as Peter Haas have asked. Why were the Nazis so successful in co-opting so many into their system? For Bernauer a response to this question requires an understanding of the spiritual dynamics present in Germany as the Nazi party arose. He argues that there was a strong thirst for spiritual renewal in Germany at the time. But the Christian churches were ultimately unable to meet this quest for spiritual transformation because of the spirit-flesh dichotomy in Christian spirituality. The Nazis did a much better job in presenting a kind of "infleshed spirituality." The moral lesson we gain from a study of the period of the Shoah is that a successful ethic must take into account the vitalistic dimension of the human person. One cannot challenge the appearance of evil only on the intellectual plane. That was the failure of liberal morality during the Nazi era as Irving Greenberg has emphasized in his writings.

The volume concludes in sections five and six, with two essays and two more reflective pieces. Fr. Remi Hoeckman, O.P., Secretary of the Holy See's Commission for Religious Relations with Jews, offers a survey of Pope John Paul II's statements on good and evil in the light of the Shoah. Overall the present Pope has continued to remember the Shoah and its victims in order to ensure that evil does not prevail over good once more as it did under the Nazis.

Professor David Blumenthal presents a detailed plan for moral education after the Shoah. It is part of a larger project on "The Banality of Good And Evil: A Social-Psychological and Theological Reflection" which has appeared in book form. His goal is to ascertain why so many participated in the evil of the Nazis and equally why some did not. How did both responses come about? His tentative conclusion, on which a post-Shoah program in moral education must be based, includes a conviction that insertion into a social hierarchy in which legitimate authority does, or tolerates, evil or good strongly influences individual moral responses. Here he seems close to Haas' perspective, that teaching exclusiveness/inclusiveness affects the choices for evil or good, that the normal social processes of modeling, identification, peer support and incremental learning promote the doing of good or evil depending on the thrust of those processes, and finally that the style of childhood discipline impacts adult moral choices.

Jean Halpern and Joseph Sievers bring the volume's reflections to an end with, in Halpern's case, a strong call for moral responsibility in light of the Shoah with reference to a number of essays in the volume, and, in the case of Sievers, with texts from three participants in the experience of the Shoah–Moshe Flinker, Etty Hillesum and Dietrich Bonhoeffer. The volume thus concludes appropriately not with theological or philosophical analysis but with actual voices of the victims of the Shoah. This is as it should be, for as Metz and others have emphasized, post-Holocaust theology must be person-centered theology.

It is clear from all the essays in this volume that Professor Steven Katz's dictum is quite true: the evil that was the Shoah cannot be explained solely within traditional theological or philosophical categories. To understand its depth, to confront it in a morally responsible way, will involve new theological and philosophical categories that must break through previous boundaries of understanding. Theological and philosophical insights must be brought together in a new way, with the writings of Emmanuel Levinas providing an example for many of the contributors of how this might be done.

John T. Pawlikowski

PART I
Thinking About God After Auschwitz

Abraham's Covenant Under Assault:
The Need for a Post-Holocaust Theology, Jewish, Christian and Muslim

Emil L. Fackenheim

"Forgetfulness leads to Exile, but Memory leads to Redemption": these words of the Baal Shem Tov (Besht for short, the "Master of the Good Name") are at the exit of Yad Vashem, the Holocaust Memorial Institute in Jerusalem. The eighteenth-century founder of Hasidism may have meant remembering the mitzvot (the 613 commandments of the Torah, traditionally given on Mount Sinai), but also the destruction of the second Temple (70 C.E), this latter with Rabbi Akiba in mind. Once several rabbis were walking in Jerusalem near the destroyed sanctuary, and a fox came from the under-brush where the Holy of Holies had been. The others wept but Akiba laughed. "Now that the threatened punishment has come," he said, "the promised redemption is sure to come."

But would the Besht have said any such thing about the Holocaust? Jewish catastrophe, this time, did not relate to beliefs or actions, *but to birth*, and birth does not call for punishment. Indeed, to have children, for Jews, is a mitzvah.

Is it better to forget, then? It is late anyhow. The survivors are nearly gone, and the third or fourth generation— Jews, Germans, Christians, the world— has other concerns. Perhaps theologians had better forget as well, or (which amounts to the same) pretend that the disaster was no different from others long theologically accounted for. The original Christian Good Friday antici-pated all guilt and suffering, and Easter "overcame" in advance. As for Jews, are past catastrophes not enough—the two destructions of the Temple, the eleventh-century Crusader massacres, the fifteenth-century expulsion from Spain, the seventeenth-century Chmielnicki slaughter? A noted Jewish histo-rian objects to this "lachrymose view" of Jewish history, and the tradition con-fines mourning and fasting for all the above to just one day.

It may be late—even too late—for *experience*; but is it too late for *thought*, theological thought? If faced with "Alpine events" (Franklin Littell, a Christian theologian), must theology—*can* it—respond at once? Surely not always. Although history is full of "murder and manslaughter" (Franz

3

Rosenzweig, a Jewish theologian), the Holocaust is so shockingly unprecedented that even facts long known to scholars are reaching public awareness
only now, more than fifty years later. "Perpetrator–Victim–Bystander": once
ordinary folks had clear concepts of these. No longer.

The perpetrators were SS robots, thoughtless executioners sworn to obedience? But among them were also "ordinary men" who had not murdered
before and were free to refuse now. And the Wehrmacht—this is now publicly
accepted, and nearly every German has soldiers for ancestors—was implicat-
ed.

If Germans must engage in newly shocked thought, so must the world.
The sin of the bystanders was standing by? But passivity was not all. They
also helped themselves to—to say it bluntly, stole—the property of murdered
Jews. Who besides Swiss bankers? Just other Europeans? A stone is dropped
into the water, and who knows where the ripples will end? Shock and rethinking are necessary, then, not just about the Third Reich but also about its startling success in corrupting the world.[1]

But theology begins with the victims. Once Jews and their friends were
arguing between "why didn't they fight?" and "in the Warsaw Ghetto they
did," and between "the authentic ones kept the faith" and "for the honest there
was no God." And while Diaspora Jews always tend to evade the worst—soft-
en the impact, find hope and comfort where there is neither[2]—in Israel they
are arguing still, as some join the "March of the Living" to see Auschwitz for
themselves, while others are afraid of right-wing lessons. "It was not
Germans who murdered Jews," a left-wing cabinet minister has said, "but
people murdering other people." (Both have a point, of course.) As regards
thinking about the unthinkable, then, it is not too late: it may still be too soon.

Thus in 1958, even as ruthlessly honest a survivor-witness as Primo Levi
wrote of the *Muselmänner*—skin-and-bones "non-men," already "too empty
really to suffer," the "divine spirit dead within them"—only as *victims*. Not
until 1986 did he write that they are also *witnesses*—the *complete* ones.

> The *Muselmänner*, the submerged, [are] the complete witnesses, the
> ones whose deposition would have a general significance. They are the rule,
> we [the survivors] are the exception. When the destruction was terminated,
> the work accomplished was not told by anyone, just as no one ever returned
> to recount his own death. Even if they had paper and pen, the submerge
> would not have testified because their death had begun before that of their
> body. . . . We speak in their stead, by proxy.[3]

A theology that attends to partial witnesses—the resistance fighters, the unbroken believers, the Gentiles who risked their lives to help, righteous beyond belief—but ignores the *complete* ones? None but the *Muselmänner* force theological thought *directly*—pitilessly, without cushioning comfort—to a world without pity and comfort, that of the perpetrators. But just these witnesses are speechless and voiceless. And as we listen, even if just by proxy, we are stunned.

Our thought is stunned by Auschwitz but also by the regime that created it. Sixty years ago I understood "Heil Hitler," or thought I did: I had six years of it before I fled.

Now I don't understand. Is it like "Hail Caesar," with one Caesar following another, and the "Hail" for Rome? But just this was denied by the Nazi philosopher Alfred Bäumler, for whom Germany was an "abstract idea," and Hitler, "more" than an idea and "concrete."[4] A thousand-year Reich, and its Fuehrer "concrete"? It survived Hitler by just one week, and who remembers Admiral Doenitz?

But is it *really* gone? Alan Bullock and Hugh Trevor-Roper, expert historians, are still at a loss to explain Hitlerism.[5] And on the fiftieth anniversary of V-E Day, *Time* had the Fuehrer on its cover, with this screaming legend: "Hitler: The Evil That Won't Die."

THE INADEQUACY OF FRANZ STANGL'S ANSWERS

"What did you think at the time was the reason for the extermination of the Jews?"

The question was asked of Franz Stangl, the *Kommandant* of Sobibor and Treblinka. It was the high point of a seventy-hour-interview that Gitta Sereny conducted in 1970. Stangl had fled to Brazil, was tracked down many years after, extradited to Germany, and found guilty of co-responsibility for the murder of between 700,000 and 900,000 Jews.

"They wanted their money," Stangl answered. He said it without hesitation—"at once," she reports.

Sereny went on:

"If they were going to kill them anyway, what was the point of all the humiliation, why the cruelty?"

"To condition those who actually had to carry out the policies. To make it possible for them to do what they did."[6]

These were Stangl's two answers, and Sereny thought his second, if not the first, was correct. However, they were both false.

They wanted their money? But they had already taken it; and if to kill was necessary for getting a hidden remainder they should have taken the rich. But it was extermination for all Jews, as if they were rats or vermin.

The perpetrators needed to be "conditioned"? But the "sardine method" had been harder on the *Einsatztruppen*, earlier in the war, and Himmler decided on gas to make it easier, not for the victims, of course, but for the perpetrators.[7] (Sometimes they had to get drunk, and Himmler didn't like SS drunkenness.) That method had been as follows: one drives the victims into mass-graves, forces them—with dogs, rifle butts—to lie, face-down, sardine-like, closely together to save space, shoots them in the neck, gets others on top— some below are still alive—shoots those, and so on, until the grave is full. Press buttons for gas? Not easy, exactly, but much, much easier.

There were two goals aimed at in the Holocaust, not just one; humiliation and cruelty not merely as means to the killing but also as ends in themselves.[8]

The goals were perfected in 1942, with Stangl at Treblinka. They existed already in 1939 when the war had just begun. The chronicler Shimon Huberband writes:

> When in September 1939 the wicked ones came to Bendin [a town in Poland] they headed straight for a synagogue and set fire to it. Any Jew who tried to escape was shot. But lo, even as the fire engulfed the synagogue a certain Schlesinger, his son and son-in-law, rushed into it, ran toward the holy Ark, took two Torah scrolls, one in each arm, in order to save them. When they emerged from the doors of the synagogue they were shot by the wicked ones. Thus they died as martyrs.[9]

Rush *into* the burning buildings? Not rats, only humans do that, for something valuable, even holy. But *for them* Torah scrolls were demonic, even diabolical, and Jews had to be "punished." When the three men emerged from the burning synagogue the "wicked ones" did not lower their rifles.

Progress from Bendin to Treblinka? *They were robbed of the freedom to die their own death.* No more heroes, no more martyrs, no more chroniclers, all of whom formerly rescuing Jewish self-respect, faith, hope for a future, for the Messiah. Now the victims would be *spurlos verschwunden*, "vanish without a trace." No memory, no hope, no Jewish history, past or future. And, of course, no Messiah.

Stangl endorsed that progress—legitimized it—when he viewed and treated Treblinka Jews, not as human beings but as "cargo." Asked about this, he replied:

"They were so weak: they allowed everything to happen to them. They were people with whom there was no common ground, no possibility of communication—that is how contempt is born."[10]

In earlier times they had driven Jews into moneylending, then despised them for it. Stangl's qualitative jump is from Shylock's few choices for fighting back to no choice at all; and he conveniently forgot the Treblinka Uprising.

WHY STANGL DIDN'T KNOW

Had Sereny asked why *he* had "exterminated" the Jews—humiliated them, been cruel to them—Stangl would have resorted to lies and evasions. Asked why *they* did it, he had no reason not to say what he thought: after all, he had volunteered for the interview. Then why not at least *hesitate* about answers *when he had been there*? And there was plenty of time to think, for all those hours of the interview, to say nothing of the quarter-century gone by.

Stangl is thus a candidate for Hannah Arendt's "banality of evil." She did not ascribe stupidity to Eichmann: one cannot achieve what he did—or Hoess in Auschwitz and Stangl himself in Treblinka—and suffer from outrageous stupidity. His banality was thoughtlessness. "He 'merely,' to put the matter colloquially, never realized what he was doing,"[11] the enormity of it, not even fifteen years later, not during all those weeks of the trial. (I like her "merely," with her quotation marks.)

But Arendt overlooked one fact that alters everything. Eichmann did not *happen* to be thoughtless. (Nor did Hoess or Stangl.) The SS was *supposed* not to think; not to think was its "honor" and its "fidelity": indeed, its defining principle.[12] Not even the Nazis' very own *Weltanschauung* was to interfere with their fidelity; or, more precisely, little of it in relation to *Menschentiere*, and not at all with Jews.

The distinction is made by Himmler himself, in a speech to the SS, on October 4, 1943, at Poznan, secret at the time, but now, rightly, much quoted and anthologized. Although Germans are "kind" to *Tiere* (animals), it is "criminal" for them to be kind to Czechs, Slavs, and other *Menschentiere*.

"I cannot build the anti-tank ditch with women and children: it is inhuman, they will die in the process."

Anyone acting in this way is a "murderer" of his own "blood," for "if the ditch is not built, German soldiers will die." "Honest, decent, loyal, and comradely to members of [their] own blood, and to nobody else": this all Germans ought to be. For the SS it is a "basic principle" that "must be absolute."[13]

Himmler justifies SS behavior toward *Menschentiere* in terms of his *Weltanschauung*, thus making it debatable, and—note well!—others high in

Nazi circles debated it. They wanted kindness to Ukrainian nationalism, and, who knows, this might have made Ukrainians into allies and won Hitler the war.

But as Himmler's speech turns from *Menschentiere* to Jews there is no debate and nothing debatable. All "party members" agree on their "annihilation": it is self-evident, a given, worth mentioning only to emphasize—their "honor," their "fidelity" had proved itself—that the SS had done it.

> Most of you know what it means when 100 corpses lie there, or 500 lie
> there, or 1000 lie there. To have gone through this and—apart from excep-
> tions caused by human weakness—to have remained decent, that has hard-
> ened us. That is a page of glory in our history never written, and never to be
> written.[14]

The speech is widely known, quite a few quote this particular passage, but most seem to miss the main point. Himmler wanted no misunderstanding: "One needs no *Weltanschauung* to remove lice: it is a question of cleanliness."[15] This in another speech, also to the SS, also about Jews.

Meine Ehre heisst Treue: this was on SS belt buckles. I saw these men sixty years ago in Sachsenhausen. I also knew their motto. But only now do I understand Franz Stangl and all the others.

WE DO NOT KNOW WHY THEY DID IT

But surely there *are* "whys" for SS fidelity coming, of course, from the Fuehrer himself.[16] (They are parroted in Himmler's speech.)[17]. However, no even moderately informed, honest, and thoughtful person can take them at face value now.

Hitler had planned the war (see his second "Secret Book") at least since 1928; introduced his generals to his plans (see the Hossbach Protocol) in 1937; unleashed war itself in 1939; and made it worldwide (the attack on the Soviet Union, the declaration of war on the United States) in 1941. Moreover, he *wanted* war, even *for its own sake*: read about—and be surprised by!—his lasting regret that at Munich they had "tricked" him into peaceful victory: he had wanted that triumphant ride into the conquered Sudetenland, even into Prague, right away. Indeed, unlike other Social Darwinisms, his own *Weltanschauung* knew *nothing* but war, with peaceful interludes only in preparation. "The German nation," Nazi ideologist Alfred Rosenberg famously said at the time, "is on the way finally of finding its lifestyle . . . , of a marching column, regardless of where and to what purpose [it] . . . is employed."[18]

Now, after all this, hear Hitler as follows:

> Today I wish to be a prophet once more. If international finance-Jewry, within and outside Europe, succeeds once more in hurling the nations into world war, the result will not be bolshevism on earth, and with it victory for Jewry, but the annihilation of the Jewish race in Europe.

This in a Reichstag address before the war started. With war ending, his "political testament" blamed the Jews once more.[19]

Was he serious? The Reichstag members thought he was, and responded with "lasting and stormy applause." And of the "testament," some say that no one tells lies when near death.[20]

But can *anyone* take it serious by *now*? The Jews plot war, plot all wars, wage this war, every war, *Cosmic* wars? (On the "cosmic," see further below.) And he, Hitler, is only defending himself, defending Germany, defending the world?[21]

What holds for this particular "reason" for his Jewish policy—the "prophecy" was self-fulfilling—holds also for the *Sammelsurium* of all the others. Maggots, bacilli, tuberculosis, parasites, vampires, syphilis, world-pestilence—these metaphors, taken from medicine and parasitology, are no more credible than others taken from politics: communism, mammonism, international plotting, plotting-in-general. Eberhard Jäckel's term "*Sammelsurium*"[22] ("random medley" comes closest in English) is perfect: there is no filth, foulness, creepy-crawly-scary thing, *unadulterated shit* that Hitler digs up in others, concocts himself and splashes about—at friends, enemies, the world—that expresses, to be sure, his own fears, hates, nauseas, disgusts, and that foments, certainly, the same in others: but that utterly fails to add up to *reasons* for a policy of staggering cost (not just in money); first nation- then continent-wide, and that culminates in Stangls and their "cargo."

Not even the Jewish-blood myth is enough. It speaks poorly for pre-Hitler Vienna—and Austria, Germany, much of Europe, some of the world—that this "threat" was peddled in drugstore pamphlets, even got into books. But a mind-boggling leap is required from pamphlets and books to a systematic policy that, first, defines the victims, then proceeds to laws—marriage, sexual relations, the age of "Aryan" household help permitted in "non-Aryan" homes, in short *Rassenschande*—and ends with complex schedules for special trains to take the long-defined victims to a still more complex machinery built for mass murder. As for tracing *this* end—quite unprecedented then, with nothing really similar since—back to an "ultimate" cause in private phobias: Hitler's unknown grandfather, possibly, was Jewish; Heydrich's father's "real" name, Suess, sounded Jewish—it calls for a redefinition of the absurd.

In a good account that says everything in a mere ten pages, Karl Dietrich Bracher writes: "The extermination [of the Jews] grew out of the biologistic insanity of Nazi ideology, and for that reason it is completely unlike the terror of revolutions and wars of the past."[23]

"Biologistic"—not "biological"!—"insanity": you'll never find a better definition, yet both terms are inadequate. The adjective may encompass *Untermenschen, Menschentiere,* and—with difficulty—even Jews-as-rats-to-exterminate, but never Jews-as-devils-to-humiliate, torture, in any case to "punish."[24] As for "insanity," one understands Nero setting Rome on fire to inspire his fiddling, but all the little Hitlers who fiddled, even after the big one's death? Insanity looks like an explanation, but only means that explanations have come to an end. The whole Reich one vast madhouse? That is throwing up one's hands.

The deeds were those that Himmler praised and the SS performed. But of reasons Hitler's are not credible, and the SS had none of their own. "There is no 'why' here," a murder camp guard said to Primo Levi.[25]

"Banal" evil, "radical" evil, "demonic" evil—forget these abstractions. But "evil has addresses," and I have suggested a good many.

AN ASSAULT ON THE COVENANT OF ABRAHAM

Why it happened continues to elude us, but theologians must face *what* happened: *the Holocaust was an assault on the Covenant of Abraham, the only truly radical one ever made.*

"Get thee out of thy country, thy kindred, thy father's house" (Genesis 12:1). Thus it begins, and the text then has God promise life and blessing. Without a word, Abraham goes, and his fidelity is the model through the Jewish generations. *But in the Holocaust blessing was made into curse—*"don't get near them, their breath poisons"—*and life into death.* "They were not merely destroyed," thus Paul Bailey on Primo Levi's testimony-by-proxy. "They were blotted out of existence."[26]

But Jews still circumcise their sons, the "token" that sealed Abraham's covenant with God (Genesis 17:10 ff.).

Theology is familiar with controversy about Sinai, with the Jews defending their covenant and Christians and Muslims viewing it as just a stage in an ongoing *Heilsgeschichte*. But assailing *Abraham's* covenant, the very start of *all Heilsgeschichte* and, moreover, threatening to terminate it forever? This was unprecedented, and no theology was prepared.

But is Abraham's God not also the God of the Christians? And is not Ishmael the patriarch's very own son? *The Nazi attack on the Jews was also a visitation on Christians and Muslims, but they failed to recognize it and abandoned the Jews.*

POST-HOLOCAUST THEOLOGY

Half a century later, can theology make a reckoning? Is the time ripe for a post-Holocaust theology?

"In dialogue, Jews and Christians want different things from each other; Christians, legitimation from Jews, and Jews, for Christians to keep their hands off their kids."

This was said at an early post-Holocaust Christian-Jewish dialogue—privately, by one Jew to another. The subject was "Ethical Monotheism," "The Brotherhood of Man," or something similarly innocuous. The Holocaust was not on the agenda.

In 1974 it *was*. At a conference co-sponsored by Jews and Christians, Irving "Yitz" Greenberg must have found it no easy task to report how a Slovak rabbi had asked Archbishop Kametko to save Slovak Jews from deportation. The rabbi had grounds for hope, for he knew that Josef Tiso, the pro-Nazi head of the Slovak government, was the archbishop's former secretary. But Kametko replied:

> It is not just a matter of deportation. You will not die there of hunger and disease. They will slaughter all of you, old and young alike, women and children, at once—it is punishment that you deserve for the death of our Lord and Redeemer, Jesus Christ. You have only one solution. Come over to our religion, and I will work to annul this decree."[27]

There were many Kametkos during the Holocaust, some even after, and now there is Claude Lantzmann's film *Shoah*. But Greenberg testified, not to accuse or to express despair, but within a shared Jewish-Christian search for hope.

But with the SS as the Christian God's very own executioner, how *can* there be hope? The conference was entitled "Auschwitz: A New Beginning?" The organizers had not forgotten the question mark.

"Then answered all the people and said, 'His blood be on us and our children'" (Matthew 27:25).

I permit myself just one *cri de coeur:* in all of Christian history, why was there not one Christian—courageous, compassionate, and authoritative enough to make an impact—to toss just this passage out of the Christian canon? It has cost much blood of Jewish children.

Christian theology tolerated Jew-hatred in its Holy Scripture until the nemesis came: Christian love overwhelmed by Nazi hate.[28] What if Kametko's kind of Christianity had destroyed true Christianity, ever after? Alfred Kazin, Greenberg's Jewish respondent, made the once-sacred-hatred into an "old theological infamy," but also expressed his belief that, without Christian "brothers in hope," Jewish hope could not survive alone.

"Without hope, Jewish history utterly nullifies itself, and the many-thousand-year history of our unworldliness . . . becomes meaningless."[29]

After the Holocaust, theology must be other than what it was before. As generation follows generation, others may forget. But *for theology the Holocaust must be unforgettable.*[30]

Himself acting against "old theological infamies," in 1986 Pope John-Paul II visited a Rome synagogue. Fifty years had passed since the missed visitation. Now the pontiff responded by stressing that Jews and Christians "share a spiritual heritage," and Jews are "older brothers." The assault had been on Abraham; the pontiff harked back to the patriarch himself.

If he also stressed differences that remain, it was perhaps because in 1984 he had gone further and failed. In *Salvifici Doloris*, he had written:

> The suffering of Christ created the good of the world's redemption. This good in itself is inexhaustible and infinite. No human can add anything to it. But at the same time, in the mystery of the church as his body, Christ has, in a sense, opened his own redemptive suffering to all human suffering. Insofar as a human being—*in any part of the world and at any time in history* [emphasis added]—becomes a sharer in Christ's suffering, to that extent he in his own way completes the suffering with which Christ accomplished the redemption of the world.

The pontiff then cited St. Paul, but in the passage italicized by us, went beyond him, this—I have no doubt; he had visited Auschwitz on June 7, 1979—with the Holocaust in mind. The apostle writes: "For the body of the church I complete in my own earthly life what is still missing in the sufferings of Christ" (Colossians 1:24).[31]

But Paul suffered for his faith, the Holocaust victims for their birth. He was an adult, Stangl's "cargo" included the children. Paul *chose* suffering; the Holocaust victims, robbed even of dying their own death, were choiceless.

Theologically, the third difference is crucial. On the subject of redemptive suffering, Judaism may be closer than ever to the daughter-faith when Emperor Hadrian forbade Jewish faith on pain of death, Rabbi Akiba, defying him, was tortured to death, and his martyrdom *al kiddush ha-shem*, "for the sanctification of the divine Name," redeemed, if not the world, the sanctity of the Name. But while Hadrian forbade Jewish faith, Hitler forbade Jewish life. And while the emperor created Jewish martyrs, the Fuehrer killed Jewish martyrdom.

Thus the truth in *Salvifici Doloris* is not shared redemptive suffering, but rather the shared grief of a failure. Perhaps one day Jews and Christians will bring this grief to the God of Abraham, Isaac, and Jacob.

Protestant theology has had a similar experience. In examining Dietrich Bonhoeffer's papers Eberhard Bethge found the following: "The expulsion of the Jews from the West must be followed by the expulsion of Christ, for Jesus Christ was a Jew."

This became the chief text of Bethge's lecture *Bonhoeffer und die Juden*, which then led, in 1984, to William J. Peck's following response:

> Bethge brings a syllogism to light that stuns (*macht betroffen*). If the *expulsion* of the Jews means [for Christians] the expulsion of Christ from the West, what is the *annihilation* of the Jews (which began as a political measure a few months later)? . . . Here the syllogism breaks off, and we hear Bonhoeffer speak of co-suffering with God's suffering in a world without God, just before he sealed his testimony with his own death.[32]

Christian theology can have bad Jews, so long as there are also good ones, *in extremis* at least one, Jesus himself. But if Jewish *birth* is under attack, and the aim is a world wholly *rein* of Jews, the carpenter of Nazareth is included.

IF HITLER HAD WON

Theology cannot remain *betroffen* forever: it must move on to thought:[33] If the Holocaust is unforgettable, what, nevertheless, could blot it out? Only a Hitler victory. He almost won.

A Hitler peace-after-victory boggles the mind. The architect in him could not imagine giant "Germania"—the world capital, replacing puny Berlin—without the background of skyscrapers collapsing in firestorms. With one nation's capital after the other flattened in victory, would his Germania shrivel into nothingness?

The "most brutal" war is "the most merciful," for it ends most quickly:

this was the maxim Hitler followed. With final victory, would the victims—
"let us not flinch at calling them the modern slave class"—be "happy" in his
"merciful" peace?[34]

And Jews? In a well-known passage in *Mein Kampf* Hitler writes:

> If, with the help of his Marxist creed, the Jew is victorious over the other
> peoples of the world, his crown will be the funeral wreath of humanity, and
> this planet will, as it did thousands of years ago,[35] move through the ether
> devoid of men.
>
> Eternal Nature inexorably avenges the infringement of her commands.
>
> Hence today I believe that I am acting in accordance with the will of the
> Almighty Creator: by defending myself against the Jew I am fighting for the
> work of the Lord.[36]

Note that this invokes two deities, not just one. Which would rule after
victory was certain as early as October 1939, when the war had hardly begun.
A Fuehrer decree ordered the murder of "life unworthy of living": the mentally impaired, babies with birth defects—a project, incidentally, in which
Stangl had his apprenticeship.

The murders were stopped by Christian protests, but would resume, it was
vowed, after victory. (There would be no Christians left then, or, at any rate,
none to protest.) With "life-unworthy-of-living" expanded to "otherwise-use-
less-eaters," wounded World War I veterans had already been murdered. And
after World War II?

While the war was on, Himmler's one and only sanctuary—the idyllic
"honest, decent, loyal SS comradeship"—survived. But not after. *Ich hatt'
einen Kameraden*: this song never failed to move old soldiers mourning com-
rades, faithful unto death. I was moved myself when I joined my father to
mourn an uncle I had never known. But after a Hitler victory-peace, the song
would move no more. Is the one next to me a comrade? This the SS would
have to ask. Not if I am luckless enough to get wounded rather than killed.
Just another "useless eater" then, he'll murder me, and send me up the chimney.

Hitler's deity, then, is by no means the biblical Creator who forbids
killing and delights in life, but a murderous Nature that revels in death. Hitler
spells out her "inexorable" commands as follows: "Nature is cruel; therefore
we also are entitled to be cruel."[37]

The Muslim God would not be spared, anymore than the God of
Abraham, Isaac, and Jacob. Allah shows mercy to his followers. Real mercy,
not Hitler's kind.

But Hitler lost the war, and we have another chance.

HOPE LOST AND RECOVERED

When the Jewish people returned to Jerusalem they recovered hope. But a hope recovered after it was murdered is more fragile than a hope that never died. May Jews hope for "brothers in hope"? There are signs of it, from an emerging post-Holocaust Christian theology. A Muslim theology might begin also, if it is recalled that when Abraham died, Isaac and Ishmael buried him together (Genesis 25:9).

EPILOGUE

Had the nations realized what a boon the Temple was to them, they would have built fortifications round about it to safeguard it. For it was a greater boon to them than to Israel, as in the prayer of Solomon on its initiation: "Moreover, concerning the stranger that is not of thy people Israel. . . Thou shalt give all the stranger asks" (1 Kings 8:41, 43). But of Israel he asks. "Thou shalt render to every man according to his ways" (2 Chronicles 6:30). If the Israelite was worthy He should grant his prayer; if not He should not.[38]

With the Temple still standing, would Christians, worshiping with such as Hillel, Akiba, or, for that matter, Joshua ben Levi, have considered them deicides, or Judaism superseded?

With the Temple still standing, would Muslims have destroyed it, to put the al-Aqsa in its place, or erected the mosque beside it?

NOTES

1. Hitler did not want to export National Socialism but only antisemitism. Naturally, his efforts were more welcome in some countries, such as Vichy France, than in others.
2. Cf. Lawrence Langer, *Admitting the Holocaust* (New York: Oxford, 1995). The very title of this book, together with its date of publication, speaks volumes.
3. *Survival in Auschwitz* (New York: Collier, 1961), p. 82; *The Drowned and the Saved* (London: Abacus, 1988), p. 64.
4. In his inaugural lecture at Berlin University, reprinted in Leon Poliakov and Josef Wulf, *Das Dritte Reich und seine Denker* (Berlin: Arami, 1959), pp. 267 ff.
5. See Ron Rosenbaum, "Explaining Hitler," *New Yorker*, May 1995.

6. Gitta Sereny, *Into That Darkness: From Mercy Killing to Mass Murder* (London: Andre Deutsch, 1974), pp. 101, 232.

7. See Mathias Beer, "Die Entwicklung der Gaswagen beim Mord an den Juden," *Vierteljahreshefte für Zeitgeschichte* 1987, pp. 413, 417.

8. I am puzzled by Sereny's assent to Stangl's second answer, when she herself writes: "The killings were organized systematically to achieve the maximum humiliation and dehumanization of the victims before they died. The pattern was dictated... not by 'mere' cruelty or indifference: the crammed airless freight-cars without sanitary provisions, food or drink, far worse than any cattle-transport; the whipped-up (literally so) hysteria on arrival; the immediate and always violent separation of men, women and children; the public undressing; the incredibly crude internal examination for hidden valuables; the hair-cutting and shaving of the women; and finally the naked run to the gas chambers, under the lash of the whips." *Into That Darkness*, pp. 100–101.

9. Shimon Huberband, *Kiddush ha-Shem* (Tel Aviv: Zachor, 1969), p. 27.

10. Sereny, *Into That Darkness*, pp. 232–233.

11. *Eichmann in Jerusalem* (New York: Penguin, 1963), pp. 51, 287.

12. Arendt's Eichmann is banal because "unable to think from the standpoint of somebody else" (p 49). But in his report for the 1964 Frankfurt Auschwitz trial, Hans Buchheim shows that among required SS virtues were (1) unthinking obedience, (2) hardness of character immune to cries for pity, and (3) considering no feat impossible (*Befehl und Gehorsam* [Munich: Kösel, 1964], p. 277). Eichmann's behavior is fully accounted for by these virtues, the last-named of which, to be sure, includes famous, derring-do Otto Skorzeny's rescue of Mussolini from captivity, but also Franz Stangl's less-glamorous "cargo" and Eichmann's jolly, backslapping talk with unsuspecting Jews about to be murdered.

I am indebted to this and Buchheim's other works, and also to Josef Ackermann's *Himmler als Ideologe* (Göttingen: Musterschmidt, 1970). The *Reichsführer* wouldn't let SS men decide for themselves even whom to marry or whether to smoke.

Were Eichmann's crimes against humanity (as represented by the Jewish people), the Nuremberg view, or against the Jewish people, Israeli law and Ben-Gurion's view? The first supposes a permanent humanity, to be appealed to for one and all; the second supposes— with Jews practically outside humanity, in an exile culminating in the Holocaust—that the newly founded Jewish state was duty-bound to correct that abnormality. Arendt never examined the second view. She also accused Ben-Gurion—who, through the testimony of the survivors, sought to unite Diaspora Jews (who didn't know) with Israelis (who didn't understand)—of wanting a show trial. General Dwight Eisenhower ordered GI Joes to a concentration camp, to learn, if not what they were fighting for, at least what against. Did he want a "show"?

13. In Lucy Dawidowicz, *A Holocaust Reader* (New York: Behrman House, 1976), p. 131.

14. Ibid, p. 133.

15. Himmler's speech in Kharkov, April 1943, quoted by Ackermann, *Himmler als Ideologe*, p. 163.

16. Raul Hilberg told me a good many years ago that he had dealt only with the "small" questions of the Holocaust—how it was done—for fear of giving "too small" an answer to the "big" question—why it was done at all. Since I still believe this fear sound, I here omit any reference to prior antisemitism, the German included: the gulf between all of this latter and the Holocaust is an abyss. But in attributing to pre-Hitler Germany an "eliminational" antisemitism, Daniel Jonah Goldhagen, in *Hitler's Willing Executioners* (New York: Knopf, 1996), practically does away with the abyss; and while John Weiss's *Ideology of Death: Why the Holocaust Happened in Germany* (Chicago: Ivan R. Dee, 1996) may get us a lot closer to why it happened in that country, it does not answer why it happened at all.

17. Himmler claimed not to have wanted to perpetrate the Holocaust, that it was a hard duty imposed on him by the Fuehrer. (Goebbels supported this; see Martin Broszat's "The Genesis of the Final Solution," *Yad Vashem Studies* 13 [Jerusalem, 1979], especially p. 107.) Hence his Poznan "the Jews want to murder us, so we must kill them" must be taken as parroting Hitler's view.

"The SS has remained decent in mass murder" is generally considered the core of the Poznan speech, but the reference is to doing what all party members agree ought to be done but lack the SS virtues to do, i.e., make no exceptions to murdering Jews.

18. Cited in Karl Dietrich Bracher, *The German Dictatorship* (New York: Praeger, 1970), p. 252.

19. The "prophecy" speech was made on January 30, 1939, but Hitler later referred to its date, mistakenly, as September 1, 1939, the start of the war. The last sentence of his "political testament" is: "Above all I obligate the leaders of the nation and their followers to the strict adherence of the racial laws and to merciless resistance to the world-poisoners of all nations, international Jewry." After a similar outburst near the end, Hitler states: "In saying this, I promise you I am quite free of all racial hatred." *The Testament of Adolf Hitler* (Icon Books, 1962), p. 62.

20. This is suggested several times by Robert G. L. Waite's thought-provoking *The Psychopathic God: Adolf Hitler* (New York: Basic Books, 1977).

21. Hitler claimed much the same about the Soviet Union: he had to defend himself and the world. There is no evidence that the Soviet Union planned an attack.

One obviously is tempted to resort to pathology, but I avoid this, for fear of trivializing either the crime or the responsibility of the criminals.

22. Jäckel, *Hitlers Weltanschauung* (Tübingen: Wunderlich, 1969), p. 64.

23. Ibid, p. 430. Bracher ends his chapter as follows: "The reality and irreality of National Socialism were given their most terrible expression in the extermination of the Jews" (p. 431).

24. Someone in Himmler's circle produced this definition: "The Jews are not a people like others, but a pseudo-people (*Scheinvolk*) united by hereditary criminality." Quoted by Ackermann, *Himmler als Ideologe*, p. 162.

25. *Survival in Auschwitz*, p. 25.

26. See Primo Levi, *The Drowned and the Saved*, p. ix.

27. In Eva Fleischner, ed., *Auschwitz: A New Beginning?* (New York: Ktav, 1977), pp. 11 ff.

28. "Torture was no invention of National Socialism. But it was its apotheosis. The Hitler vassal did not achieve his full identity if he was merely as quick as a weasel, tough as leather, hard as Krupp steel. . . . He had to torture, to destroy, in order to be great in bearing the suffering of others. . . . They tortured with the good conscience of depravity. . . . They placed torture in their service. But even more fervently they were its servants." Jean Amery, *At the Mind's Limits* (New York: Schocken, 1986), pp. 30 ff.

The Protestant theologian Roy Eckardt once defended the New Testament as Holy Writ before a Jewish audience. When someone quoted Matthew 27:25 at him, he responded, "The word of the devil." "Joint authorship," someone behind me whispered.

29. In Fleischner, *Auschwitz*, pp. 65–72. The old theological infamy is "that a whole people should feel guilty throughout history, and continuously be made into a sacrifice."

30. The use of the term "Auschwitz" does not guarantee attention to Jews, victims or survivors. Thus, for historian Juergen Foerster, Auschwitz symbolizes "racial madness" and "murder of peoples," while for theologian Dorothee Soelle, theology after Auschwitz symbolizes divine powerlessness which requires care for the powerless poor in South America; but of the nonsymbolic victims of Auschwitz, i.e., Jews, she has nothing to say. See J. Moltmann, ed., *Wie ich mich geändert habe* (Gütersloh: Kaiser 1997), pp. 31 ff. See also below, n. 33.

31. "On the Christian Meaning of Human Suffering," Apostolic Letter *Salvifici Doloris*, February 11, 1984 (Washington, D.C.: United States Catholic Conference, 1984), p. 27.

32. *Konsequenzen*, ed. Ernst Feil and Ilse Toedt (Munich: Chr. Kaiser 1980), pp. 171–222; *Ethik im Ernstfall*, ed. W. Huber and Ilse Toedt (Munich: Chr. Kaiser 1982), pp. 25–40. Bethge shows admirable integrity in detailing his friend's struggles with theologies (punishment theology, supersessionist theology, etc.), but it is sad to read of his theological troubles that he reached conclusions that—without theology but as a *Mensch* and a Christian —he had known all along. *In times of crisis, is theology a help or an impediment?*

33. "The ghost of one of the victims comes to a lecture, attracted by the theme of Auschwitz, happy to know that someone remembers him. The lecturer speaks of the unspeakable, the unimaginable, the inexpressible. The ghost asks himself why his murder should be 'unspeakable' when there is a good German word for it: he was shot through the neck. And why 'unimaginable' when it was no mystery, but a bloody swinishness committed in the broad light of day. Gradually he realizes that the speaker is not talking about him at all, but merely the *Erschütterung* of the speaker, who is displaying his capacity for sympathy to the public. Disappointed and insulted, the ghost leaves." Cited from Ruth Klueger, in *Freiburger Rundbrief* 3 (1997): 178.

The last sentence is a bit nasty, but may be needed to shock theologians into awareness that Jews are flesh-and-blood people, not a symbol or theological category.

34. For convenience's sake I cite from Joachim Fest, *Hitler* (New York: Vintage 1974), pp. 667 ff. Fest cannot bring himself to give these texts except under "Lost Reality," as if they had not always been Hitler's reality: he had wanted the "removal" (if not necessarily yet the Holocaust) of the Jews since 1919; world conquest since 1928, and kept invoking Nature throughout *Mein Kampf*. Fest also finds it necessary to preface the book with seven tortured sentences on whether Hitler was "great."
35. In the second edition, Hitler changed "thousands" to "millions."
36. *Mein Kampf*, trans. Ralph Mannheim (Boston: Houghton Mifflin, 1943), p. 65. The struggle with the Jews appears here as cosmic; I cannot deal with this in the present context, but hope to take it up elsewhere.
37. Fest, *Hitler*, pp. 679 ff.
38. Rabbi Joshua ben Levi (3rd cent. C.E.), in Midrash Numbers Rabbah 1:3.

Between Remembering and Forgetting:
The Shoah in the Era of Cultural Amnesia

Johann Baptist Metz

I.

I belong to that generation of Germans who slowly, much too slowly, learned to understand themselves as a generation "after Auschwitz," and I sought in my way of doing theology to do justice to this understanding insofar as possible. Auschwitz signaled for me a terror beyond all familiar theology, a terror that left any noncontextual talk of God empty and blind. I asked myself: With such a catastrophe at one's back, is there a God to whom one can pray? Can any theology worthy of its name simply continue to speak, continue to speak of God and human beings, as if in the face of such a catastrophe one must not scrutinize the assumed innocence of our human words? My intention with such questions is not to stylize Auschwitz into a negative myth that would again remove this catastrophe from our theological and historical purview. First and foremost it was all about the unsettling question: Why is this catastrophe—as with the history of human suffering itself—so little, or even not at all, apparent in the words and images of theology? The noticeably apathetic content of Christian theology, its astounding resistance to being disconcerted in the face of the Shoah, upset me. From that point on, I have attempted to do Christian theology with full consciousness of the situation "after Auschwitz." My purpose, however, is not to give this catastrophe a Christian meaning, let alone a Christian "reception," but rather to do "theology after Auschwitz" primarily as critique of theology.

II.

"The Shoah between Remembering and Forgetting." With this theme I am addressing not only theology, but the "very spirit (*geistige Situation*) of our time" (K. Jaspers). In my opinion, there has been in this regard a momentous shift or a change of mentalities. In sum, I could say, the mystery of redemption is no longer called remembrance, but rather forgetting. We are living more and more in an era of cultural amnesia.

Under the title of postmodernity are we not slipping increasingly into a world that cultivates forgetting? Human beings are less and less their own memories, ever more only their own unlimited experiments. Friedrich Nietzsche, who as the presence behind the spirit of our times has long supplanted Hegel and Marx, connected his "new way to live," with which he tried to do away with Christianity and all monotheistic religion, with the triumph of cultural amnesia.

> In the smallest and greatest happiness there is always one thing that makes it happiness: the power of forgetting. . . . One who cannot leave himself behind on the threshold of the moment and forget the past, who cannot stand on a single point, like a goddess of victory, without fear or giddiness, will never know what happiness is.[1]

The vision of human happiness is grounded now very simply in the capacity to forget, in the amnesia of the victor or at least the one who has made it through. "Blessed are the forgetful,"[2] declares Nietzsche, and juxtaposes his "beatitude" with that of Jesus of Nazareth: "Blessed are those who mourn," those who cannot overcome the pain of remembrance.

But how can this be true? Isn't there enough talk of the past and of overcoming the past in Germany? Of the Historians' Controversy and its consequences? Isn't our public domain characterized by discussions about "monuments of warning," about Holocaust memorials, by controversies about the Armed Forces exhibition in Germany and Austria, and about Daniel Goldhagen's book, *Hitler's Willing Executioners*? Where is the predominance of forgetting, the era of cultural amnesia in which we are supposedly living? Let us see!

In my estimation, the totally networked information society that we are becoming cannot resist this forgetting. On the contrary, this society is in danger of becoming a "forgetting machine," because storing information is, in fact, not remembering. In the words of H. M. Enzensberger: "Storing—that means forgetting."[3] To get to the bottom of our question, I would like to quote Nietzsche again, Nietzsche in his entire ambivalence, Nietzsche who was not at all the blind fanatic of forgetting. In his thoughts in *The Genealogy of Morals* he writes:

> How can one create a memory for the human animal? How can one impress something upon this partly obtuse, partly flighty mind, attuned only to the passing moment, in such a way that it will stay there? . . . If something

is to stay in the memory it must be burned in: only that which never ceases to *hurt* stays in memory.[4]

Cultural amnesia means shutting down the pain of remembrance in the cultural memory of human beings. Jean-François Lyotard rightly emphasizes that there are actually two kinds of forgetting. On the one hand, there is the destruction of all evidence, so that there is nothing more to remember (as the Nazis tried to do with the death chambers). On the other hand, there is also the "perfect" memory, namely, the presumed certainty that the event in and with its (later) representation has been preserved and understood.[5]

III.

The contemporary triumph of amnesia rests on different foundations.

1. The first, in my opinion, is Christian theology itself. Has it not always used much too strong categories for its perception of history, categories that all too quickly cover up all the historical injuries, all the gaping wounds, all the collapses and catastrophes, and that spare the talk of God from the pain of remembering? Must not the Shoah, at least, work as an ultimatum to an all-too-easy theological intercourse with history? Must not, in any case, the question of the locus and the degree of the horror turn up in the midst of the logos of theology? Must not theology, in any case, now be convinced that it does not heal all wounds?

The evidence of cultural amnesia in Christian theology reaches far into the past—back to the history of its separation from Jewish tradition. Very early on, Christianity deployed a questionable and momentous strategy of an institutional and intellectual disinheritance vis-à-vis Judaism. On the one hand, Christianity understood itself as the new Israel, as the new Jerusalem, as the true people of God. The originary importance of Israel for Christians, as Paul urgently warns in his letter to the Romans, was too quickly displaced: Israel was demoted to an obsolete precondition for Christianity in the scheme of salvation history. At the same time, there began what I call the "halving" of the Christian spirit, as Christianity became theologized. The faith tradition of Israel was ostensibly invoked, but the spirit was taken exclusively from Athens, more precisely from the Hellenistic tradition. In other words, from a subjectless and ahistorical thought structure of Being and Identity, in which ideas are always more foundational than memories and time knows no boundaries. Athens versus Jerusalem? Didn't Jerusalem, didn't the biblical Jewish traditions and Jewish experience of the postbiblical era, didn't Jewish thought right up to our time offer any specific intellectual paradigms? Naturally these

Jewish intellectual paradigms exist. There is thinking as "being mindful of" (*Eingedenken*), there is that anamnestic culture that does not spare itself the pain of remembering and which knows that not time, but rather the eschatological God, heals wounds, if they are healed at all.

2. Certainly modern science does not break the spell of the cultural amnesia that I have described. In our civilization, science is the paradigm of normality, and thus one can say of science that it heals all wounds and does not know the pain of remembering. I would like to make a special remark regarding the human sciences. As I see it, since the German Historians' Controversy (*Deutscher Historikerstreit*, 1986–88), the historicization of National Socialism and its crimes has more or less come to be the prevailing view in the human sciences.[6] Regarding Auschwitz, the question remains for me of how a terror that repeatedly threatens to remove itself from historical consciousness can nonetheless be kept in memory. This can only be accomplished by a historiography that is supported by an anamnestic culture, by a memorial culture that knows about the sort of forgetting that is still ingrained in every historicized objectivization.

For the most part, we are deprived of such a culture in Europe because we lack the spirit that Auschwitz was supposed to extinguish once and for all. In the last analysis, it is the Jewish spirit that is the privileged carrier of such an anamnestic culture. Therefore, I tend to speak of a double-destruction, a double-death, so to speak, in the Shoah. Not only were the Jews murdered with technical-industrial perfection; with them that very spirit was supposed to be extinguished, and once and for all destroyed, that makes us capable of remembering this unimaginable horror and keeping it present in memory: the anamnestic culture of the human spirit itself. Over and over again I have asked myself whether we deal so ambivalently and uncertainly with Auschwitz because we lack this anamnestic spirit that would be necessary to perceive and express appropriately what also happened to us, to what we call spirit, in this catastrophe. In short, whether we deal ambivalently with Auschwitz because we lack a memorial culture that is more deeply rooted than our scientific perception of history and that knows the pain of memory.

3. "Science heals all wounds." Doesn't this also apply to the major and influential portion of contemporary philosophy? In a text entitled "Israel and Athens; or, To Whom Does Anamnestic Reason Belong?", the famous German philosopher Jürgen Habermas tried to make clear that the anamnestic spirit of biblical thought has long since penetrated European philosophical reason.[7] Why then, for example, in Habermas's work itself, does the catastrophe of Auschwitz appear in his "Minor Political Works"—and there, as is known, quite clearly and in a very influential and convincing fashion—but

with not even a single word in his major philosophical writings concerning communicative reason? Does the theory of communicative competence, perhaps, also heal all wounds? How then would one speak in a generalizable fashion of what remains a disaster, of what cannot be healed, of what cannot be allowed to disappear behind the curtain of cultural amnesia, of what does not allow itself to be shut away behind an impervious wall of normality? How could one speak of that which demands, when at all, another kind of forgiveness than the forgiveness of time that supposedly heals everything, or than the forgiveness of theory that closes all wounds.

IV.

Nonetheless, there is something remaining even when all wounds have seemingly been closed. What remains is hard to describe. It is an unusual feeling of something missing that resists the complete assuaging of the pain of remembering, whether purely theoretically, psychologically, aesthetically, in rituals of memory, or even religiously. What is it? This something missing in the present is least understood when it is ascribed to a typical sensitivity of the older generations, as is most often done. It is much rather the case, in my opinion, that the younger generation exhibits precisely this sense of something missing. It fuels the skepticism of the young, their indifference, at times their anger toward "the" experience, "the" point of view, "the" lesson of history which the older generation has offered them, has imposed on them, and has elevated to the canon of normality. What is most remarkable for me about the recent discussion in Germany of Daniel Goldhagen and his book subtitled *Ordinary Germans and the Holocaust*[8] is that the practically unanimous and —according to the criteria of professional historiography—fully correct critique of the experts has nonetheless failed to soothe the upset of so many younger people over the magnitude of the guilt involved.

Being mindful of the suffering of others remains a fragile category in our time, a time in which human beings in the end are of the opinion that it is only with the sword of forgetting and the shield of amnesia that they can arm themselves against the latest waves of the history of suffering and evil deeds: yesterday Auschwitz, today Bosnia and Ruanda, and tomorrow? But this forgetting is not without consequences.

For many, Auschwitz has certainly long since disappeared beyond the horizon of their memories. Yet no one can avoid the anonymous consequences. The theological question after Auschwitz is not only: Where was God at Auschwitz? It is also: Where was humankind at Auschwitz?

What has always particularly touched and troubled me about the situation "after Auschwitz" was the affliction, the hopelessness of those who survived this catastrophe—so much silent misery, so many suicides! Clearly these people were shattered by their despair about the human race, about that which human beings are capable of toward one another. This catastrophe vastly lowered the metaphysical and moral threshold of shame among human beings; it injured the bands of solidarity between all those who bear a human face. Only those without memory survive something like this; or those who have already successfully forgotten that they have forgotten something. One cannot sin randomly at the expense of humankind. Not only the individual human being, but also the idea of human beings and of humanity can be injured. Only a few connect the current crisis of humanity with the Shoah, for example, the so-called crisis of values, the increasing deafness to demands for "greatness," the crisis of solidarity, etc. Isn't this all a vote of no-confidence against human beings and their morals?

It is not just the superficial history of the human species that is real; there is also a deep history, and it can be wounded through and through. Don't the contemporary orgies of violence and rape reap the benefits of the normative force of the factual? Don't they, behind the mask of amnesia, break down the original trust of civilization, those moral and cultural reserves that ground the humanity of human beings? How exhausted are these reserves? Are we witnessing, perhaps, the end of the paradigm of humanity to which we have been historically accustomed until now? Could it be that human beings in the grip of cultural amnesia have lost not only God, but also, increasingly, themselves, insofar as they have lost what previously was emphatically known as humanity? What remains, therefore, when we have repeatedly successfully closed all wounds? When cultural amnesia is complete? What remains? Human beings? Which human beings? The appeal to humanity is itself highly abstract. It frequently has its source in a naively optimistic anthropology that long ago lost sight of the problem of evil and of a view of human history from the vantage point of theodicy.

In order not to allow the pain of history, the pathos of memory, to evaporate in this time of cultural amnesia, we need the power that is the converse of what I have termed anamnestic culture. Religion, in its essence, is characterized by this anamnestic culture. It has its first home in the monotheistic root religion of Judaism. Therefore,

> the mass murder of the European Jews and Hitler's attempt to annihilate the Jewish people, at least in Europe, can be seen as an unparalleled and unprecedented attack upon the cultural memory of humanity, as the murder

of memory on the scale of millions (memory-cide), if this term is appropriate. Nowhere in the world was memory, as religious and cultural force, so fully enfleshed in a human collective as in the Jewish people from Moses to Moses Mendelssohn and beyond.[9]

This resistance to cultural amnesia has allies not only in religion. Religion finds assistance in a body of literature that teaches us to see the panorama of history through the eyes of the victims, and in art that comprehends and expresses itself as the visualization of the memory of the suffering of others. In addition, we should mention here cinematic art works that call to mind the situation of pain and guilt in a way that the objective lens of scientific historicization cannot achieve. All of these arts have an essence that "carries after." They carry after us, who are enamored of forgetting, the pain of remembering. If we take things very exactly, there is for us no time "after" the Shoah in the way that there can be a time after Hitler and after Stalin.

Translation: Leo J. Penta

NOTES

1. "Thoughts out of Season II: The Use and Abuse of Memory, 1," in F. Nietzsche, *The Use and Abuse of History*, trans. Adrian Collins, 2nd ed. (Indianapolis, 1980), p. 6 ("Bei dem kleinsten aber und bei dem grössten Glücke ist es immer Eines, wodurch Glück zum Glücke wird: das Vergessen-können. . . . Wer sich nicht auf der Schwelle des Augenblicks, alle Vergangenheiten vergessend, niederlassen kann, wer nicht auf einem Punkte wie eine Siegesgöttin ohne Schwindel und Furcht zu stehen vermag, der wird nie wissen, was Glück ist." *Unzeitgemäße Betrachtungen II.1*, in F. Nietzsche, *KSA* I, 250).
2. *Beyond Good and Evil*, p. 217, in *Basic Writings of Nietzsche*, trans. and ed. Walter Kaufmann (New York, 1968), p. 336 (*Jenseits von Gut und Böse* 217, in F. Nietzsche, *KSA* 5, 153).
3. *Gedankenflucht* (Frankfurt, 1995): "Stored, that means forgotten." Formerly I used an opposite formulation that nonetheless makes the same point: "The computer cannot remember because it cannot forget anything."
4. *On the Genealogy of Morals*, II.3, in *Basic Writings of Nietzsche*, trans. and ed. Walter Kaufmann (New York, 1968), pp. 497 ff. ("Wie macht man dem Menschen-Thiere ein Gedächtnis? Wie prägt man diesem theils stumpfen, theils faseligen Augenblicks-Verstande, dieser leibhaften Vergesslichkeit Etwas so ein, dass es gegenwärtig bleibt? . . . Man brennt Etwas ein, damit es im Gedächtnis bleibt: nur was nicht

aufhört, weh zu thun, bleibt im Gedächtnis." *Zur Genealogie der Moral II.3*, in F. Nietzsche, *KSA* 5, 295.)

5. See U. Bernhardt, "Die Kehrseite des abendländischen Geistes," *Merkur* 43, 931.

6. M. Broszat, who recommends and defends the concept of historicization, does not understand it in the sense of memory-distant "removal" of the German past (*Entsorgung der Vergangenheit*). "Whoever wishes to talk the citizens of the German Federal Republic out of their self-critical consideration of their older and more recent history, robs them of one of the best elements of the political culture that has slowly developed since the late fifties in this nation. What is most treacherous in this regard is the fundamental misconception that the moral sensibility vis-à-vis their own history achieved through necessity was a cultural and political disadvantage compared with other nations."

7. In J. B. Metz et al., *Diagnosen zur Zeit* (Düsseldorf, 1994), pp. 51 ff.

8. New York: Alfred A. Knopf, 1996.

9. H. Weinrich, *Lethe: Kunst und Kritik des Vergessens* (Munich, 1997), p. 232.

What Can We Jews Affirm About God After the Holocaust?

Jack Bemporad

I would like to address myself to the theological aspect of the problem of evil and, in a narrower sense, to the problem of the Holocaust. I do so, not because I am foolhardy enough to believe that I have any definitive answers to these problems, but because I believe that it is only through groping together with the questions they raise that we can begin to pave the way for a viable Jewish theology.

If we maintain a belief in a God who creates and sustains the world, we come up against one of the most fundamental enigmas of religion—the problem of evil.

The path that many medieval theologians took in dealing with the problem of evil was quite simply to say that it is not real. They say evil is privation. Now, I think that all of us, especially after Auschwitz, will recognize the limitations of this view. If evil is not real, but just a privation, then it is nothing to avoid. Or, if we say that evil is necessary to the perfection of good, then why combat it, or replace it, if good would be diminished and not increased through rejection of the evil.

Those theories that define evil as negation or privation or unreal must themselves be rejected. Evil may be defined as irreparable loss, as Thomas Aquinas and Whitehead define it, the absence of that which might have been. And evil, it seems to me, has to be seen as the irreparable loss of the good. Evil is that which is, but ought not to be. But then we ask, of course, what is good? And this is the crucial question, since whether a good God could have created this world depends in large measure on what we take to be good in the highest sense.

The most common doctrine of the nature of the good is hedonism, which maintains that pleasure is the highest good, and pain is the worst evil. But I don't think I need to refute the doctrine of hedonism before this group. I can challenge it in the form of a question. Can one say that insofar as a life fails in pleasure, it also fails in worth? Obviously it is conceivable for us to think of an individual whose life is eminently worth living but whose quantity of pleasure in that life is minimal. An example of this kind of life was that of the great Jewish theologian Rosenzweig, who for years suffered from multiple sclerosis, and gradually died. He was only capable, at the end, of blinking his eyes, and his wife, through some kind of extraordinary method of communication, was able to write down his books while he was in this state. He certainly had little pleasure, but can one say that Rosenzweig's life had no worth? The simple identification of pleasure with worth simply won't hold. Furthermore, can one really believe that pain as such is evil? Isn't this, as Harris has stated,

> as questionable as the converse that pleasure is good? At least we should say that neither all pleasures are good nor all pains evil. Biologically pain serves the function of warning an animal of danger, and stimulating it to avoidance. The burnt child shuns the fire and so is protected from greater harm. Without pain we should be continually in danger of serious injury, and even of destruction against which we have not learned to take precaution. It cannot, therefore, be maintained without qualification that pain is evil, for it often serves a beneficent function. Things are evil, not because they are painful, but because they frustrate our efforts to obtain the ends we most value.

And what are the ends that we most value? We don't really have the time here to go into all the various ends that people value, so let me dogmatically assert what I take the good to be in the highest sense. The highest good is the free act of virtue for its own sake. It requires individuals who are free to act virtuously, that is, free to choose good or evil. Similarly, the ideal that the good is chosen for its own sake must be viewed as diametrically opposed to the doctrine which says that the good can only be chosen through coercion. A moral agent cannot do the good naturally, but must do it by an act of self-transcendence. As Tennant says, "character is made, not born; it is not given, nor ready-made." What I am saying is that the highest good obtains where each individual will do the good for its own sake, and through doing the good for its own sake will realize, as Kant said, "a kingdom of ends" where each individual is treated as an end, and not a means to someone else's end.

The doctrine of the good as the free act of virtue for its own sake implies not merely free agents, but also the recognition of the dignity and sanctity of each individual. It is this view that is implicit even in the hedonistic doctrine and underlies whatever value the concept of justice has.

Hedonists have no satisfactory way of explaining why, if the goal of life is simply the greatest amount or sum of pleasure, it is wrong for a few to have extreme pleasure and many none, if the total sum of pleasure is the same.

Bentham's motto, "Each one to count for one, and one to count for more than one," illegitimately introduces a principle of equality which cannot be deduced from the sum of pleasure as such.

However, as we shall see, even the doctrine of equality or justice presupposes for its very possibility the higher doctrine of virtue for its own sake, for it seems to me that we must make a basic distinction between justice as paying due respect or obligation to one another, and the attitude of the saint, of a person who gives, who cares, who loves, not for reward, but for its own sake.

If we consider justice, namely, the doctrine that justice is the arrangement wherein the good are rewarded and the evil are punished, one finds oneself in continual difficulty. Not that I deny the relationship between good and reward, or evil and punishment, but rather that the only way that statement can be defended is negatively, and not positively. Because, as a matter of fact, justice originated as a negative concept. The doctrine of "an eye for an eye, a tooth for a tooth," which is a great doctrine and a great improvement on any prior ethics of the ancient world, is basically a negative concept. It says that for the damage done to this individual we must somehow recognize that a like damage should be done to the perpetrator of the damage. In other words, if a person is hurt, that person or his family should not destroy the whole clan or society of the person who perpetrated the damage. There must be some kind of balance between the hurt and the restitution.

In this instance justice's main purpose is to suppress evil rather than create good. It can be seen also that strict justice does not allow for the remaking of man, for repentance and self-transformation. However, when one says that a person should be punished, does one really mean only that he should be punished, or does one mean that this individual should recognize the evil he has done, and repent and change? Similarly, if by justice we mean rewarding the virtuous, then we confront the strangest paradox of all. Virtue, if genuine, is done for its own sake; a genuinely virtuous person feels embarrassed by praise or thanks. And in the religious realm, the best take on the heaviest burdens, as exemplified in the concept of *noblesse oblige*. In the religious world, individuals are privileged to bear the burden of ascent, and here self-sacrifice and devotion are most significant. As Jonas has indicated,

> we must, in other words, distinguish between moral obligation and the much larger sphere of moral value. (This, incidentally, shows up the error in the widely held view of value theory that the higher a value, the stronger its claim and the greater the duty to realize it. The highest are in a region beyond duty and claim.) The ethical dimension far exceeds that of the moral

law and reaches into the sublime solitude of dedication and ultimate commitment, away from all reckoning and rule—in short, into the sphere of the
holy. From there alone can the offer of self-sacrifice genuinely spring, and
this, its source, must be honored religiously.

So I repeat, the highest good, the good that should be realized, is the good
where the individual can freely choose the virtuous as opposed to the selfish,
self-centered task.

Now, two questions face us: First, what is required so that this goodness
can be achieved, and second, is the world that we know one that is consistent
with such an idea of goodness? Rather than deal with these two questions separately, I would rather phrase the question negatively and ask, What are the
factors that make for evil in the world, and would we relinquish any of them?
Would we choose not to have these factors even though they are the factors
that make for evil, or would we say, Yes, that these factors are necessary in
any world that we could conceivably accept?

The first factor that makes for evil is the law-abiding nature of the universe, which will not vary to save anyone. The universe is a cosmos, not a
chaos; it is law-abiding, not whimsical; it expresses natural order. The question that arises is the status of the contingent. The contingent is that which
appears to be simply determined by law and cannot be brought within the
scope of any rational or beneficent purpose. But once brought under some
moral purpose, would we then wish the law-abidingness to cease?

Let us take the example of disease and cure which requires law and order.
Would we wish that disease not be rational or lawful? Only if disease has a
certain lawful structure can it be understood and abolished. If it were chaotic,
can it be understood and abolished? if it were chaotic, if it were whimsical, if
it were not subject to law and order, then we could in no sense understand it
or control it. Whitehead correctly stated "it is not that there is a world that
happens to have an order—but no order, no world."

The second basic factor that makes for evil in the universe is that the universe is a place where the possible is realized and in which it can only be realized in time. If we were to have a so-called perfect universe, we would have
a static universe, one that would be completely immobile and finished. But in
a universe that is completely finished, all the things that give us joy would be
eliminated. When we see a mother look at her child grow and develop and
prosper, and see both her joy and her apprehension the first time he goes to
school, or the first time he has a birthday, or the first time that the child smiles
at her, we recognize that over the years people grow through their sorrows and
joys to achieve a bond, a sense of joy and mutual affection. This is not possi-

ble in a static universe. It is only possible where there is realization, where time and process are real.

Furthermore, all realization is limiting; thus, the actualization of one set of events precludes the actualization of an alternative set of events.

Thirdly, the universe is unfinished and, therefore, has an open future, and the openness of the future gives man a task, for something is at stake. The rabbis spoke of this in the Doctrine of Tikkun Ha-Olam—the world is unfinished; it needs human beings to freely complete it. But if it is genuine freedom that human beings have, then this means that individuals can complete the world for good or for evil. Nothing takes place morally that does not take place through self-determination. It is this that converts a mere occasion into an action. The concept of human beings as moral beings requires that they make choices, and that these choices be available to them. Thus, they must exist in a world where evil is possible and can be actualized, but also where it can be avoided. It then follows that if a human being has the liberty to choose the worst, he or she cannot be compelled to choose the best. How can we conceive of a person's character or moral nature at all, except as that element of his or her being which is created in the crucible of crisis and temptation? If we had a choice, would we really prefer not to be free and that human beings act mechanically? Would we really prefer that God had created the kind of a universe where any action, however evilly motivated, would, without any loss to anyone, turn out in every way to be good and all right for all? If we really had that kind of universe, the ultimate distinction between good and evil would have disappeared.

Finally, the world must be such that our intermeshing relationships will affect others, too. The influences of the will that chooses the evil in preference to the good cannot fail to affect others in a world of free wills, freely interacting. But could we wish the reverse, that there be no interaction, that there be no influence of one person on another, could we really wish that? Could we wish there were no freedom, or realization? Could we wish that there were no law in nature or no possibility of fulfillment?

The essence of what I have been trying to say is that the world order is such that if all that makes evil possible is eliminated, then all that makes good possible is eliminated as well, because law, realization, freedom, and interaction make both for evil and for good.

Now, the answer that I have given is one that differs with two other traditional solutions to the problem of evil. The first one, quite simply, says that there is no undeserved human suffering, that is, that all people who suffer are guilty of sin. This was a position that was refuted with the Book of Job and needs no refutation today. Can anyone imagine that the million children who died at Auschwitz were in any way guilty of any sin deserving such punishment? The second doctrine that tries to deal with the problem of evil is the doctrine of immortality. It says that all evil is made good in the future life, in the world-to-come. But Hans Jonas has clearly criticized this view in his Ingersoll Lecture on Immortality, in which he maintains that "True justice would consist not in another life, but in a new chance at the same life, on the same terms." He further states:

> Missed fulfillment could only be made up for in its original terms, that is, in the terms of effort and obstacles, and uncertainty, and fallibility and unique occasion, and limited time—in short, in terms of nonguaranteed attainment and possible miss. These are the very terms of self-fulfillment, and they are precisely the terms of the world.

If immortality is to have any value at all, it is not because of the compensatory claim of justice, but because it is a consequence of the realization of the highest value, and being highest has the greatest claim to eternal endurance. But then, immortality must be seen as something separate from its traditional relation to evil in this world.

Underlying the question of evil is a basic misunderstanding that one must explore carefully as to the nature of God and how God works in the world. And this is the question of the power and purpose of God, as well as the kind of universe we have.

God is the creator of creators. In creating the world, God brings into being wills that are distinct from His own. A concept of God which allows free beings to exist beside Him is a much worthier concept than that of a God who is the cause of everything that happens.

God as creator has traditionally been conceived as a great architect, mechanic, or watchmaker who produces a mechanical model. On the contrary, it is a much greater God who allows free beings to act in such a way as to realize His purposes, or to frustrate them, a God who does not, indeed cannot make all the decision if a universe with being order, value and freedom is to come into being. In creating the world God gives full significance to creation so that He acts not through coercion or manipulation, but through persuasion, appeal, and revelation.

God would be responsible for evil if He were the sole agent of all that happens, and all other beings merely instruments or vessels of His will. But in a world where there is genuine freedom, which means personal discovery and production of values, in such a world God can only work as a persuasive being, and not as a coercive being.

Professor Howison put it very well:

> The divine love is a love which holds the individuality, the personal initiative of its object sacred. The father of spirits will have its image brought forth in every one of his offspring by the thought and conviction of each soul itself. Therefore the moral government of God, springing from the divine love, is a government by moral agencies purely, leaving aside all the juridical engineering of reward and punishment . . . that the cause of God may everywhere win simply upon its merits.

The divine purpose can only be realized by human beings freely making God's purpose their own. From this comes both the possibility of cooperating with God and estrangement from God's purpose, or sin. It means that the future is not given, it means that not everything is already determined, it means, as William James said,

> If this life be not a real fight in which something is eternally gained for the universe by success, it is no better than a game of private theatricals from which one may withdraw at will, but it *feels* like a real fight, as if there was something really wild in the universe which we, with all our idealizations and faithfulness, are indeed to redeem.

Or, as Sorley stated, "If there were no possibility of missing the mark, there would be no value in taking aim."

In a world that is open, where man is free, where he can frustrate or realize God's will, and where he can only gain the ultimate good through inner growth and moral action, such a world, I say to you, is the world we live in. Of course, there is evil, great evil; but human beings have the task to transcend and transform that evil. Of course, human beings are not in the center of the universe; it is humanity's task to reorder the universe so that human beings can indeed be at its center.

And so we finally reach the problem which all of us are haunted with today, and that is the problem of the Holocaust. Let us review several recent attempts to deal with this issue and contrast them with the view presented above. Professor Fackenheim, in his book *God's Presence in History*, has said that from Auschwitz there emerged a divine commandment, and that the divine commandment was to deny Hitler a posthumous victory; that we Jews should do everything we can to preserve Judaism, and thus ensure that Hitler does not ultimately win. "The religious Jew who has heard the voice of Sinai,"

Professor Fackenheim asserts, "must continue to listen as he hears the commanding voice of Auschwitz." He prefaces his chapter entitled "The Commanding Voice of Auschwitz" with an interesting if somewhat bitter tale by Elie Wiesel. It is a tale of a madman, a pious Jew, who comes back to a little synagogue in Nazi-occupied Europe, and during services suddenly says to the Jews, "Don't pray so loud, God will hear you. Then he will know that there are still Jews left alive in Europe, and you, too, will be destroyed."

Professor Fackenheim has done a remarkable service for our generation in pointing out the unique horror of the Holocaust, and in that respect his many writings have been of great help to all of us. However, the formulation of his theology in the activist form of not giving Hitler a posthumous victory is subject to at least a two-fold interpretation. Granting that the destruction of European Jewry was unique, it is still not clear what theological consequences are to be drawn from it. For example, Michael Wyshogrod said that should there be a tyrant who wanted to eradicate all stamp collectors, does that mean we should all take up stamp collecting not to give this tyrant a posthumous victory?

In other words, is this an aberration of a person and people that albeit has historic precedence or is there a deeper theological meaning to this. Is it, in fact, that Judaism stands for ideals, visions, religious truths which Hitler thought were inimitable to Nazism. If it is the latter, than it is not so much that Hitler should win but that the great Jewish teachers and teachings should not lose. And then if that is the case, unless one wants to have a Judaism with God under a question mark, then one must confront the theological issues of the nature of God and how God acts in the world which I think must be confronted for a viable religion.

What Professor Fackenheim has postulated is a demonic God and, in fact, he says that the religious Jew today must be revolutionary, for there is no previous Jewish protest like his protest. Continuing to hear the voice of Sinai as he hears the voice of Auschwitz, may require him to cite God against God in ways even more extreme than the challenges of Abraham, Jeremiah, Job or Rabbi Levi Yitzhak. And here are the forms which Fackenheim says this must take:

> You have abandoned the covenant . . . we shall not abandon it, you no longer want Jews to survive . . . and we shall survive, as better, more faithful, more pious Jews. You have destroyed all grounds for hope. We shall obey the commandments of hope which you yourself have given. Nor is there any previous Jewish compassion with divine powerlessness like the compassion required by such powerlessness. The fear of God is dead among

the nations; we shall keep it alive and be its witness. The times are too late for the coming of the Messiah; we shall persist without hope and recreate hope and, as it were, divine power by our persistence. For the religious Jew who remains within the Midrashic framework, the voice of Auschwitz manifests a divine presence which, as it were, is shorn of all except commanding power. This power, however, is inescapable.

Now, it seems to me that Fackenheim's proposed solution to the spiritual dilemma of the Holocaust is inadequate. If Sinai is genuine, then we don't need Auschwitz to learn that Hitler should not win. We don't need six million people to suffer and die for us; one doesn't need an experience like that to get the special commandment that Hitler should not succeed. If Sinai is genuine, than God could not be demonic. The God of Abraham, who could be challenged to fulfill his obligations, to whom Abraham said, "Shall not the judge of all the earth do justice?", could not be demonic. Abraham proclaimed that God was just. Fackenheim seems to be saying that we are just, but God is demonic. He is holding God responsible for the evil men do, a view I cannot share. God is a persuasive, not a coercive being, as I have already discussed. He has created a world from which man emerged as the last stage of evolution, but man must bring about justice in the earth; God does not take on the task of man. Man must take on his own task with God's help. It seems to me that the real issue the Holocaust raises is not whether Hitler should win, but should Abraham, and Akiba, and Jeremiah lose. Those truths which they stood for and which many died for, the truth which completely revolutionized the world, necessitates that we bear witness to them, for if we do not carry on for them, then the gift that the Jews gave to mankind may perish. If any truth comes from this, it is not that Hitler should not win—we knew that Hitler should not win—but that Abraham and Isaac and Jeremiah should not lose. There have been, however, several other ways of dealing with the Holocaust, two of which I would like to briefly analyze. The first is the view of a man of outstanding genius, tremendous character and heroism, one of the great leaders and teachers of our time, the late Professor Henry Slonimsky. In his brilliant paper, "The Philosophy Implicit in the Midrash," he states the following:

> The core of Jewish belief is that Israel must bear the Torah from God to the world, but the world is unwilling and resists all three: God, Torah, and Israel. And the protagonist who does the actual bearing must also bear the brunt of the suffering. . . . the Torah stands for goodness, for the vision, and ideals, and values, or light of God in which we see light. God, besides being this light and vision which we behold, is also such power, such real actual

power in the universe as is committed and has already been marshaled for the victory of the good. This power must be increased, the ideal must be translated into the real, and the active agent in this crucial event is man, who is thus destined for tragic heroism by the very nature of his situation. Israel, of course, stands for the ideal Israel, and is paradigmatic of the good and brave man everywhere. That the best must suffer the most, must assume the burdens and sorrows of the world, constitutes the most awesome phenomenon and paradox of the whole spiritual life. God in the full meaning of the term is seen to stand at the end, not at the beginning; on that day He shall be one and His name shall be one. He must be made one, man is the agent in whose hands it is left to make or mar that supreme integration. The assertion of God in a Godless world is the supreme act of religion.

For Slonimsky, this task is the true meaning of the covenant. It embodies the principle of noblesse oblige, which requires those who have witnessed the unity of God to bear witness and stand for God in a Godless world, to stand for justice in a world that denies justice, to stand for truth where truth is despised. In this way, Slonimsky accounts for our countless suffering. I believe Slonimsky is essentially correct in this evaluation. Yet, as impressive and brilliant as this view is, it seems to me to be defective insofar as it leads to an ultimate dualism between the universe and God. God is characterized only as an ideal which must be actualized and therefore, as a growing god, who either emerges or is held back by man's action. Evil, according to Slonimsky, can be explained as a concomitant of the unfinished character of the universe, which I believe is correct, and as a result of a God who does the best He can, but without man's help, is not strong enough to overcome evil, a view I hold to be incorrect.

For Slonimsky, God is not a creator, but is that aspect of reality that is good and holy, and which must overcome the other aspects of reality which are recalcitrant. His view of God is coupled with a belief in progress. Here he was true to his great teacher Hermann Cohen, and true to that Biblical phrase which he so often quoted, "on that day He shall be one and His name one." According to Slonimsky, the demand of the heart that God be one and that man succeed in making Him one overrides whatever rational doubts one may have as to the success of this end.

Unless, as I have indicated, God is in some sense the creator, then there are no guarantees about God's emergence. Rather than emerge, He may be defeated. What turned Slonimsky away from the concept of a creator God was the reigning view that a creator God not only is responsible for all that happens and, therefore, must be responsible for evil, but also that such a God denies human freedom. But if we conceive creation as an act wherein God allows other beings full power to act for good or ill, then we can conceive of a God who is a creator and revealer, yet not responsible for evil. God, in my view, respects the integrity and freedom of human beings and thus works through persuasion and revelation, and not coercion. Tennant expressed this well when he stated that God, "in revealing himself . . . will respect the moral personality of the persons who he would enlighten." This is the ethical condition of revelation to human beings.

Professor Hans Jonas has developed a position that in many ways is similar to Slonimsky's but differs from it in certain crucial respects. Jonas has devised a staggering myth in which he describes a God who, for reasons known only to Himself, allowed the universe to come into being, and in doing so, divested Himself of all power to direct, correct, or ultimately guarantee the devious working out of creation.

> God renounced His own being, divesting Himself of His deity—to receive it back from the Odyssey of time weighted with the chance harvest of unforeseeable temporal experience transfigured or possibly even disfigured by it. . . . Man was created "for" the image of God, rather than "in" His image, and our lives become lives in the divine countenance. . . . Our impact on eternity is for good and for evil—we can build and we can destroy, we can heal and we can hurt, we can nourish and we can starve divinity, we can perfect and we can disfigure its image—and the scars of one are as enduring as the luster of the other.

Addressing the question of Auschwitz, he continued:

> What about those who never could inscribe themselves in the Book of Life with deeds either good or evil, great or small, because their lives were cut off before they had their chance, or their humanity was destroyed in degradations most cruel and most thorough, such as no humanity can survive? I am thinking of the gassed and burnt children of Auschwitz, of the defaced, dehumanized phantoms of the camps, and of all the other numberless victims of the other man-made holocausts of our time. Among men, their sufferings will soon be forgotten, and their names even sooner. Another chance is not given them. . . . are they, then, debarred from an immortality which even their tormentors and murderers obtain . . . leaving their sinister mark on eternity's face? This I refuse to believe. And this I like to believe: that there was weeping in the heights at the waste and despoilment of humanity; that a groan answered the rising shout of ignoble suffering, and

wrath—the terrible wrong done to the reality and possibility of each life thus wantonly victimized, each one a thwarted attempt of God. "The voice of thy brother's blood cries unto me from the ground": Should we not believe that the immense chorus of such cries that has risen up in our lifetime now hangs over our world as a dark, mournful, and accusing cloud? That eternity looks down upon us with a frown, wounded itself and perturbed in its depths? The image of God is in danger as never before. . . . An eternal issue is at stake together with the temporal one—this aspect of our responsibility can be our guard against the temptation of fatalistic acquiescence or the worse treason of *apres nous le deluge.* We literally hold in our faltering hands the future of the divine adventure and must not fail Him, even if we would fail ourselves.

When Jonas discusses the philosophical consequence of his myth, he postulates a suffering God, a God affected by man's action, which implies a becoming God. He is also a caring God, and finally, He is not, for Jonas, an omnipotent God.

The similarity between Jonas's and Slonimsky's views is obvious. Both Slonimsky and Jonas seem to argue for a doctrine of a God who risks something, and that what God risks entails His very being. The being of God is itself dependent on man's action. Jonas sees this as a direct result of the existence of a universe, and thus, as one of the effects of creation, which makes it, in my opinion, more satisfactory than the dualism proposed by Slonimsky. I would accept the doctrine that in creating the world, God did take a risk, in the sense that the world is open, and thus, contingency, temporality, and freedom are real. I would not, however, go so far as to say that man can create or annihilate God. He can, however, annihilate and destroy himself and God's creation. Here his freedom is clear.

Fackenhelm, Slonimsky, and Jonas all seem to agree that there is a kind of drastic limitation of God's activity in the world. However, I believe this limitation is not such as to render the divine powerless or impotent. This does not mean that God is finite, for the limitation of God's power is not, as Slonimsky states, due to man or any other external cause. Rather it is a necessary condition of there being a world at all.

The old theism is no longer meaningful today. A God who creates a finished universe, down to its last detail, who is the creator of all, the evil as well as the good, who knows all, so that man's actions are merely a reenactment of what is eternally in God's mind—such a view makes a mockery of the agony and tragic heroism of man. By making God the cause of all, it makes Him directly responsible for the evil in the world and, therefore, either makes God demonic or denies the reality of evil. In either case, humanity is denied any significance. Human beings really make no difference in a universe where God's whim could at any point make everything different, or in which God could have worked everything out at the beginning for the best. Such a view simply cannot account for the reality of time, process, novelty, and risk.

We must affirm the creation of a cosmos, but one that is unfinished, incomplete in the making. Creation must be the "creation of creators." There are both order and chance in the world, both being and process, law and freedom. But novelty makes risk as well as loss and evil real.

God creates continually the universe with possibilities for life, mind, and value. Now the good, the true, and the beautiful become goals to be achieved, ends to be realized.

It is due to God that there is a world order rather than chaos, the primacy of good and not the primacy of evil. Neither being, nor order, nor aim at value is intelligible without some reference to God as Creator, an impetus to greater differentiation, organization, and harmony. However, it is a mistake to assume that order is all of a type. There is logical, natural, and moral order. There is no moral order apart from logic, pattern, and value. Moral order is a goal to be achieved and not a fact. This presupposes man's task. God must be such as to allow for man's task. In creating the world, God decided on the side of having man be the decider of his fate, and not fate the cajoler of man.

It is a mistake to see creation as a finished product. Creation is a process with an open future. It is not the case that God creates a finished universe. God has created and is creating with His creatures a basically unfinished universe. The goal of creation is the actualization of an ideal order of things.

The positive fact of evil is the conclusive proof that there is an unfinished character to reality. Science deals with an ideally closed world. The laws of nature are there to be discovered. Religion deals with an essentially unfinished world. Religion is concerned with what needs completion, with a universe in the making. It must actualize the truths it stands for. The ultimate resolution of the problem of evil is the affirmation that being, with its risks and possibilities of irreparable loss, is more valuable than nonbeing and nothingness; that time and temporality are real and not merely appearance. A perfect universe is a static universe. It is an impossibility, everything at once. Here realization is impossible.

God creates the formative elements and acts as the divine inspiration to man's task, but God does not take on humanity's task. It is human beings that are to help and continue the process of creation and be co-creators with God.

God is the basis and ground of the novelty of the world. God is necessary for the universe and man to be intelligible. Only through belief in God as Creator and sustainer, as the ground of being and order, as the source of inspiration in worship, as the ground for the values man must realize—only through such a belief in God can man find meaning and value to his existence.

So, perhaps we may summarize by saying that evil is the irreparable loss of good, that the individual's greatest good is not pleasure or justice but soul-making, the realizing of the good, and that human beings must take upon themselves that task, that burden of ascent. The rabbis taught this in a splendid midrash in which they say, "Those who are persecuted and do not persecute in return, those who listen to contemptuous insults and do not reply, those who act out love and are glad to suffer, concerning them, Scripture says, they that love God are like the sun going forth in his strength."

"Whoever Does Not Experience the Hiding of the Face Is Not One of Them" God's Hiding of Himself, Good and Evil

Benedetto Carucci Viterbi

INTRODUCTION

Talking about the Shoah is always a hard decision, especially for someone like me, who was born afterwards. There is always the temptation to keep silent out of a kind of fear of speaking of the unspeakable, for we wonder what right we have to say anything. As others have suggested, the biblical episode of Lot's flight from Sodom comes to mind: we must not look back at the destruction, under pain of being turned into pillars of salt. However, memory—always a fundamental obligation in Jewish tradition—is something different.

There is another fear too; that of being even distantly tempted to take part in the process of theological justification-explanation of the Shoah. There have been various approaches and attempts at a response of this kind, many of them from opposing viewpoints—sin, Israel, the rejection of the messianic figure of Jesus, the assimilation of Jews and their loss of tradition, non-Zionism—and I would stress that I intend steering well clear of anything of this kind. There is a danger that such "reasons" for the Shoah, seen in these somewhat trivial terms, could become the greatest justification of aberrant human behavior and the excuse for suffering. And we cannot allow this, just as God did not allow Job's friends to do so, when they tried their best to find the source of his misfortune in himself.

Having said this, I also think (as the title of our meeting indicates) that for us who have the Shoah behind us and did not experience it, the correct focus for our reflections is that of theoretically and ethically based action. I shall try to throw more light on the question by developing some elements found in Jewish tradition, both biblical and rabbinical, as it reflects on *hester panim*, the hiding of God's face. Many others have considered this subject in a whole range of perspectives, but perhaps it can provide some faint pointers on the path to be followed.

HESTER PANIM: THE CHAOS OF CHANCE

The principle of the hiding of God's face—what Buber calls the eclipse of God—appears a number of times in the Bible. References are found in Isaiah, Job, and the Psalms, but the clearest source is in the following passage from Deuteronomy, in which we should particularly note the interesting alternation of singular and plural—perhaps a reference to the unity of destiny of the whole people, on the one hand, and individual involvement, on the other:

> Then My anger will flare up against them, and I will abandon them and hide My countenance from them. They shall be ready prey; and many evils and troubles shall befall them. And they shall say on that day, "Surely it is because our God is not in our midst that these evils have befallen us." Yet I will keep My countenance hidden on that day, because of all the evil that they have done in turning to other gods.[1]

A rapid analysis of these verses allows us to list certain facts: God's face is hidden and no longer looks at the people; the absence of this gaze, caused by a betrayal, is the source of the misfortunes that affect the whole group, which explains these misfortunes by saying that it has been abandoned by God, and wonders about His absence, and perhaps His nonexistence. The text is a harsh one, speaking of abandonment. The commentator Rashi explains that this hiding is, on God's part, a non-looking at the people's sufferings; in a certain sense—and here we find a first major theological question—it is the interruption of sympathetic attention, of providence, of what Jewish tradition calls *hashgahah pratit.* However, if this is a punishment (as it appears to be), it is so in a special way, and one that deserves further investigation. It is not a direct divine intervention, as is found in the Torah on other occasions; rather, it is a withdrawal or absence, as the commentator Rabbi Levi ben Gershon observes.[2] The difference is considerable: in the first case punishment is addressed to the guilty, while in the second it is chance, as Maimonides stresses, that is unleashed against man, against the people. Thus a betrayal of the original covenant, with man hiding himself from his responsibilities, unleashes chance, which overwhelms each and every one, the good and the wicked, the guilty and the innocent.

However, it should be noted that it is pointless looking to the immediate pre-Shoah period for the sin that gives rise to the abandonment; as some people have suggested, this source moment is to be sought much further back, at the source of the Exile, in the destruction of the Temple—not by chance the place of the face-to-face meeting between God and humankind, the place that guarantees the divine presence among human beings.

In the Mishnah, the fundamental text of rabbinical literature, this event is already seen as the turning point, a hiatus in Jewish history, which, although remaining addressed toward an end, spends a long parenthesis in random chaos. History is no longer the place of God, as it obviously still was in biblical literature: God has withdrawn (perhaps, in an incredible existential theological oxymoron, following the exile of His people). The following are a few of the many texts that could be quoted in support of a working hypothesis along these lines:

> When it [the Temple] was burned, the Holy One, blessed be He, said, "I no longer have a dwelling-place in this land; I will withdraw My *Shechinah* [presence] from it and ascend to My first habitation."[3]

> Rabbi Yohanan said: Since the Temple was destroyed, prophecy [the semblance of the divine voice] has been taken from prophets and given to fools and children.[4]

> Rabban Simeon b. Gamliel says: R. Joshua testified that from the day the Temple was destroyed, there is no day without a curse, the dew has not descended for a blessing, and the flavor has departed from the fruits. Raba said: And the curse of each day is severer than that of the preceding.[5]

The view of historical and even natural reality, like the dimension of God's audibility and comprehension, steadily narrows and deteriorates. In this perspective, Jewish history after the destruction is placed—and it may not be too paradoxical to say this—under the sign of chance (as we shall see, chance with some major limitations); despite its aberrant enormity, the Shoah thus becomes another of the days, the darkest day—here in the literal sense of being bereft of the light of the divine face—in the Jewish historical continuum as it gathers debris. The worst, but not the only one. This is the view of those in the religious and Orthodox Jewish world who reject the principle of the uniqueness of the Shoah.

HESTER PANIM: GOD'S WITHDRAWAL AND HUMAN RESPONSIBILITY

Solitude in the apparent absence of God places the Jewish people and humanity in a situation of abandonment, but also in the face of stark responsibility, with no possibility of any heavenly postponement or providential alibis, almost at the origin of being. The hiding of the face can then perhaps be compared with the primal dimension of creation, using some categories of the Jewish mystical and philosophical tradition, as Hans Jonas does.

According to the Lurianic Kabbalah, the world's being is possible only with the concentration of God in one point: the existential conceptual "space" for reality requires this. In his hypothesis of threefold movement, Luria states that the first stage is *tsimtsum*, explained by Scholem as withdrawal. Creation, which opens human beings to the solitude of responsibility—almost immediately disregarded—requires a moving away of God, a "dilution" of his presence, as guarantee of human freedom. In this perspective, *hester panim* and *tsimtsum* could be read in parallel: the former as a punishment that threatens, in the form of chance, to leave man a prey to the destruction of others and himself; and the latter as inevitable openness to the autonomous history of man and his associated necessary responsibility. In both cases, we can perhaps speak of a return of God to his deepest, innermost, and most hidden "core," which, by no coincidence, is called *'ain*, or "nothing," in Jewish mystical tradition: at the moment of creation, man is faced with the nothingness of still-unexplored existence; and, at the moment of hiding before his own nothingness, his own possible nullification.

A great master of contemporary Orthodox Judaism, Rav Joseph Soloveitchik, seems to be saying something fairly similar, although he starts from a non-kabbalistic philosophical viewpoint.[6] For him, *hester panim* represents a return to the phase following the creation *ex nihilo*, but prior to that of the true physical dimension of reality, a hylic and chaotic phase, without physical structures or real existence. The assurance of the being of the world is maintained, but in a particular condition, prior to the applicability of the divine ethical system: the rules have become void, so that man is a prey to chance in this perspective too.

Taken together, the two perspectives seem to indicate clearly the link between *hester panim* and man's ethically responsible solitude, which is then the source of his being in the world. The punishment represented by *hester panim* is the return to the primal phase in which man has no excuse at all, perhaps partly because as soon as he first appeared he rejected the principle of responsibility (Adam blames Eve, who blames the serpent).

CAIN HIDES HIMSELF: BEING HIDDEN FROM THE DIVINE FACE

The episode of Cain's punishment—which is, in fact, contradictory— seems to provide a further point of confirmation. This is the text where the idea and verb of *hester* appear for the first time, albeit in a passive form— being hidden from the face of God. A rabbinical tradition, taken up by modern-day commentators, suggests seeking the first appearance of a word in the Torah in order to understand its true significance. The following verses may thus be of help:

> Cain said to the Lord, "My punishment is too great to bear! Since You have banished me this day from the soil, and I will be hidden from your face (*umipanekha 'assater*) and become a restless wanderer on earth—anyone who meets me may kill me!"[7]

This text is of considerable interest for our discussion. In terms of man-man relations, Cain is the first to face the consequences of evildoing. The punishment described in the previous verse is harsh for Cain, but it is interesting to see what he in a sense adds to the divine edict: being banished from the soil (something immediately contradicted in the following verse) and hiding from God's face—in other words, not being seen, not the object of attention, as many commentators stress. Cain is in exactly the situation described by Rav Soloveitchik: in the nothingness of chance. *Na' vanad*, the Hebrew for "exiled, wandering," is the condition of foreignness to a predictable structure of existence, and leads, despite having to wander on earth, to being banished from the soil—exiled to where anyone we meet can become our killer. However, the dangers of chance have a limit: the sign that God gives to Cain and that will prevent others from destroying him. According to the Midrash,[8] the rabbinical interpretative-narrative tradition, the sign is not something generic, but an aid against one's own destruction; some teachers say that it is the sun, which would save Cain from wild beasts (who else could kill him, since there are no other human beings there?), and would also represent a never-denied possibility of redemption; according to others, it is Abel's sheep dog, which also is a defense against wild beasts and a constant reminder— salvific in the most concrete sense of the term—of the murdered man.

At this point it seems that abandonment to chance—in the view of all those who interpret *hester panim* in this way—cannot ever entail total annihilation, perhaps on condition of certain choices: a readiness to rethink and reconstruct human relationships in memory and practice (as Cain teaches).

HESTER PANIM AS NECESSARY, AND THE PRIESTLY BLESSING

In its paradoxical contradiction (a frequent and rich element in rabbinical texts), the following talmudic passage throws fresh light on our subject:

> "Then My anger shall be kindled against them in that day, and I will forsake them and I will hide My face from them" (Deuteronomy 31:17). R. Bardela b. Tabyumi said that Rab said: To whomever *hester panim* [hiding of the face] does not apply is not one of them [the Jewish people]; to whomever [the phrase] "and they shall be devoured" (Deuteronomy 31:17) does not apply is not one of them. . . . Raba said: Although I hide My face from them, I shall speak with them in a dream. R. Joseph said: His hand is stretched over us, as it is said, "And I have covered thee in the shadow of My hand" (Isaiah 51:16).[9]

The first part of this text contains very strong words: being in the condition of *hester panim* and a prey to others is a constituent part of being Jewish, of belonging to the people; it seems a necessity in the framework of history (a statement the teachers come to on the basis of a careful interpretation of the structure of the text of the Torah, and not on that of simple intuition or historical experience). It is a bitter and terrible confirmation of the hermeneutic direction proposed above, which, we would stress, never indicates the immediate cause behind the Shoah. However, the second part of the text—as is also true of the episode of Cain—indicates that there is still some link with the Hidden One. It may be tenuous and oneiric (and hence, according to the teaching in other points of the rabbinical tradition, random), but it exists: the shadow of the hand (which in a certain sense hides) does protect, as does the sign of Cain.

This text seems to lead us toward the end of our journey. For those who are part of the Jewish people, there is no possibility of escaping the hiding. Perhaps in the chaos of history (in which, as Norman Lamm suggests,[10] shadow is always present but to varying degrees), it may be necessary to persist in seeking a possible link, albeit tenuous and dim, with the One who is hidden and masked, and hence ever more incomprehensible—a possibility of making real the Priestly Blessing, which is, not by chance, repeated in the synagogues by the kohanim, the priests, as their sole remaining prerogative in the world of the destroyed Temple (and hence of the necessarily now distant and hidden God), and must thus be understood as a future invoked goal and not a present reality. In this sense, the threefold blessing represents the hidden God's gradual self-revelation: "The Lord bless you and keep you! The Lord make His

face to shine upon you, and be gracious to you! The Lord lift up His countenance upon you, and grant you peace."[11] The initial phrase seems a first slight
change from the perspective of *hester panim*: as we have seen, protection is
always present, at least in general terms; here the blessing is added. In the following verse, the face that illuminates appears, but does not yet turn toward—
and is thus not yet wholly attentive—although assuring grace; the last verse
is the overturning of *hester panim*, or *nesi'at panim*, in which the face is
turned toward, observes, and lastly gives *shalom*—peace, completeness, and
completion; it is the end.

HIDE-AND-SEEK, GOOD AND EVIL

So what remains to be said of good and evil after the Shoah? Is there
something other than what could have been said before it, or, despite its enormity, is there very little to be added?

The approach we have taken thus far seeks to follow certain pointers from
the Jewish rabbinical tradition—although others, of a contrary nature, are
obviously possible—and I think it leads to some working hypotheses and
bases for reflection.

We Cannot Stop Playing Hide and Seek

For a large part of history the Jewish people—the world?—has been in
the condition of someone unable to see where God is, someone who is a prey
to the unpredictability of events, which cannot be anything but indiscriminate.
The overall sense of history remains, but the sense of this escapes us, perhaps
because it does not exist. The only possible response to the challenge is not to
give up the game of hide-and-seek: humanity's main role in this phase is that
of seeking and asking, not of finding and receiving answers. Two texts, one
talmudic and one hasidic, emphasize this.

> There was never a more difficult hour for the world than that hour at
> which the Holy One, blessed be He, said to Moses, "And I will surely hide
> My countenance from them in that day" (Deuteronomy 31:17). From that
> hour, "I will wait for the Lord, who is hiding His face from the House of
> Jacob, and I will trust in Him" (Isaiah 8:17), for thus did He say to him on
> Sinai, "My covenant will live unforgotten in the mouths of their descen-
> dants" (Deuteronomy 31:21).[12]

The certainty proclaimed on Sinai that the covenant will not be forgotten by the descendants of the Jewish people is what allows hope. Fidelity to the covenant, which in Jewish tradition represents the foundation and reference point of ethics, allows a wait that can be ended with the Priestly Blessing. In this perspective, the dramatic game of hide-and-seek must always be kept alive, through study and behavior in line with the Torah.

> Rabbi Barukh's grandson Yehiel [Rabbi Barukh was himself a grandson of the Baal Shem Tov] was once playing hide-and-seek with another boy. He hid himself well and waited for his playmate to find him. When he had waited for a long time, he came out of his hiding-place, but the other was nowhere to be seen. Now Yehiel realized that he had not looked for him from the very beginning. This made him cry, and crying he ran to his grandfather and complained of his faithless friend. Then tears brimmed in Rabbi Barukh's eyes and he said: "God says the same thing: 'I hide, but no one wants to seek me.'"[13]

Hiding and Autonomy—Freedom—Responsibility

As indicated, the world of *hester panim* is the world of freedom. With *tsimtsum*, reality was born under this sign, and, painfully for humankind, *hester panim* accentuates autonomy, and also the risk of evil performed and borne. In all this, an opportunity is provided, on the one hand, by the ethics of responsibility, which broadens each person's sphere of awareness beyond the individual dimension and projects him or her toward those who live in his or her own time, and also those who are to come; on the other, in line with Jewish tradition, we must bear in mind a heteronomous, divine ethical system, which puts human beings on guard against taking themselves as the measure of all things, the parameter of good and evil, the masters of God's will. It is no coincidence that the sinister sign of the Nazis' delusion of omnipotence was *Gott mit uns*.

Relationality/Solidarity: Job's Trial

Lastly, rereading Job—the text where *hester panim* is, perhaps, most clearly reflected—we see how important it is to recompose relationships, and to lay the foundations for a humanity in solidarity. Rav Soloveitchik points to solipsism—the limited individual dimension—as the stain on Job's righteous behavior prior to his misfortune. At the end of the book, Job shares in other people's humanity, even that of those who have until then tried to throw the responsibility onto him for the sin at the source of his ills. Rebuked by the intervention of God himself, his friends must bring a sacrifice, and Job must pray for them, for only then will God accept the offering. And Job prays for his friends.[14]

NOTES

1. Deuteronomy 31:17–18.
2. Cf. Ralbag, ad loc.
3. Eicha Rabbah 24.
4. Babylonian Talmud, Baba Batra 12b.
5. Babylonian Talmud, Sotah 49a.
6. See "The World Is Not Forsaken," in *Reflections of the Rav* (Jerusalem, 1979), pp. 31–39.
7. Genesis 4:13–14.
8. Bereshit Rabbah 22:12.
9. Babylonian Talmud, Hagiga 5ab.
10. Cf. N. Lamm, "The Face of God: Thoughts on the Holocaust, " in Bernhard H. Rosenberg and Fred Heuman, *Theological and Halakhic Reflections on the Holocaust* (Hoboken, NJ: KTAV, 1992), pp. 119–136.
11. Numbers 6:24–26.
12. Jerusalem Talmud, Sanhedrin 51;1,
13. M. Buber, *Tales of the Hasidim: Early Masters* (New York: Schocken, 1947), p. 97.
14. See Job 42:8–10.

God:
The Foundational Ethical Question after the Holocaust

John T. Pawlikowski

Back in the early seventies, two futurists introduced us to a fundamentally new reality with which religious ethics has yet adequately to grapple. Victor Ferkiss, a political scientist out of the Catholic tradition, and Hans Jonas, a social philosopher of Jewish background, served warning that humankind had reached a new threshold in its evolutionary journey. The human community now faced a situation whose potential for destruction was equal to its possibilities for new levels of human creativity and dignity. What path humanity would follow was a decision that rested with the next several generations. Neither divine intervention nor the arbitrary forces of nature would determine the choice in the end. And the decision would have lasting impact, well beyond the life span of those who are destined to make it. It would, in fact, determine what forms of life, if any, will experience continued survival. Buckminster Fuller did not exaggerate the profundity of the choice before us when he asserted that contemporary humanity now stands on a threshold between utopia and oblivion.

Ferkiss's 1974 volume, *The Future of Technological Civilization*, put the late-twentieth-century challenge to humankind in these words: "Man has . . . achieved virtually godlike powers over himself, his society, and his physical environment. As a result of his scientific and technological achievements, he has the power to alter or destroy the human race and its physical habitat."[1]

Hans Jonas, in a ground-breaking speech in Los Angeles in 1972 at a gathering of learned societies of religion, and subsequently in published writings, conveyed essentially the same message as Ferkiss. Ours is the very first generation to have to face the question of basic creational survival. In the past, there was no human destructive behavior from which we could not recover, largely through nature's self-recuperative powers. But today we have reached the point, through technological advancement, where this principle no longer automatically obtains. Humankind now seems increasingly capable of actions which can inflict terminal damage on the whole of creation and raise serious questions about the future of life itself.[2] The emergence of cloning has brought us to yet another level in terms of human power. We now appear to have the capacity to engage in actions previously considered the exclusive domain of God.

For me, the Holocaust represents perhaps the clearest twentieth-century example of the fundamental challenge now facing humanity as described by Ferkiss, Jonas, and Fuller. I have emphasized in a number of published essays that in the final analysis the Holocaust must be viewed as inaugurating a new era in human self-awareness and human possibility, an era capable of producing unprecedented destruction or unparalleled hope.[3] With the rise of Nazism, the mass extermination of human life in a guiltless fashion became thinkable and technologically feasible. The door was now ajar for the dispassionate torture and murder of millions not out of xenophobic fear, but through a calculated effort to reshape history supported by intellectual argumentation from the best and brightest minds in the society. It was an attempt, Emil Fackenheim has argued, to wipe out the divine image in history. "The murder camp," Fackenheim insists, "was not an accidental by-product of the Nazi empire. It was its essence."[4]

The basic challenge of the Holocaust lies in our changed perception of the relationship between God and humanity and its implications for the basis of moral behavior. What emerges as a central reality from the study of the Holocaust is the Nazis' sense of a new Aryan humanity freed from the moral constraints previously imposed by religious beliefs and capable of exerting virtually unlimited power in the shaping of the world and its inhabitants. In a somewhat indirect, though still powerful way the Nazis had proclaimed the death of God as a governing force in the universe. In pursuit of their objective, the Nazis became convinced that all the "dregs of humanity," first and foremost the Jews, but also Poles, Roma and Sinti (Gypsies), Gays, and the disabled had to be eliminated, or at least their influence on the culture and human development significantly curtailed.[5]

The late Uriel Tal captured as well as anyone the basic theological challenge posed by the Holocaust. In his understanding, the so-called Final Solution had as its ultimate objective the total transformation of human values. Its stated intent was the liberation of humanity from all previous moral ideals and codes. When the liberating process was complete, humanity would be rescued once and for all from subjection to God-belief and its related notions of moral responsibility, redemption, sin, and revelation. Nazi ideology sought to transform theological ideas into exclusively anthropological and political concepts. In Tal's perspective, the Nazis can be said to have adopted a kind of incarnational ideology, but not in the New Testament sense of the term. Rather, for the Nazis, "God became man in a political sense as a member of the Aryan race whose highest representative on earth is the Fuhrer."[6]

If we accept this interpretation of the ultimate implications of Nazism, we are confronted with a major theological challenge. How does the human community properly appropriate the genuine sense of human liberation that was at the core of Nazi ideology without surrendering its soul to massive evil? However horrendous their legacy, the Nazis were correct in at least one respect. They rightly perceived that some basic changes were underway in human consciousness. The impact of the new science and technology, with its underlying assumption of freedom, was beginning to provide humankind on a mass scale with a Promethean-type experience of escape from prior moral limits. People were starting to perceive, however dimly, an enhanced sense of dignity and autonomy that went well beyond what Western Christian theology was prepared to concede. Traditional theological concepts that had shaped much of the Christian moral perspective, notions such as divine punishment, hell, divine wrath, and providence, were losing some of the hold they had exercised over moral decision-making since biblical times. Christian theology had tended to accentuate the omnipotence of God, which in turn intensified the impotence of the human person and the rather inconsequential role played by the human community in maintaining the sustainability of creation. The Nazis totally rejected this previous relationship. In fact, they were literally trying to turn it upside down.

Numerous Jewish writers have attempted to respond to the fundamental implication of the Holocaust in terms of human and divine responsibility for the governance of the world. Emil Fackenheim, David Hartman, Richard Rubenstein, Elie Wiesel, the late Arthur Cohen, and David Blumenthal are authors who have made significant contributions to the post-Holocaust discussion. One of the most intriguing responses has come from Rabbi Irving Greenberg. His is a perspective with both theological and practical dimensions.

For Greenberg the Holocaust has destroyed all further possibility of a command dimension to our understanding of the God–human community relationship. "Covenantally speaking," he says, "one cannot order another to step forward to die."[7] Any meaningful understanding of covenantal relationship between God and humanity must be understood as voluntary. The voluntary nature of the post- Holocaust covenantal relationship unquestionably heightens human responsibility in Greenberg's eyes:

> If after the Temple's destruction, Israel moved from junior partner to
> true partner in the covenant, then after the Holocaust, the Jewish people are

called upon to become the senior partner in action. In effect, God was saying to humans: you stop the Holocaust. You bring the redemption. You act to
ensure that it will never again occur. I will be with you totally in whatever
happens, but you must do it.[8]

Based on this theological reversal in divine-human responsibility after the
Holocaust, Greenberg strongly argues for the assumption of power on the part
of the human community. For Greenberg it would be immoral, in fact it would
likely prove fatal for humanity, to abandon the quest for power after the
Holocaust. "Power inescapably corrupts," he writes, "but its assumption is
inescapable after the Holocaust." The only option in the post-Holocaust world
that will enable us to avoid the repetitions of human degradation and evil of
the Nazi period is to combine the assumption of power with what Greenberg
terms the creation of "better mechanisms of self-criticism, correction and
repentance." Only in this way can we utilize power "without being the unwitting slave of bloodshed or an exploitative status quo."[9]

I remain sympathetic to Greenberg's understanding of the heightened role
of humanity in the governance of creation. I also concur with his position that
such governance will require the assumption of power, even though the understanding of power may need some alteration. Nonetheless I have had difficulty in the past with some of Greenberg's applications of his theory of human
power to concrete situations, particularly to issues in the Palestinian-Israeli
conflict.[10] Clearly, developing the "better mechanisms of self-criticism, correction and repentance" for which Greenberg himself has called is a far more
challenging task than he may have realized. It necessarily involves, in my
judgment, a merger between an ethic of power and an ethic of solidarity. Only
a firm commitment to solidarity, something that Pope John Paul II has underlined as a fundamental virtue for our time,[11] can mitigate the excessive use of
power in the assumption of human co-creational responsibility.

Apart from the misapplication of power to concrete situations, such as the
current Middle East conflict, I would fault Greenberg on a more principled
basis. As a social ethicist I find myself at odds with the unqualified pacifist
position (though I remain a nuclear pacifist) and the deep ecological vision
that tends to submerge humanity within creation as such. But I do feel that
Greenberg has carried the theological role reversal too far. Viewing God as the
junior partner renders God overly impotent. I would opt for a more co-equal
relationship, though with a redefined understanding of divine agency.

The language of co-creatorship, developed mostly in Christian theological literature but also present in some Jewish writers, such as the eminent
Orthodox rabbi Joseph Soloveitchik and the contemporary scholar David

Hartman, who draws heavily on Soloveitchik,[12] represents the most promising paradigm after the Holocaust. While the notion of co-creatorship has roots in the biblical tradition,[13] its full magnitude has become apparent only in light of events such as the Holocaust and Hiroshima, and, as theologian Philip Hefner has emphasized, "with our enhanced appreciation of the vast evolutionary process in which the role of human responsibility emerges as absolutely decisive."[14]

While I am aware that it is open to misuse, I do not agree with those ethicists, such as Stanley Hauerwas, who have strongly criticized Pope John Paul II's appropriation of co-creatorship in his encyclical *Laborem Exercens* on the grounds that it would lead to a Nazi-like mentality regarding human superiority within the human community,[15] or those who reject it out of hand on the premise that it would open the door to ecological destruction. Surely the affirmation of co-creatorship must be tempered by the notion that the Creator God retains a central role. Hence my rejection of Greenberg's junior partner status for God after the Holocaust.

Hauerwas's call for humility in light of the Holocaust sounds an important cautionary note for any co-creatorship paradigm. But as the prevailing motif for understanding divine/human responsibility, it would likely prevent humankind from assuming full governance of creation, a failure that might, as well, entail economic, ecological, and nuclear disaster on a global scale. Unless we recognize that human responsibility for creation has been raised to a new level in consequence of the Holocaust and through our improved understanding of the evolutionary dynamic, the human community will likely refrain from taking those decisive steps that will ensure the continuity of life at all levels of creation. To follow Hauerwas or the deep ecologists in terms of envisioning humankind's role in creational governance could result in people of faith becoming bystanders rather than central actors in human history.

To ensure that the notion of co-creatorship does not wind up elevating human power to a destructive level, we need to reaffirm the role of divine agency, but in a refined sense. The paradigm of an all-powerful God who will intervene to halt human and creational destruction is dead after the Holocaust and in light of our contemporary evolutionary consciousness. On this point the Nazi ideologies were perceptive. Where their vision was fatally flawed, and so humanly destructive, was in responding to the death of the interventional God with an assertion, as Michael Ryan has put it, of all-pervasive power for themselves minus any transcendent moral referent.[16]

If we are to curb successfully the excessive use of human power within a paradigm of co-creatorship, we must reintroduce into human consciousness, especially in our highly secularized societies parented by the Enlightenment and its revolutionary heritage, a deep sense of what I have called a compelling God. This compelling God whom we must come to experience through symbolic encounter that is both personal and cultural will result in a healing, a strengthening, an affirming that will bury any need to assert our humanity, to try to "overpower" the Creator God in Nazi-like fashion through the destructive, even deadly, use of human power. This sense of a compelling God who has gifted humanity, whose vulnerability for the Christian has been shown in the Cross (as Jurgen Moltmann has articulated in *The Crucified God*),[17] is the indispensable foundation for any adequate paradigm of co-creatorship today.

I remain convinced that the notion of a compelling God must be sustained both in our personal consciousness and in our societal awareness. I fully concur with Professor Donald Dietrich when he writes, "As Christian theologians have faced the post-Holocaust world of environmental degradation, political brutalization, and social oppression . . . a concept of evil embedded in an individual's relation to God does not seem sufficient because it cannot explain macroevil."[18] "The human condition and its foundational values are intimately connected," Dietrich continues, "to the control fostered by the institutional environment. . . . From a social psychological perspective, the evidence seems to indicate that there is a critical interaction between the person and society that needs to be understood before the development and formulation of a moral grid can be accomplished."[19]

The importance of restoring a sense of the compelling God in public culture poses a special challenge to those of us who generally subscribe to the vision of church-state separation enshrined in Western democracies, and which, for Catholicism, was raised to the level of theological principle by the Second Vatican Council in its Declaration on Religious Liberty.[20] Nonetheless we also need to take very seriously Vatican II's Declaration on the Church in the Modern World, which strongly emphasized the centrality of culture in contemporary morality. Unless a sense of a compelling God is integrated into Western communal consciousness, not in a fundamentalist way but as a true moral benefactor, I fear that personal consciousness of a compelling God by itself will prove ineffective in guarding against the abuse of human co-creatorship. It could easily result, as the church historian Clyde Manschreck warned some years ago, in "naked state sovereignty."[21]

For the Christian, speaking about God after the Holocaust inevitably involves speaking about Christ as well. In light of the above discussion on how the Holocaust has impacted the God question in our time, we can move on to a brief discussion of its significance for Christology.

In the first instance, we must recognize the immorality of Christological claims that totally displace Jews from the covenantal relationship with God. Vatican II's Declaration *Nostra Aetate* undercut the very basis for displacement Christologies. Given the impact of an antisemitism rooted in such Christologies on the Christian masses at the time of the Holocaust, we need to recognize the removal of all traces of displacement Christologies from theology, catechetics, and liturgy as the first moral imperative emerging from the experience of the Holocaust.

Upon the elimination of displacement Christologies, we must begin to restate our understanding of Christ in terms more faithful to the teaching of Paul in Romans 9–11 that God's covenant with the Jewish people is enduring. Understanding the ministry of Jesus as emerging from the heightened sense of divine-human intimacy that surfaced in the Pharisaic revolution in Second Temple Judaism,[22] Christological claims made by the Church in reflection on that ministry can be seen as attempts to articulate a new sense of how profoundly humanity is imbedded in the divine. God's humanity became transparent in Christ in a unique way.

The ultimate significance of Christology so understood lies in its revelation of the grandeur of the human as a necessary corrective to the demeaning paternalism that often characterized our sense of the divine-human relationship in the past. In this sense all authentic Christology, in the final analysis, is theological anthropology. As Gregory Baum has stressed in commenting on Pope John Paul II's first encyclical, *Redemptor Hominis*, human dignity is presented as integral to Christological doctrine in the papal perspective.[23]

In my view, the fear and paternalism associated in the past with the statement of the divine-human relationship were at least partially to blame for the attempt by the Nazis to produce a total reversal of human meaning and values, as Uriel Tal has put it. Incarnational Christology can help the human person understand that he or she shares in the very life and existence of God. The human person remains creature; the gulf between humanity in people and humanity in the Godhead has not been totally overcome. The human struggle vis-à-vis the Creator God, the source of the misuse of human power in the past, has come to an end in principle, though its full realization still lies ahead. In this sense we can truly affirm that Christ continues to bring humankind salvation in its root meaning—*wholeness*.

With a proper understanding of the meaning of the Christ, even people can be healed, they can finally overcome the desire to supplant the Creator in power and in status that lay at the heart of Nazism. Critical to this awareness is the sense of God's self-imposed limitation manifested, as Jurgen Moltmann has underlined, on Calvary. This sense of divine limitation or divine self-construction, I might add, is also to be found in the Jewish mystical literature. The notion of divine vulnerability can become a powerful Christological symbol in terms of morality. It reminds us that one need not exercise power, control, and dominance to be godly.

But let me say that if the notion of divine vulnerability is to serve in this way, it must be disassociated from direct linkages to Jewish suffering above all, as well as to the suffering of other victims of the Nazis. From a theological perspective Jesus' suffering must not be seen as voluntary and redemptive. But such claims cannot be made in good conscience for the sufferings endured by Jews and other Nazi victims.

What I wish to argue is that the Holocaust represents, at one and the same time, the ultimate expression of human freedom and evil—the two are intimately linked. The ultimate assertion of human freedom from God that the Holocaust represents may in fact prove to be the beginning of the final resolution of the conflict between freedom and evil. When humanity finally recognizes the destruction it can produce when totally rejecting dependance on its Creator, as the Nazi leaders did in the Holocaust, when it perceives that such rejection is a perversion and not an affirmation of human freedom, a new stage in human consciousness may be dawning. We may finally be coming to grips with evil at its roots. The power of evil will wane only when humankind develops, along with a profound sense of the dignity it enjoys because of its direct links to God, a corresponding sense of humility occasioned by a searching encounter with the devastation it is capable of producing when left to its own wits. A sense of profound humility evoked by the experience of the healing power present in the ultimate Creator of human power—this is crucial. In this context Hauerwas's plea for humility as a critical response to the Holocaust makes sense, even though I cannot accept it as the prevailing paradigm. Clearly a Christology focused on divine vulnerability will enhance this process considerably.

Thus far I have emphasized the relationship between post-Holocaust human consciousness and Christology and how this relationship impacts morality. As central as this issue remains, by itself this approach is incomplete. Here is where the inchoative reflections of a group of Christian scholars who stress the human response dimension of post-Holocaust Christology assume great significance. Clearly the emphasis by theologians such as Rebecca Chopp and David Tracy on a person-centered theology, on a theology that directly relates to the victims of current history, is very much to the point in light of the Holocaust. Christology needs to become more than a theoretical affirmation of the human dignity that, in the words of John Paul II, lay at the heart of authentic Christology. It must also become the impetus for concrete manifestations of that belief through identification with, and support of, the victims of oppression through personal and political means. This will enhance the dignity not only of the victims, but also of the person who reaches out. Only through this kind of bonding can the instinctive patriarchal impulse, rooted in relationships based on power rather than mutuality, be overcome and a central force for the continued misuse of technological capacity be neutralized. Only in this way can we guarantee that killing, to paraphrase psychologist Robert Jay Lifton, will never again become a force for supposed human healing.

In this approach to Christology after the Holocaust, the emphasis on Jesus' sufferings on the Cross surely has a place. But this suffering must not be seen in isolation from his public ministry. For it is the period of the public ministry which Jesus often went out of his way to identify with, and personally affirm, the social outcasts of his time that gives significance to his experience on the Cross. His continual affirmation of human dignity in very concrete ways is what brought him a death sentence.

In a volume I find particularly perceptive and challenging, Vytautas Kavolis, a distinguished professor of comparative civilization and sociology at Dickinson College in the United States, argues that while the sacred will continue to influence culture, it will do so in a different way. In *Moralizing Cultures* Kavolis speaks of a movement toward the humanization of morality.[24] This movement involves a fundamental shift from the dominance of abstract principles requiring adherence, whatever the consequences, to a more directly practical concern with the reduction of human suffering and the enhancement of nondestructive capacities within humanity. For this to continue in a socially constructive way, we require moral leaders perhaps more than abstract principles.

Applying Kavolis's perspective to Christology after the Holocaust, we can say that Jesus' own public ministry becomes a prime example of moral leadership. But important as well is the witness of countless martyrs, whether during the Holocaust or subsequently, who have embodied Christology in acts of concrete witness on behalf of the victimized. The personal, and even communal, cleansing of human consciousness from the temptations toward the destructive use of enhanced human power is a necessary first step, in my judgment, in the humanization of morality. But the process cannot stop here. If reflection on the Holocaust leaves us merely with a Christology of divine vulnerability, we have failed in our basic responsibility as post-Holocaust Christians. We must also develop a Christology of witness which encompasses, as James Moore has insisted,[25] both rescue and resistance. I would add that it also needs to embrace the notion of authentic reconciliation, as described in recent writings by Robert Schreiter,[26], Donald Shriver,[27] and L. Gregory Jones,[28] and wrestled with by various commentators in the revised edition of Simon Wiesenthal's classic *The Sunflower*.[29]

Several closing points are in order. First, there are certainly more specific ethical issues connected with the Holocaust. I have examined these in several other published writings.[30] I remained convinced, however, of the centrality of the God/Christ question for morality after the Holocaust. That is why I have made it a focal point of this presentation. Secondly, while I have devoted most of this essay to highlighting the fundamental theological challenges for ethics in light of the Holocaust. I wish to underline again a point made at the outset, namely, that the issue of classical Christian antisemitism remains a moral challenge. I have spoken often of the need for the Church to confront it head-on, most recently in my 1966 Kenrick lecture.[31] I share the perspective of John Paul II that ultimately antisemitism must be labeled a sin.[32]

Thirdly, we need to ask the question, How can the compelling God spoken of above serve as a foundation for contemporary ethics? Strange as it may seem, the Holocaust provides us with some assistance in responding to this question. For if the Holocaust reveals one permanent quality of human life, it is the enduring presence of, the continuing human need for, symbolic affirmation and communication. What Reinhold Niebuhr termed the vitalistic dimension of humanity has not been permanently obliterated. But increasingly in the West it has been relegated almost exclusively to the realm of play and recreation. The Enlightenment and its aftermath caused a bifurcation in Western dominance which has catapulted reason to a place of overwhelming consciousness in the definition of the human person. All other human dimensions tend to be relegated to an inferior position. In this setting, ethics has become too exclusively rational a discipline and far too dominated by the scientific mentality. The liberals in Germany were powerless in fighting Nazism, not because they did not care, but because they naively assumed that the masses would respond to merely rational moral argumentation. The Nazis were far more perceptive in recognizing the centrality of the vitalistic in human life, as George Mosse's analysis of the Nazi "public liturgies" amply demonstrates.[33]

To sum up, the Holocaust and our contemporary evolutionary consciousness force upon us a major reformulation of our understanding of divine and human agency. In speaking of the need to rediscover a compelling God as the ground of post-Holocaust ethics, I believe I am close to the stage Elie Wiesel has reached as he has probed the depth of the Holocaust these many years. Despite the remaining ambiguities from God's side, atheism is not the answer for contemporary humanity, according to Wiesel. After we have exhausted ourselves in protesting against God's nonintervention during the period of night, we still are unable to let God go away permanently. Any attempt, Wiesel insists, to make the Holocaust fit into a divine plan, any belief that somehow we can imagine a universe congruent with it, renders God a moral monster and the universe a nightmare beyond endurance. But, as Robert McAfee Brown, has put it,

> for Wiesel and for many others the issue will not go away. He must contest God, concerning the moral outrage that somehow seems to be within the divine plan. How can one affirm a God whose "divine plan" could include such barbarity? For Wiesel, the true "contemporary" is not the modern skeptic, but the ancient Job, the one who dares to ask questions of God, even though Wiesel feels that Job gave in a little too quickly at the end.[34]

Wiesel hints that after all is said and done, the Holocaust may reveal that divine and human liberation are very much intertwined, and that, despite continuing tension, both God and humanity yearn for each other as a result. In consequence of this linkage, Wiesel is prepared to say that human acts of justice and compassion help to liberate God, to restore the divine image as Fackenheim has phrased it. Job, says Wiesel, "did not suffer in vain; thanks to him, we know that it is given to man to transform divine injustice into human justice and compassion."[35] But they also show the need for God's continuing presence, for the human person who claims total freedom from God will not likely pursue such a ministry of justice and compassion for very long, if at all. So the human person is also liberated from the corrupting desire to sever all ties to the Creator.

Restoring a *compelling* God to a central place in contemporary ethics will require taking account of the prophetic words spoken by the Catholic philosopher Romano Guardini soon after World War II: "In the coming epoch, the essential problem will no longer be that of increasing power—though power will continue to increase at an even swifter tempo—but of curbing it. The core of the new epoch's intellectual task will be to integrate power into life in such a way that man can employ power without forfeiting his humanity, or to surrender his humanity to power and perish."[36] Neither a return to religious fundamentalism, the growth of Western democratic secularism, nor a paradigm of junior-level divine agency can respond adequately to this challenge. Only a vision of human co-creatorship anchored in a personal and cultural sense of a compelling God, and bolstered for the Christian by a Christology of witness, has the possibility of measuring up.

NOTES

1. V. Ferkiss, *The Future of Technological Civilization* (New York: George Braziller, 1974), p. 88.

2. H. Jonas, *The Imperative of Responsibility* (Chicago: University of Chicago Press, 1984); also cf. idem, *Mortality and Morality: A Search for the Good after Auschwitz*, ed. L. Vogal (Evanston: Northwestern University Press, 1966).

3. Cf. J. T. Pawlikowski, *The Challenge of the Holocaust for Christian Theology* (New York: Anti-Defamation League, 1982); "Christian Theological Concerns After the Holocaust," in *Visions of the Other: Jewish and Christian Theologians Assess the Dialogue*, ed. E. J. Fisher (New York: Paulist Press, 1994), pp. 28–51; "The Holocaust: Its Impact on Christian Thought and Ethics," in *New Perspectives on the Holocaust: A Guide for Teachers and Scholars*, ed. R. L. Millen (New York: New York University Press, 1996), pp. 344–361; and "Penetrating Barriers: A Holocaust Retrospective," in *From the UNTHINKABLE to the UNAVOIDABLE: American and Jewish Scholars Encounter the Holocaust*, ed. C. Rittnet and J. Roth (Westport, Conn.: Praeger, 1997), pp. 99–109.

4. E. Fackenheim, *The Jewish Return into History* (New York: Schocken, 1978), p. 246.

5. Cf. J. T. Pawlikowski, "Uniqueness and Universality in the Holocaust: Some Ethical Reflections," in *Biblical and Humane: A Festschrift for John F. Priest*, ed. L. Bennett Elder, D. L. Barr, and E. Struthers Malbon (Atlanta: Scholars Press, 1996), pp. 275–289.

6. U. Tal, "Forms of Pseudo-Religion in the German *Kulturbereich* Prior to the Holocaust," *Immanuel* 3 (1973–74): 69.

7. I. Greenberg, "The Voluntary Covenant," *Perspectives #3* (New York: National Jewish Resource Center, 1982), p. 15.

8. Ibid., pp. 17–18.

9. I. Greenberg, "The Third Great Cycle in Jewish History," *Perspectives #1* (New York: National Jewish Resource Center, 1981), pp. 24–25.

10. Cf. J. T. Pawlikowski, "Ethical Issues in the Israeli-Palestinian Conflict," in *Beyond Occupation: American, Jewish, and Palestinian Voices for Peace*, ed. R. Radford Ruether and M. H. Ellis (Boston, Beacon Press, 1990), pp. 167–168.

11. Cf. M. Vianney Bilgrien, "Solidarity: The Newest Virtue," *New Theology Review* 10, no. 3 (August 1997): 82–90.

12. Cf. D. Hartman, *A Living Covenant: The Innovative Spirit in Traditional Judaism* (New York: Free Press, 1985), pp. 60–88.

13. Cf. J. T. Pawlikowski, "Participation in Economic Life," *Bible Today* 24, no. 6 (November 1986): 363–369.

14. P. J. Hefner, *The Human Factor: Evolution, Culture, and Religion* (Minneapolis: Fortress Press, 1993); also cf. J. T. Pawlikowski, "Theological Dimensions of an Ecological Ethic," in *The Ecological Challenge: Ethical, Liturgical, and Spiritual Responses*, ed. R. N. Fragomeni and J. T. Pawlikowski (Collegeville, Minn.: Liturgical Press, 1994), pp. 39–51.

15. S. Hauerwas, "Jews and Christians Among the Nations," *Cross Currents* 31 (Spring 1981): 34; also cf. idem, "Resurrection, the Holocaust, and Forgiveness: A Sermon for Eastertime," in *Removing Anti-Judaism from the Pulpit*, ed. Howard Clark Kee and Irvin J. Borowsky (Philadelphia and New York: American Interfaith Institute and Continuum Books, 1996), pp. 113–120.

16. M. Ryan, "Hitler's Challenge to the Churches: A Theological-Political Analysis of *Mein Kampf*," in *The German Church Struggle and the Holocaust*, ed. F. H. Littell and H. G. Locke (Detroit: Wayne State University Press, 1974), pp. 160–161.

17. J. Moltmann, *The Crucified God* (New York: Harper & Row, 1974).

18. D. J. Dietrich, *God and Humanity in Auschwitz: Jewish-Christian Relations and Sanctioned Murder* (New Brunswick, N.J.: Transaction, 1995), p. 294.

19. Ibid., p. 295.

20. Cf. J. T. Pawlikowski, "Catholicism and the Public Church: Recent U.S. Developments," in *The Annual of the Society of Christian Ethics*, ed. D. M. Yeager (Washington: Georgetown University Press, 1989), pp. 147–165; and idem, "Walking With and Beyond John Courtney Murray," *New Theology Review* 9 (August 1996): 20–40.

21. C. L. Manschreck, "Church-State Relations: A Question of Sovereignty," in *The American Religious Experiment: Piety and Practicality*, ed. C. L. Manschreck and B. Brown Zikmund (Chicago: Exploration Press, 1976), p. 121.

22. Cf. J. T. Pawlikowski, *Jesus and the Theology of Israel* (Wilmington: Michael Glazier, 1989) and idem, "Ein Bund oder zwei Bunde?" *Theologische Quartalschrift*, Begrunder 1819, 176. Jahrgang 4, Heft 1996, 325–340.

23. G. Baum, "The First Papal Encyclical," *Ecumenist* 17 (May–June 1979): 55.

24. V. Kavolis, *Moralizing Cultures* (Lanham, Md.: University Press of America, 1993).

25. J. F. Moore, *Christian Theology After the Shoah* (Lanham, Md.: University Press of America, 1993), pp. 145–146.

26. R. J. Schreiter, *Reconciliation: Mission and Ministry in a Changing World* (Maryknoll, N.Y.: Orbis, 1992).

27. D. Shriver, *An Ethic for Enemies: Forgiveness in Politics* (New York: Oxford, 1995).

28. L. G. Jones, *Embodying Forgiveness: A Theological Analysis* (Grand Rapids, Minn.: W. B. Eerdmans, 1995).

29. S. Wiesenthal, *The Sunflower: On the Possibilities and Limits of Forgiveness* (New York: Schocken, 1997).

30. Cf. J. T. Pawlikowski, "Christian Ethics and the Holocaust: A Dialogue with Post-Auschwitz Judaism," *Theological Studies* 49 (December 1988): 649–669; "The Shoah: Its Continuing Challenges for Religious and Secular Ethics," *Holocaust and Genocide Studies: An International Journal* 3, no. 4 (November 1988): 443–455; and "The Holocaust: Its Implications for the Church and Society Problematic," in *Christianity and Judaism: The Deepening Dialogue* (Scranton, Pa.: Ridge Row Press, 1983), pp. 95–106.

31. Cf. J. T. Pawlikowski, "A Faith Without Shadows: Liberating Christian Faith from Anti-Semitism," *Theology Digest* 43, no. 3 (Fall 1996):203–217.

32. Cf. Pope John Paul II, "The Sinfulness of Anti-Semitism," *Origins* 23, no. 13 (September 5, 1991) 204; and *Crossing the Threshold*, ed. Vittorio Messori (New York: Alfred A. Knopf, 1994), p. 96.

33. Cf. G. Mosse, *The Nationalization of the Masses: Political Symbolism and Mass Movements in Germany from the Napoleonic Wars Through the Third Reich* (New York: New American Library, 1977).

34. R. McAfee Brown, "The Holocaust as Problem in Moral Choice," in *When God and Man Failed: Non-Jewish Views of the Holocaust*, ed. H. J. Cargas (New York: Macmillan, 1981), p. 94.

35. E. Wiesel, *Messengers of God* (New York: Random House, 1976), p. 235.

36. R. Guardini, *Power and Responsibility* (Chicago: Henry Regnery, 1961), p. xiii.

Steadfast Love and Truth after Auschwitz

Maureena Fritz

When I was young and doing undergraduate work in the 1950s, a professor of English literature made this statement: All the wars fought since the beginning of Christianity are the result of the answer given to the question Jesus asked of his disciples, "Who do you say that I am?"[1] I was disturbed by this statement, although I didn't understand it then. Years later, in 1978, I was on sabbatical in Israel when one day, while standing in line at the main post office in Jerusalem, a woman pointed to the cross about my neck and said, "I hate that. For me and my people that is a sword." Because of that encounter and those with other Holocaust survivors, I began to study the history of the relationship of the Church with the Jewish people. My eyes were opened to a dark side of Church history.[2] Then, in the spring of 1997, I read an article written by a Catholic professor of theology at a major university in the United States who repeated teachings of the Church regarding the Jewish people: that this people is still most dear to God, that the covenant has not been revoked, and so forth. He concluded with the words, "But we await and pray for the day when the Jewish people will recognize Jesus as their Messiah." I was stunned by that last sentence. If it is true that we await the day when they will recognize Jesus as their Messiah, then they are still blind! And how can they be most dear to God if they are still blind. Is it not a contradiction in terms? So again the question, "Who do you say that I am?"

I want to make a plea, therefore, that we seriously look at the Church's Christology in a way that can maintain steadfast love in Jesus yet have the courage to look at the truth of what we have done in Jesus' name.

To rethink Christology in the light of the Church's new thinking about the Jewish people, that is, that they are most dear to God, that God's covenant with them has not been revoked, is to initiate a paradigm shift. A paradigm is a mental map, a way of seeing and perceiving that organizes pieces of a system or situation into an understandable whole. A change in one piece of this mental map shifts all the pieces and creates a new map of reality. When there is a major shift in teaching in one area (such as that regarding the covenant with the Jewish people which has not been revoked), the whole corpus of the Church's teaching is affected.

PARADIGM SHIFTS ARE NOT NEW IN THE ROMAN CATHOLIC CHURCH

One such shift was occasioned by the Church's collision path with science in the latter Middle Ages. Up until this time, the Church held staunchly to the Ptolemaic worldview, in which the earth was perceived as the center of our solar system. But Copernicus and Galileo laid this theory to rest with their discovery that the sun, not the earth, is the center of the planetary system. Displacing the earth from center stage had far-reaching effects in many areas of life.

That was very threatening to many, including Church leaders of the highest rank, and so Copernicus was persecuted and Galileo was condemned for heresy by the Inquisition. It took centuries for the Church to accomplish all the necessary elements of this paradigm shift, to be reconciled with reality through recognition of error, repentance for arrogance, and resolution for a change of behavior.

Another paradigm shift occurred during the Second Vatican Council concerning the Church's perception of herself. Recognizing that there were signs of the one true church of Christ existing in other Christian denominations, the Church made a simple word change. She replaced the word "is" (*est*) with the phrase "subsists in" (*subsistit in*). In previous perceptions of herself, the Church of Christ *is* the Roman Catholic Church.[3] In the new formulation, the Church of Christ *subsists in* the Roman Catholic Church, but not exclusively. The substitution of these words provided the leverage by which the Roman Catholic Church moved itself from an earlier self-understanding of centrality, of absolute uniqueness and elitism, to the recognition that "many elements of sanctification and of truth can be found outside of her visible structures" (*Lumen Gentium*, Art. 8).

Another paradigm shift is in the offing with the publication of *Nostra Aetate* and subsequent ecclesial documents. The proclamation that the Jews are most dear to God and that God's covenant with them has not been revoked becomes real in the measure that Christians depart from the road that denies these realities, namely, a Christology that did not leave authentic room for the "other." But what would such a process of reconciliation involve?

THE PROCESS OF RECONCILIATION

The Catholic definition of reconciliation and the Jewish teaching on *teshuva* have identical components, and these are contained in the Jewish confessional formula prayed on the Day of Yom Kippur:

I beseech Thee, O Lord,
(Recognition:) I have sinned, I have acted perversely, I have
      transgressed before Thee.
(Repentance:) I repent and am ashamed of my deeds,
(Resolution:) And I will never do this again.

These steps make up the action of reconciliation: recognition, repentance, and resolution. In this development, we begin with our focus on the first two steps in the process of reconciliation, recognition and repentance, and apply them to the Church's relationship with the Jewish people. With this introduction in place, we continue on to the third step, the resolution not to sin again in Jesus' name.

RECOGNITION OF SIN

Recognition, the first step in reconciliation, involves standing before God and making a public and communal confession of sin: I have sinned, I have acted perversely, I have transgressed.
Maimonides says,

> It is very praiseworthy for a person who repents to confess in public and to make his sins known to others, revealing the transgressions he committed against his colleagues. . . . Anyone who, out of pride, conceals his sins and does not reveal them will not achieve complete repentance, as Proverbs 28:13 states: "He who conceals his sins will not succeed."[4]

While the Church has always encouraged individual confession and contrition, it has not, until recently, made a practice of corporate confession.[5]
Rabbi David Polish referred to *Nostra Aetate* as a "unilateral pronouncement by one party which presumes to redress on its own terms a wrong which it does not admit."[6] To the extent that this is true, there is a serious flaw in the document. How can the Church redress a wrong without first admitting guilt and sin?[7]
Bruno Hussar, a Dominican priest, and the founder of Neve Shalom in Israel, wrote,

> When we know the history of the persecution of Jews by Christians, by Bishops, by the Heads of Churches; when we know the consequences of what Jules Isaac calls "the teaching of contempt in our catechisms"; when we know what really happened, how can we fail to be ashamed that people

of our own faith, belonging to our Church could so disfigure the Gospel of Jesus Christ?. . . . When forgiveness has not been sought there can be no sincere reflection or prayer in common. We may talk, discuss, have interesting theological dialogue, but the essential condition for true dialogue is that the Church asks pardon officially and from the heart.[8]

Recognition of sin and public confession are the first steps of *teshuva*. "Speak to the Israelites: When a man or a woman wrongs another, breaking faith with the LORD, that person incurs guilt and shall confess the sin that has been committed" (Numbers 5:6–7).

THE EXPRESSION OF REPENTANCE

The second step in reconciliation, of *teshuva*, is repentance: "Behold, I regret and am embarrassed for my deeds." Remorse and shame give us the right perspective on the value of confession. Feelings, emotions, thoughts, and ideas become clear and are grasped only after they are verbally expressed by the lips, in an audible voice.

Hence the highest teaching authority of the Church must yet publicly express regret and be embarrassed by her specific actions and by statements which had the effect of saying to the Jews, "You have no right to live among us as Jews." The secular states added, "You have no right to live among us." And the Nazis cried out, "You have no right to live."[9]

THE COMMITMENT TO RESOLUTION

The final step in reconciliation is a resolution not to commit the same sin again. This requires an examination of the teachings that led to anti-Judaism and antisemitism, particularly interpretations based on New Testament texts and expressions of Christology.[10]

Anyone who surveys the current debate on a Christian theology of religions and on interreligious dialogue and antisemitism in the churches will agree that Christology is a key element in the movement toward repentance. "Who do you say that I am?" St. Paul, in the letter to the Ephesians, writes of his vocation to "preach the unsearchable riches of Christ" (Ephesians 3:8). If the riches of Christ are "unsearchable," then the task is a never-ending one, and generation after generation of Christian theologians must revisit Christology, so that faith seeking understanding will find more adequate expressions. History itself helps us to weed out what is erroneous in our teaching, points to new directions, and provides a record of how well we have treated "the other." Treatment of the other is a good gauge for examining the truth of our Christology and our type of Christianity, which proclaims love of God and all others as foundational.

That is why the Shoah forces us anew to examine our Christology, for we have sinned in Jesus' name. ". . . the Church, which we proclaim as holy, and which we all know as a mystery, is also a sinful church and in need of conversion."[11] Following upon the Shoah, and influenced by it, the Pope's proclamation that the Jews are most dear to God and that God's covenant with the Jewish people has not been revoked is the piece in our mental map that shifts all the other pieces in the paradigm into a new map of reality. How can we now include this new teaching, which was not there before, into our understanding of the uniqueness of Jesus for the Christian?

Theologians from a wide range of Christian denominations are attempting to express a Christology open to the encounter with world religions.[12]

A sampling of these efforts will point to some of the directions and issues at stake. With old models of astronomy in mind, where one body, either the earth or the sun, is at the center of the system, we have a model by which to view our Christology. That is, is Christ the center of the theological planetary system, or is God? In the Christocentric paradigm, all things point to Jesus Christ and radiate from him to God. In the theocentric paradigm, God is the center, and the different religions are various paths that lead to God. Within these two broadly contrasting models are various nuances.

A CHRIST-CENTERED CHRISTOLOGY

In the Christocentric model, Christ may be seen in an exclusive or an inclusive way. In an exclusive model, belief in Jesus and baptism are necessary for salvation. Jesus is the only way to the Father, and those who wish to be saved must be baptized into him. Two supporting scriptural texts for this view are: "I am the way, and the truth, and the life. No one comes to the Father except through me" (John 14:6) and "The one who believes and is baptized will be saved; but the one who does not believe will be condemned" (Mark 16:15–16).

An inclusive Christology, on the other hand, does not demand explicit belief in Jesus Christ or ritual baptism into him, yet salvation comes through Christ. A scriptural text to support this view can be found in 1 Timothy 2:4–6: "This is right and is acceptable in the sight of God our Savior, who desires everyone to be saved and to come to the knowledge of the truth. For there is one God; there is also one mediator between God and humankind, Christ Jesus, himself human, who gave himself a ransom for all." Although it can be said that peoples and nations of other religions are saved through fidelity to their own faith traditions—a Hindu is saved as a faithful Hindu, a Jew as a faithful Jew, a Moslem as a faithful Moslem—yet without knowing it, they are all "anonymous Christians,"[13] and are saved through the grace of Christ.

Karl Rahner, the Roman Catholic German theologian whose theology had a strong influence on several of the documents of Vatican II, was one of the first to define the notion of the anonymous Christian. In developing this notion, Karl Rahner was inspired by the writings of Teilhard de Chardin. Much of Roman Catholic Christology following upon Karl Rahner has been influenced by the doctrine of the anonymous Christian. Others, however, question it.[14]

A GOD-CENTERED CHRISTOLOGY

In a theocentric model, God is the center and the focus of all human aspirations.[15] Even those who hold to a Christocentric view of the world admit that God is the goal and end of human striving.

Before the birth of Jesus, God was present in the world as Creator and Redeemer, and dwelt among peoples of all races and colors and belief systems. After the birth of Jesus this has not changed; God is still the focus of the lives of many people, and they will be saved, even though the majority of them are not Christians. An open Catholicism accepts the mystery of the divine presence dwelling amidst humanity, dwelling among men, women, and children, all of whom are made in the divine image and participate in God's being.

As we have seen, Karl Rahner advocated such an open Catholicism in his notion of the anonymous Christian, but while Rahner admits the omnipresence of God's saving and revelatory actions in non-Christian religions, he affirms that the saving and revelatory actions of God in them are made possible by Christ. Dialogue with Judaism and world religions is encouraged, but ultimately the non-Christian world is interpreted in terms of Christian categories.

Opposed to Rahner's stance are those who maintain that it is not necessary or even possible to judge among religions or their founders. Such judgments are unverifiable and without basis. They are unnecessary, for the non-Christian world is also a place of genuine revelation and the action of God. This positive attitude to the world does not open the door to relativism, they say, but rather it points to the incomprehensibility of God. Even God's revelation of the divine self in Jesus does not remove the mystery but only deepens it. Hence, the followers of Jesus must continue to learn from non-Christian religions, especially from Judaism, in which it is rooted and has a continual relationship, about the same God it sees revealed and present in Christ.

CRITERIA BY WHICH TO JUDGE OUR CHRISTOLOGY

The criteria with which to judge the Church's Christology, whether it is of God or not, is, I believe, clear. The Church's Christology is of God if it is marked by openness, love, compassion, and understanding for all peoples and religions; if it is respectful and in awe of the divine found present in the most unlikely places; if it has the ability to wonder at the multiplicity of divine expressions in the various cultures and to see God's Word incarnate, not only in Jesus of Nazareth, but implanted in all children, women, and men. If faith in Jesus causes these attitudes to be experienced and expressed, then such faith and belief is of God, and God's Kingdom is near at hand. His followers will be a force for good in the world and will have power to help build and bind together the building blocks of humanity into the living Temple of God.

When the Church focuses on the uniqueness of Jesus Christ, she does not thereby dismiss others but rather has further reason to embrace others. Because she believes in the particularity of God's presence and incarnation in Jesus, she can believe in the universality of God's presence and incarnation in others. Because she believes that she is chosen by God for a specific mission, she can thereby believe that there are other chosen peoples and races. In the foreground of this belief today is the affirmation that the Jewish people are still the chosen people of God, that the covenant with them has not been revoked. Belief in Jesus does not take away from God's revelation or presence among the Jewish people or in the non-Christian world, but adds to it and complements it.

This has not always been the stance of the churches, for, as we have said, in the name of Jesus we have sinned.[16] In his name there have been discriminations, expulsions, prison, and murders. Historical events have demonstrated the harm occasioned in former formulations of Christology. Theologians must therefore continue to probe the mystery of Jesus.[17] Old answers are not adequate for today's issues. Words of the past are no longer sufficient for the task at hand. There is need to go beyond what was said before. As competent theologians engage in this task, the official church must encourage them in their pursuits. God is present as leaders listen to those seeking new formulations of Christology. We must pray for those who silence research and discussion, who build walls around the faith and rob it of the rich insights that it can enjoy from the sharing and interchange with the Spirit's presence manifest outside these same walls.

Sometimes it seems as though a breakthrough has been achieved, as, for instance, at the Councils of Nicaea and Chalcedon. But on such occasions it soon becomes clear that the alleged "breakthrough" has left unanswered questions and these have to be taken up again. What is the case in the history of theology is replicated in the experience of each individual theologian who enters the field of Christology. Wittingly or unwittingly, he or she has engaged on a quest to which it will be necessary to return again and again.[18]

In conclusion, the statement that the Jewish people are still the beloved of God, that God's covenant with them has not been revoked, is a new piece in the Church's teaching. It changes and reshuffles all the other pieces of the paradigm. Consequently, the Church needs to concern itself with the fourth element of *teshuva*, resolution[19]—to examine all elements in her teachings about Jesus that in the past led to sin, discrimination, and hatred.

For Christians, confirmed in their espousal of the Gospel values that Jesus proclaimed as the marks of the Kingdom of God, reconciliation is both a requirement of faith and a resolve for behavior. While this is a work of *teshuva*, it is also a work of love. A scribe came to Jesus and asked him which was the greatest commandment. Jesus answered, "The first is, 'Hear, O Israel, the LORD is God, the LORD is one; you shall love the LORD your God with all your heart, and with all your soul, and with all your mind, and with all your strength.' The second is this, 'You shall love your neighbor as yourself.' There is no other commandment greater than these" (Mark 12:28–31). *Shema Israel, Adonai Elohenu, Adonai ehad.*

NOTES

1. This paper was first presented at the International Symposium "Good and Evil After Auschwitz," Rome, September 22–25, 1997. In this revision I have expanded my thesis by including references to recent ecclesial documents.

2. See M. Fritz, "*Nostra Aetate*: A Turning Point in History," *Religious Education* 81 (Winter 1986): 67–78.

3. See A. Dulles, *Models of the Church* (Garden City, N.Y.: Doubleday, 1974), esp. chap. 8, "The True Church."

4. Maimonides, *Mishneh Torah: Hilchot Teshuvah, the Laws of Repentance*, trans. with commentaries by Rabbi Eliyahu Touger (Jerusalem: Moznaim, 1990), chap. 2, p. 30. For a commentary on this tractate, see Pinchas Peli, ed., *On Repentance in the Thought and Oral Discourses of Rabbi Joseph B. Soloveitchik* (Jerusalem: Oroth, 1980).

5. For the statement made by the German bishops on January 23, 1995, marking the fiftieth anniversary of the liberation of Auschwitz, in which they acknowledge the Church's share of blame for the Holocaust, and for a similar statement by the Polish bishops marking the fiftieth anniversary of the liberation of the Auschwitz-Birkenau concentration camp, see *Origins* 24 (February 16, 1995): 586–588. For the statement of corporate confession made by the French Bishops' Conference on September 30, 1997, see the *Catholic International*, December 1997. And more recently, "We Remember: A Reflection on the Shoah," March 16, 1998, prepared by the Holy See's Commission for Religious Relations with the Jews, under the directorship of its president Edward Cardinal Cassidy. This twelve-page document deals with matters related to the Holocaust, the role of the Church during that period, and the Catholic understanding of the Holocaust in Jewish and Christian history.

6. Walter M. Abbott, ed., *The Documents of Vatican II*, pp. 669–670. After quoting Rabbi Polish, Claud Nelson, the author of this entire response to *Nostra Aetate*, continues: "Some Jews, however—perhaps most—while not enthusiastic find substantial grounds for hope for the future" (p. 670). He concludes: "It [*Nostra Aetate*] provides the basis, from the Catholic side, for a united and thoroughgoing Christian campaign against anti-Semitism" (p. 671).

7. James Parkes, *The Conflict of the Church and the Synagogue* (Temple Books, 1981). This is a comprehensive study of the origins of antisemitism beginning with the Jews in the Roman world and continuing to the beginning of the Middle Ages. See also Edward Flannery, *The Anguish of the Jews* (New York: Macmillan, 1965). A serious criticism of the document "We Remember" (see above, n. 5) is that it stopped short of admitting that anti-Judaism is related to antisemitism. Anti-Judaism in many respects prepared the way for the pagan antisemitism of Nazism; hence it is difficult to fully affirm that the antisemitism of Nazi ideology had its roots outside of Christianity.

8. See *Sidic* 29, no. 1 (1996): 18.

9. See Grosser and Halperin, *Anti-Semitism: The Causes and Effects of Prejudice* (New York: Citadel Press, 1979).

10. In his speech of welcome to sixty scholars whom he had called together on October 3–November 1, 1997, to consider the roots of anti-Judaism, Pope John Paul II said that "erroneous and unjust interpretations of the New Testament regarding the Jewish people and their presumed guilt circulated for too long" and "contributed to a lulling of many consciences at the time of World War II."

11. See the German document, n. 5 above.

12. Paul Knitter, *"No Other Name?" A Critical Survey of Christian Attitudes Toward the World Religions* (Maryknoll, N.Y.: Orbis, 1985); John Hick and Paul Knitter, eds., *The Myth of Christian Uniqueness: Toward a Pluralistic Theology of Religions* (Maryknoll, N.Y.: Orbis, 1987); Leonard Swidler, ed., *Toward a Universal Theology of Religion* (Maryknoll, N.Y.: Orbis, 1987); Avery Dulles, *Models of Revelation* (Garden City, N.Y.: Doubleday, 1983); Jacques Dupuis, *Jesus Christ at the Encounter of World Religions* (Maryknoll, N.Y.: Orbis, 1991); Robert Schreiter, "The

Anonymous Christian and Christology"; John Pawlikowski, *Christ in the Light of the Christian-Jewish Dialogue* (New York: Paulist Press, 1982).

13. See M. Fritz, "Karl Rahner and Theological Anthropology," in "Revelation and Self-Understanding" (Ph.D. diss., University of Ottawa, 1971), pp. 29–51, and Joseph Wong, :Anonymous Christians: Karl Rahner's Pneuma-Christocentrism and an East-West Dialogue," *Theological Studies* 55 (1994).

14. See above, n. 12, esp. Paul Knitter and Robert Schreiter.

15. For a comparative analysis of different models of Christology, see J. Peter Schineller, "Christ and Church: A Spectrum of Views," *Theological Studies* 37 (1976): 545–566.

16. As a reminder, there are the famous statues in the south transept of the Cathedral in Strasbourg. In the Middle Ages a type of symbolic art developed portraying two graceful female figures in which the Church is shown erect and triumphant, bearing a cross, and the synagogue is usually blindfolded and dejected and bearing a broken staff. Statues of this type are found in Bamberg, Rheims, Paris, and Bordeaux. Medieval Christian manuscript art is also filled with this type of presentation.

17. Fr. Jacques Dupuis, a professor of Christology at the Gregorian in Rome, in his *Toward a Christian Theology of Religious Pluralism* (Maryknoll, NY: Orbis, 1997), tries to answer the question "whether theology is able to assign to the plurality of religious traditions a positive meaning in God's overall design for mankind." Fr. Dupuis gives an historical overview of Christian approaches to other religions through the centuries and examines the axiom "There is no salvation outside the Church." He argues that religious pluralism is part of God's plan and says that the various paths to human salvation and fulfillment can be seen to converge in history.

18. John Macquarrie, *Christology Revisited* (Harrisburg, Pa.: Trinity International, 1998), p. 9.

19. Peli, *On Repentance in the Thought and Oral Discourses of R. Joseph Soloveitchik*, pp. 64–65. ". . . in regard to purification, abandoning the act of sin is only a partial remedy. . . . One must turn away from any temptation to talk in the 'path of sin.' 'Let the wicked man leave off his way, and the man of evil deed his thoughts.' The reference here is not to refrain from sin itself, but to avoid the path leading towards it."

God Between Mercy and Justice:
The Challenge of Auschwitz and the Hope of Universal Reconciliation

Dirk Ansorge

GUILT, FORGIVENESS, AND THE QUESTION OF VICARIOUS PARDON

In his famous novel *The Brothers Karamazov* (1880), Fyodor Dostoyevsky recounts a passionate dispute between Ivan Karamazov and his brother Alyosha.[1] The subject of the dispute is the suffering of innocent children and its impact on man's belief in God.

At the end of the dispute Ivan mentions a short article he has found recently in a newspaper. According to the article, it happened that some time before a general, a very prosperous landowner, had ordered the killing of the eight-year-old son of one of his serfs by setting dogs on him. The only reason for this order was that the day before the boy had unintentionally injured the leg of one of the general's hunting dogs. The boy was hunted down and torn to pieces by the dogs while the serf folk and the huntsmen watched—in front of them all the boy's mother. The general, Ivan ends his report, was not even convicted for this murder but was merely put in ward.

Ivan tells Alyosha this story as a "very characteristic" example of the suffering of innocent children. He regards their suffering as a refutation of the belief in a God who is both good and almighty. Ivan does not doubt the existence of God; but he denies that God is at any time able to realize genuine reconciliation. For such a genuine reconciliation would not only have to undo the suffering of the boy who had been killed, but furthermore, it would have to include forgiving the general's crime.

But who is *allowed* to forgive the general's crime? The boy's mother, who watched the horrible crime? But what sort of authority, Ivan asks, would entitle her to take the place of her murdered child? She may only forgive the sufferings she herself endured, but she may not forgive on behalf of her child: "She dare not forgive his torturer," Ivan exclaims, "even if her child himself forgave him!"

The assertion that the child's mother is not allowed to forgive the general's crime even if the child himself forgave him is grounded in Ivan's conviction that every kind of suffering is to be respected without any restriction. No one is entitled to integrate it into a sort of final harmony. Because according to Ivan's view, such a final harmony would conclude by rendering creaturely suffering inoffensive.

Certainly, Ivan is not consistent on this point, because at the same time he concedes that the child's mother may forgive what she herself suffered as a result of the general's cruelty. However, it is through his very assertion that the mother is not allowed to forgive in her murdered child's place that Ivan denies the moral legitimacy of vicarious pardon—a sort of pardon that is not based on personal suffering.[2]

While denying the possibility of vicarious pardon, Ivan's objection contains a far-reaching challenge to Christian theology. Alyosha correctly remarks that it is the redeeming work of Christ that is fundamentally doubted by Ivan's assertion.

But the ecclesiastical doctrine and practice of reconciliation is also called in question by Ivan.[3] For in the past the notion of reconciliation was very often restricted to the relationship between God and the individual sinner. Consequently, reconciliation seemed to be possible provided that the sinner repented sincerely, confessed his guilt in the face of God, and promised to compensate for the damage done as far as it was possible for him.

But what about the *victims* in this context? Aren't *they* the very ones who suffered at the hands of the torturers? Don't *they* possess, for that reason, the moral right to pardon *first*—a moral right that is even prior to the right of God?

Correspondingly I interpret Ivan's anger in a way that demands for the victims a right to a say in their own affairs. Encouraged by Ivan's objection, I ask: Is God really allowed to forgive the torturers without listening to the victims first? Moreover, should God only be permitted to forgive on condition that the victims have pardoned their torturers first? Should God even be bound to the victim's willingness to forgive with respect to the alternative of eternal life and everlasting perdition? But what if the victims, even at the Last Judgment, refuse to forgive their torturers? Is universal reconciliation made impossible then?[4]

Looking at the horrible suffering and the mass genocide brought upon the people of Europe by Nazi Germany, one finds a power in Ivan's thesis that considerably surpasses what Dostoyevsky obviously intended to say. As a Christian theologian I feel prompted by Dostoyevsky's work to reformulate the content of the hope that is in me (see 1 Peter 3:15): Who is that God in whom I believe and in whom I dare to trust even in the face of the crushing history of suffering, guilt, and injustice? What does my hope of universal reconciliation consist of in the face of millions of tortured and murdered human beings—in Auschwitz and elsewhere in the world?

THE PIVOTAL ROLE OF THE VICTIMS

In 1968 the Jewish philosopher Emmanuel Levinas discussed the question of reconciliation by commenting on a rabbinical interpretation of the Day of Atonement (Yom Kippur):

> For transgressions that are between man and God, the Day of Atonement effects atonement, but for transgressions that are between a man and his fellow, the Day of Atonement effects atonement only if he has appeased his fellow (Mishnah Yoma 8:9).

Commenting on this text and its discussion in the Gemara, Levinas shows himself to be impressed by its outrageousness:

> The fellow, my brother, a human being, who is infinitely less other in comparison to the absolute Other, is in a certain sense for me more Other than God Himself. To receive his pardon on the Day of Atonement, I first have to achieve that he lets himself be appeased.[5]

The victim—"in a certain sense . . . more Other than God Himself"! And Levinas does not hesitate to stress the offensiveness of this interpretation by emphasizing that he even considers the victim's possible refusal to pardon:

> And if he does refuse? As soon as two persons are involved, everything is at risk. The other one is able to refuse pardon and leave me without pardon forever.[6]

"To leave me without pardon forever"—that is very close to the challenge to the hope of universal reconciliation we derived from Dostoyevsky. Levinas, like Ivan Karamazov, clearly rejects the idea that the victim's assent is only of secondary importance with regard to God's plan of universal reconciliation.

> No, it is the offended individual who always has to be appeased, who has to be addressed and consoled personally. God's pardon—or the pardon of history—cannot be granted without the individual being respected.[7]

Pardon, according to Levinas, following the Gemara, can only be granted if the perpetrator asks the victim to forgive. But what if pardon is refused? This possibility, too, is taken into consideration by Levinas. And he seems to insist on the legitimacy of revenge and retribution. The reason, for him, is that the Other is an epiphany, a manifestation of the Divine in the world: the Other is the "image" of God (see Genesis 1:26). Therefore the Other is to be respected without any restriction. Revenge and retribution seem to be justified when this responsibility is neglected by anyone.

Nevertheless, the right of revenge and retribution does not appear to be without mercy. Levinas hopes for a kind of "superior justice":

> The Talmud teaches us that it is impossible to oblige people who claim the right of retribution to forgive. It teaches us that Israel does not deny anyone this unimpeachable right. But above all it teaches us that Israel, by acknowledging this right, does not claim it for itself, that belonging to Israel means not to claim it.[8]

What kind of justice, then, is this "superior justice" that distinguishes Israel? According to Levinas, it is the individual readiness of a person to refrain from the legitimate right of retribution when confronted by the concrete need of another person. Such a readiness, as Levinas points out, finds "in the midst of all the dialectical setbacks of justice and its contradictory ups and downs a straight and secure passage without any hesitation."[9]

Hence, Levinas's ultimate perspective is by no means an abstract right of retribution. The very opposite is true: the right of retribution is realized—at least for Israel—by not claiming it.

THE CONFLICTIVE RELATIONSHIP BETWEEN MERCY AND JUSTICE

What is the outcome of these deliberations with regard to the notion of universal reconciliation that we are searching for? It is the conflictive character of the relationship between the victim, the perpetrator, and God, which we may understand more deeply in the light of Levinas's interpretation of the talmudic tradition. Levinas criticizes any request for an abstract and universal kind of justice. Such justice puts the Other in a totalitarian system. It subordinates Him to an ontology that abandons His absolute transcendence. The absolute transcendence of the Other, according to Levinas, is only safeguarded in the ethical relationship between the Self and the Other.

But this intimate relationship is immediately disturbed by the presence of the "Third," the presence of the "real society." Even if the Third is regarded as a "second fellow" together with the "first fellow," a level of social relationship is established.

The figure of the Third in Levinas' writings indicates a formal authority that introduces the level of right into the relationship between the Self and the Other. He indicates the shift from morality to justice as the principle of right.

The Third bestows a form of objectivity on justice. However, to be morally responsible for the Other who faces me remains the fundamental principle of justice.

> It is always by facing the Other, it is by reason of being responsible for the Other, that justice arises—justice that introduces judgment and comparison of what is never to be compared—because every being is unique, every Other is unique.[10]

Levinas's assertions about the position of the Third remain very ambiguous. Nevertheless, they indicate the conflictive character of justice. This conflict cannot be avoided once the intimacy between the Self and the Other is "disturbed" by the introduction of claims that are both different and legitimate.[11]

With regard to our question concerning the possibility of universal reconciliation at the end of time, we may identify the emergence of the Third with the intervention of the victims: by the moral authority of their suffering, they claim a kind of justice that at first sight seems to enable them to forgive—or to refuse pardon.

In the perspective of the Last Judgment, the possibility of conflict between different claims cannot be excluded, because we are not permitted to suppose, without further inquiry, that God and the victims will act unanimously. On the contrary: according to Levinas the victims will "inevitably" perceive a possible renunciation of compensation on the part of the perpetrators as a form of violence. "They feel in their flesh the horrible price of the pardoned injury .. , the danger of merciful pardon of the crime." Therefore Levinas indicates the possibility that at the time of the coming of the Messiah the perpetrators are to be sacrificed to the victims—because "in every righteous action there is a kind of violence that causes suffering. Even if the action is righteous it contains violence."[12]

Interpreting the Talmud, Levinas points to the conflictive and violent structure of justice. It is not even perfect justice—justice that Levinas connects with the coming of the Messiah—that will be realized without violence.

Because the conflict is introduced by different legitimate claims: the victims' claims for compensation based on the moral authority of their personal suffering, the possibly repenting torturers' claim for mercy, and God's self-imposed claim to act righteously with regard to the victims as well as to the perpetrators. How is one to reconcile these different claims?

Within the theoretical framework of Levinas's philosophy, it is hardly possible to reconcile these different moral claims. Levinas's anthropology is based on the presumption that the human being is an epiphany, a sort of a revelation of the Divine in the world. Therefore every human being has to be respected even if he has done wrong.

The idea that every human being is an epiphany of the Divine enables Levinas to argue in favor of the moral authority of the victims who have suffered at the hands of their torturers. But the same idea inhibits him from reconciling conflicting moral claims. Because the claim for revenge and the claim for pardon are both based on the same ground, the "honor of the Divine Name." The only solution Levinas can offer is hesitation: the hesitation of Israel to claim the right of retribution, and the hesitation of the Messiah to realize his perfect justice.

But can we really accept hesitation as the last word in realizing universal reconciliation? In order to escape the dilemma outlined by Levinas, we have to scrutinize more closely what exactly we have in mind when we speak about pardon.

THE MEANING OF PARDON IN TERMS OF FREEDOM

Responsibility, guilt, pardon, reconciliation—all these notions point to fundamental dimensions of humanness where man's subjectivity and freedom are deeply involved. At the very latest, it is since Immanuel Kant (1724–1804) that the notion of freedom has been put at the center of most philosophical and theological efforts to understand the human being. But it was Johann Gottlieb Fichte (1762–1814) who, for the first time, not only centered his deliberations on the moral individual, but considered intersubjectivity to be essential for understanding humanness. Intersubjectivity is fundamental in the process of developing human self-consciousness, for human self-consciousness is formed by external moral demands. In order to realize myself I have to accept the other's freedom to be the normative content of my own freedom.[13]

Accordingly, refusing to accept the other's freedom as part of my own freedom is Fichte's very definition of guilt: he conceives guilt as the self-centering of human freedom.[14]

Following Fichte, the German philosopher Hermann Krings (b. 1913) stresses that the opening of freedom toward another freedom—that is, toward another human being—implies an acknowledgment of the other freedom for its own sake—that is, an acknowledgment of another freedom with respect to its unconditional self-determination.[15] For only that which is determined by unconditional freedom is able to fulfill the freedom we are ourselves.[16]

If this unconditional acknowledgment of another freedom is realized as a redetermination of freedom against a background of a preceding self-center-ing or self-absolutization—in other words, against the background of a pre-ceding guilt—then we have obtained a primary and formal notion of repen-tance as the beginning of reconciliation.

Repentance is initiated by the acknowledgment of personal guilt. It points to the dialectical unity of affirming and simultaneously negating a committed crime that a person accepts as his own deed. Repentance reopens this person to admit a non-self-conceived promise of pardon. By his confession of guilt and by his free assent to such a promise, the perpetrator agrees to redetermine his own freedom. This redetermination should be directed by an acknowledg-ment of the other freedom in order to be the essential subject of one's future actions.

Reconciliation, then, means to overcome the self-centering of human freedom, to redetermine freedom by the unconditional acknowledgment of another freedom, and to be accepted by that other freedom.

Because the promise of pardon does not pin down the perpetrator to his crime but offers him the possibility of a redetermination toward goodness, it opens up the prospect of a new and common future.

> Pardon . . . does not consist of denying former actions . . . but means instead not fixing another person's freedom to what one has done, i.e., to acknowledge freedom in its transcendence to its actual achievement, to release it into the possibility of its original capability to begin anew and, by way of this very acknowledgment, to offer this freedom the possibility of a new self-determination.[17]

Hannah Arendt, in her *Human Condition* (1958), stresses the imperative character of pardon.

> Without being forgiven, released from the consequences of what we have done, our capacity to act would, as it were, be confined to one single deed from which we could never recover; we would remain the victims of its consequences forever.[18]

But don't Arendt's deliberations contain a kind of moral obligation to forgive in order to realize universal reconciliation?

A MORAL OBLIGATION TO FORGIVE?

The experience of Auschwitz poses serious questions to such a conception. In the face of the horrible evil symbolized by the very name of Auschwitz, are we not constrained to suppose a legitimate refusal of pardon? Isn't that refusal legitimate with regard to the inconceivable dimensions of suffered pain? Can we really demand that the victims forgive their perpetrators for what has been done to them? Can we really demand that they forgive Adolf Hitler and his tormentors?

It is true: if we conceive reconciliation in terms of freedom, forgiveness appears to be a moral obligation—a moral obligation of a very high dignity. As such it can be compared with the appeal to love another person. To love somebody means to acknowledge him for his own sake, to act in favor of him and to provoke his best capacities. But even if to love one another appears to be a divine commandment (see John 13:34), it can be nothing but an appeal directed to man's free will. Love cannot be imposed by enforcement, because any form of imposed love is a contradiction *eo ipso*.

This is also true with respect to the commandment to love one's enemies (see Matthew 5:44, Luke 6:27). This moral demand can only be realized if a person gives his free assent to it. Moreover, to be able to love somebody— perhaps even to love one's enemies—very often is not perceived as an obedient fulfillment of a commandment, but as a freely given grace.

The awareness that love, the principal ideal of being human, cannot be imposed by force may help us to understand better the nature of the moral obligation of pardon. The call for pardon can be nothing but an invitation. Forgiveness can only be granted if it is initiated and conducted by free personal assent. Just as it is impossible to compel anyone to love some person, it is impossible to compel a victim to pardon his torturer. To be able to pardon somebody, then, appears like an event of grace. It is just as unconditional as freedom.

With special regard to Auschwitz, we are too easily able to imagine experiences of maltreated and abused persons that justify their refusal of pardon. The Bible tells us that God is fully aware of the possibility that human beings who have suffered abundantly will refuse to be comforted (see Jeremiah 31:15, Matthew 2:18). Will they be able to forgive? And if not, aren't they to be respected in their sorrow even by God?

But what would be the consequences of God's respect with regard to the hope of universal reconciliation? Isn't universal reconciliation made impossible forever if God respects the victims' possible refusal to forgive? Or should God be allowed to dismiss the victims' refusal and forgive vicariously?

IS GOD ALLOWED TO PARDON VICARIOUSLY?

This question leads us back to the initial problem of this essay. It receives its full weight in the perspective of God's intention to realize universal salvation at the end of time. If God is goodness, which means that He is a morally acting being,[19] then He seems to be obliged to respect any free decision of a human being on condition that it is morally legitimate to some extent.[20] And we stress that the refusal of pardon can be legitimate with regard to one's awful suffering. Therefore the suffering of the victims seems to grant them a moral authority that is to be respected even by God—and even in the case where God's intention of universal salvation calls for another decision.

But would this not mean that human beings are left at one another's mercy? Wouldn't it mean that mortal men and women are to decide on reconciliation and damnation, on eternal life and everlasting perdition?

I am not dealing here with the case that the torturers do not repent and refuse to accept pardon—a case that points to the possibility of self-imposed everlasting perdition.[21] But if the victims do not forgive their torturers even if they repent, is universal reconciliation then impossible? Would God be bound to the victims' refusal even in this case? Or would He be entitled to substitute the victims' refusal by pardoning in their place? Would God be entitled to dismiss the victims' refusal? Yet what sort of right would authorize such a dismissal? The right, for instance, to realize universal salvation at the very end of history? Or the right to keep human beings from being at the mercy of one another? But why didn't God intercede in history—at Auschwitz, for instance?

Hence the question concerning the possibility of pardon receives its ultimate significance with regard to the Last Judgment, when the fate of human beings is finally decided on.

What will be the nature of the human being reinstituted by God in the context of the Last Judgment? I wish to argue here that all our deliberations concerning the nature of guilt, freedom, and pardon will not lose their significance with regard to the Last Judgment. Because in the Last Judgment man will not simply be a passive recipient of the divine judgment. Since the human being essentially is created as free, his or her freedom will neither be extinguished after the individual's death nor done away with in the course of the Last Judgment. On the contrary: man's freedom will be released from all the restricting factors it was influenced by while living upon earth. At the Last Judgment, I presume, every human being will be released to a truly free relationship toward his own life, toward God, and toward his fellow-creatures.

Therefore at the Last Judgment the individual will not stand alone before God: with him and around him will be assembled all those to whom he has done good or evil in the course of his life. And the human being, as a concrete person characterized by possibilities both realized and unrealized, will be restored as that unique subject whom God originally intended and created him or her to be—a being that includes the restoration of the unconditional freedom that he or she originally as well as ultimately is.

I have to admit that neither theological tradition nor present theology is free of ambiguity on this point.[22] However, fully aware of the fact that the freedom of human beings living on earth is influenced by many factors, I suppose that there are good reasons to hope that at the Last Judgment the torturers actually will be free to repent and to ask pardon and mercy. And that the victims actually will be free to pardon their torturers—or to refuse pardon.

But if this is true, the complex structure of reconciliation and the conflictive relationship between God, the victim, and the perpetrator will by no means have ceased to exist in the context of the Last Judgment. And our key question still requires an answer: Will God be bound by the victims' definitive refusal?

My tentative answer is: If the perpetrators as well as the victims are able to act freely in the context of the Last Judgment, and if the self-engagement of God in human freedom is not to remain conditional, so that His self-engagement is not without any further obligation for God Himself, then we have good reason to say that the decision of the victims to grant or to refuse pardon is to be respected even by God.[23]

My tentative answer, however, is located on a very formal level. It does not regard the *content* of our hope for universal salvation. Therefore we have, finally, to scrutinize more closely what exactly we hope will be realized in the course of the Last Judgment.

THE HOPE FOR UNIVERSAL RECONCILIATION

Neither Jews nor Christians believe in a passionless God residing somewhere in heaven. On the contrary, the biblical God is deeply involved in history—the history of Israel as well as the history of Jesus of Nazareth. Therefore we believe that God knows about the sufferings of His creatures.

And His knowledge is by no means merely theoretical: God knows about the victim's sufferings just as a lover knows about the sufferings of a loved one, and His knowledge is a personal suffering for Himself.[24]

At the Last Judgment God's unconditional love for the victims will be revealed without any uncertainty. Becoming aware of the fact that God loves them passionately—may this not free the victims to refrain from their legitimate right of retribution and invite them to pardon their tormentors? Will they really be able to insist on the restriction of God's love to only a certain number of human beings?[25]

These reasons encourage us to hope that God's wooing love will enable the victims to pardon their torturers without any restriction.

God's wooing love, however, remains nothing but an invitation to human freedom. His invitation to forgive respects human freedom even with regard to universal salvation:

> Even as the One who effects salvation, God respects the freedom He gave to His creatures. And He will never overwhelm this created freedom by the power of His absolute freedom, because by doing this He would contradict Himself.[26]

Here we face the helplessness of God's love, a helplessness that consists of the absolute refutation of any form of violence and enforcement. Wooing for a free response, God takes over the consequences of having created a human being that is free to choose between good and evil. It points to God's risk that the victims refuse pardon, because neither love nor pardon can be imposed by any sort of external commandment. And it points to our hope that in His glory God will meet the victims with His love, which is, at the same time, both powerless and overwhelming.

Prompted by our reading of Dostoyevsky, we asked about the role of the victims in realizing universal reconciliation. At the very end of our deliberations, we have nothing other than our firm hope in God's wooing love. Regarding the horrible suffering in the world, we have learned to recognize the pivotal role of the victims in realizing reconciliation. It is their subjectivity that has to be restored at the Last Judgment. Only by addressing them by their names (see Isaiah 43:1) does God instill something their torturers withheld: that is, to be free subjects. At the Last Judgment they are no longer indifferent bystanders to a granting of pardon exclusively restricted to God and the torturers. By authority of their dignity as subjects, having been restored by God, the victims will be granted a unique and irreplaceable ministry in the realization of universal reconciliation (see Revelation 20:4).

In this special regard, reconciliation is conceived as an event that is no longer restricted to the relationship between sinner and God alone, but instead is expanded to encompass the vision of the universal solidarity of all human beings.

A theology that insists, even in the face of Auschwitz, on the fact that God has created the human being in His own image and as His free counterpart, is also taught by Auschwitz that by creating man, God began a history with an indeterminacy even for God Himself. To speak of reconciliation within this history—and at its very end—points to our firm hope[27] that not only God, but the victims as well—and they first and foremost!—will forgive their torturers.

NOTES

1. (London and New York: Penguin Books, 1993), pt. I, 5.4: "Mutiny."
2. Ivan's denial of the possibility of vicarious pardon presupposes that guilt refers to individual human relationships. According to this position, guilt is not an obligation that can be shifted from one person to the other—a view stressed by the German philosopher Immanuel Kant (*Die Religion innherhalb der Grenzen der bloßen Vernunft* [1794], B 94). If guilt cannot be shifted from one person to another, both perpetrators and victims with regard to pardon and reconciliation are called upon in a unique capacity: they cannot ever be substituted by anybody. A similar problem with special regard to the Nazi genocide is discussed by Simon Wiesenthal in his famous story *The Sunflower* (New York: Schocken Books, 1977). See also the enlarged edition: S. Wiesenthal and H. J. Cargas, *The Sunflower: An Inquiry into the Possibility and Limits of Forgiveness* (New York: Schocken Books, 1997).
3. This conclusion is by no means surprising. Because the ecclesiastical doctrine and practice of reconciliation are fundamentally based on the redeeming work of Christ. See Council of Trent (1545–63), 14th session (1551), *Doctrine on the sacrament of penitence*, esp. chap. 1: Through the sacrament of penitence the repenting sinner receives the benefits of Christ's redeeming death (Denzinger-Schönmetzer 1668).
4. One might doubt whether universal reconciliation is really aimed at by God at the end of time. Can't we imagine that eventually there will be a "great gulf" fixed between the good and the evil (see Luke 16:23–26)? Contrary to this position, I presume that God's creation would not have achieved its primary purpose if there were no universal salvation at the end of time (see 1 Timothy 2:4) and if God will not be "all in all" (see 1 Corinthians 15:28).
5. *Quatre lectures talmudiques* (Paris: Les Editions de Minuit, 1968), pp. 36–37 (my translation).
6. Ibid., p. 37.
7. Ibid., p. 44.

8. Ibid., p. 63.

9. Ibid., p. 64.

10. "Philosophie, justice, et amour," in *Entre nous* (Paris: Grasset & Fasquelle, 1991), p. 122 (my translation).

11. Concerning the notion of disturbance with regard to social relationship, see Torsten Habbel, *Der Dritte stört. Emmanuel Levinas—Herausforderung für die Politische Theologie und Befreiungsphilosophie* (Mainz: Grünewald, 1994).

12. *Difficile Liberté. Commentaire*, 4th ed. (Paris: Albin Michel, 1995), pp. 108–9 (my translation). Commenting on Walter Benjamin's "Zur Kritik der Gewalt," the violent character of justice is stressed by Jacques Derrida, "Deconstruction and the Possibility of Justice," *Cardozo Law Review* 11 (New York, 1990): 919–1045. Concerning the notion of justice in Levinas and Derrida, see Drucilla Cornell, "From the Lighthouse: The Promise of Redemption and the Possibility of Legal Interpretation," *Cardozo Law Review* 11 (1990): 1687–1714.

13. See particularly *Grundlage des Naturrechts nach Prinzipien der Wissenschaftslehre* (1796), §§ 1–4; *Vorlesungen über Moral* (1796); *System der Sittenlehre* (1798).

14. See Marco Ivaldo, "Das Problem des Bösen bei Fichte," *Fichte-Studien. Beiträge zur Geschichte und Systematik der Transzendentalphilosophie III. Sozialphilosophie* (Amsterdam, 1991), pp. 154–69.

15. The characterization as "unconditional" points to the spontaneity of human freedom. It is used here in a strictly *formal* sense. In a *material* sense, human freedom is obviously subject to many conditions. It is God's freedom alone that is subject neither to formal nor to material conditions.

16. See Hermann Krings, *System und Freiheit* (Freiburg: Alber, 1980).

17. Thomas Pröpper, *Erlösungsglaube und Freiheitsgeschichte*, 3rd ed. (Munich: Kösel, 1991), p. 203 (my translation).

18. *The Human Condition* (New York: Doubleday, 1959), p. 213.

19. See 1 Chronicles 16:34, 2 Chronicles 5:13, Mark 10:18. For the rabbinical tradition concerning God's goodness, see Hermann L. Strack and Paul Billerbeck, *Kommentar zum Neuen Testament aus Talmud und Midrasch*, 10th ed. (Munich: Beck, 1994), vol. 1, p. 809. The assumption that God is a morally acting being is fundamental not only for theologians but also for philosophers. In the context of the discussion of theodicy, it was already presented by Epicurus, resumed by Descartes, and developed by Leibniz. Yet for what reasons—apart from revelation!—do philosophers assume that God is good?

20. It is obvious that God is not obliged to respect *any* free decision of a human being, particularly if it is directed to something wrong or evil.

21. Nevertheless it has to be underlined that the possible refutation of God's inviting love maintained by only one single human being—which points to the real possibility of what tradition calls hell—would be a defeat for God Himself!

22. For the recent discussion, see the comprehensive survey presented by Hans Halter, "Deutungen des göttlichen Endgerichts in der modernen Dogmatik," *Hoffnung über den Tod hinaus: Antworten auf Fragen der Eschatologie*, Theologische Berichte

19, ed. Josef Pfammatter and Eduard Christen (Zurich: Benziger, 1990), pp. 184–206.

23. The victims' decision seems to be respected even if Alyosha's argument is valid that Jesus Christ is the only being who has the right to forgive "everything and every-one" because he gave his innocent blood "for all things and all men" (*Brothers Karamazov* I 5.4). To be aware of Christ's sacrifice might even more strongly invite the victims to forgive, but it does not replace their free assent. Ivan's well-known response to Alyosha's proposal is his enigmatic poem of the Grand Inquisitor, where human freedom is one of the principal topics. And what might be the meaning of Alyosha's reference to those who do not accept Christ as the incarnate Son of God? This crucial question with regard to Auschwitz cannot be discussed here.

24. This supposition by no means denies the doctrine of God's immutability. However, that God is the plenitude of being *in se* does not mean that He cannot change with regard to what is different from Him, namely creation. See Karl Rahner, "Zur Theologie der Menschwerdung," *Schriften zur Theologie*, vol. 4 (Einsiedeln: Benziger, 1960), pp. 137–55, esp. 147.

25. In my opinion this is a very strong argument. Will I really be able to enjoy the eternal communion with God in awareness that by my very decision other human beings are excluded from this communion? It is hard enough to imagine an eternal life in communion with God knowing that there are—or at least may be!— persons who refuse God's grace of their own free will. Therefore the insistence on the real possibility of hell ought to be counterbalanced by the hope that in fact it will not be possible for human beings to refuse God definitively.

26. Johannes Brantschen, *Hoffnung für Zeit und Ewigkeit. Der Traum von wachen Christenmenschen* (Freiburg: Herder, 1992), p. 150 (my translation).

27. This hope is different from certainty; it is hope in a strict sense. But, as Saint Paul affirms, "we are *saved* by hope" (Romans 8:24).

PART II
An Ethical Challenge

Between Will to Power and Dereliction:
Speaking of Man after the Shoah

Emilio Baccarini

INTRODUCTION

Fifty years after the mortal silence of Auschwitz, and of all the other death camps, a powerful accusation is still raised, an accusation with the force of a categorical imperative, insisting on the assumption of responsibility for guilt in its moral and metaphysical dimension, to use Karl Jaspers's expression. Intellectuals—or, more specifically, philosophers and theologians—have not yet assumed responsibility for the guilt, despite the huge amount of evidence already at their disposal. The works of E. Wiesel, P. Levi, E. Hillesum, J. Amery (H. Mayer), J. Semprun, and many other witnesses are waiting to be thought through, at the crossroads of history. This situation may be the result of superficiality or fear, but more probably of the fact that it is impossible to apply the ontological categories normally used by philosophers and theologians. The notion of guilt has not yet found a real space in which to be thought out or at least conceptually clarified, which would allow light to be shined on its underlying implications. Philosophy has reflected on it exclusively, or almost so, in the context of personal morality or of the punishment that it requires as its direct compensation. Guilt also, however, has an anthropological nature that links it indissolubly to the structure of human beings.

In his precious text of accusation, first published in 1947, *The Question of German Guilt*, K. Jaspers speaks of metaphysical guilt as the most radical type, and writes:

> There exists a solidarity among men as human beings that makes each co-responsible for every wrong and every injustice in the world, especially for crimes committed in his presence or with his knowledge. If I fail to do whatever I can to prevent them, I too am guilty. If I was present at the murder of others without risking my life to prevent it, I feel guilty in a way not adequately conceivable either legally, politically or morally. That I live after such a thing has happened weighs upon me as indelible guilt. . . . That somewhere among men the unconditioned prevails—the capacity to live only together or not at all, if crimes are committed against the one or the other, or

93

if physical living requirements have to be shared—therein consists the substance of their being. But that this does not extend to the solidarity of all men, nor to that of fellow-citizens or even of smaller groups, but remains confined to the closest human ties—therein lies this guilt of us all. Jurisdiction rests with God alone.[1]

The basic solidarity structure of human beings has certainly attracted considerable attention in the history of Western thought, but this has been focused almost exclusively on the ethical and the political sphere, and less on the ontico-ontological sphere, which is the perspective I want to examine here. The Aristotelian definition of human beings as social animals, which was taken over by the Western ethical and political tradition, is of most importance in the sphere of politics or *societas*, but less in terms of the substantial determination of the human person. And it is symptomatic that it is precisely in the ontological perspective—that of necessity—that the person does not see this fundamental dimension ratified, but, on the contrary, relegated to the sphere of morality, which is that of freedom, but also that of arbitrariness. Here we can recall two perspectives that do not speak explicitly of the solidarity structure, but are certainly a presupposition and deepening of it; moreover, they both use the same expression, *systematische Verbindung*, albeit with slightly different meanings. Thus, in Kant's *Foundations of the Metaphysics of Morals*, it is used to define the structure of the "realm of ends," the realm of persons in their demand for absolute value, and in Husserl's work it is used to define the structuring of the "monadic community."

Jaspers's statements imply that silence is unjustifiable. As philosophers and theologians, we have the duty to come to radical grips with the tragic nature of the event, showing a conscious will to understand why, at a certain moment in its history, humanity entered a blind alley from which it has not yet managed to emerge. Two paths therefore have to be followed, one leading backward, in order to identify and understand the causes of the tragedy, and the other forward, in order to emerge from the blind alley. The post-Auschwitz category of thought, no longer seen simply as a chronological category, becomes particularly precious here, as we shall see.[2]

As evidence, I shall introduce some "voices" that can help focus our thinking on the problem. On March 1, 1995, in memory of the fiftieth anniversary of the liberation of the concentration camps, the French-German television company ARTE broadcast a dialogue between two famous survivors, J. Semprun and E. Wiesel, which was then published under the title *Se taire est impossible*. Wiesel very bitterly observes that "evil survived Auschwitz"[3] in the thousand forms of the genocide and wars and killings that fill our century, and he closes with a question that explains the title I chose for my present reflections: "If Auschwitz and Buchenwald did not truly change man, then what *will* change man?"[4]

Even the title of the Italian writer Primo Levi's most famous work, *If This Is a Man*, indicates that what happened in the camps was the pure negation of what is human, and deliberately advances the suspicion—which is in fact a certainty—that "*this* . . . is not a man—is no longer a man."

In 1934, shortly after Hitler's rise to power, Levinas published an article in the journal *Esprit*. Lucidly prophetic and overwhelmingly decisive, it was entitled "Some Reflections on the Philosophy of Hitlerism,"[5] and managed to identify the theoretical coordinates of National Socialism: the cult of the body as opposed to the culture of the spirit, and the will to power as struggle for self-affirmation and self-dissemination as against the affirmation and dissemination of ideas, leading to a fundamental modification in the very idea of universality. In his conclusion, Levinas writes:

> Force is marked by another type of propagation (as opposed to that of ideas). It does not leave the person who exercises it. Force is not dispersed among those subject to it, but is a part of the personality or society exercising it, and increases them by subordinating everything else to them. Here universal order is no longer established as a corollary to ideological expansion; rather, it is this very expansion that constitutes the unity of a world of masters and slaves. The Nietzschean will to power that modern Germany is rediscovering and glorifying is not merely a new ideal, but an ideal that also brings its own particular form of universalization: war and conquest.

He ends by declaring that what is at stake here "is the very humanity of man."[6]

In 1949, some years after the war, Emmanuel Mounier, the founder of *Esprit*, published his famous little book on *personalism*. In a very succinct passage denouncing the crisis of European classical man, he observes:

> Today, European nihilism is spreading and organizing its forces in every field left vacant by the retreat of those substantial beliefs which kept our fathers in heart—the Christian faith, the culture of science, of reason and of duty. . . . The reign of satisfied mediocrity is, without doubt, the contemporary basis of nihilism and, of the demoniac.

> One can longer tell what man is, and as we watch him today undergoing such astonishing transformations, some think there is no such thing as human nature. For some people, this idea becomes translated into 'every-

thing is *possible* for man', and in that they find some hope; for others, 'everything is *permissible* to man', and with that they abandon all restraint; for others, finally, 'everything is *permissible against* man', and with that we have arrived at Buchenwald.[7]

Mounier's statement can be rephrased: "Everything is *permissible* against man when he is no longer considered such."

We find a disturbing confirmation of this in Gitta Sereny's book *Into That Darkness*,[8] which contains an interview with Franz Stangl, commandant of the Treblinka camp. The author observes that Stangl "still avoided referring to them [the prisoners] as 'people,'"[9] and when she asked him, "So you didn't feel they were human beings?" he answered: "Cargo. They were cargo." "When do you think you began to think of them as cargo?" persisted Sereny, and Stangl replied: "I think it started the day I first saw the *Totenlager* in Treblinka. I remember Wirth standing there, next to the pits full of blue-black corpses. *It had nothing to do with humanity. . . . It was a mass—a mass of rotting flesh*. Wirth said: 'What shall we do with this garbage?' I think unconsciously that started me thinking of them as cargo." "Could you not have changed that?" asked the journalist. "No, no, no. This was the system. Wirth had invented it. *It worked. And because it worked, it was irreversible*" was the answer.[10]

Stangl's words give a very clear picture of the correlation between the will to power expressed in the technicization of death and the reduction of people to an anonymous mass, and the extreme dereliction to which people are abandoned. In the death camps, the will to power reached its ultimate expression in the reduction of people to nothing—their annihilation. Suffice it to think of the tragic, bitter sound of the words set over the gate to the camps, *Arbeit macht frei*, precisely where there was no longer any sense of work, and still less of freedom. Falsehood and lies provided the very structure of the system. Can we see here what Nietzsche called the transmutation of values—the essence and consequence of nihilism? In any case, we are duty-bound to ask ourselves if this is not also the truest result, in its tragic quality, of a millenary path followed by philosophical, theological, and political thought.

WILL TO POWER, AND DERELICTION

The historical phenomenology of anthropological thought constantly shows this dramatic swing between will to power and dereliction in which the splitting of self-awareness is clear—or, better, a split and contradictory self-awareness in which the two elements destroy one another. In the title of the present study, will to power and dereliction are in fact seen as consequential in the correlation of cause and effect. In the brief analyses that follow, we shall try to take account of this consequentiality, which, in a variety of forms, seems to be a very specific feature of Western thought. I am not using the expression "will to power" in the technical sense intended by Nietzsche—at least according to Heidegger's conceptual clarification[11]—even though in the final analysis it coincides with the affirmation of self, and with the recognition of self-affirmation as the *proprium* of being. I cannot see the "metaphysical" dimension that Heidegger attributes to Nietzsche's perspective, even though it is no longer an onto-theological dimension. The will to power coincides in its foundation with a will to dominate, "the will to be master," says Nietzsche, which is an inherent part of man and defines him in his essential, and in this sense "metaphysical," features. I shall try to clarify the perspective I intend here by using some interpretative models that read the violence in the very heart of the possibility of what is human. In chronological order, the first appeals to F. Ebner, who speaks of a *Menschenverachtung* (contempt for human beings), while the second is taken from E. Weil's *Logique de la philosophie*, and sees violence as the other face of philosophical reasonableness. A third interpretative approach is found in E. Levinas's *Totality and Infinity*. These models will help us to work out a kind of etiology of the evil that man produced in Auschwitz, even though the radical nature of the phenomenon is situated in the realm of the unthinkable and hence the unjustifiable. Interpretative attempts are simply stumbling efforts that can in no way calm the conscience.

According to the Austrian thinker F. Ebner,

"Evil" in man is above all the blind drive and the inner urge to make others suffer. But where does it spring from? Simply from a dim sense of powerlessness and the "will to power."[12]

Human beings appear to have a kind of innate negativity. There is

a constant temptation of hatred for human beings, so that in the face of most people there can be nothing but a conception of life that despises people and is almost nihilistic. It is not so easy to find a person in whom we can recognize humanity. The majority of people are proof that it is possible to be human beings and to exist without a spiritual content of life, without any sensitivity to spiritual values,[13] which can be grasped only "directly." This last adverb also provides the key to Ebner's position, which is not pessimism, but recognition that every universalizing "idealistic" position entails a kind of *Menschenverachtung*. Thus he writes:

> Idealism can never show a person the path on which the I finds the you in the other person. It lands and is finally always wrecked on the reef of contempt for man. . . . Platonism, moreover, in a way meets man's deep-rooted need to dream the life of the spirit—simply to dream instead of living it.[14]

He is still more explicit in another passage:

> In the sphere of Platonism, individuals will always be seen merely as a constant pretext for *Menschenverachtung* and *Menschenhass* (hatred for human beings). In its sphere, there will always be the temptation of that half-truth of the saying of the *Cherubinischer Wandersmann* which says: "That you do not love man is right and good; it is humanity that we must love in the man." This can also basically be the confession of direct hatred of man.[15]

The challenging of Platonism as idealism should be seen within the framework of Ebner's essentially dialogical existential realism. He is concerned to rediscover the authenticity of the spiritual realities (I–you–God) without distorting mediations, in the "involving" relationship.[16] This obscure Austrian schoolmaster wrote these things in the first years of this century, and his contribution was that of using a relational-dialogical perspective in order to move beyond *Menschenverachtung* toward *Menschenliebe* (love of man), thus opening the way for a new way of speaking of the human, which is still very valid today.

Unlike Ebner, who more or less consciously sets himself outside a two-thousand-year-old tradition, moving toward what Rosenzweig would a few years later call "new thought," Weil is positioned squarely within the Greek *logos*, which is seen as the horizon of meaning through which violence itself is overcome. Hegel had, of course, advanced a phenomenology of the life of the spirit as a deployment of reason, in other words as a totally coherent discourse without any breaks.

As has been said, Weil's approach can in fact be seen as that of a post-Hegel Kantian. The general introduction to his *Logique de la philosophie* opens with an analysis of man as oscillation between *reason* and *violence*.[17] Even in its basic definition, the structure of the human being, according to Weil, is ambiguous in its bringing together of the animal and rational elements, inasmuch as the one is irreducible to the other. Thus Weil writes:

Man is an animal endowed with reason and language: this means and is destined to mean exactly what seemed at first so surprising, in other words that men do not ordinarily possess reason and reasonable language, but that they *must* have them in order to be *fully* men. Natural man is an animal; man as he wants to be, as he wants the other to be so that he can recognize him as an equal, *must* be reasonable. What science describes is simply the material on which a form must still be stamped, and the definition *human* is given not so that man can be recognized, but so that he can be realized.[18]

If we accept this perspective, we have to say that Auschwitz—but in the sense of any other previous or later production of evil—means the negation of the specificity of humanity, while manifesting man's capacity for negativity. In the classical view, the nondialectical mastery of negativity consists of living according to reason, in other words in the elimination of the elements of violence innate in man. In this sense, for Weil, philosophers' and philosophy's reflection is the path of philosophy in the world so that violence may vanish from the world. However, living according to reason is not a necessity, but a choice—a "first choice," as Weil defines it.[19] Violence and freedom are elements that define man; violence is innate, radical and irreducible, and freedom is affirmed only against the background of violence. Taking pure violence seriously means highlighting the foundation of philosophy, which is not some necessity, but man's freedom with his will to coherence and wisdom, which raise him above his finitude. Weil echoes Kant in understanding man as reasonable (the adjective is taken as indicating a possibility), redefining him as *animal rationabile*. He can choose reason:

Instead of saying that man is a being endowed with reasonable discourse, we shall say that he is a being who can be reasonable, if he so chooses; in other words, that he has freedom with a view to reason (or for violence).[20]

Thus, philosophy exists because being human is to seek meaning, is to demand a meaningful world. Philosophy is the discourse of an ambiguous being whose other possibility is the negation of meaning, or violence. "The discourse is formed—man forms his discourse—in violence against violence, in finite against finite, in time against time."[21] Eric Weil, a German philosopher of Jewish origin, wrote his *Logique de la philosophie* as a state doctoral thesis directed by J. Wahl in 1950, having left Nazi Germany in 1933. His stance can be read as a choice of life according to freedom and humanity, but we may wonder whether it is also an implicit accusation against the German philosophy of his time, which instead made a choice of violence, or at least kept silent in the face of the violence that was taking place. This was also Jaspers's conviction, as we said above.

In this sense, E. Levinas's viewpoint is more radical, for he moves from explicit awareness of the violence that took place not against or despite philosophy, but because of it and its reasoning, especially ontology. All his thinking can be seen as an attempt to leave behind the logic of being in order to affirm the rights of exteriority, even to the extent of rethinking the meaning of subjectivity on a new basis. In the preface to his *Totality and Infinity*, Levinas writes:

> We do not need obscure fragments of Heraclitus to prove that being reveals itself as war to philosophical thought, that war does not only affect it as the most patent fact, but as the very patency, or the truth, of the real. . . . War is produced as the pure experience of pure being.[22]

In a few lines he launches a radical accusation against over two thousand years of history of Western philosophy. Despite its brevity, however, it bears no trace of approximation, but has the decisive nature of a denunciation on the basis of which to promote an alternative path.

> The ontological event . . . is a casting into movement of beings hitherto anchored in their identity, a mobilization of absolutes, by an objective order from which there is no escape. The trial by force is the test of the real. But violence does not consist so much in injuring and annihilating persons as in interrupting their continuity, making them play roles in which they no longer recognize themselves, making them betray not only commitments but their own substance, making them carry out actions that will destroy every possibility for action. Not only modern war but every war employs arms that turn against those who wield them. It establishes an order from which no one can keep his distance; nothing henceforth is exterior. War does not manifest exteriority and the other as other; it destroys the identity of the same.
>
> The visage of being that shows itself in war is fixed in the concept of totality, which dominates Western philosophy. Individuals are reduced to being bearers of forces that command them unbeknown to themselves. The meaning of individuals (invisible outside of this totality) is derived from the totality. The unicity of each present is incessantly sacrificed to a future appealed to to bring forth its objective meaning.[23]

Levinas suggests that we can escape from the continuity of totality by taking a path that still requires thinking out as regards its anthropological possi-

bilities and that could be summarized as a "thinking on the basis of the other";
however, we cannot even begin to describe it here.

The models of thought referred to above show the urgent need for an
alternative way of knowing about man, a new way of speaking of him, and
therefore of looking at him. This also presumes a new perspective guided by
a new ontological approach. A first interesting—and, I believe, particularly
fruitful—attempt at an investigation along these lines was recently made by
G. Agamben in his book *Homo Sacer*,[24] where he uses the categories of bio-
politics to approach thinking about "the death camp as *nomos* of the modern."
Speaking explicitly of the camps, he observes:

> Whoever entered the camp moved in a zone of indistinction between
> outside and inside, exception and rule, licit and illicit, in which the very con-
> cepts of subjective right and juridical protection no longer made any sense.
> What is more, if the person entering the camp was a Jew, he had already
> been deprived of his rights as a citizen by the Nuremberg laws and was sub-
> sequently completely denationalized at the time of the Final Solution.
> Insofar as its inhabitants were stripped of every political status and wholly
> reduced to bare life, the camp was also the most absolute biopolitical space
> ever to have been realized, in which power confronts nothing but pure life,
> without mediation. . . . The correct question to pose concerning the horrors
> committed in the camps is, therefore, not the hypocritical one of how crimes
> of such atrocity could be committed against human beings. It would be more
> honest and, above all, more useful to investigate carefully the juridical pro-
> cedures and deployments of power by which human beings could be so com-
> pletely deprived of their rights and prerogatives that no act committed
> against them could appear any longer as a crime.[25]

In another approach, post-Auschwitz thought means considering this failure as what has been called a starting-point for a new era, or a kind of new
creatio ex nihilo, to use the words of Neher, who also writes:

> Auschwitz was a total collapse: quite simply the abandonment of
> men—of men, women, and children—who died an entirely mortal death
> whose disatrousness is demonstrated in its very limits. . . .
>
> Auschwitz is like some perilous passage between the rocks where the
> millenial adventure of human thought met with absolute disaster. It went
> down in darkness, without even the ray of a lighthouse to indicate where it
> had been. It is a return to chaos, which we must first have the courage to
> enter if we wish to find our way out of it; otherwise there can be only false

exits, spurious thought without any grasp of reality. Perhaps, moreover, entering into Auschwitz may encourage thought to make its dwelling there, and will spur it on to renew itself from within and to take, at last, the first step, which alone is absolutely free and which consists of self-creation out of nothingness. Did the world not spring up *ex nihilo*, out of such a creative act? The first step after Auschwitz then seems to be the one which would place us at the exact moment when nothing any longer exists but when all may be again.[26]

J. Amery also invites us to set out on new paths and to think of man on the basis of the tragic suffering of the ghetto. Thus he writes in conclusion to his clear-thinking study "In the Antechamber of Death":[27]

> The history of the ghetto is not over yet. It is still acting and must go on doing so. The impossibility of reconciliation with the murderers who may still be among us, and with others who still stand, ghostlike, before us as horrifying reminders, is the highest moral commandment, the sole admissible historical lesson of what the anti-man was able to create. Many concepts have received a wholly new content through the ghetto. Vengeance, irreconcilability. We have to relearn from the beginning, just as the inhabitants of the ghetto had to have a totally new experience of the world. Christian ethics, like Jewish ethics, was able to offer so little. A new philosophy of history has to be outlined; more precisely, perhaps, it is already being born, and the people of the ghetto have written the first words. Nothing will ever again be the way it was. One day people may be able to say that the history of a more human humanity started in the inhumanity of the ghetto.[28]

All the voices we have heard here, from both inside and outside the Jewish world, urge us to focus anew and with fresh seriousness on man, the meaning of his being, and his way of being in the world with others. As philosophers and theologians—thinkers—we must consider the Shoah as an event that forces us to think, especially today when we have seen it repeat itself in forms of extreme dehumanization that have found us totally lacking in any new interpretative categories. In the third part of my reflection I shall try to present, in a very schematic and hence incomplete way, certain elements that can become pieces of a new theory of man.

SPEAKING OF MAN AFTER THE SHOAH

We can take our cue from a fact that has played a crucial role in the history of thought, inasmuch as it is a demand for meaning and a manifestation of an ontological need for meaning: the philosophy of history. Philosophers always ask themselves this final question about the definitive meaning of history, or at least its inner meaning. The Shoah is the tragic manifestation of the possibility of a break in the meaning of history, a break wrought by the will that considers evil the result of a perverse logic that allows it to appear as good. This interruption in the meaning of history indicates that good and evil can become confused, where their relationship can no longer be defined by abstract criteria. Neither are norms helpful that precede or set aside specific reference to an attitude of goodness or badness. History is not only the story of the struggle between good and evil seen as principles of an abstract metaphysics, but is above all the story of the will to good or evil, in other words the story of a gift of meaning that is always at the mercy of its opposite, and thus never totally ascertained. Human beings have a constitutional ambivalence which structures them in their personal behavior, and nothing and nobody can ever guarantee them in the exercise of their freedom. In this perspective, the meaning of history coincides perfectly with the sense that human beings give it, without appealing to abstract interpretative principles. On the basis of these premises, there would appear to be grounds for saying that after Auschwitz even the possibility of a philosophy of history vanished, and that the shattering of meaning that took place cannot be grasped except through acceptance of its fragmentariness. The consequences of this are far from clear from the viewpoint of ontology, or from that of ethics and anthropology, and refer us to a metaphysical perspective that no longer has anything in common with ontotheology. Let us try to reflect more specifically on the *fragmentariness* which seems to some one of the unthought-of features defining human beings, but one that allows us to understand the impossibility attributed to the philosophy of history as a single whole.

The elementary fact with which philosophy has worked from its earliest days is that of the categorical determination of being, which has allowed it to speak of the being of beings through recourse to the structure of the identity of essence. In history this has been translated, especially in modern European thought, into the anthropological-political—and hence ethical—concept of equality; all men are equal (ethics adds "in dignity and value"). The Greeks knew and recognized an *isótēs*, an equality, only as *isonomía*, in other words as equality of rights established by law, but also by custom and usage. This refers us back, almost in contraposition, to an unthought-of, perhaps because inconceivable, *isótēs phýsei* (equality of nature), which is, on the contrary, what interests us most today. Natural equality is indeed the gain of modern times, which focuses its reflection on it not only in ethical-juridical and anthropological terms, but also in theoretical terms.

Each person is thus equal to every other through their *common human nature*. In other words, using more abstract language, equality is established by identity of essence. The confusion of equality and identity has in fact provided the basis for a major part of modern thought, which therefore cannot use this path to leave behind it the reference level of essential identity.

Identity of essence, moreover, as we have said, guarantees the possibility of defining the being's being. However, this identity is, in the last resort, the disappearance of uniqueness, with which philosophy has always had a conflictual relationship. The identity of the identical and the nonidentical is produced in the essence, but the existence that is the very condition of the possibility of the same thinkability vanishes, reduced to its conditions of thinkability.

The objective identity of the ego is recognized in the essence of a definition,[29] but subjective identity, on the other hand, discovers itself in the difference of name. Beyond the naturalness and hence the generality (genus) of the essence, the condition of nameability of the name lies in creatureliness, which, here and now, shows all its newness. If I ignore many moves intermediate to the question "Who am I?" and in the first instance I answer, "I am a creature of God," I probably disconcert philosophers, who do not find it easy to gain a clear picture of creatureliness but above all of what this implicitly says; in other words, to use Rosenzweig's expression, the authentic concept of creation refers back to one's own fulfillment in the miracle of revelation. The reality/notion of man-image/son-of-God provides us with a correlative reality which is also the third magical word in the revolutionary triad, together with equality and freedom—in other words, *fraternity*. Paradoxically, however, the correlation of fraternity, which thus refers back to a shared father, is the one that has historically proved less effective (it is practically absent even in the *Encyclopédie*, where it is allotted a few lines that affirm its parental and juridical structure), and been relegated to a theological and broadly religious context. Rather, if philosophy really wants to tackle equality, it seems to me urgent to think through creation, the reality of man as son of God. What I am saying here is that philosophers should also assume this as a possible way of speaking of man—a possibility we also find in the Jewish scriptures. It is not intended as a *metabasis eis allo genos*, an invasion of the theological sphere; I am simply trying to make the idea of a scripture that does not belong to the Greek philosophical tradition philosophically effective (in the specific sense of philosophy as "providing the reason for").[30]

It is impossible first to think and then to bring about a world of different equals except through the explicit thematization of this inherent given: equality of sons and diversity of brothers; unity of kind and difference of name. Each one is himself an identity and difference, or, if you like, a different identity and an identical difference. This means that the identity of the subject is seen only through relations. This identity, which is never definitively given, is brought about through responsibility for redemption; in other words, in making the world the Kingdom of God. This results in abandonment of an abstract and isolated concept of identity in favor of one that reveals its pole of consistency and effectiveness outside itself.

The point of arrival is only in appearance religious. In fact, it is the assumption of a hypothesis that allows us to grasp, at its roots, difference as a value: the utopia of equality, not despite being different, but *because* each one is different. Redefinition of equality without identity.

The reasoning on which the West is built is that of the necessitating identity that recognized the other as self. The "like me" is a less innocuous model than might be thought. "Despite" the difference: this statement displays an attitude of egocentric benevolence, which allows the other to enter into our own cultural, political, and religious circles, and so on. Even so, entry of the other into my life is conditional on the *nihil obstat* that I grant. However, the priority of the I has charge of supervision.

In the second case, on the other hand—the *because different*—the reference levels are overturned. My subjectivity could become an obstacle. The other's face is the difference which, as visitation, breaks forth with the force of its naked need and calls me to responsibility, becoming in fact the condition for the possibility of my identity.

In the move from one attitude to the other, the logic of creation is the determining factor, making each subject unrepeatably unique and therefore making him a value to be met, and above all assigning him a radical gratuity that makes any reduction whatsoever impossible. Recognizing a value in the face of the other person, always and under all circumstances, means introducing the notion of difference as structure of thinkability into our conceptual framework. Here we have a new "transcendental," but one that shatters the logic of identity, rendering it ineffective. According to the logic of difference, however, fragmentariness becomes fully meaningful and is no longer marked by negativity. Creatureliness says that every "fragment" is totally significant, and that every person refers exclusively to himself without needing any other models.

Extraneousness or hostility toward others is often caused by fear of difference or by the impossibility of making the other the same as myself, reducing him to me. However, on the very basis of the consideration that the other is a value, we have to accept difference, and indeed promote it. This means that we have to tread a long, hard path leading from tolerance to conviviality. Tolerance—one of the major conquests of modernity—is acceptance of difference, whereas conviviality is its promotion and defense. Our culture and society are very sensitive to plurality, which is seen as a fundamental element, and people have in fact realized that true conviviality is possible only where plurality is safeguarded.

Giving up the concept of the identifying identity of essence—which led, in its nihilistic degeneration, to massification and the objectivizing quantification of the human—is not intended as a choice to give up being able to speak of the meaning of man, but rather as the will to start on a path of qualitative thinking—necessarily entailing difference—in order to speak of man. It seems to me that gratuity is a category still requiring much attention in this perspective, for gratuity does not invite us to a devaluation but to think in the perspective of discontinuity—or, to use the term already used above, that of fragmentariness. In this sense the Shoah has shown us the most tragic of the possible conclusions of the guarantee of continuity. Let us note this, in order to affirm the absolute discontinuity of difference and personal uniqueness.[31] However, this also means affirming, through the principle of difference, that the human being is absolutely meaningful already in the naked life that has no need of any extrinsic recognition of value, whether juridical, ethical, or political. Indeed, an ontology of need is seen even in his naked life, calling for an assumption of responsibility and benevolence.

The gratuity in its manifesting itself as difference—an ontic rather than ontological difference—is also a manifestation of the radical mystery of man, who dwells within it and expresses it. Thus the new possibility of speaking of man has to pass through this new recognition, apart from that of Hegel's dialectics, of a being, man, who can be spoken of only as a surplus of meaning, an excess, a fullness that, despite its fragmentariness, has God as its only possible paradigm of comparison. Then, if the starting point is that *God is dead*, man himself, every single man in his gratuity, which is cast adrift from any totality but is itself totality of significance, is the bearer of an absolute meaning that makes him the paradigm for himself and hence inviolable. Perhaps this is where we find the utopia of the human that we have been dreaming of since the Shoah, although we cannot forget Dostoevsky's warning that "If God is dead, everything is possible." Man's whole future lies in this terrible fragility. However, this fragility becomes an ethical imperative, a moral commandment, "Thou shalt not kill," and hence the start of sociality as mutual recognition of the other's need, my need of him and his need of me.

NOTES

1. K. Jaspers, *The Question of German Guilt* (New York, NY: Capricorn Books 1961), p. 32.

2. The many thought-provoking observations advanced regarding the radical challenge that Auschwitz and its power for evil have also raised for theological thought include that of P. De Benedetti, who wrote a postscript to P. Ricoeur's small but very important work, *Le Mal: une défie à la philosophie et à la théologie* (Geneva, 1986), in which he posits the correlation between guilt and evil. De Benedetti writes: "The reassuring metaphysical horizons of Leibniz and Hegel, and even Thomas Aquinas, Augustine and Vatican Council I, evaporated like a mirage in the face of experiences that reduced to dust their majestic constructions of theodicy, rational theology, apologetics, and the *De Deo* tract; and the dust rose up until it hid even God. When people realized this ruin, the problem of evil was seen in all its renewed and pristine immensity" (p. 60).

3. J. Semprun and E. Wiesel, *Se taire est impossible* (Paris: Mille et une nuits-Arte Editions, 1995), p. 25.

4. Ibid., p. 26.

5. Published in English in *Critical Inquiry*, 17,1 (1990) pp. 62–71.

6. Ibid.

7. E. Mounier, Personalism (Notre Dame, IN: University of Notre Dame Press 1952), pp. 98-99.

8. Gitta Sereny, *Into That Darkness: An Examination of Conscience* (New York: Vintage, 1983).

9. Ibid., p. 170.

10. Ibid., pp. 201–202 (emphasis added). A very clear passage in E. Jünger's *Über die Linie*, a study first published in 1949 in a collection for M. Heidegger's sixtieth birthday, seems to provide a fundamental theoretical context for the above dialogue. Jünger writes: "It is by now clear that nihilism can certainly be harmoniously combined with large-scale order systems, and that it is indeed the rule that it is active and displays its force in such systems. For nihilism, order is a fertile ground which it shapes for its own ends. It is simply presupposed that the order is abstract and hence of a spiritual nature. This comprises firstly the well-structured State with its officials and mechanisms—especially in an era when the main underlying ideas, with their *nomos* and their *ethos*, have been lost or have declined, although they may superficially appear to live on more visibly than ever."

11. Cf. M. Heidegger, *Nietzsche* (San Francisco: Harper & Row, 1979).

12. F. Ebner, *Schriften* (Munich: Kösel, 1963), vol. 1, p. 925. In a passage just before this, he states: "There is no man who does not suffer through the evil that is in him, through the blind impulse to make others suffer" (p. 922).

13. Ibid., pp. 38–39.

14. Ibid., pp. 40–41.

15. Ibid., vol. 2, p. 459.

16. He writes in another aphorism: "The real, true, concrete person: this is you, this is me. Does idealism never understand this simple truth? The idea is not the spiritual bond between persons, between the I and the you, but only between the individual and humanity, a humanity, however, which exists only in the idea" (ibid., vol. 1, p. 40).

17. E. Weil, *Logique de la philosophie*, 2nd ed. (Paris: Vrin, 1985).

18. Ibid., p. 5.

19. Ibid. p. 59.

20. Ibid., p. 68.

21. Ibid., p. 69.

22. E. Levinas, *Totality and Infinity: An Essay on Exteriority* (The Hague: M. Nijhoff Publishers, 1969), p. 21.

23. Ibid., pp. 21–22.

24. G. Agamben, *Homo Sacer: Sovereign Power and Bare Life* (Stanford, Calif.: Stanford University Press, 1998).

25. Ibid., pp. 170–171.

26. A. Neher, *The Exile of the Word: From the Silence of the Bible to the Silence of Auschwitz* (Philadelphia: Jewish Publication Society of America, 1981), p. 143.

27. First published in G. Deschner, ed., *Menschen im Ghetto* (Gütersloh, 1969), then reprinted in J. Amery, *Widersprüche* (Stuttgart: Klett, 1971).

28. Ibid., pp. 213–14.

29. With a clear contradiction which matches the first-person singular of the pronoun with the third-person singular of the verb.

30. An international congress held in Mainz, July 14–17, 1996, investigated the ethical implications of this assumption. See the proceedings of the meeting, "Created in God's Image: The Imperative for Moral Action," in *From the Martin Buber House* 2 (Spring 1997): 24.

31. We can find help here in what Theodor W. Adorno wrote in the meditations on metaphysics which closed his *Negative Dialectics* (New York: Continuum, 1983), p.362: "the dialectical motif of quantity scores an unspeakable triumph. The administrative murder of millions made of death a thing one had never yet to fear in just this fashion. There is no chance any more for death to come into the individuals' empirical life as somehow conformable with the course of that life. The last, the poorest possession left to the individual is expropriated. That in the concentration camps it was no longer an individual who died, but a specimen—this is a fact bound to affect the dying of those who escaped the administrative measure.

Genocide is the absolute integration. It is on its way wherever men are leveled off—"polished off," as the German military call it—until one exterminates them literally, as deviations from the concept of their total nullity. Auschwitz confirmed the philosopheme of pure identity as death. . . . What the sadists in the camps foretold their victims, "Tomorrow you'll be wiggling skyward as smoke from this chimney," bespeaks the indifference of each individual life that is the direction of history. Even in his formal freedom, the individual is as fungible and replaceable as he will be under the liquidators' boots.

But since, in a world whose law is universal individual profit, the individual has nothing but this self that has become indifferent, the performance of the old, familiar tendency is at the same time the most dreadful of things. There is no getting out of this, no more than out of the electrified barbed wire around the camps."

Doing Ethics in an Age of Science

Peter J. Haas

I.

In 1615, Galileo Galilei wrote a letter to Madame Christina, Grand Duchess of Tuscany, explaining why the Church ought to allow him to publicize his thesis that the earth revolves around the sun. What he wants to say as a scientist, he claimed in the letter, should not be seen as any kind of threat by the Church. After all, he said, the Church's expertise, and legitimate teaching authority, concerns the salvation of the soul. The intention of the Holy Spirit, he averred, "is to teach us how one goes to heaven, not how heaven goes."[1]

In one sense, of course, Galileo was right. Church teaching, religious teaching in general, does not depend on scientific validation. What religion has to teach stands on its own authority. It is, or certainly ought to be, possible for us to accept new scientific theories without having to change our religious beliefs. To be sure, Galileo's claims were radical, and yes, they did fly in the face of long-standing Church teaching on cosmology. But the Church was also teaching about human morality, and those teachings remained in essence true, even if we come to think of the world differently.

But at another level, Galileo was surely wrong. We do not think of the structure of the cosmos, on the one hand, and the nature of being human, on the other, as though these were separate and distinct topics. The way we conceive the natural world has always, at least in the West, had a major impact on what we think it means to be human, and to act human. As we have experienced changes in scientific paradigms, we have in fact come to new understandings of what constitutes the moral life. In the long term, then, history has proven Galileo wrong. Science and morality are intimately linked. As Western science has evolved, it has not only changed the technical possibilities of what we as humans can do, but it has also changed our attitudes as to what it is conceivable, or even permissible, to do. It is this that brings me to the Holocaust. The Holocaust, as I shall argue below, is both a reflection and a critique of modern Western science. By this, let me make it clear, I do not mean Western technology. I mean how the West has come to understand what constitutes the good in the modern era.

In what follows I want to cover two themes. The first is that the Holocaust was not the random acts of a few thugs, but was the result of a systematically thought out scientific ethic. This is why, as I shall argue in a moment, it was able to gain the support, or at least the acquiescence, of so many intellectuals, such as physicians, biologists, and theologians. This is the basic argument of my book *Morality After Auschwitz*.[2]

In the second part of this paper I want to move beyond this argument and my book to reflect on the meaning of the Holocaust for modern scientific and moral thinking. What does it mean that science can spawn this kind of ethic? What does this tell us about science, and about the study of ethics, in the modern world? In essence, I shall argue that the Holocaust, through its sheer gruesomeness, has forced us to look at science, and at moral philosophy, with much more modest expectations. In this, I argue, the Holocaust makes the exact opposite point of Galileo's letter to Madame Christina: science and ethics cannot be torn apart as if activities in one sphere had no impact on those in the other.

II.

The thesis with which I propose to begin grows out of my book *Morality After Auschwitz*. The question that provoked the book was how could modern, twentieth-century, cultured people think that genocide was the right thing to do. My answer was, briefly, that the perpetrators thought that killing Jews and other racial enemies was the most scientific and therefore the best strategy available to them to solve their problems. Science is ultimately instrumental, it is designed to yield answers to questions that trouble us. I argued in the book that scientific studies of society seemed to be saying that it was necessary for the greater good to get rid of certain segments of the population, to cleanse the gene pool. This the Nazis then proceeded to do. They were able to conceive of their genocide, and convince others of its need and urgency, because it was clear to everyone that things in Germany were not going well and that some solution had to be found. Germans felt, and I think with some justification, that their society was collapsing. I think that throughout the 1930s the Nazi propaganda machine made this alternative view of the world, what I called the "Nazi ethic," more or less self-evident to many Germans. That is, the Nazi reading of history and current events became the norm, and like any reading of events produced an ethic. College students, professors, doctors, lawyers, theologians, fathers (and mothers) could live with the destruction of the Jewish community, and then of Jews and Gypsies and others, because, distasteful as it might be, it was the "right" thing to do.

The reason what I call the Nazi ethic enabled otherwise normal people to override their moral heritage was that it was based on what appeared to be a coherent scientific moral theory, that of Social Darwinism. This theory took shape in specific response to the mounting social problems of nineteenth-century Europe. It drew together elements of mainline biology and Darwinism, on the one hand, and Romantic theories of nation and *Volksgeist*, on the other, to create a scientific explanation for the social malaise Europe was experiencing. It provided a paradigm within which the reliable insights of science could be harnessed by men of insight and understanding to manage, if not master, the deteriorating social situation. By the late nineteenth and early twentieth century, it claimed to offer the most plausible and coherent account of reality as people were experiencing it. To explain how this worked, I need to say a few words about the intellectual background against which scientific racism took shape.

The nineteenth century developed a particular meaning for the word "nation." A state was a political entity, a jurisdiction with a ruling establishment, laws, clear boundaries, and the like. A nation, however, was much more. At its simplest level, a nation was taken to be a group of people who shared a history, culture, and tradition. Under the influence of Romanticism, however, the concept took on a more mystic or occult meaning. For the Romantics, a nation was made up of people who shared in their blood a certain life-force that made them what they were: French, German, Italian, Jewish, or whatever. This force was taken to be an innate essence that was stable and unchangeable such that each nation retained its essential nature over time and space. This essence could be detected from the characteristic creations of the nation, or the *Volk*: its language, religion, folktales, and so forth. This vague sense of cultural kinship lay at the foundation of the creation of the modern nation-state.

As it happens, a similar question having to do with the taxonomy of the natural world was raging in the biological sciences. The discovery of the new and strange flora and fauna in the New World, along with the discrediting of Aristotelian essences, had led to attempts to rethink the order of nature. Probably the earliest systematic attempt to do so was the work of Carl Linnaeus. His efforts, however, only fueled the question of whether or not there were real taxonomic distinctions. Some biologists argued that all such grids were nothing more than human inventions, a trick of the mind to produce meaning in an otherwise meaningless world. What was becoming clear is that if such distinctions were real, the dividing lines were subtle. They could not be based on outer form and appearance alone. For those arguing for the ontological existence of order, the problem was how to recognize and establish difference on some objective basis. It was at this juncture that the rise of historicism in the nineteenth century suggested another strategy, that of historical development. The essential identity of an individual was adducible not from its outward accidents, but from its genealogy. This is where the debate stood in the middle of the nineteenth century. Darwin provided a scientific way to account for the persistence of genetic identity in the midst of ongoing historical change. Through the mechanics of adaptation and survival of the fittest, he could show how, in nature, change was both possible and logical. He of course meant his scheme to apply only to the natural world, not to human society. Yet some Romantic historians thought that human history and the clash of rival cultures could also be explained through his scheme. He offered a way to make human history a function of the laws of biology. This Romantic reading of the human situation remained pretty much out of the mainstream of scientific thinking, more a part of popular myth and rhetoric than anything else, during the bulk of the nineteenth century. It entered the mainstream, in some ways the forefront, of modern science near the turn of the century because of what turned out to be the fortuitous collaboration of two great scientists: Walter Weldon, a biologist, and Karl Pearson, a mathematician, both teachers at University College in London. Through their application of mathematics to biological inheritance, they supplied the missing ingredient that turned Social Darwinism from an interesting, though rather mystic and romantic way of thinking about the human condition, into an apparently objective science.

More importantly, perhaps, than their reception in the scientific community was the enthusiasm with which their work was accepted by Social Darwinists and the public at large. Social Darwinists seized on their work as a way of showing in stark mathematical terms the effects of certain social policies on the national gene pool. Within a few years, the approach these men took to understanding the details of the natural world was being applied to human society. Eugenics societies sprang up across England in London, Birmingham, Cambridge, Manchester, Southampton, and Liverpool. The United States was not far behind, with several local eugenic societies (in New York, Chicago, and St. Louis, for example) plus many at the state level; with state fairs giving out awards in "human husbandry." It was simply assumed that proper management of human breeding would solve social problems.

When applied to the problems of society, this kind of thinking could, and did, have terrifying results. Because of the tendency of a species to "regress" to the norm, offspring which exhibited desirable traits had to be bred generation after generation, while individuals with undesirable traits had to be weeded out and, as far as possible, prevented from reproducing. The logic of inherited traits led to widespread governmental support for programs of genetic counseling and, when necessary, forced sterilization of the unfit. All this seemed perfectly logical, the application of demonstrable scientific principles to the creation of an enlightened public health policy. Yet such policies did seem to run counter to human rights and so were implemented slowly and carefully by most Western governments. Only in Germany, under the Nazis, did Social Darwinism become the unquestioned ideology of government policy.

Let me recapitulate where the argument is so far and reflect on what I see as some of its major ramifications. First of all, I want to say that the theories of Social Darwinism, and the eugenic sciences it created, constitute an encompassing and internally consistent worldview. That is, once one accepts the biological/medical paradigm of Social Darwinism, there is no way from within to prove it wrong. Second, Social Darwinism had deep roots in legitimate science, especially biology. Third, Social Darwinism, unlike most other scientific theories, was able to energize a social paradigm as well. That is, one could take the insights of Social Darwinism and transfer them to the social sphere. I contend that what made Social Darwinism attractive is that it offered a scientific way of understanding and solving Germany's problems. Once people entered this way of thinking, it became self-validating, and the atrocities of the Holocaust in a sense follow logically therefrom. My argument also is that so many intellectuals—college students, professors, physicians, etc.—were caught up in the ethic precisely because of its coherence, its scientific foundation, and its elegance, if I can say so. It was a powerful and magnificent way to account for everything in large scale and in detail. For an age that trusted immensely in science and technology, the worldview offered by Social Darwinism proved irresistible to a Germany reeling from defeat in war, social anarchy, and economic collapse. Here was a scientific system that could not only explain what was happening, but also how to fix it. And so step by step Auschwitz was built and operated by people just like you and me and in good conscience.

III.

This brings me to my second point, namely, the question of what this tells us about making modern scientific ethics. I think the basic lesson is that people will accept as their ethic any system of morality that is internally consistent and in accord with their view of the world, regardless of the content of that ethic. Let me restate the point in other words so that my meaning is clear. People will make a reasoned decision as to what is right or wrong on the basis of how they understand the world to work. The choice of a paradigm for understanding how the world works is not so much a rational choice as one that is emotional and maybe cultural. The Nazis did not choose Social Darwinism and modern racism as the basis of their ethics on any objective, disinterested grounds. They did so because these assumptions and methods helped establish as scientific fact the conclusion that people were already willing to accept. The fact that it meant mass killing and other atrocities was in a sense bracketed out or overcome in the interest of maintaining the integrity of the larger system and in the service of the larger good.

In my book I made the assumption that Social Darwinism was there and, once adopted, allowed the result to emerge. I did not at the time consider the prior question, the ethics, as it were, of the Nazi choice of just that particular science in the first place. That is, I simply assumed that the availability of a coherent and scientifically sophisticated system for defining good and right was sufficient reason in and of itself for adopting that point of view. The book has often been criticized on just those grounds for being rather too relativistic. Readers have said, with some justification, that it in essence leaves no way of adjudicating among different moralities. Since the content is irrelevant, a morality needs merely to meet certain formal requirements to be as good as any other. I could see no way of showing that what the Nazis were doing was wrong in their own frame of reference, and I did not deem it appropriate to judge their actions in their system on the basis of a different ethic.

I now wonder whether there is indeed the possibility of creating a meta-morality, as it were, a way of addressing in moral terms the decision of people to choose one morality over another. In other words, I wonder if there is indeed a way to grant that once the Nazis had adopted the morality they did, they were bound to commit certain acts because that is what the system demanded, but to be able still to say that the choice of that system to begin with was bad. The trick would be to find such an Archimedean point that is not simply within another system of morality. I think I have the beginnings of an answer, and I would like to think aloud with you about it.

I am going to take my starting point from the history of science. I do so because I think that in our own day, science gives a clearer reflection in the public sphere of how we implicitly see reality than does philosophy. In the end, I think that modern philosophy and modern science are in fact working out of the same worldview, as they always have. But for my purposes here, I find the debate among historians of science to be the most helpful in elucidating our problem.

Among the most important have been Ludwik Fleck and Thomas Kuhn. I think I can best state my starting point by referring to Ludwik Fleck. He states in the prologue to *Genesis and Development of a Scientific Fact* that

> we have even lost any critical insight we may once have had into the organic basis of perception, taking for granted the basic fact that a normal person has two eyes. We have nearly ceased to consider this as even knowledge at all and are no longer conscious of our own participation in perception. Instead, we feel a complete passivity in the face of a power that is independent of us; a power we call "existence" or "reality."[3]

What Fleck was getting at, it seems to me, is the unconscious assumption on the part of scientists and philosophers that what they perceive or experience is intimately connected to what is really out there, that the "facts" of scientific or philosophical observation are given, and it is only up to us to perceive and interpret them. His book is rather a long argument the other way around (and so parallel in many ways to Niels Bohr), that the observer is in fact an active agent in the very formation of the perceived "facts" and the "meaning" they bear. Whitehead paraphrasing John Locke, puts it this way: "nature gets credit which should be reserved for ourselves: the rose for its scent; the nightingale for his song."

Fleck in fact pushes his argument one step further. In his case, the "fact" under investigation is the existence of a disease called syphilis. For Fleck the nature of this disease and what it "means," medically and socially, are not defined by the data themselves. Rather, there were, and are, a variety of ways in which the "disease" can be defined. This means, argues Fleck, that the one that was adopted by the scientific community was in fact a choice. To be sure, the choice had a certain self-evidence to it because it was part of a larger universe of discourse, but it was a choice nonetheless.

The danger comes in, Fleck clearly tells us, when the scientist forgets that he or she has had a hand in constructing the facts. The living relationship between the observer and the observed, between the one and the other, is ignored. The fact becomes dead, a sort of Buberian "it," and the scientist's understanding takes on the status of being the only possible reading of reality. The very possibility that another equally valid reading or paradigm might exist is dismissed out of hand. The scientist thus becomes "right," and every other statement is *ipso facto* wrong.

I would like to take this same logic back to ethics. In ethics and moral philosophy, we deal with certain facts in much the same way the scientist does. We know, for example, that there is a distinction between killing and murder. Killing is not necessarily deemed bad in our culture; we do it everyday in order to eat, to prevent disease, etc. That is not to say that we all think killing is good; we regard it as an unpleasant but often necessary evil. Murder, on the other hand, is clearly bad. And for most of us most of the time, the distinction is clear enough to make rough-and-ready moral decisions possible. I know usually when an act is killing and when it is murder. To be sure there are gray areas, and times in which I recognize that people seeing the same situation can honestly disagree. But I can still take it as a moral "fact" that there is such a distinction.

The problem is that a moral system, especially one that is thought out and elaborated along "scientific" lines, that is, through the application of a strict logic, hardens such facts into universal givens. In this case the distinction between, say, killing and murder becomes harshly and unequivocally defined. It presents itself to me as a given. It is simply a matter of determining which act fits which taxon. I then lose sight of my own moral agency, of my own power to create not only the acts through my observation of them, but also to create the taxa that give the act its moral value. I at that moment stop being a moral agent and become instead a passive actor in someone else's drama.

This brings me back to the Nazi ethic. What I think I am now prepared to say is that what was wrong with the Nazi ethic was that it was too worked out, too coherent, too cut-and-dried. It did the thinking for people. It announced as a scientific and so unassailable given not only what was right and what was wrong, but which acts fell into which category. The result was that people did atrocious things because they took them to be morally mandated. The Nazi morality predefined what was acceptable to such an extent, and in such an authoritative, scientific way, that many people, especially intellectuals, simply fell into line. The living relationship between the human as moral agent, on the one hand, and the moral act, on the other, was lost.

Fleck's writings, and developments in relativity and quantum mechanics, were showing already at the time of the Nazis' rise to power that this givenness of taxa and data is not scientific. Modern science has been teaching us that the things we take for granted out there in the physical world are not really out there at all. We now know that even space and time are constructions of our perceptions. Heisenberg and quantum mechanics have made it clear that while we can have true knowledge, we can never have complete knowledge of everything all at the same time. These are important insights even in the moral sphere. We cannot continue as if there are absolute moral facts out there that some of us can know and which must be imposed on all others. Science and philosophy both tell us that our knowledge is limited and our complicity in the creation of "facts" is significant. When we lose sight of this and let the perceptions out there harden into a given and unquestioned reality, we lose control of our own moral destiny.

Where exactly this leaves us in terms of constructing a morality for the twenty-first century I am not sure. It does seem clear to me that the paradigm will have to discard the idea of hard facts and given truths, and depend more on the dynamics of relationship, cooperation, openness to the other, and compassion for the Other. It will have to respect contingency more than Western ethics have so far been willing to do. I cannot help but think in this regard of another line in Galileo's letter to Madame Christina. He pleads at one point, "Let us confess quite truly that those truths which we know are very few in comparison with those which we do not know."[4] The masses of corpses which represent the consistent and dedicated application of a scientific ethic in our own century stand as a reminder of how wrong we can be even about the facts we declare with great scientific conviction. What the Holocaust reminds us of is how little we know, and how dangerous a science claiming exclusive knowledge can be.

NOTES

1. *Discourses and Opinions of Galileo*, transl. and introd. by Stillman Drake (New York: Doubleday, 1957), p. 186.
2. *Morality After Auschwitz: The Radical Challenge of the Nazi Ethic* (Philadelphia: Fortress, 1988).
3. (Chicago: Univ. of Chicago Press, 1979), p. xxvii.
4. *Discourses and Opinions*, p. 187.

The Morality of Auschwitz?
A Critical Confrontation with
Peter J. Haas's
Ethical Interpretation of the Holocaust

Didier Pollefeyt

INTRODUCTION

For the American ethicist and rabbi Peter J. Haas, ethical reflection on the holocaust has been dominated by the wrong question, namely, how people in Auschwitz were able to do what they recognized, or should have recognized, as evil.[1] In his pioneering ethical study, *Morality after Auschwitz*,[2] as well as in numerous articles, he demonstrates how the fundamental question is not why the Nazis did evil, but why they did not recognize evil as evil and therefore why they did not distance themselves from it. Haas answers this question by referring to the prevalent patterns of ethical argumentation and acting among the Nazis that predetermined their perception of Jews in a very specific way. In the light of this ethical framework, the effort to persecute and exterminate the Jewish people appeared for the Nazis as an ethically acceptable part of a greater good. However shocking Haas's thesis may be, it has become, in the words of Richard Rubenstein, "impossible for future researchers to work in the field [of ethics after Auschwitz] without taking serious account of his [Haas's] findings."[3] Haas's analysis has provided a new paradigm[4] in holocaust studies,[5] a paradigm that enables us to understand some difficult aspects of the Nazi genocide, but that at the same time entails serious limits and weaknesses.

ETHIC AND MORALITY: A CRITIQUE OF MODERN ETHICS

In the interpretation of Haas,[6] the Nazis were neither diabolical (Steiner)[7] nor banal (Arendt),[8] but remained ethical throughout the course of the war. For them, the development of genocidal policy had an ethically logical progression with which they could consciously, voluntarily, and even enthusiastically identify. Given this, the holocaust proves the exceptional human capacity to redefine good and evil, reconstructing reality in the light of these new ethical categories. The Germans did not suddenly become savages in 1941, nor did they accidentally return to humanity in 1945. Through the entire period of the war they remained the same people, doing their jobs professionally and with dedication, devoted to their families, and functioning in society in a normal way.

At the core of Haas's position is a critique of the prevailing notion of modern ethics. In Western thought about the good life, one usually begins with the presupposition that all ethical systems rest on propositions that are universally valid and that determine what is good and evil. All ethical theories are thought to be rooted in universal and rational premises, a common basis upon which all people agree and which functions as the objective foundation for all ethical systems. For Haas, however, an ethical system does not acquire its validity from a universal, rational principle, but from the coherent patterns of thinking and speaking it incorporates.[9] As such, ethical judgments are not objectively or scientifically provable, but are the result of the interaction of individual personalities, human relationships, cultural ways of thinking, juridical and social habits, generally accepted linguistic conventions, and experiences of the past.[10] Mistakenly, this description can give the impression that Haas views an ethic as an arbitrary system. This is far from the case. An ethic can only work if it conforms to some formal criteria; it must be coherent, noncontradictory, and intuitively right.[11] For Haas, the deep structure of an ethic is based on a coherent and logical structure of binary oppositions.[12] On a conscious level, every part of the opposition helps to define the other part. Good and evil mutually call each other into being. An ethic makes it possible to divide the cosmos into forces of good and evil, in an unambiguous way. An ethic is intuitively right when it is the expression of dominant values and interests, both individual and collective.[13]

Haas distinguishes such an ethic from what he calls morality.[14] While he means by ethic a systematic way to understand good and evil, in and by which a society shapes itself, he defines morality as those values which we think *should* be incorporated or developed in an ethic. This distinction has the advantage of describing the holocaust as an ethic without immediately assessing its moral character. Haas is not *a priori* excluding the possibility that moral reality coincides with the ethical structure.[15] He merely wants to stress how in reality people only live out of an ethical system immediately.

When an ethic can produce such a coherent and intuitively right discourse about good and evil, and the results of such an ethic meet the wishes and needs of a community, then, for Haas, it is possible for people to be ethically motivated to do any action, even the most immoral. The Nazi genocide would be the most extreme and clear illustration of this thesis. Haas argues that the carrying out of the holocaust manifests all the characteristics of an ethic. Nazism created a specific public discourse about good and evil within which genocide became an ethically acceptable, even laudable, policy. Nazi propaganda portrayed the extermination of the Jews as a good by connecting it to the ethical principle of the right to self-defense. The Jew was presented as a mortal threat to Germany's cultural and biological patrimony. In the light of the age-long history of anti-Judaism and antisemitism, this was not even a difficult task.

THE NAZI ETHIC

In the interpretation of Haas, the Nazi ethic can be seen as a new construction, but put together from the old building blocks of Western ethics. And this explains, at least in part, the success of the Nazi ethic in and outside of Germany. This brings us to one of the most challenging and startling of Haas's conclusions: that the ethical framework of Nazism stood in continuity with the formal framework of Western ethical discourse. In this view, Nazism ensues from the intellectual and ethical history of modern Europe, and its politics of extermination stems from ethical convictions and symbols that have influenced Western moral theology and philosophy for centuries. With this idea, Haas is criticizing the idea of aberration which portrays the holocaust as a sudden and formal rupture with the political, juridical, and moral thinking of the last centuries. Auschwitz has its roots in a complexity of moral and political lines of thought that were long evident and seemingly innocent. This is, in fact, a fundamental idea of Haas's: the holocaust was only able to take place because it appeared ethically acceptable in the light of Western history.

The choice of the Jew as the archenemy of the Aryan race could be readily convincing within the Nazi ethic, since it fit perfectly into the long Christian history of systematically depicting the Jew as the mythical symbol for evil,[16] as well as the nineteenth- and twentieth-century theories of eugenics.[17] Building further on these traditions, the Nazi ethic could easily color the notions of good and evil by using the opposition Aryan and Jew. The real battle against this evil only became possible within the political constellation of fascism, which was not an invention of Nazism, but the historical synthesis of three important intellectual elements of recent European history: economical socialism, nationalism, and racism.[18]

When the Nazi Party came to power in 1933, the most important components of its ethic were already in place. While Nazi discourse was a complete and functional system, within which every action could in principle be interpreted in terms of good and evil, it was initially a very formal, abstract, and even sectarian announcement of a platform, without real impact on concrete political and social structures. When Nazism came to real political acts, this ethic became more and more concrete, attempting to forcibly shape reality within its formal ethical discourse. The wrestling of Nazi bureaucrats with the question of who was finally a Jew is a classic example of the way in which Nazism, with ups and downs, tried to accommodate reality to its predetermined ethical framework.[19] The definition of a Jew seemed to be a Gordian knot that could only be cut in two after long discussions. In a certain sense, the Nazi bureaucracy *created* an inferior race, using a complex of laws.

Once the Jewish evil was clearly localized, its persecution could begin. Still, the activities of murder were too concrete and too direct to keep the executioners wondering about the inhuman consequences. Haas does not explain this aspect of the Nazi genocide as the result of the distant, bureaucratic attitude of its perpetrators, as Arendt did. Rather, he thinks that only a thoroughly convincing ethic could explain the unwavering conviction of the perpetrators. In spite of the repulsion and the physical and psychological problems with which, for example, the *Einsatzgruppen* were confronted,[20] they continued to carry out their jobs. Haas does not explain this as due to some diabolical hunger for evil, or to mechanical and blind obedience to authority, but refers instead to the enormous influence of the Nazi ethic upon their minds and deeds. Moral and emotional feelings can be put aside more easily than one often thinks, especially when one employs a framework within which morally or emotionally difficult acts can be legitimized in an ethical way. There were, of course, emotions among the perpetrators, but any difficult emotions were considered to be human weakness, or the necessary price one had to pay to be ethical.[21] Every ethic has its painful and emotionally difficult moments. The Nazi ethic was a powerful way to trivialize, ridicule, and falsify emotional constraints as reminiscences of the old ethic.

Another convincing factor that established the persuasive power of the Nazi ethic and its genocidal policy was its economic advantages for Germany.[22] The Nazi ethic borrowed the old image of the Jew as an economic force and bloodsucker. From an economic point of view, the holocaust could be characterized as an enormous and systematic transfer of possessions from victims to perpetrators. While there were no conflicts among the Nazis about the deportation of the Jews, considerable discussions were held about the destiny of Jewish properties.

Haas can also explain why the Western world protested so little during the period 1933–1945.[23] Despite being told of the atrocities, the Allied powers were unable to react against the Nazi ethic precisely because they, like the Germans, were caught in the same web of moral presuppositions. Since at that time the entire West thought in terms of such principles as race, the sovereignty of the state, the right to self-defense, the war against Bolshevism, anti-Jewish ideas, etc., the Allies could not react forcefully and adequately to the Nazi policy of extermination. Even more, their attitude toward Jewish refugees indirectly abetted the Nazis' genocidal policy. By closing their borders and refusing Jews the right to asylum, the Allies disrupted the efforts of the Nazis to cleanse their territories of Jews. This can also be seen as a reason why the anti-Jewish policy in Germany accelerated so steadily. Moreover, Western passivity also gave the Nazis the impression that their enterprise was acceptable in the eyes of the Western world. More than once, the Nazis used the unwillingness of the Allied powers to accept Jewish refugees as an argument for the ethical legitimation of their expulsion and extermination policies. In this way, it becomes clear that the Allied powers employed the same basic values. It became impossible for the Western world to launch a credible ethical critique of Nazi policy. It seemed more and more clear that the Nazis were working in behalf of a "good cause" that was justifiable in the light of Western morality.

A good illustration of the ethical framework of the judeocide can be found in Haas's penetrating analysis of the medical experts working in the genocide process.[24] According to Haas, most of the Nazi doctors had a good conscience about working in the genocide program since they saw themselves as selective killers in the service of the life and health of the German people.[25] The principle of their ethical reasoning was the so-called killing-healing paradox. According to this principle, selective killing is sometimes a necessity in order to protect and promote the well-being of a society. Nazi doctors believed that the elimination of certain people was a painful but necessary duty, required of them in the service of public health. The presupposition that life is not possible without some kind of killing has a long history. It accepts the idea that death feeds life. Only through this ethical argumentation of killing in the service of life were the Nazi doctors capable of collaborating on such a large scale in the mass murder while still considering themselves inside the ethical framework within which medicine has understood itself since the time of Hippocrates.

In a certain sense, the perpetrators were also victims of the all-powerful Nazi ethic. This can be illustrated with the hyper-ethical decision of Eichmann to withdraw trains from the eastern front at a decisive point of the war in order to use them against the Jews.[26] But it is not only the choices of the regime's supporters, but even those of the adversaries fighting the system, that are understood by Haas as expressions of their individual character and of their social, political, or religious position.[27] Whatever attitude one had vis-à-vis the Nazi ethic, it was always provided with (and thus predictable from) the story, the personal and social background of the individual.

In the end, it was not the power of argumentation of Western ethics that finally eliminated Nazism, but the contingent military victory of the Allied armies. The internal or external critique of morality was entirely powerless. Only thanks to military intervention was the Nazi ethic ultimately defeated. With his thesis that an ethic depends upon the political exertion of power, Haas comes very close to the interpretation of Rubenstein. In Rubenstein's view, people have no natural rights, they have only the rights that are guaranteed by an organized community that is powerful enough to protect these rights.[28] When Nazism deprived the Jews of their citizenship, it at the same time robbed them of all claims to so-called human rights. Human rights only have meaning when there is a political power that can demand that they be enforced. Stateless people have no rights because there is no institution that can guarantee and enforce them. People without political rights are superfluous, and ultimately expendable. They lose all claim to dignity, human protection, and life.

For Haas, individuals do not act as independent moral agents. They make their ethical decisions within certain preordained ethical frameworks. The origin of the catastrophe of Auschwitz is not to be found in its individual perpetrators, but in the ethical universe in which they lived. As such, we can only formulate an adequate and authentic response to Auschwitz insofar as we come to develop an alternative ethical discourse. While holocaust theologians are continuing to think, and their theologies can therefore be seen as an internal critique of the inherited ethic of Western thinking, it has been the great merit of Elie Wiesel to develop an entirely new and unusual manner of speaking ethically and theologically.[29] Wiesel no longer believes that truth and morality are automatic products of scientific rationality. In Haas's view, the success of Wiesel is proof that the age-old coalition between Judaism and Enlightenment has come to an end. Wiesel's stories open a new framework in which we can meaningfully situate our own existence, with all its paradoxes and tensions. The story of Auschwitz is a story of fear and death. By contrast, the stories of Wiesel open perspectives on reconciliation, healing, and respect for human life.

A CRITIQUE OF PETER HAAS'S POSITION

How should we evaluate the interpretation propounded by Peter Haas? Explaining the holocaust as an element of an ethical system is, of course, a precarious enterprise. Haas seeks to make his interpretation acceptable by distinguishing ethic from morality. In this way, he is able to call the holocaust a component of the Nazi ethic without saying that the Nazi genocide was morally permissible. But it is precisely this distinction in his thought that is, in my view, very vulnerable. It is not clear *on what grounds* a certain ethical system can be qualified as moral or immoral in Haas's interpretation. Each and every ethical judgment is determined by the ethical system in which one stands. A critique of one ethical system can only be formulated from within another ethical system that has the same formal characteristics (coherence, noncontradiction, intuitive rightness). There is no Archimedean point from which all ethical systems can be evaluated as to their content, using a kind of universal standard. As such, it would be impossible to find in Haas's thinking a real criterium by which to judge that Nazism is immoral, because there is no intra- or trans-ethical touchstone for preferring one ethical system over another.

When Haas defends the stories of Elie Wiesel, and asks that moral duty be discovered within such an alternative ethical structure, the question arises as to *how* one can be sure that this framework is indeed right and humanly authentic. Weren't the Nazis convinced of the rectitude of their ethical thinking, as we are of ours? Were they unable to justify their actions, as we do, in a coherent, logical, and intuitively right way? In short, when the persuasive power of ethical systems depends only on their semantic and syntactic form, we can only conclude that it is impossible to compare and qualify them from a moral point of view.

On this point, the interpretation of Rubenstein, who is one of Haas's sources of inspiration, appears to be more fecund. It is no accident that Rubenstein wrote one of the most favorable reviews of Haas's book.[30] Rubenstein thinks that after Auschwitz, there is no longer a higher, universal morality by which all peoples and nations can be judged. People only have rights as members of a *polis*. Persons who do not have the power to protect themselves must always be prepared to become the victims of the obscenities of their opponents. What Bauman, in his *Modernity and the Holocaust*,[31] has called the spontaneous ethical inclination of human beings is for Rubenstein nothing but the expression of the sentimental, yet completely powerless, desire of human beings to be respected. Thus, moral indignation and justice are only relevant in situations where people understand themselves to be members of the same community. Auschwitz is proof that such considerations become totally senseless in a society where more and more people lose their right to dignity and life. In the ethical system of Nazism, it was an illusion for the victims to think that they lived in the same moral universe as the perpetrators.[32] Moral indignation is only relevant in situations where people are connected in a community that shares the same story about what is decent human behavior. People have no spontaneous moral orientation, as Bauman suggests, that would regulate their behavior towards fellow human beings in a natural way. By exterminating the stateless, the Nazis did not violate any law, since these people were not protected by any law. In this way, Rubenstein comes to one of his most paradoxical and controversial, but logical conclusions: not one crime was committed in Auschwitz.[33]

What Haas seeks to do is to avoid *in extremis* Rubenstein's ethical relativism by introducing the distinction between ethic and morality. In our view, Rubenstein's theology reveals the real consequences of Haas's interpretation. When the moral quality of an act is justified only from within and by the ethical framework of the (ruling) group, and when the validity of this ethical structure depends only on formal criteria, then there can be no moral story against evil deeds that arise from such stories, except for the story of another ethical system with the same formal characteristics, defended with the same ethical passion. Ethics then becomes a question of the strongest, the most beautiful, the most intelligent, the most influential, the most privileged, the most numerous, etc. Ultimately, the result is power positivism. For Rubenstein, then, the only response of the Jews to the holocaust would be the establishment of their own community which can enforce their rights politically and militarily. On this point, however, the story of the holocaust risks becoming an ethical legitimation for new forms of injustice, an ethic can easily become ideology.[34]

With this last statement, we come to the heart of our critique. Haas's distinction between ethics and morality can be best substituted by the distinction between ideology and morality (in Haas's sense). The characteristics that Haas uses to describe an ethic, namely coherence, noncontradiction, and intuitive rightness, do not seem to be the essence of moral discourse. In a critical essay, Emil Fackenheim similarly argues against Haas's position, contending that his use of the terminology "Nazi *ethic*" is inaccurate.[35] The concrete content of Haas's notion of ethic is for Fackenheim closer to the German notion of *Weltanschauung*.[36] A *Weltanschauung* has some formal attributes: cosmic dimensions, internal coherence (*Geschlossenheit*), and unconditional devotion. A *Weltanschauung* provides an all-embracing system of explanation, according to which all natural and historical facts can be interpreted. It is characterized by a self-grounding, closed, and internal coherence. External criteria to evaluate its truth do not exist. A *Weltanschauung* demands total dedication and obedience from its followers. It not only creates a system of values from which one can live, but also values for which one is prepared to die. The devotion of its followers is necessary because a *Weltanschauung* (in contrast to a religion or a metaphysical system) is never true as such, but always needs to be made true. And this entails a difficult struggle wherein those elements of the *Welt* that do not fit into the *Weltanschauung* are forged in such a way that they fit into it anyway. According to Fackenheim, Nazism was established on such a *Weltanschauung*, formulated by Hitler.

In this interpretation, the holocaust is not seen as working toward a greater good, but as a component of a coherent system that tried in the first place to establish itself. This *Weltanschauung* gave its followers a closed framework that enabled them to legitimate their actions. As a result, one cannot conclude from the fact that the Nazis legitimated their crimes that they acted out of ethical concerns. Perhaps Haas too easily believes the Nazis' self-presentation. Their so-called ethical language could also be the expression of the need they felt to legitimate themselves in the face of what they recognized as unambiguous evil, and this for themselves as well as for others. The Nazi *Weltanschauung* can be interpreted as the supplier of an arsenal of skillful pretexts and ethical sophisms to do evil (and not good) with a more peaceful (but not good) mind. Here we encounter the phenomenon of self-justification becoming self-deception.[37]

It seems to us that to argue that an ethical view can only be asserted within a contingent ethical framework is both unwarranted and even dangerous. While Bauman's theory of the presocial origin of morality needs to be criticized because it denies the fact that an ethical attitude always originates within a certain intersubjective and narrative context, we must also formulate the opposite critique against Haas. He overemphasizes the social origin of morality insofar as he holds that an ethical view can only be argued for from within a contingent ethical framework. But how can one be certain that one's own ethic is not merely an ideology, attempting *in medias res* or *post factum* to give one's crimes an ideological legitimation? For Haas, ethical options are always given within the story in which individuals situate themselves. Is this not a kind of ethical determinism?[38] If this were true, then the Nazis, given their ethical framework, could not possibly have made any other choice. Moreover, within Haas's interpretation, it becomes impossible to explain how different individuals coming from the same story can arrive at entirely different ethical attitudes. In the end, one can forget that people always live in different, even contradictory and mutually questioning stories.

When the differentiation between good and evil is only at the disposal of social groups that are capable of controlling social reality, then there is no longer any ground for protesting against the crimes perpetrated against those who are outside this group. If there were no inter- or trans-narrative foundation on which the actions of the Nazis can be evaluated, then there would also

be no argument against the thesis that their punishment was merely the vic-
tors taking revenge on the losers, as Goering claimed about the verdicts of the
Nuremberg trials.

In the postscript of her *Eichmann in Jerusalem: A Report on the Banality
of Evil*, Hannah Arendt developed a notion of moral responsibility in which
resistance to social forces is possible.[39] Human beings must be capable of distinguishing good from evil, even if they can only rely upon their own judgment, and when this judgment is in conflict with the dominant and univocal
opinions of their environment.[40] While Haas sees the holocaust as proof for
the overpowering influence of the ethical framework in which one lives and
acts, Arendt's interpretation shows how the normative forces of good and evil
can never be finally legitimated by referring to the social forces that call them
into life, preserve and sanction them. An action can have moral meaning even
if it is condemned by the dominant group, and it can be an immoral act even
if it is accepted by the whole society. Put the other way around, this means
that resistance against a dominant immoral social norm can never restrict
itself to a reference back to an alternative normative system of another community that one thinks to be better, for example, a system of values that has
been abandoned. Ultimately, the social foundation of moral authority is irrelevant.

Bauman argues that the human capacity to distinguish good from evil is
ultimately built on something other than the collective conscience of a particular community. Instead, Bauman stresses the role of moral emotions as they
emerge from a confrontation with human suffering. Haas, however, does not
seem to appreciate the positive meaning of emotions for moral life. In his
view, emotions can disturb ethical performance, but they do not play a positive, constitutive role in the genesis of moral choices.[41] Still, one can ask
whether the spontaneous emotional disgust of the Nazis for their own crimes
should not have had a warning function in their own moral lives. Moreover, it
is not clear how the perpetrators could feel that the genocide was intuitively
right while shuddering at the consequences of their own jobs. In general, the
question remains as to whether Nazi criminals believed their own ethical
story.

If their story were to become the final norm for good and evil, and insofar as this story presents genocide as an acceptable means, then we would
have to accept that people acted in good conscience when they followed this
story. In the end, it would be impossible to distinguish moral from immoral
stories, and the possibility of describing the holocaust as evil would vanish.
As Berel Lang has pointed out, when the holocaust can be seen as working
toward a good, it becomes impossible to ground the notions of good and bad.

"If . . . we still conclude that the Nazis were only doing what they *thought* to be right . . . we give up all hope of distinguishing morally significant judgment or action from whatever it is that anybody, at any particular moment, *does*. . . . In short, the possibility of evaluation is threatened as it applies to *all* moral action."[42]

The problem with Lang's position is how to discover a foundation for good and evil in a postmodern world where there no longer seems to be any Archimedean point from which to defend such a position. For Haas, ethical values are temporary and fragile preferences of a particular social group at a certain place and time. Rubenstein is even more clear. For him, there are no longer transcendent values after Auschwitz to do what Berel Lang wants to do, that is, to call the holocaust an absolute evil, *le mal pour le mal* (Levinas). If there are no transcendent standards (and it matters not whether these be considered divinely ordained or simply natural or fated—the key question is whether they *are* at all!), there are no grounds for saying that what the Nazis did was wrong.[43]

This brings us to an exceptionally paradoxical conclusion, namely, that such a terrible evil as the holocaust, which asks in fact for an immediate and absolute condemnation, brought into life a sincere process of thought that seems to undermine the very foundations of morality. And if there is no longer a foundation for good and evil, why then should not the strongest rule over and even eliminate the weakest?[44] In our view, it is precisely this basic intuition that Emil Fackenheim formulated so acutely in his new moral imperative after Auschwitz: not to grant Hitler posthumous victories.[45] How ethical relativism also played a role in the foundation of Nazism is illustrated by the thinking of one of the most important Nazi philosophers, Alfred Rosenberg. In his *Der Mythus des 20. Jahrhunderts* ("The Myth of the 20th Century"),[46] of which more than one million copies were sold in 1943, Rosenberg strongly attacked the empty, universal, and logical truth of modern philosophy and argued for a more organic conception of truth, the truth of blood and race. In short, values were not to be discovered in logical analysis, but were to be created by a race. Moreover, no communication between the races was possible. When one detached humanity from its racial origin, it became a senseless notion. For the successful philosopher Rosenberg, truth is always culturally relative and subordinated to the practical purposes of the *Volk*.[47]

In our view, the powerlessness and bankruptcy of objective morality in Auschwitz need not, and should not, lead to ethical relativism and power positivism. Fact and norm should not be confused. Nazism was created in a relativistic and nihilistic spirit, but this does not mean that it illustrates the excellence of this ideology. One needs to distinguish the ethical categories that established Nazism from the ethical conclusions that can be deduced from the study of it. In other words, it is not because there was an Auschwitz that the possibility of authentic moral action is impossible after Auschwitz. As the French ethicist Todorov indicates in his ethical study of the holocaust, *Face à l'extrême*, factuality and conviction do not coincide.[48]

This means that the Nazi ethic should not simply be seen as a reorganization of the values of Western ethics. It is not a rearrangement of the classic values of our moral tradition, but a *perversion* of its ethical principles. In Nazism's ideological abuse and corruption, the basic inspiration and main concerns of Western values were completely lost. For instance, the ethical paradox of healing by killing is dissociated from the rational principle of proportionalism, the Kantian categorical imperative is dissociated from the principle of autonomy, the Christian idea of ascesis is detached from the desire to be in harmony with what is human.[49] In killing for killing, in obedience for obedience, and in ascesis for ascesis, Nazism cut Western ethics from its source and basic concerns. What was left was only the veneer of an ethic. While sometimes, and mistakenly, the total discontinuity between Western history and the holocaust is emphasized, Haas too easily stresses the fact that the Nazi genocide was in continuity with our Christian and humanistic civilization. Nazism, however, is more a manipulation than a continuation of Western ethics. This can be illustrated with the Nazis' use of the theory of the just war that was developed in the Christian tradition. Historically, the notion of a just war is not so much a strategy to justify war as a theory that was orientated toward the introduction of a certain circumspection, trying to postpone the mortal use of violence as long as possible. It was a theory that, on the one hand, tried to delay the violence of war as long as possible, without, on the other hand, completely delivering the victims of evil to the arbitrariness of tyrants. Because of this reserve about the use of violence, one would better speak of the theory of restrictive or limited war. In the Nazi ethic, however, the notion of just war functioned in an entirely different manner. Hitler thought he had the right to kill the Jews. At the core of his view was no longer the radical imperative of love, an imperative that in exceptional cases asks, in the name of human dignity, to use, with fear and trembling, power and violence, but was instead a misuse of this complex notion of Western history in the name of pure *Wille zur Macht* (will-to-power).

Moreover, a consistent ethical relativism is internally destructive. To say that all ethical argumentation is determined by the story from which one speaks is also a statement colored by a particular story that is logically and historically relative. The question becomes whether there is no form of ethics that might transcend different stories and with which one can criticize one's

own story, escaping ethical relativism. An answer to this question presupposes the identification of a number of values or characteristics that in some way
surpass the particularity of different stories or traditions. These values, however, can no longer be thought to be story-independent, objective characteristics. They will always be expressed in and supported (or not) by particular
narrative communities. An essential task of ethics after Auschwitz is to identify ethical-religious and fundamental human experiences in different ethical
traditions that transcend their original cultural and historical circumstances,
and thereby can have a liberating and humanizing meaning in other times and
places. Because these kinds of values, traditions, or stories have proven to be
transcultural and even transreligious, it is the task of the ethicist to make them
understandable and communicable.[50] In this way, characteristics and criteria
that enable criticism of ruling cultures, ethics, and religions can emerge.

We can illustrate this with one formal criterion that we find crucial for an
authentic ethic: openness to positive alterities. Through such a criterion,
Nazism can be rejected from an ethical point of view because it is not characterized by this kind of openness, but by a deadly closedness. Closedness is
characteristic of unauthentic ethical systems. This characteristic can be found
by analyzing Haas's philosophy of language. The whole production of meaning in the language of Nazism is thought of in Haas's interpretation as an ideal
and closed syntactic-semantic design of the Nazis world, which has not produced itself, but has been given in the form of binary opposition prior to all
production of meaning. Understood in this way, the production of meaning in
the Nazi language is seen as and subordinated to the constant reproductive
reactualization of this pre-given, indisputable, and self-satisfied ideal structure. As such, there is no room for creative transcendence within a language
and within an ethic itself, a creativity that could break open the existing and
fixed binary oppositions of the pre-given ethic. In this way, ethical language
is simply reduced to nomenclature.

Lacan indicated that language is only possible in confrontation with otherness. Similarly, the precondition for the production of ethical meaning is not
a closed and absolute self-satisfied system, but the unremovable difference
between the system and the possibility of deviations of meaning. In other
words, no system can be closed and definitive, because there are always pro-
ductions of meaning possible that escape the power and the rules of the system. An authentic ethical discourse differs precisely from a *Weltanschauung*
thanks to its principal openness to new meaning, to otherness, to the new, to
that which calls the *Geschlossenheit* of the system into question, time and
again. While it is true that human morality always takes form within a particular and contingent community, with its own history, language, social struc-

ture, and political interests, an ethic can never derive its validity from this community itself. On the contrary, the concrete ethic of a community receives its legitimacy precisely from a point that lies outside its homogeneous structure and can never be captured by it. An ethic becomes immoral when it eliminates or strangles this point of transcendent otherness.

The difference between a society based on biblical-humanitarian values and a society based on totalitarian and racist values is not that the former has ethical and theological concerns, and the latter does not. Nazism also had a conception of goodness ("Good is what is good for the German people") and a conception of God (*Gott mit uns*). On this point, we agree with Peter Haas. What makes the difference is that the basic structure of the Judeo-Christian ethic is characterized by an openness *in concreto*, an openness to the vulnerability of the face of the other, which continually and unpredictably calls my closed system into question, as Levinas says,[51] while totalitarian and extreme nationalist discourses are typified by closedness. In biblical ethics, for example, centrality is given to the unpredictable coming of God, always in new, different, and challenging perspectives, so that people and communities might perpetually grow in their humanity. Herein God is not *Gott mit uns*, who can be used for one's own purposes, but the total Other who always represents what is irreducible, what escapes my power and the power of my story, what can never be defined in terms of economic value, gender, national identity, religious belief, or race. It is a God who can never be used in order to legitimize evil in any form. Finally, it is a God who never definitively encloses human beings in their own failures, but who always offers them new chances, if they are prepared to take them. There are numerous examples of life in the camps where the experience of openness within victims could never be entirely extinguished.[52]

In a totalitarian ethic, on the contrary, priority is given to sameness. Closed totalitarian stories always seek to reduce otherness to sameness. In such a logic, difference is the greatest danger, even a crime. Everything that cannot be assimilated into the beautiful, safe, and closed identity must be excommunicated and even exterminated. All that is unprepared or unable to integrate in the wonderful harmony, thereby questioning the closed system, must be destroyed. A closed ethic knows no mercy. Instead it becomes ideology[53] and brings with it a legitimation of all evil, anxiously undertaken against the disturbers of the closed order. In such a system, God is not the Other who constantly challenges self-righteousness in the name of more and more humanity, but a *Gott mit uns*, a pseudo-God who legitimizes the closed and murderous order. Such a God does not, indeed cannot, know mercy.

In this sense, Nazism is a politics without an ethic, meaning it had no respect for alterity and it required the eradication of everything that could not be reduced to the closed system. As such, Nazism was an idolatrous effort that radicalized itself and eliminated everything that did not conform, in its own name. In idolatry, one tries to adapt God to the ideological ends of one's own group. Precisely as a fundamental critique of such an idolatrous use of God, the biblical tradition asks us not to make images of God, or even to pronounce His name. When the Bible says that human beings are created in the image of God, this also means that the essence of being human can never be defined in closed terms. When we try to seize the essence of being human into binary, manichaean categories, we always risk that we do so according to our own benefit. This is, for us, the primary lesson of the Nazi genocide, but also of other forms of racism and discrimination, such as nationalism, sexism, or religious fundamentalism. Every effort to grasp the essence of being human in closed terms opens the way, mostly in the name of one or another so-called human or pseudo-religious good, to violence against the dignity of men and women, as well as against the dignity of God.

NOTES

1. Peter Haas's father was born in Germany, and his mother has a Polish-Jewish background. During the war, his parents were arrested by the Nazis in the Netherlands and were deported to the Nazi camps of Westerbork, Voeght, and Bergen-Belsen. In 1944, they were exchanged for German prisoners-of-war in France. The last year of the war, they lived in a refugee camp in North Africa. After the war, they went to the United States, where Peter was born in 1947, in Detroit, Michigan. Peter Haas received his doctoral degree in Jewish ethics in 1980 as a student of Jacob Neusner. He became a professor of holocaust studies at Vanderbilt University and has recently accepted an appointment at Case Western Reserve University.

2. P. J. Haas, *Morality after Auschwitz: the Radical Challenge of the Nazi Ethic* (Philadelphia: Fortress Press, 1988). Some important reviews by M. Brearley in the *Scottish Journal of Theology* 46 , no. 4 (1993): 550–553; L. Rasmussen in the *Journal of Religion* 71 no. 1 (1991): 119; R. L. Rubenstein in the *Journal of the American Academy of Religion* 60, no. 1 (1992): 158–161; A. M. Suggate in the *Expository Times* 101, no. 7 (1990): 220; A. Toubeau in *Nouvelle Revue Théologique* 115, no. 3 (1993): 420; M. Baird in the *Journal of Spiritual Formation* 15, no. 1 (1994): 21]; and the *Jewish Quarterly Review* 83, nos. 1–2 (1992): 167–172. See also our own review in *Driemaandelijks tijdschrift van de Stichting Auschwitz* 32 (1992): 78–80.

3. Rubenstein, review of *Morality after Auschwitz*, in *Journal of the American Academy of Religion* 60, no. 1 (1992): 158.

4. For the notion of paradigm, see T. Kuhn, *The Structure of Scientific Revolutions* (Chicago: University of Chicago Press, 1970).

5. For an interpretation of holocaust ethics in three paradigms, see D. Pollefeyt, "Vergeving na misdaden tegen de mensheid? Een christelijke antropologie van kwaad en vergeving," in *Tijdschrift voor theologie* 36, no. 2 (1996): 155–178.

6. P. J. Haas, "The Morality of Auschwitz: Moral Language and the Nazi Ethic," in *Holocaust and Genocide Studies* 3, no. 4 (1988): 385: ". . . two other general conclusions about good and evil that have emerged in the confrontation between the Holocaust and moral theory, both of which I find inadequate and which I mean to reject." This article was first published as "The Morality of Auschwitz: Moral Language and the Nazi Ethic," in Y. Bauer, *Remembering for the Future: Papers to be Presented at an International Scholars' Conference to Be Held in Oxford, 10–13 July, 1988), Theme II: The Impact of the Holocaust on the Contemporary World* (Oxford: Pergamon Press, 1988), pp. 1893–1902.

7. G. Steiner, *In Bluebeard's Castle: Some Notes Towards the Re-Definition of Culture* (London, Faber & Faber, 1971).

8. H. Arendt, *Eichmann in Jerusalem: A Report on the Banality of Evil* (Harmondsworth: Penguin Books, 1984).

9. P. J. Haas, "Morality of Auschwitz," p. 385: "I propose a theory of ethics which makes our conceptions of right and wrong ultimately a function largely of discourse, that is, of patterns of thought, language and action."

10. P. J. Haas, "Toward a Semiotic Study of Jewish Moral Discourse: The Case of Responsa," *Semeia* 33 (1983): 60: ". . . moral discourse is *moral* discourse because it expresses its conclusions in a way that links them to the grid values and principles which implicitly constitute the hearer's notion of the good or proper life. This means that moral discourse consists not only of what is said, but also of how and in what context it is said. In short, the rhetoric of moral discourse is itself an integral expression of that culture's moral universe."

11. *Morality after Auschwitz*, pp. 1–3.

12. Ibid., p. 175: ". . . ethical systems posit pairs of evaluative definitions (good-bad, right-wrong), the members of which are binary opposites. This means that at a deep, preconscious level, positive and negative evaluations will always be mirror images of each other."

13. The structuralist approach of Patte and Greimas is at the background of Haas's interpretation of ethics. See, for example, D. Patte, *What Is Structural Exegesis?*, 2nd ed. (Philadelphia, Fortress Press, 1976), and idem, *The Religious Dimension of Biblical Texts: Greimas' Structural Semiotics and Biblical Exegesis* (Atlanta: Scholars Press, 1990). Compare with G. Schiwy, "Strukturalismus," in *Katholisches Soziallexikon*, ed. A. Klose, W. Mantl, and V. Zsifkovits, 2nd ed. (Innsbruck: Verlag Tyrolia, 1980), pp. 2989–2992.

14. P. Haas, "Morality of Auschwitz," pp. 383–384.

15. Ibid., p. 388.

16. See, for example, the early Church Father Gregory of Nyssa (330–394) on the Jews. Quoted in L. Poliakov, *The History of Anti-Semitism*, vol. 1, *From the Time of Christ to the Court Jews* (New York: Vanguard Press, 1965, p. 25: "Murderers of the Lord, assassins of the prophets, [who] resist grace, repudiate the faith of their fathers. Companions of the devil, race of vipers, informers, calumniators, darkeners of the mind, pharisaic leaven, Sanhedrin of demons, accursed, detested, lapidators, enemies of all that is beautiful."

17. P. Haas, "The Killing-Healing Paradox" (Paper presented at the University of California Medical School, San Francisco, August 21, 1992), p. 7.

18. Haas refers to A. S. Lindemann, *A History of European Socialism* (New Haven: Yale University Press, 1983), pp. 8–25.

19. See further R. Hilberg, *La destruction des juifs d'Europe*, Folio Histoire 39 (Paris: Gallimard, 1988), vol. 1, pp. 61–74.

20. *Morality after Auschwitz*, p. 86.

21. Ibid., p. 86.

22. Ibid., pp. 169–172.

23. Ibid., pp. 191–199.

24. Haas, "Killing-Healing Paradox."

25. P. J. Haas, "Auschwitz: Re-envisioning the Role of God," in *Contemporary Jewish Religious Responses to the Shoah*, ed. S. L. Jacobs, Studies in the Shoah 5 (Lanham, Md.: University Press of America, 1993), p. 130: "People could devote themselves to this new ethic with good conscience, feeling that they were still fulfilling their moral duty and serving a higher good. . . . They were not moral cripples, they were normal, well-intentioned people who could, and did, do their jobs with dedication and return home at night to be average husbands and fathers."

26. *Morality after Auschwitz*, p. 109.

27. Ibid., p. 181: "In other words, conformity or opposition to an ethic is rarely, if ever, a matter of philosophical analysis. It is almost always a matter of accident, of where one happens to find oneself along the way."

28. See R. L. Rubenstein, *The Cunning of History: The Holocaust and the American Future*, 2nd ed. (New York: Perennial Library, 1978), p. 91: "We are sadly forced to conclude that we live in a world that is functionally godless and that human rights and dignity depend upon the power of one's community to grant or withhold them from its members."

29. *Morality after Auschwitz*, pp. 226–229: "After all, he [Wiesel] writes for, and is read by, the same general audience. He needs to hold on to some image of God, as does Berkovits, and he relies heavily on the power of memory, as does Fackenheim. But Wiesel has fused these elements into a new form of discourse that has proved surprisingly powerful" (p. 226).

30. *Journal of the American Academy of Religion* 60 , no. 1 (1992): 158–161.

31. Z. Bauman, *Modernity and the Holocaust* (Cambridge, Polity Press, 1989).

32. R. L. Rubenstein and J. K. Roth, *Approaches to Auschwitz: The Holocaust and Its Legacy* (London, SCM, 1987), p. 191: "How shall we understand these men who in their daily lives were not sadistic brutes but respected business leaders of their community during the period of National Socialism and afterwards? . . . It would appear that these men felt no remorse because they regarded their victims as wholly outside of their universe of moral obligations."

33. Ibid., p. 14.

34. For the complex meaning of "ideology," see the five meanings described in H. Schneider, *Ideologie*, in *Katholisches Soziallexikon*, ed. A. Klose et al., 2nd ed. (Innsbruck: Verlag Tyrolia, 1980), pp. 1140–1141: "(a) Ideologie als eine *praxisferne Bewußtseinsorientierung* . . . (b) Ideologie als *falsches Bewußtsein*, d.h. als ganz oder teilweise unwahrer Gedankenbestand, der die Realität einseitig darstellt, entstellt, verhüllt oder verklärt . . . (c) Ideologie als *illegitimer Ersatz* für wissenschaftliche Erkenntnis, etwa als *System scheinbarer Tatsachenaussagen*, die jedoch *Werturteile* enthalten (d) Ideologie als *Komplex von Ideen, Wertvorstellungen, normativ bedeutsamen Überzeugungen*, der praktischem Handeln *Orientierung* gibt, *Gemeinsamkeit* stiftet u. insbes. politische oder gesellschaftliche *Ziele* definiert (e) Ideologie als *innerweltliche Heilslehre*."

35. E. L. Fackenheim, "Nazi 'Ethic,' Nazi Weltanschauung and the Holocaust: A Review Essay," *Jewish Quarterly Review* 83, nos. 1–2 (1992): 167–172.

36. See H. Gunkel and L. Zscharnack, eds., *Die Religion in Geschichte und Gegenwart: Handwörterbuch für Theologie und Religionswissenschaft*, 6 vols., 2nd ed. (Tübingen: Mohr, 1927–32), s.v. "Weltanschauung" (vol. 5, pp. 1911–1918).

37. S. Hauerwas and D. B. Burrell, "Self-Deception and Autobiography: Reflections on Speer's *Inside the Third Reich*," in *Truthfulness and Tragedy: Further Investigations in Christian Ethics*, ed. S. Hauerwas, R. Bondi, and D. B. Burrell (Notre Dame: University of Notre Dame Press: 1977), pp. 82–98.

38. Fackenheim, "Nazi 'Ethic,'" p. 169: "One is tempted to say 'made it necessary'; the word 'inevitable' appears frequently—too frequently—in Haas' account as, somewhat reminiscent of a Greek tragedy, the process which he sees leading to Auschwitz unfolds."

39. For Haas's critique of the position of Arendt, see P. J. Haas, "Auschwitz: Re-envisioning the Role of God," pp. 110–111 and *Morality after Auschwitz*, p. 1: "It seems to me that if the Holocaust does have any lesson to teach, it is precisely because its perpetrators were not banal or unthinking people."

40. H. Arendt, *Eichmann in Jerusalem*, pp. 294–295: "What we have demanded in these trials, where the defendants had committed 'legal' crimes, is that human beings be capable of telling right from wrong even when all they have to guide them is their own judgment, which, moreover, happens to be completely at odds with what they must regard as the unanimous opinion of all around them. . . . Since the whole of respectable society had in one way or another succumbed to Hitler, the moral maxims which determine social behavior and the religious commandments—*Thou shalt not kill!*—which guide conscience had virtually vanished. Those few who were still able to tell right from wrong went really only by their own judgments, and they did so freely."

41. *Morality after Auschwitz*, p. 86: "To hear the perpetrators themselves explain their reactions and experiences is to hear how fully the Nazi ethic was allowed to override contradicting feelings and moral concerns."
42. B. Lang, "The Concept of Genocide," *Philosophical Forum* 16, nos. 1–2 (1984–85): 16.
43. W. H. Becker, "Questions Out of the Fire: Spiritual Implications of the Holocaust," *Journal of the Interdenominational Theological Center* 10, nos. 1–2 (1982–83): 23.
44. Cf. E. Berkovits, *How Can a Jew Speak of Faith Today?* (Philadelphia: Westminster Press, 1969), pp. 33–34: "If there is no transcendent standard of holiness by which all men are bound, then why should the strong not rule and torture and destroy? If God is dead, then, as Ivan Karamazov said, then [*sic*] all things are possible."
45. E. Fackenheim, "The 614th Commandment," *Judaism* 16 (1967): 271: "The authentic Jew has the duty not to hand Hitler posthumous victories."
46. A. Rosenberg, *Der Mythus des 20. Jahrhunderts: eine Wertung der seelisch-geistigen Gestaltenkämpfe unserer Zeit* (Munich: Hoheneichen, 1930).
47. See also J. Bernauer, "Nazi Ethics: On Heinrich Himmler and the Origins of New Moral Careers," in *Remembering for the Future: Papers to be Presented at an International Scholars' Conference Held in Oxford, 10–13 July 1988*, ed. Y. Bauer (Oxford: Pergamon Press, 1988), pp. 2071–2082. Also see idem., "Beyond Life and Death: On Foucault's Post-Auschwitz Ethic," *Philosophy Today* 32 (1988): 128–142.
48. T. Todorov, *Face à l'extrême* (Paris: Seuil, 1991), p. 337.
49. Haas, "Killing-Healing Paradox."
50. See also the project of D. J. Fasching, *Narrative Theology after Auschwitz: From Alienation to Ethics* (Philadelphia: Fortress Press, 1992), and idem, *The Ethical Challenge of Auschwitz and Hiroshima: Apocalypse or Utopia?* (Albany: State University of New York Press, 1993).
51. D. Pollefeyt, "The Trauma of the Holocaust as a Central Challenge of Levinas' Ethical and Theological Thought," in *The Holocaust: Remembering for the Future II on CD-ROM (Papers Presented at the International Annual Scholars' Conference held in Berlin, 13–17 May, 1994)*, ed. Marcia L. Littell, E. Geldbach, and G. J. Colijn (Stamford, Conn.: Vista InterMedia Corp., 1996).
52. D. Pollefeyt, "Victims of Evil or Evil of Victims? Towards a Hermeneutic to Understand the (un)Ethical Behavior of Victims of the Holocaust," in *Unique Moral Problems of the Holocaust*, ed. H. J. Cargas (St. Louis, Webster University Press, 1998).
53. See also P. Lacoue-Labarthe and J.-L. Nancy, *Le mythe nazi* (Paris: Editions de l'Aube, 1991), p. 22: "Ce qui nous intéresse et nous retiendra, en d'autres termes, c'est l'idéologie en tant, d'une part, qu'elle se propose toujours comme une explication de l'*histoire* . . . à partir d'un concept unique: le concept de race, par exemple, ou le concept de classe, voire celui 'd'humanité totale'; et en tant, d'autre part, que cette explication ou cette conception du monde (*Weltanschauung*: vision, intuition, saisie compréhensive du monde) se veut une explication ou une conception *totale*."

Auschwitz from a Nuremberg Perspective:
Medical and Ethical Implications

Etienne Lepicard

> I set before you life or death, blessing or curse. Choose life, so that you and
> your descendants may live . . .
>
> —Deuteronomy 30:19

Before turning to deal with good and evil *after* Auschwitz, I would like to
draw your attention to the very evil we usually summarize with the word
Auschwitz, but from a medical point of view. From this point of view,
Auschwitz is firstly the end of some practices, before being, perhaps, the
starting point for reflections. I would like to apologize for the crudity of my
language, but it is not possible to kill millions of people without technical
training and know-how. My claim is that the technical training and the know-
how which were necessary "to do the job" at Auschwitz and the other extermination camps were, from beginning to end, essentially medical in nature.
Physicians were in charge, from the selection on the ramp through the opening of the gas chambers, to verify the deaths of the victims and to give the
order to have them cremated. Medical rhetoric had a vital part in a process
which called the victims "parasites" and "infected people," and the whole
process, "purification" or "hygienic measures." This whole process did not
appear overnight at the order of the Führer, but has a much longer history, and
this history is relevant to contemporary reflections on medicine and ethical
issues. In my talk, I would like to do two things. I would like to tell you a
story—a story which I think has to be told in a forum such as ours; and I
would like to indicate some directions for future reflections starting from the
medical Nuremberg Trials in 1946–47.

Given this difficult subject, it seems appropriate to start by defining some
of the words I will use. The term "Auschwitz" is used today to summarize a
number of things. One of them is a change in our perception of human values. There is a "before and after Auschwitz" related to the value we attribute
to each individual human life, in contrast to the power of the state over human
life. For example, most Western legislation abolishing capital punishment
dates from after Auschwitz. It is possible that the reflections of Albert Camus

and Arthur Koestler on the subject are more connected to the Liberation than to Auschwitz, but it is no coincidence that today the abolishment of capital punishment is connected to Auschwitz and not to the abuses of the period after Liberation.[1] The word "Auschwitz" seems to summarize more than what took place there, but not without relation to it. In short, it seems to me that we sum up in this word "Auschwitz" a scale of values where life and death are in first place, and where good and evil are related to them. The word "Auschwitz" is thus a symbolic word.

From a medical perspective, the term now covers all the crimes of German medicine under the Nazis. From a strictly historical point of view, this assumption can be debated, as there is a matter of historical methodology. We must distinguish here between two aspects of historical work: in research, the historian must take into consideration the sources and their context without a consideration of what came after, but in presenting the historical narrative, the same historian has a moral duty to remind his reader what crimes were committed in the name of the activities he has researched. Here, for example, we speak of "Good and Evil after Auschwitz, medico-ethical implications for today," and thus it is legitimate to prepare this sort of summary. The question at stake is a question of transmitting a message, sufficiently short and clear, that will bring people to think.

After telling the story, I would like to elaborate on the ethical implications that may be seen in it. But are there ethical implications in the story of Auschwitz? This is a very sensitive question. Some people say there are always lessons to be learned from the past. Others wish to respect the uniqueness of this crime against humanity and prefer that Auschwitz remain what it was and not turn it into a subject of discussion, even a discussion on ethics. For my own reasons, I prefer to start my discussion and elaboration of ethical proposals with the Nuremberg Trials of 1946–47. There, historical events were brought back into the public sphere through the deliberations of the court. This public aspect is of some importance when dealing with such difficult issues.[2] At the same time, however, one must remember that not all of what happened in Auschwitz was examined in Nuremberg, and *a fortiori* not all that is put under this term today, but only a small part of it.[3] Nevertheless, the public acts of calling for witnesses and judgment of what happened there took place in Nuremberg, and these should be used as a reference point for transmission to future generations. Indeed, the court made a symbolic act calling for further reflections when it published a code of medical ethics, now known as the Nuremberg Code.

After these very preliminary remarks, I will summarize some aspects of the history of medicine during the Nazi regime, without stressing the general framework of eugenics and Social Darwinism in which they took place.[4] Two programs may be seen as the main steps leading to the medicalized "racial cleansing" of Germany: the Nuremberg law on sterilization of 1933, which was reinforced by the Nuremberg Laws of 1935, and the euthanasia program.

THE 1933 LAW ON STERILIZATION

Hitler was called to the chancellery on January 30, 1933 with a conservative coalition cabinet.[5] By March 23, he succeeded in passing the Enabling Act, which authorized him to rule by decree for the next four years. On July 14, 1933, at the same cabinet session which approved the Concordat with the Vatican, the Nazi government passed a law for the "Prevention of Hereditarily Diseased Offspring" (*Gesetz zur Verhütung erbkranken Nachwuchses*), better known as the "Sterilization Law."[6] The Concordat was made public on July 20, and the sterilization law a few days later, for obvious diplomatic reasons. The law allowed the forcible sterilization of anyone suffering from one of nine hereditary illnesses, including feeble-mindedness, epilepsy, genetic blindness, deafness, and "severe alcoholism." The conclusion that these diseases were hereditary was part of the general hereditary conceptions of the time and was not specific to Germany. During the next year, 181 Hereditary Health Courts and Hereditary Health Courts of Appeal were established throughout Germany in connection with the regular courts. The president of these courts was a judge, who was helped by two physicians, a state physician and a specialist in hereditary diseases. They were called "technical assessors." However, as a simple majority was all that was required to decide on sterilization, the doctors obviously had the last word. The procedure was not public. While there was a possibility of appeal, the confirmation of the decision to sterilize by the Court of Appeal was final, and no escape was possible; force could be used if the condemned did not submit voluntarily to the decision. The sterilization was carried out in a hospital by an officially accepted physician. Physicians who did not report known cases of hereditary illness could be prosecuted. In addition, physicians were trained in hereditary pathology in the racial institutes founded all around the country. Finally, the German Medical Association founded a journal, *Der Erbarzt* ("The Heredity Physician"), dedicated to this issue.

The sterilization law was passed on July 14, 1933 and came into force on January 1, 1934. It was then slowly but strongly radicalized. In November 1933, a Law Against Compulsive Criminality was passed, enabling the preventive detention and castration of supposed criminals. This law was expressed in sufficiently vague terms that it quickly became possible to sterilize anyone categorized as antisocial. For example, by June 1935, castration was extended to homosexuals. By 1936, an antisocial person was defined as an individual who merely "shows by his behavior that he did not want to be integrated into the community." In the fall of 1935, after the promulgation of the Nuremberg Law on citizenship to "Protect German Blood and Honor," there appeared a law on marriage to "Protect Hereditary Health." Even if these laws differed in tone, reflecting two different currents among the Nazi administration, an ideological one led by Wilhelm Wagner, the Reichsärzteführer, and a more administrative one represented by Gütt Leiter of the Reich Ministry of Health, the important point here is that both were considered public health measures, and both were administered primarily by physicians.

According to the historian Gisela Bock, the number of people sterilized in Germany between 1934 and 1945 according to the law could be as high as 360,000.[7] This law also created "one of the largest medical industries" of the time, as new techniques and medical equipment were required. For example, Proctor notes that more than 180 doctoral theses were written on this subject within a few years. In 1943, Carl Clauberg, a gynecologist experimenting in Auschwitz, reported to Himmler, head of the SS and Minister of Interior, that he had found a way to sterilize as many as 1,000 women a day, with a staff of only ten people. The only organized resistance to the sterilization law was that of the Catholic Church.

The law caused a debate within the Catholic Church from the very beginning, as it directly opposed the moral law of the Church, which had once more been publicly formulated at the Fulda Conference of bishops in May 1933. In August 1933, the Church presented a memorandum to the Reich Ministry of Interior requesting that Catholics not be subjected to a conflict of conscience. They wished to exempt the directors of Catholic institutions from the duty of applying for the sterilization of patients under their care. According to the compromise reached with the Church, these directors had only to report the names of patients afflicted with diseases mentioned in the law. The Church did not declare a public attack on the law as such, but rather attempted to preserve the autonomy of Catholic institutions. The Church received "the right to inform the faithful that according to Catholic doctrine it was forbidden to volunteer for sterilization or apply for another's."[8] Thus the Church was firmly against the law on the theological level; in practice, it had to cope with the legal pressure of the state. Should a Catholic agree to lose his job in order to be loyal to the law of the Church? Should a Catholic priest inquire in confession about this particular issue? The history is not clear-cut. Some priests lost their right to teach religious instruction in the public schools. Sometimes parish priests were told not to ask questions about the subject and to leave their parishioners in their "good faith," or to distinguish between "material and formal cooperation," reporting to the authorities versus submitting applications for the sterilization of a person.

Clear in theory, much more difficult in practice, Catholic resistance to the sterilization law seems nevertheless to have been one of the main reasons why the Nazis waited until the beginning of the war to start the second part of their medical racial policy: the euthanasia program.

THE EUTHANASIA OF MENTALLY ILL PERSONS

Some things are possible in wartime but not during peacetime; one was the massive euthanasia program of mentally ill people in Germany between October 1939 and the fall of 1941.[9] The power given by the Führer on October 1 was predated to the beginning of the war, September 1, 1939. Unlike sterilization, there was no law creating this program, nor was there an order from the Führer. The physicians were simply given permission to kill. The wording of the announcement is as follows: "Reichsleiter (head of Hitler's chancellery) Bouhler and Dr. med. Brandt are charged with the responsibility to extend the powers of specific doctors in such a way that, after the most careful assessment of their condition, those suffering from illnesses deemed to be incurable may be granted a mercy death."[10] In short, murder became one of the tools used by the physician to heal.[11]

At the Nuremberg Trial, Brandt recalled the beginning of the program in an answer the Führer gave in the fall of 1938 to the parents of a mentally deficient, blind, and deformed baby who wished him to have a quick death. However, the question had long been debated in medical circles and among the Nazis. Hitler, at the Party rally in 1929 in Nuremberg, claimed that "if each year among one million new-born children in Germany, 7 or 8 thousand of the weakest were eliminated, the result would probably be a growth in the national strength." Even so, the Nazis, and especially the Nazi doctors of Wagner's League, were well aware of the difficulty in implementing such "medicine." Some people, among them racial hygienists, might be in favor of the sterilization of mentally ill people, but it was quite another thing to be in favor of killing them. Propaganda had to be used to prepare the public to receive such ideas. One of the main arguments used was the cost of institutional care. Scientific surveys were conducted among the municipal authorities. Schoolchildren learned to calculate the costs in mathematics lessons and visited asylums in order to write on racial degeneration and its meaning in biological and economic terms. Wagner's Nazi Doctors League arranged debates on the subject among medical practitioners. They also used other means; in 1936, Wagner's assistant, Hellmuth Unger, wrote a novel, *Mission and Conscience*, which was adapted for the theater and film. Another movie on the same issue was produced in 1941; the name of this movie quite ironically alludes to Zola's defence of Dreyfus: *Ich klage an* ("J'accuse!").

In the spring of 1939, an advisory committee was formed to prepare for the killing of deformed and retarded children. It was under the direct supervision of Hitler's Chancellery. For reasons of secrecy, it was named the Committee for Scientific Research into Severe Hereditary and Congenital Diseases, and included renowned professors of medicine and administrators. On August 18, 1939, the Reich Ministry of Interior decreed that doctors and midwives must register children under three years with local health authorities. The official reason given was "to clarify certain scientific questions in the areas of congenital deformity and mental retardation," but the actual result was the selection of 5,000 children to be killed. The methods of killing included lethal injections and tablets, and gassing. Parents were informed by letter of the sudden death of their child and also of his or her cremation due to the danger of an epidemic.

This child-murder operation is thus a clear link between the sterilization laws and the euthanasia program. At the same time, Conti replaced Wagner as Leader of the Reich Physicians, but significantly enough his title became Reich Health Leader. Gütt, the former head of the Health Administration of the Reich, resigned the same year, and Conti's new title signified the unification of the Health Administration with the Party office for public health. By the summer of 1939, Conti, Philipp Bouhler (head of Hitler's private chancellery), and Herbert Linden (a psychiatrist and head of the department of health institutions at the Ministry of Interior) planned the extermination of all of Germany's mental patients. Three official bodies cooperated in this action: the Working Committee for Hospital Care provided administrative cover, the Charitable Foundation for Institutional Care provided the subsidies, and the Nonprofit Corporation for the Transportation of the Sick provided transportation to the six Euthanasia Institutes that were created. This last group was located at Tiergartenstrasse 4 and gave its name to the operation: T-4. The directors of asylums received a questionnaire with a request to divide their patients into four main categories: persons with specific diseases, persons who had been in the asylum for more than five years, mentally ill criminals, and foreigners who did not belong to the German race. The forms were sent back to the administration, where colors were used to indicate who would be killed and who would be deferred. The file of a deferred person was sent for further investigation. Thus, absolutely no connection existed between those who made the decisions and those who carried them out, nor was there any personal contact between the sick person and the expert who decided whether to kill or defer him. Even so, the authorities insisted that the operation be carried out only by physicians; the motto was: "The needle in the hand of the doctor."

After several attempts to use a lethal injection of morphine and scopolamine, methods of gassing were developed. After gassing, the bodies were burned and the ashes returned to the families, who received a fictitious death-certificate. The cause of death was chosen at random from an official list. Over time, people became suspicious, and similar death notices were published in the newspapers. Some prosecutions were started but were quickly stopped when it became apparent that the empowerment came directly from the Führer. Historians agree that the protests by clergymen, especially those of Bishop von Galen, brought Hitler to stop the program on August 24, 1941, less than two years after it began.[12] According to Benno Muller-Hill, from a total of 283,000 applications evaluated, roughly 75,000 patients were marked to die, and more than 70,000 were killed by the time the program was officially stopped.[13] In fact, despite its official end, the program continued to run throughout the war and even a little bit after. This phenomenon is known as "wild euthanasia." Physicians in the asylums continued to kill patients; they just changed the method. Some used repeated injections of morphine and scopolamine, while others starved the patients to death. According to Paul Weindling, "more were killed in this way than in the T4 programme, and there was a greater integration with the normal structures of medical 'care'."[14] Proctor reports an incredible story that mentally ill patients were killed even after the war, a story which emphasizes the routine character of this operation in German psychiatric institutions during these mad years.[15]

The medical character of the euthanasia operation and its timing at the beginning of the war provided a medical and scientific background for mass murder and training for people who, after the official end of the program, would be sent to the extermination camps to do their deadly "work." The latter part of their "work" is better known, and I need not describe it here.[16] It is sufficient to stress once more the medical character of the crimes committed there. I will, however, say a few words about the presentation of the Nazi doctors at the Nuremberg Trials, which took place between December 9, 1946 and August 20, 1947.

THE MEDICAL TRIALS AND THE NUREMBERG CODE

After the war, the four Allies brought to trial before an International Military Tribunal (IMT) the major war criminals they were able to capture.[17]

They decided on an international legal framework to judge the Nazi criminals at the London Convention of August 1945, and on December 20, 1945 Law number 10 of the Control Council for Germany was signed. This established a uniform legal basis in Germany for the prosecution of war criminals other than those dealt with by the IMT. Shortly after, the Cold War began, and there were no other trials under the Allied banner. Even so, the individual Allies retained the right to establish a military tribunal, independent from the others but on the same legal basis. Only the United States used this right in the following years, holding sixteen other trials. Among them, and the first chronologically, was the Medical Nuremberg Trial. As Paul Weindling has recently suggested, the reasons for this trial, well covered by the press, were not only humanistic but also fit American political interests at the time, the beginning of the Cold War.[18] For similar reasons, the Americans promised to be silent about Japanese war crimes; in return, they received scientific and medical data resulting from Japanese war experiments that were very similar to the medical experiments judged as criminal at the Nuremberg Trial. The Japanese data were classified top secret by the U.S. Army and were revealed only very recently, after fifty years of secrecy. Another important factor in the Medical Nuremberg Trial is the narrowness of the crimes judged. The prosecution charged Nazis who had perpetrated crimes on prisoners in the name of medical science during wartime, no matter the reason why these people became prisoners. Medical experiments, such as high-altitude experiments, freezing experiments, malaria, typhus, and other epidemic experiments, mustard gas experiments, and seawater experiments, were judged. Sterilization and euthanasia were not put on trial. Many physicians and medical professionals who had participated in these two programs remained free. Here it has to be clear that history will never replace justice.

Nevertheless, the results of the Medical Nuremberg Trial can be of some help in an understanding of what happened to medicine during the Nazi years and how it is related to today's medicine. On August 20, 1947, when the Nuremberg court delivered its judgment, it included ten points of medical ethics that are now known as the Nuremberg Code of medical ethics. There was no necessity to do so. These ten points were based on a certain misunderstanding of medical deontology, but, nevertheless, by their decision the judges included them in international law. From a strictly legal point of view, the London Charter and Law number 10 were sufficient to judge these crimes as war crimes and crimes against humanity. The judges did not really justify themselves or explain why they included these points of medical ethics in their judgment, nor did they suggest that their judicial concern should lean on ethical requirements rather than legal ones. Michael Grodin has suggested that "the Nuremberg Tribunal attempted to pave the way for a reconstituted moral vision" which the judges expressed in the sentence prefacing the Code: "All agree, however, that certain basic principles must be observed in order to satisfy moral, ethical and legal concepts."[19]

The main element of the code—the principle of consent—is formulated in the first point and was originally based on a misunderstanding of Hippocrates. As Jay Katz has said about the formulation of the first point, "Never before in the history of human experimentation, and never since, has any code or any regulation of research declared in such relentless and uncompromising a fashion that a psychological integrity of research subjects must be protected absolutely."[20] This first point is formulated as follows:

> The voluntary consent of the human subject is absolutely essential. This means that the person involved should have [the] legal capacity to give consent, should be so situated as to be able to exercise free power of choice, without the intervention of any element of force, fraud, deceit, duress, overreaching or other ulterior form of constraint or coercion; and should have sufficient knowledge and comprehension of the elements of the subject matter involved as to enable him to make an understanding and enlightened decision, etc.[21]

If this is not sufficient, the ninth principle added:

> During the course of the experiment the human subject should be at liberty to bring the experiment to an end if he has reached the physical or mental state where continuation of the experiment seems to him to be impossible.

These two principles may today seem so obvious and basic that we do not understand the revolutionary perspective they contain. They are based on a misunderstanding of Hippocrates and medical deontology. What does this mean? For the judges, it was obvious that a consensus existed in the medical and scientific research community, and that this consensus stemmed from the Hippocratic Oath. However, never before and never after has such a consensus existed. Never before: the idea that the subject of medical experimentation has something to say, that he has the right to say something, seemed to the judges to be a commonsense conclusion, but in the history of human experimentation it had never before appeared. Claude Bernard, for example, who has written extensively about medicine and experimentation, and who has considered the ethical implications of human experimentation, finally refers to the physician and to his professional consciousness, but not to the opinion of the experimental subject.[22] The common good, the advancement of science, and the professional consciousness of the experimenter seemed sufficient to him.

The two experts for the prosecution, Dr. Leo Alexander and Dr. Andrew Ivy, experimenters themselves, referred to the Hippocratic deontology and even suggested part of the wording of this new concept of informed consent. The Hippocratic Oath refers to the relationship between physician and patient, and explicitly expresses the duty of the physician to help the patient. This was later expressed in the Latin formula: *Primum non nocere*. But, as Grodin notes, "during the Hippocratic period benefit to the patient was determined by the physician,"[23] and there is no trace in the Oath of any such notion as informed consent. "Alexander and Ivy confused therapeutic treatment with non-therapeutic experiments on prisoners and thus incorrectly cited Hippocrates as the source for the ethics of human experimentation." The judges took for granted a Hippocratic consensus for informed consent in the medical research community when such a consensus had never existed.[24]

The Nuremberg Code, grounded in an international judgment, may well have founded a tradition, but the history of medical ethics since the Nuremberg Trial in general, and the history of human experimentation in particular, shows exactly the opposite. Until now there has been no real legacy of the Nuremberg Code in medicine, at least not where one may expect it: in medical deontology and the ethics of experimentation.

Developments in medical ethics after the Second World War were instead a confirmation of traditional Hippocratic deontology. The Medical Oath promulgated by the World Medical Association in Geneva in 1948 was written in this spirit. Another example may be found in the conclusions of the two Congrès Internationaux de Morale Médicale that took place in Paris in 1955 and 1966.[25] On the other hand, the history of human experimentation ethics may be followed through the various Helsinki Declarations; the latest revised version of which dates back to 1989. As Jay Katz has shown, even in the latest version: "Clearly the integrity of the scientific enterprise comes first, though it must be balanced against unspecified 'interests of the subject.'"[26] In the first version of 1964, the notion of consent does not appear at all. It is as if, notes Katz, "The spirit of the Nuremberg Code was not, and perhaps could not be, taken seriously. Its language was too uncompromising and too inhospitable to the advancement of science that subsequent codes reintroduced by giving physician-scientists considerable discretion in pursuing their objectives."[27]

What is the significance of this perhaps inapplicable code?

I began this talk by saying that the word "Auschwitz" may perhaps sum up a new scale of values, one born after Auschwitz. In this scale of values, life and death have first place, and good and evil are related to them. This is perhaps too general a statement. An analysis of the Nuremberg Code and the particular case of medicine under the Third Reich show a disappearance and then a reintroduction of the patient as subject in medicine, but that is not all. Auschwitz has also revealed, in an unprecedented way, the capacity for aggression inherent in medicine. We now know that it is a matter of life and death. And indeed we touch here the essence of contemporary medicine, which has gained more and more power over life itself. The Code may seem inapplicable, but it stands in such a way that it may signify for us the change which has appeared in our understanding of what medicine is and which role we may or may not attribute to it.

Selected Bibliography

On the general organization of medicine under the Nazi regime, see:

Kater, Michael H. *Doctors under Hitler*. Chapel Hill: University of North Carolina Press, 1989.

On the general background of eugenics and social Darwinism:

Weindling, Paul. *Health, Race and German Politics between National Unification and Nazism, 1870–1945*. Cambridge: Cambridge University Press, 1989.

On the 1933 sterilization law, its consequences, and the euthanasia program:

Burleigh, Michael. *Death and Deliverance: "Euthanasia" in Germany, 1900–1945*. Cambridge: Cambridge University Press, 1994.
Muller-Hill, Benno. *Science Nazie, Science de Mort, l'extermination des juifs, des tziganes et des malades mentaux de 1933 à 1945*. Paris: Odile Jacob, 1989.
Noakes J. "Nazism and Eugenics: The Background to the Nazi Sterilization Law of 14 July 1933." In *Ideas into Politics: Aspects of European History, 1880–1950*, ed. R. J. Bullen, H. Pogge von Strandmann, and A. B. Polonsky, pp. 75–94. Beckenham: Croom Helm, 1984.

Proctor, Robert. *Racial Hygiene: Medicine under the Nazis.* Cambridge, Mass.: Harvard University Press, 1988.

On Church attitudes:

Dietrich, Donald J. *Catholic Citizens in the Third Reich: Psycho-Social Principles and Moral Reasoning.* New Brunswick, N.J.: Transaction Books, 1988.
————."Catholic Eugenics in Germany, 1920–1945: Hermann Muckermann, S.J. and Joseph Mayer." *Journal of Church and State* 34 (1992): 575–600.
Lepicard, Etienne. "Eugenics and Catholicism: An Encyclical Letter in Context, *Casti connubii*, December 31, 1930." *Science in Context*, Fall 1998.

On the Nuremberg trial of the Nazi doctors, and its relation to experimental medicine and to today's medicine:

Ambroselli, Claire. *L'Éthique Médicale.* Paris: P.U.F., 1988.
Annas, George J., and Michael A. Grodin, eds. *The Nazi Doctors and the Nuremberg Code: Human Rights in Human Experimentation.* New York: Oxford University Press, 1992.
Lepicard, Etienne. "L'Offense de la raison ou la satisfaction du regard! Qu'en est-il du silence des médecins au lendemain des procès de Nuremberg?" *Revue d'Histoire de la Shoah, le Monde Juif*, 1997, pp. 136–146.
Seidelman, William E. "Whither Nuremberg? Medicine's Continuing Nazi Heritage., *Medicine & Global Survival* 2 (1995): 148–157.

Some elements for a reflection on science, culture, and society since World War II:

Chrétien, Claude. *La Science à l'oeuvre, mythes et limites.* Paris: Hatier, 1991.
Weisz, George, ed. *Social Science Perspectives on Medical Ethics.* Philadelphia: University of Pennsylvania Press, 1991.

NOTES

1. Albert Camus and Arthur Koestler, *Réflexions sur la peine capitale* (Paris: Calmann-Lévy, 1957).
2. Hannah Arendt, *The Human Condition* (Chicago: University of Chicago Press, 1958).
3. Alexander Mitscherlich and Fred Mielke, *Medizin ohne Menschlichkeit, Dokumente des Nürnberger Ärzteprozesses* (Frankfurt: Fischer Taschenbuch, 1960); 1st ed.: *Das Diktat der Menschenverachtung* (Heidelberg, 1947); trans. as *Doctors of Infamy: The Story of the Nazi Medical Crimes* (New York, 1949).
4. For further reading on these topics, see the selected bibliography at the end of this essay.
5. For this section, see Proctor, *Racial Hygiene*, p. 95; Weindling: *Health, Race and German Politics*, pp. 450–457, 522–534.
6. The main difference between the law that was drafted and the one that was implemented by the Nazis is between voluntary and compulsory sterilization. In May 1933, sterilization was legalized by a clause in the revised criminal code; this clause declared that sterilization did not constitute assault. On June 2, 1933, Reich Interior Minister Wilhelm Frick announced the formation of an Expert Committee on Questions of Population and Racial Policy (Sachverständigen-Beirat für Bevölkerungsfragen und Rassenpolitik).
7. Quoted by Weindling, *Health, Race and German Politics*, p. 533.
8. Dietrich, *Catholic Citizens in the Third Reich*, pp. 119–121.
9. For this section, see Proctor, *Racial Hygiene*, pp. 177–194; Weindling, *Health, Race and German Politics*, pp. 393–398, 541–551.
10. Burleigh, *Death and Deliverance*, p. 112.
11. Following the title of the film of Nitzam Aviram, *Healing by Killing* (Tel Aviv: Per Capita, n.d.).
12. See, for example, Burleigh, *Death and Deliverance*, who discusses Gitta Sereny's position; see also Dietrich, *Catholic Citizens in the Third Reich*.
13. Cited in Proctor, *Racial Hygiene*, p. 189.
14. Weindling, *Health, Race and German Politics*, p. 550.
15. Proctor, *Racial Hygiene*, pp. 192–193.
16. See, for example, Lifton, *The Nazi Doctors*, and Proctor, *Racial Hygiene*.
17. For this section, see *The Nazi Doctors and the Nuremberg Code*, pp. 61–120; see also Ambroselli, *L'Ethique Médicale*, pp. 81–116.
18. Paul Weindling, lecture given at the Edelstein Center for the History of Sciences, May 24, 1997.
19. Grodin, in *Nazi Doctors and the Nuremberg Code*, p. 140.
20. Katz, in ibid., p. 227.
21. Ibid., p. 2.
22. Quoted in Lepicard: "Le Silence des Médecins," *Revue d'Histoire de la Shoah*, 1997, pp. 142–145.

23. Grodin, in *Nazi Doctors and the Nuremberg Code*, p. 123.

24. In fact, the Nuremberg Code is based on directives of the German Reich Health Office (1931) that were never applied, and at the time of the Nuremberg Trials, for obvious reasons, such a paradoxical origin was not imputed; see Grodin, in *Nazi Doctors and the Nuremberg Code*, pp. 127–131.

25. For the traditional aspect of postwar medical ethics, see, for example, George Weisz, "The Origins of Medical Ethics in France: The International Congress of *Morale Medicale* of 1955," in *Social Science Perspectives on Medical Ethics* (1991), pp. 145–162.

26. In Annas and Grodin, *Nazi Doctors and the Nuremberg Code*, p. 231.

27. Ibid., p. 235.

PART III
Philosophy Faced with the Shoah

Moral Principles in Extreme Situations:
Auschwitz and the Truth about the Human Condition

Armando Rigobello

THE TERMS AND SHAPE OF THE QUESTION

In a speculative context such as this—in *dürftiger Zeit*—it is hard to produce an overall description or a really full evaluation of the human situation, and even more so to produce a definition of humanness. However, it would seem that an approach seeking to grasp human nature in its concrete exercise will offer pointers for a knowledge of human nature. This means shifting the focus of research from human *nature* to the human *condition*, using a phenomenological method in the initial phase, and then a hermeneutic one. After identifying eidetic constants in the various manifestations of human action, we can then depict the *human condition*. Although the task is neither easy nor straightforward, we can obtain some significant results if the human condition is examined in *extreme situations*—at the limits of its very possibility of being. In other words, we can understand who human beings are not so much in the harmonious composition of their classical form (although only rarely is this form found in its perfection, in a very exceptional condition of balance), but in radically extreme situations. As an analogy, we recall the prolegomena to any future anthropology that Sartre reaches through his existential analysis.

We can reach a description of the human condition through a phenomenological reduction *von oben* ("from above") or *von unten* ("from below"). A reduction *von oben* gives us the eidetic structure of heroic virtues, of total self-giving—the poetics of agape, to use an evocative phrase of Paul Ricoeur's. A reduction *von unten*, on the other hand, offers us the eidetic structure of the darkest and cloudiest tortuosities of lived experience. This linking up of centers of negative meaning is the phenomenological image of the Auschwitz experience, *an extreme von unten situation* of the human condition. This image is marked by the disturbing presence of fragments of lucid and logical consequentiality, which act in a radical neutralization of values and sentiments connected with them. It is not pure and simple brutishness, for the organization of acts with a view to a specific end still persists, as well as the search for—or, better, the presumption of—an ideological justification. Although the principles of moral conscience are neutralized and hence exposed to every type of transformation and reversal, an internal logic of behavior remains operative. The principles and their connecting logical structure, devoid of their content, become *schemata* capable of facilitating the connection between the actions and any content. In our case, the content-motive is typically ideological, i.e., the Nazi doctrine, which became a project for destruction.

We have appealed to the Kantian concept of *schema*, for here too it is a case of connecting very different elements: action as expression of pure activism, and gratuitous, or basically irrational, motivation. Reference points (principles emptied of content) and the logical connection between them (as a purely technical exercise of logic) operate as framework for the final definition of a line of conduct that is, on the one hand, rigorously logical, and, on the other, irrational—the reversal of values, the arbitrary choice of a totalizing ideology. Thus we find a closed, totally doctrinaire ideological system, which operates through an unscrupulous logical formalism, presenting us with the image of man at the nadir of his rational barbarity, in the ultimate negative possibility of his condition—the eidetic X-ray of the Auschwitz persecutor.

THE AUSCHWITZ MODEL: THE LIMIT *VON UNTEN*

The considerations outlined above were expressed in the technical language of phenomenological philosophy, but can be restated in a somewhat streamlined form. The above reflection sought to grasp the internal structure and dynamics of the attitude that, while still being an attitude of human beings, must have marked the Auschwitz persecutors and also, before them, those who drew up the extermination plan as the Final Solution of the Jewish question.

This picture of the perverted conscience seemed to us to be both rigorously logical and unfailingly irrational. A conscious effort is evident in a succession of methodological choices, and hence of actions performed in order to implement the clear and fully structured plan of destruction as effectively and widely as possible. This is naturally a formal rationality, a rationality confined to the logical consistency of the process with no reference to its motives or underlying principles. Consistent implementation, in fact, leads to a subjective conviction of rightness in the person performing it, with applicability eventually silencing human sentiments, the sense of formal duty disguising cynicism, and cruelty being justified by the efficiency of the method with which it is performed. All this constitutes a terrible alibi, which is then strengthened by collective participation—or participation in organized groups operating in a disciplined manner within a system.

In the case of the acts of concentration camp persecutors, the aberrant matrix of action also tends to find justification in a compact and fully structured ideological context. The method, in itself neutral and in any case logical, is the stock, while the content is a strong but extrinsic graft. Common to the motivation and the method of implementation is the fact that both show a systematic closure. The untroubled decision to translate the irrational into the logic of a method acts as a *schema*, a framework, for persecutory action, to return to the Kantian term used above.

This attitude is a figure of the human condition studied—almost taken by surprise—in its most barbarous manifestations; in other words, *the difference between good and evil* seems to collapse, and the meanings of the two terms become confused. Here we have an *extreme von unten situation* of the human condition. The indirect and unintended consequences of the Auschwitz tragedy include that of allowing us to identify the extreme situation that man can reach in the voluntary degradation of his humanity; thus the tragedy constitutes a chapter in an anthropology of extreme-negativity situations.

It must, however, be noted that unfortunately the phenomenology of the human condition *von unten*—i.e., seen in its extreme negative possibilities— is not necessarily confined to the Auschwitz experience. We could cite numerous other examples of barbarous human aberrations in specific situations both before and after Auschwitz. However, Auschwitz was an episode in the history and culture of the West, and thus provides us with a special spur to reflection. It shows us the thoroughgoing collapse of the whole program of liberating culture that gave rise to the modern era—that of the Enlightenment or rationality—into the abyss of non-sense.

AUSCHWITZ AS PHENOMENON OF RATIONALITY OVERTURNED

A clarification is perhaps in order at this point. What is the Western cultural identity that gave rise to the Holocaust? In particular, is it the outcome of a Christian culture? How can a religion founded on love and self-sacrifice for the redemption of others lead to such barbarities? The Nazi ideology was undoubtedly pagan, a return to the myths of earth, blood, and race. However, reference to Nazism is not enough to explain the Holocaust, for Enlightenment elements also play a warped but more subtle and more rationally lucid part. The Enlightenment arose with the aim of freeing people from prejudice, and through a strange dialectic its radical nature is reversed, turning into its own opposite, as Horkheimer and Adorno observe in their famous work, *The Dialectic of Enlightenment*.

The root of this reversal lies in the reduction of rationality to purely technical logic or formalism, which in turn becomes the supporting framework, for it is a homologizing force, reducing everything to the formal dimension. Everything is leveled in the mechanism implemented, bringing about a society in which (to quote another pungent phrase from Horkheimer and Adorno) the cruelest of humiliations takes place, fulfillment of the most ancient dread—that of losing one's own name. Enlightenment, the two authors say, bends back on itself, turning into mythology. It should, however, be stressed that the word "Enlightenment" covers a complex phenomenon and is meant here in its broad sense as critical radicalism with a formalistic outcome.

Christianity was the cradle and matrix of Western civilization, and the source of its predominant ideas. In the context of the history and culture of the West, however, the great Christian ideals have been separated from one another and from the religious context in which they arose and express their authenticity; isolated from one another, stripped of their transcendent intentionality, and inserted without mediation into secular life as lived out in history, they enter into a short circuit with the latter (given the huge difference in potential between regulative ideal and concrete situation), leading to the explosion of the irrational. For example, when freedom is split from fraternity and justice, it gives rise to the reversal of liberation into its opposite. Similarly, when the ideas of equality and justice are isolated, they become modalities of the horizontal dimension and oppressive of the collectivity. The Christian ideas are so sublime that when removed from their religious context, secularized to the limit and totally immanentized, they can degenerate to the point of self-negation.

Such figures as the curse for deicide and the wandering Jew affected by this curse appear in the collective imagination of a centuries-old Christian tradition. However, in relation to the Nazi Holocaust, these figures are a remote background, and are merely a pretext or corollary for an extraneous program.

THE EXTREME SITUATION *VON OBEN*

As indicated above, analysis of extreme situations of the human condition can also be carried out *von oben*, from above. The Auschwitz experience is certainly very significant here, allowing us to imagine the interior dynamics of such figures as Father Kolbe and Edith Stein. In terms of speculation, we can say that in the *von oben* investigation we reach the extreme limit of the possibilities of the human condition, as we did in the *von unten* investigation. While the *von unten* case brings about the emptying of the moral content of conscience, and its neutralization and reduction to *formal schemata* (then refilled with ideological content), in the opposite case we find a maximum exaltation of ethical principles, and their transformation into a spiritual full-ness that goes beyond ethics and reaches the pinnacle of total self-giving in a context of religious and sometimes mystical experience. The link between motives and actions no longer needs recourse to some contrived *schematism*, but is connatural with the positivity that is a constituent of conscience, and with its intentional infinitude. The extreme situation challenges the balance reached in terms of a functional mediocrity, placing the human condition *in a state of emergency*. Although irrationality may burst out and the abyss open up in this emergency, it can also have a maieutic function, leading toward an ethical-religious transfiguration, and reaching the heights of spirituality. The moment of truth arrives in the most extreme situations.

As in the previous case, we shall try to give the results of this phenome-nological investigation *von oben* in a smoother and more discursive form. If the persecutor's conscience is dominated by the alterity between the irration-ality of motive and the rational logic of method, the martyr's conscience is marked by unification of spiritual vitality, transfiguration of the conscience itself, and the overcoming of its own articulation in a surge of total self-giv-ing. Here is the place for a study of the contribution that the witness of Auschwitz martyrs can make to research on asceticism and mysticism—a study already partially carried out, but still awaiting fuller expression and development.

Of course not all those who were engulfed in the barbarities of the Holocaust were able to demonstrate the transformation of their experience through the transfiguration of an absolute religious faith. The age-old, nonde-nominational problem remains of the loss of meaning, of unavenged pain, and of suffering without any hope, bar that of annihilation. Here too we find extreme cases of conscience in which the dominant aspect is not the intensi-ty of unification, but the radical disintegration of identity. However, a possi-bility—or, better, a witness of indirect religiosity stands out against this dev-astated and devastating background: the abrupt awakening of dignity and of an interior force, a force in some way mysterious, even apart from a positive faith; this imperative is well summarized in Albert Camus's expression with regard to the absurd condition in which we are involved, when he calls us to be more just than the unjust condition imposed on us.

From what has been said, fresh reflection on Auschwitz also represents an authentic contribution in the more specific sphere of speculation, for the experience of Auschwitz becomes a phenomenological report on the human condition in a state of emergency, or in its extreme possibilities. This certainly does not fully solve the problem of how we can still think of God after Auschwitz, and leaves a major ethical and theological question-mark over evil and the permission of evil, on the *kenosis* of God and man. There is also the unanswered question, here barely mentioned in passing, of how modernity and the Enlightenment were able to give rise to the reverse of their program. And perhaps this is the question most closely connected with our present subject, although it is in fact a different subject. We could simply say that extreme situations reveal the ideological basis that theories, even the most widely accepted and solemn, conceal within their genetic nucleus. In conclusion, the tragic experience of Auschwitz is a devastating document on which to meditate with regard to the extreme possibilities of man's wretchedness and greatness.

Our analysis is of primarily theoretical value, throwing light on conceptual connections, in accordance with the task we set ourselves. Even in the context of the present meeting, there are other people more competent to deal with the historical, theological, and religious ramifications of the problem.

Good and Evil after Auschwitz:
Judgment

Gianfranco Dalmasso

SPEAKING OF GOOD AND EVIL

How can we *speak* of good and evil today? What significance do these terms possess? Despite the general deterioration of the ontological and ethical dimensions, and whatever we *think* about good and evil, even prior to and apart from the formulation of any theory, good and evil *have always existed and operated—and still do—in a discourse.*

Classically and biblically, good and evil exist and operate in relation to knowledge and speech, insofar as the word, the *logos*, seems right from the start to be inseparable from a sign and a destination. Good and evil are inconceivable outside the structure of discourse and its effective exercise—outside a judgment in both the gnosiological and ethical senses.

There is no good and no evil outside *judgment*. Judgment, prejudice, prejudgment. The I who speaks, and thus becomes aware of himself, experiences *the problem of his place* in the practice of his discourse—*place* with respect to his discourse and reality, in an originally ethical position. The influence of Levinas and his teaching is clear in these first lines of my contribution.

The theory—classical in the Greek and Christian tradition, and taken up again by Levinas, and forcefully reintroduced in the present theoretical perspective—that the problem of ethics constitutes the problem of taking up a position with regard to oneself and one's own discourse sees the root of the problem of knowledge in the source point of the constitution of a *conscious "I"* in the relationship with self and things; this constitution of self is prior, and escapes the full control that an "I" could exercise over self.

ETHICS AND REASON

The individual who is conscious, or partially conscious, of self, a speaking subject who is also an ethical subject, necessarily *represents himself*; in other words, if he is to be able to function, he needs a *self-image*. What is the relationship between the problem of the place and genesis of one's own discourse and the question of self-image? How does all this make the taking up of position, choice, and moral life possible?

Here we have the classic problem of *freedom* in its biblical, Greco-Christian, and, more recently, romantic versions. How far can the problem of the positioning of the "I" be controlled by the individual and his knowledge, however conceived of? In contemporary theoretical language, the question is not asked in exclusively philosophical terms; in other words, in terms of speculation and reflection, of a fully conscious self-awareness. In Freud's psychoanalysis, this question is asked as the question of the *superego*, as the unconscious structure of a law around which the ego is organized, and on the basis of which the ego operates in the tissue of its desires and hence of its relations with reality.

The theory of the Freudian superego, in any case, marks the start of a conception of reason and consciousness that goes beyond simple logic and beyond a rationality that can be perfectly controlled in its laws and mechanisms; a law structuring the ego, and on the basis of which the ego is constantly thrown out of position and brought into question, or judged; prejudged, in a kind of guilt which, prior to being exclusively moral, religious, or theological, concerns the question of destination, in other words, the question of *what comes to me* and *what returns to me* from the positions I take and from my actions.

Pre-judged,[1] as we say of a criminal wanted by the police, someone who has an identity and is identifiable by the forces of law and order. These dynamics and this fate operate within the very structure and exercise of reason. By transverse and simultaneous paths, this order of considerations confirms traditional theories according to which evil means failure, destruction, and violence, as against the vital and luminous givenness of beauty and constancy. Identification, also in the specific sense of the forces of law and order, is constituted within an order that is also social, an order that is both natural and social according to post-Enlightenment rhetorical discourse, which has by now shaped Western styles of thinking.

After this brief overview and with no more ado, we now consider whether the word is truly pre-logical or outside logic for Nazis, or whether it is ethically set in a certain *place*, or connected with the *place* as structure of the discourse. In other words, the question is whether in Nazi thought the word does not concern the structure of the relationship between the individual and his self-image, that is, *the way in which the individual thinks of himself in relation to his place, as set in his own specific place.* There is a weakness in the abstract and universalistic ideal of Enlightenment knowledge, that the knowledge at stake in Nazism seeks to deny and surpass by finding another origin, a place of membership and bond—that of body, blood, life, race. Tradition and references seem more radical than the weakness and abstraction of the agreement of wills and treaties.

This is what Emmanuel Levinas declares in a 1934 essay, "Some Reflections on the Philosophy of Hitlerism." In the face of degenerate forms of an impotent freedom, Hitlerism reintroduces certain attitudes of the German spirit based on the desire for authenticity and seriousness. This entails no longer playing with ideas, says Levinas, but being, so to speak, chained to one's own body, people, and tradition. And if body, people, and tradition are to avoid suspicion, they have to consider blood unambiguously, and must rise above the fragility of the particular, not through the ambiguity of the search for truth, but through the ideal of *expansion*.

Such expansion is a different force from the propagation of truth.

> The person who exercises it does not separate from it. The force is not lost in the midst of those who suffer it. It is attached to the personality or society that exercises it, and it broadens them, subordinating everything else to it. Here the universal order is not established as a corollary of ideological expansion; rather, the expansion itself constitutes the unity of a world of masters and slaves. Nietzsche's will to power, which modern-day Germany is rediscovering and glorifying, is not only a new ideal, but is one that brings its own particular form of universalization: war and conquest.[2]

Levinas goes on to say:

> Perhaps we have succeeded in demonstrating that racism is not opposed only to one or another particular point of Christian and liberal culture. It is not some particular dogma of democracy, parliamentarianism, dictatorial regime or religious policy that is under discussion. It is the very humanity of man.[3]

Here Levinas does not develop this radical idea further. It concerns the radical change in direction undergone in racism by the authentic demand to overcome the limitations of an Enlightenment and/or Idealist conception of *truth*, a change in direction that consists of a modification of the idea of universality, which becomes force and original exercise of a power over self and others.

In his recent *Homo sacer*, Giorgio Agamben has developed an analysis of the totalitarianisms of this century based on the *accord between biology and politics*. He writes:

The laws on discrimination against Jews have almost exclusively monopolized the attention of students of the racial policy of the Third Reich. However, it is impossible to understand them fully without restoring them to the general context of the legislation and biopolitical approach of National Socialism. The latter do not find their full expansion in the Nuremberg Laws, or in deportation to the camps, or even in the "Final Solution." These decisive events of our century are based on the unconditional assumption of a biopolitical task, in which life and politics are identified ("politics = giving form to the people's life"); and only if they are restored to their "humanitarian" context is it possible to measure their full inhumanity.[4]

These issues can be understood less inadequately if they are situated within the relationship of a subject with his own word and with his own self-image. The question is examined by Freud in *Group Psychology and the Analysis of the Ego*, where it is seen as a question of *gregarious drive* (see in particular chaps. 9 and 10).

This refers to an original membership in which self-image and relation with one's own discourse have their roots. Freud identifies the *sense of guilt* as an unconscious functioning capable of producing a *sense of duty*. The question of the *head* is the element around which the individual's constitution and representation of self are organized within the collectivity. It is not a matter of mere violence or mere weakness in the face of the play of inhibition of one's own desire. It is not simply a matter, according to Freud, of the problem of aggression and hatred in the dynamics of the frustration of desires, but rather of a *dynamics in which the role of science is proposed anew*.

In the post-Enlightenment era, ethics must be thought of, not as a relationship between man and ontology or between man and theology, but as a *relationship between science and politics*. And in the contemporary fragility of this relationship, *race bursts out*. In the antisemitic version of this process, race is considered an evil inasmuch as it is an obstacle to a *project of purity of origin*, seen as the privilege of a certain race. This purity of origin is *the source of a form of knowledge: blood, people, body, tradition* are elements of an imagery representing an origin, with respect to which people call on science to operate as a reinforcement to narcissism.

EVIL IN DISCOURSE

This leads me to consider whether the horror of the extermination camps cannot be interpreted in terms of an unbridgeable relationship between evil and judgment, between a destructive power that is the enemy of what is human, and a kind of *evil in discourse*.

I do not mean "evil in discourse" as a Socratism that could be read today in the prevalently conservative forms of a denunciation of the metaphysical and moral disorientation that is a feature of present experience. Nor do I mean, in post-Enlightenment style, a denunciation of the fall in ethical and civil values. In my view, neither of these attitudes can be reconciled with the dark, incomprehensible enigma of the origin of evil.

Philo-metaphysical approaches or philo-Enlightenment styles seem too narrow to take sufficient account of the source of the problem, which lies in an evil that works within the discourse, but cannot be appropriated by the discourse. By evil in discourse I mean an action and effects that are produced in the discourse, not in an intellectualistic sense, but rather as an act, or a taking of a position by a subject with respect to his origin and his relationship with things and with himself through things.

Before savagery, before the taste for destruction, before hatred for man, what happens? What becomes of a discourse that is conscious with regard to the other person? What happens before and beyond and through the structuring of an ethics and an attitude that can be thought of as ethical? What does it mean in Nazism, but before and beyond Nazism, to expect something for oneself from the other, to relate one's own desire to the desire of the other, to encounter the other, to open oneself to him or dominate him? What do weakness or strength, desire or passivity, hospitality or exclusion, mean within the structure of my word?

In other words, the question of evil is concealed in the issue of a supposed power that the individual exercises over and through his words. What is the effect of this power: censure, arrogance, contempt?

THE IDOL OF THE GOOD

This means that there is a destruction active in the words of a malicious discourse—what is called *speaking ill*. Lies, the theory of an inferior race, the purity of an uncontaminated origin, the triumph of a power and a plan: all this lives and is structured as a relationship of self with one's own origins.

A structure idolatrous of man as self-reference is in question here: man as absolute to himself, a blinding akin in its structure and source to a certain ethical connivance. Here too we have to refer to Levinas and his teaching. Levinas speaks of responsibility to others as the source point of the existence and structure of the ego, responsibility to others as structure of my lack, indeed of a twofold lack—my own and that of the other. According to Levinas, my own and the other's generated being, and the generated being of the discourse in which all this can be spoken, is rooted in the relationship between these two lacks.

The question of God seems not to bring much assistance to the scene of the horror of the extermination camps, but to operate as the object of a discourse: in other words, God as idol, an object that seems to be both the effect and a symptom of a structure of knowledge. The question opened by the idea of God, before and beyond the issue of His existence, seems more the form and type of knowledge in which *speaking of God* is constituted. In this structure of knowledge, *the question of the idol concerns man as relationship with himself, even before that with God*.

So does this mean that God is powerless in the face of Auschwitz? The problem seems not to be constituted by God, a God who can be conceived of as good or as evil, a God who is successful or unsuccessful in saving humanity, a God who is victorious or defeated with respect to an evil hosted within the very structure of the relationship with self. The problem springs, rather, from *the way in which people speak of God*.

With a certain lack of foresight, people in the 1960s talked a great deal about the eclipse of God and the inevitable and definitive secularization that seemed to threaten contemporary society. In theology and philosophy—and perhaps with an equal lack of foresight—people today are invited *not to speak about God*; discussions focus on the term "God" and the inappropriateness of naming Him, inasmuch as such a word is said to hide more than it reveals. Here, too, the problem seems to be radically one of method, and to concern the very structure of knowledge.

Negative theology has greatly clarified these questions in the tradition from Dionysius to Eckhart and Nicholas of Cusa. This is a Christian and not a Jewish approach, in which, in a certain sense, rather than the question of God as existent or nonexistent, perfect or imperfect, good or evil, the question asked is that of a conception of the knowledge that man has with regard to himself.

In other words, it is a question of a redefinition of the individual in relation to his evil, and of the sense of his evil. It is a case of seeking to understand—in the theoretical, or, if you like, hermeneutic perspective in which we are immersed—what John states in the Book of Revelation when he speaks of a time when "there shall no more be anything accursed,"[5] understanding this statement, if possible, in a Jewish or Christian context, or in any case in a context in which such a statement can be made and upheld. A time when there shall no more be anything accursed: the context in which this is thinkable is what is at stake in our present meeting. What is entailed is a radical redefinition of the terms of what is human, a concept that is theological in both a Jewish and a Christian sense, concerning suffering and happiness, evil and good, as aspects of a different reality that can be named in various ways.

It is a case of ceaselessly understanding the fact of the Holocaust as a sign, a universal sign. We can speak of the Holocaust on the basis of a radical subtraction of the very terms of the rationality and sense of a discourse, but we can speak of it. What *qualifies* us to *speak* of it, to *judge* it?

I believe that the thinkability of a reality like that of the Holocaust is linked, both in theological terms as well as what we can call "natural" terms, to a style of reflection and a style of language of an "I" that conceives of and associates with itself as heir. An "I" that thinks, speaks, and relates to itself as heir is not simply *one who does not possess himself.* The heritage goes beyond the weakness of the ethical intention and ontological issue. Thinking of oneself as heir and having the experience of being an heir, means being in constitutive relation with a reality arising from X, who is a father, absent but active, dead but still capable of molding the structure of the "I" and its identity. A style of functioning that surpasses and encompasses the word as form of presence—blessed or cursed[6]—is in question in the experience of inheritance. This is a resource of the discourse which, in order to constitute itself, surpasses the supposed mastery of a point of view or an action. In a certain way, this style of functioning thus also surpasses and encompasses life and death.

It is an unfathomable question, but one that defines the simple and radical structure of what is human. Being an heir after Auschwitz is an unprecedented question, but it is also the point that clarifies a deep-seated structure found within humanity itself. The heritage is an ungraspable name, unprecedented because it redefines the form of what is one's own, of the presence to self, of common sense.

A "COMPASSIONATE" KNOWLEDGE?

The subtitle of the present meeting is "Ethical Implications for Today." What does judging mean today? We could address this question by following Vico in approaching it in the form of a "compassionate" knowledge. Vico advances this formula as a conclusion to the *New Science*, which "inevitably brings with it the path of compassion." Against the "arrogance of the learned," he proposes a compassionate knowledge.

John's statement that "there shall no more be anything accursed" can be read in different ways. It can be interpreted according to a Hegelian style of knowing, in which evil and negativity work together to order everything, within a dialectically necessary structure. However, it can also be interpreted, following Vico's example, in a way that sees evil as hosted within the structure of a knowledge that is constituted as a transformation of its actor.

It is a way of speaking and judging. Following Vico's style of thought, the *nonspecific* of the word is what is in question. *Good can be born of evil* is a statement that, on the one hand, is theologically upheld, but on the other, according to Vico and a certain movement in Christian thought, concerns a knowledge *of* and *about* history. The possibility that evil can give birth to good is thinkable within a transformation of what is human; Vico says within a *revival* or *resurrection* understood as transformation of the "I" that takes place, and has already taken place, in relation to its knowledge/self-knowledge. When we speak, we remember, we judge. This takes place in the life of the individual and the life of peoples. Becoming aware in memory of a lost good or a crime committed is an experience made possible by the fact of being already transformed or regenerated with respect to a previously presumed mastery.

Here we have a kind of moving out of position of a subject, of an "I" who *thinks of himself as heir* in relation to self and to the possession of his knowledge/self-knowledge. As already noted, the structure of the heritage involves a moving out of position with respect to one's own time and to a knowledge about it and also a religious sense, however conceived of, which is enigmatic and unfathomable.

It is the question of a *dignity*, again in Vico's sense, as a relation to what generates me, as man and as subject of a knowledge. Auschwitz is a sign that makes it possible to maintain relations with the origin of my discourse.

NOTES

1. *Translator's note.* In Italian, the noun *pregiudicato* means a person with a criminal record. However, *pre-* = pre-, and *giudicato* = judged.
2. E. Levinas, "Some Reflections on the Philosophy of Hitlerism," *Esprit*, 1934.
3. Ibid.
4. G. Agamben, *Homo sacer* (Turin: Einaudi, 1995), pp. 166–167.
5. *pan katathemaouk estaieti* (Revelation 22:3).
6. *Translator's note.* In Italian, *benedetto* = blessed (*bene* = good, *detto* = spoken), and *maledetto* = cursed (*male* = evil, *detto* = spoken).

The Limit and the Unlimited

Stefano Levi Della Torre

In 1755 an earthquake hit Lisbon, killing nearly 40,000 victims and destroying thousands of buildings: it became a seminal event for the Enlightenment.

Voltaire contemplated the boundaries within which human beings can rationally be the masters of their own destinies, since chance and natural causes may suddenly swerve the picture, revealing another fate and overrunning the proudest achievements of civilization.

Likewise, the Italian poet Leopardi, in his poem "La Ginestra" ("The Broom") uses the image of an apple destructively falling onto an anthill as a metaphor:

Come d'arbor cadendo un picciol pomo . . .
d'un popol di formiche i dolci alberghi
cavati in molle gleba . . .
schiaccia, diserta e copre
in un punto . . .[1]

Ever-looming disaster lingers and is the weak point in any idea of progress: a primeval and unrestrainable event threatens linear processes and breaks them.

The thinkers of the Enlightenment perceived this threat in Nature, as in the more backward sections of society, although the Romantics had discovered the destructive side of progress itself: nature is not the only force to spawn disaster, which can ensue from the dynamics of society.

In our day and age, technology, the ever more powerful and all-pervasive prostheses that technical development offers us, is increasingly used as a destructive as well as a constructive tool. Nor is such use limited to wars or to exceptional cases, it also holds in employing it routinely. Auschwitz per se was not a war, it was a bureaucratic and technical implementation at the side of the war during the war event, in the context of the most advanced society.

In its time, some came to see the Lisbon earthquake as a symbol of the precarious existence of every achievement of civilization. Auschwitz is the same for us. The earthquake represented the external or outer boundary, limiting the triumph of progress, a limit set by Nature that cannot be mastered.

169

Auschwitz belies the inner boundary, that is to say the limit within human beings and imposed by their society; it tells us that at any time, in an unforeseen manner, basic drives can emerge from within the heart of the most advanced and developed society, availing themselves of progressively more powerful means of destruction.

Technical progress creates and destroys, providing tools and means to wisdom but also to irresponsibility, as well as to aggression: it renews the world as it ages it, smothering it with dead objects, refuse, and litter. It is an instrumental approach, the rationality linking the relationship between goal and means, without guaranteeing the goodness of the goal: it merely tells us that given an objective—be it the irrigation of barren land or extermination—one can avail oneself of rational means to carry the project out and reach the target.

Shelley's *Prometheus Unbound*, referred to by Hans Jonas in his *Principles of Responsibility*, contains the essence: for the first time, human beings can be seen as being technically able to destroy themselves and the world, intentionally or through mere lack of knowledge. No longer will it be the God of the Flood, no longer just Nature, because human society and its means can cause a catastrophe. The unlimited growth of our technical aids, our prostheses, seems not to be matched by a comparable or expected growth of our sense of responsibility. Ethics operates on a smaller scale compared to the planetary dimension chosen by the power of our means. Goethe outlines this issue perfectly in the "Sorcerer's Apprentice" as a problem inherent to civilization itself. This is precisely what Nazism reveals: the bridging element, the link establishing direct contact between mass basic drives and the technical and administrative powers.

In our day and age we perceive Hitler's short-lived regime (1933 to 1945, just twelve years) as an indefinitely long time, as undefined and extended: this is not just because of the degree and the scope of the evil it generated, but also because of the warning it holds within, a warning for the entire process of our civilization.

Why do we ask ourselves all these questions about Auschwitz, and why now more than before? I believe that the postwar period sought to distance itself from the tragedy that had just taken place. As if life were reacting, looking forward to the reconstruction process, economic development, and all its conflicts and social advancements and the conflict they entailed, as well as the social developments, the decolonization movement: all were more conducive to looking into the future rather than back into the past. There was an upsurging feeling: the future held the promise of being better than the present, and trust in progress was reaffirmed.

The East-West challenge acted as a yardstick for identities, replaced the previous antagonism against Nazism and Fascism.

What about now? Now that the pace of growth and employment has been broken into, most of the class identities have been dismembered, the bipolar simplification of the world no longer holds, and migrations and mixtures are underway, the trends in history are not so easy to decipher. The future no longer holds the promise of progress. The surge of relief for having overcome Auschwitz thanks to the victory over Nazism is warping: there have been other examples of genocide, in Cambodia, in Bosnia and Central Africa.

One wonders, now that the criminals have been defeated, whether the crime was too, or whether it lies dormant in existing social and mental processes.

The metabolization of change has always been a social issue, the more so in the event of sudden change, as happened between the two world wars, as is happening with the so-called globalization processes, migrations, and electronics. Our individual and collective subjectivities seek refuges, anchors, and constants. Yesterday's totalitarian regimes were the answer to such needs, as fundamentalist movements are today's: the two are akin.

Totalitarian regimes in this century, such as Fascism and Nazism, fed on the fear of change. Although they maintained that they were revolutionary, their vocation and their hold on the masses were based on being fixed, certain, on dogmas: they promised to control change and, wielding absolute power, to control the unforeseen through the agency of will. We have not left the sacred behind us; this is the pathology of secularization, it is the political implementation of sacredness, the incarnation of sacredness into politics. Since the loci of traditional religion have been destroyed, sacredness, the *sacrum*, has been wandering round the world with free links that bond into the State, into racial or ideological identities turning them into idols.

The imperfect, incomplete process of secularization has not dissolved the divine essence, it has rediscovered its prerogatives, placing them in humans, which has become incarnated in the "us" while the devil seeks refuge in "the other": absolute friend and absolute foe.

Totalitarianism was the messianic perversion of secularization: it held an eschatological promise, the triumph of the ultimate good against an absolute evil.

Unlike World War I, a clash of empires, nation-states, and economic interests, World War II was also a war of religion, in the Age of Secularization, a clash of civilizations, ideologies, and global identities. This is what makes it a child of our age: a landscape, a scenario announcing major future conflicts. Such conflicts are between interests, but they take the shape of a clash of civilizations. The urge for a collective identity and fundamentalism may be a symptom of this.

There was turmoil in the wake of World War I, and in this framework the control of change and the unforeseen became the obsession of every totalitarianism: people saw themselves saved through control, through power, *extra potestatem nulla salus*.

Democracy, which in principle corresponds to a form of rotation and change in political power, was seen as disquieting and is refused. Anything external, from the outside, and therefore not under control, is seen as a threat. Conquest is a means to translate anything external into something internal, and any degree of autonomy into subordination. Unlimited conquest is the only means to satisfy such an all-encompassing anxiety stemming from the outside. The greater and bigger the Reich, the more it incorporates the outside: it shifts its borders to reduce the space of the outside, it englobes its foreignness.

The extermination of Jews is part-and-parcel of this paradox: the aim of freeing the Reich of and from the Jewish ingredient using racial discrimination and then of expelling them and lastly englobing them in the conquest, the implementation of the "Final Solution." What did Jews represent for the anxiety-ridden Nazi mythology? Intruding outsiders, a controlling uncontrollable power, resistant to assimilation, yet assimilating others. In stressing the greatness of its mythological enemy, Nazism was glorifying itself, as if a Siegfried able to kill the dragon were transferring the beast's powers unto himself.

The scenario described above explains why the so-called intentionalist interpretations emerged first. According to these theories, the Nazis had intended the Final Solution since the beginning, it was the predetermined outcome in a linear program. Deep down this idea was a relief: Auschwitz in its entirety could be ascribed to the Nazi plan, limited to its time and to its ideology.

Currently the so-called functionalist theory is prevalent, a more deeply disquieting notion. It maintains that Nazism reached the Final Solution through a chain of subsequent decisions, following a "problem-solving" approach (Z. Bauman), that is, it made decisions which were functional given the circumstances that arose, thus resembling a person who proceeds along the same path in virtue or because of his previous actions. Having said this, intentionalism remains a key interpretation, insofar as extermination was never excluded, and in fact was hoped for since the very beginning.

The idea that ultimately Auschwitz was finalized thanks to a chain of decisions—each one the rational next step under the circumstances—rather than the outcome of a linear program, makes the events even more alarming and relevant to our age. In fact this interpretation divests Auschwitz of its mantle of uniqueness and reveals it as being close to other processes into which we are dragged more because we lack the boundaries to separate us rather than because we actually intend to follow a comprehensive design. It is as if we were inertly carried by a form of instrumental rationality, led step by step to an irrational and catastrophic outcome.

Hence we are denied the relief of believing that the Nazis were an alien race, that we are immune and do not share their traits. The new interpretation forces us to consider, in the words of Primo Levi in *I sommersi ed i salvati*:

> "that man, the human species—we, in short—had the potential to construct an infinite enormity of pain, and that pain is the only force created from nothing, without cost and without effort. It is enough not to see, not to listen, not to act."[2]

Compared to the intentionalist theses, the functional ones actually reach out to include larger issues. They include both the active side of the proposed ideology and the passive side: the political tailoring, where the leaders cut it to fit circumstances, the moral tailoring of the citizens living under the regime which both required adhering and "not seeing, not listening, and not doing." It can be described as hegemony—where the active subject (the party and its armed section) drew their strength from consensus, mass mobilization, and the abstention of the majority.

This is where we come across another issue: how visible were deportations, mass exterminations? If they were to be effective as instruments of terror, they had to be visible, at least to that extent; but in terms of propaganda and in the relationship with other nations, they had to be invisible. The fact is that they were unbelievable, and the euphemistic slang used—"transfers," "solution of the Jewish problem"—hid them from sight.

The regime offered two options: one could choose to know or not to know. Where there was no consent, at least they had passivity, cloaked in the alibi of not knowing. Such is the exercise of the power of hegemony. In *Se questo è un uomo*, Primo Levi wrote,

> "In spite of the varied possibilities for information, most Germans didn't know because they didn't want to know...knowing and making things known was one way (basically then not all that dangerous) of keeping one's distance from Nazism. I think the German people, on the whole, did not seek this recourse, and I hold them fully culpable of this deliberate omission."[3]

This refers to the fact that those Germans were collectively guilty of the situation described. As for the Nazis, I shall quote another "sentence" Primo Levi passed, referring to the *Sonderkommandos*, the special teams of prisoners appointed to work at the ovens:

> "Conceiving and organizing the squads was National Socialism's most demonic crime...this institution represented an attempt to shift onto others— specifically, the victims—the burden of guilt, so that they were deprived of even the solace of innocence."[4]

What I have said is not only applicable to extreme cases, such as the *Sonderkommando*: it overflows into the gray area, that fabric of coerced compromises the mass of the imprisoned gave in to.

This is how the regime, on the one hand, involved the Germans through connivance or with the alibi of (wanting) no knowledge, and, on the other, involved the victims through being forced to participate in the mechanism of extermination (Stalinism produced comparable conditions). We conclude that the ideology of purity and the cleansing process—of a race, class, or religion—generates widespread moral decay.

Let us imagine a system whose goal it is to generate unlimited production of abject behavior and events and to cause unlimited deaths. An ideology of hate is not enough, since passions soon burn out: passions are a necessary trigger, but they fail to guarantee continuity. Automatisms are needed for systematic continuity, hate frozen into doctrine, and then doctrine shaped into common sense. From a passion to a job. The irrational trigger, the intense fury thrives in the wide avenues of rationality, of bureaucratic and industrial organization. Procedures turned into a cold routine do not undergo the curve of passion which is why they can be used without any limit, extensively.

Of all Nazism's characteristic features, the one that possibly holds the greatest warning for us is the one Hannah Arendt defined as the banality of evil. Nazism was the exceptional organization of normality: assembly line type division of labor, from concept to execution, regular working hours; all these steps were per se innocent, blameless, any one of us could carry them out. However, in the case in point they become the preconditions, upstream of the gas chambers which turned taking part in the slaughter into something aseptic, each and every segment justified by the need dictated by one's private or family life, by one's job, by one's minute duty toward the hierarchy.

Hiroshima and Auschwitz share this minute fragmentation as well as the atrocity of the outcome. In fact the nuclear extermination is also the result of a series of links, each one as innocent as the next, none with blood-dripping steps, responsibilities reduced to specks of dust, a chain of impersonal actions which in the end led to the explosion of the bomb on its target.

Criminals are the necessary cadres of the entire operation, but aside from them, in the end every fragment of the extermination chain, every person who said neither yes nor no, each one who performed a negligible—in fact, possibly a routine—gesture, has a high degree of individual innocence. A marked division of labor is the hallmark of the modern technological extermination, based on a Tayloristic breakdown of our consciences: crime as the product of a chain of individually innocent events. It becomes the technologically sophisticated production of the "gray zone," a division of ethical responsibilities based on the technical division of labor.

The Nazi extermination machine shows what this organization of normality and technical breaking up of responsibility can do, what can happen to this fragmented ethics if it does not measure itself against a comprehensive picture.

All this is familiar, these are processes found within our social organization.

Hitler gained power by a democratic process, that is, a majority vote, and then he established a dictatorship: in this case not a dictatorship of the majority so much as one through the majority, which itself was subjected to the dictatorship.

This situation acted as an *ex-post* alibi for the Nazis and the Germans when they maintained that they had merely been following orders and that their leaders, those who had issued such orders, were responsible for everything. They had been coerced, and therefore were to be justified. Hitler and the other leaders, the main culprits, also became the scapegoats of collective guilt. Stalin's fate was similar, in that he was a political criminal and a posthumous scapegoat.

Unlike the autocratic governments of the *ancien régime*, which were dictatorships of a minority, this century's totalitarian regimes, whether Fascist or Communist, are dictatorships in the name of and through majorities. In this respect they are in the same sphere as democracies and socialism; they elaborate on the same theme, that is, the power of a majority, and they represent a degeneration of the process.

The majority draws strength from emphasizing the common enemy: democracy, Bolshevism, and the Jews in the case of the Nazis. By so doing, that is, by stressing the importance of enemies and of the threat they represent, it calls upon protective power able to carry out revenge and save. Lastly, this emphasis on a threat by a deadly enemy is bewitching and leads to a representation of the aggressor, themselves, as if they were the victims: we are the victims of the Versailles Treaty, we are threatened by Communism, and persecuted by the Jewish world plot. Masses and power were welded together by victimization, the masses having reason and a flair for feeling like someone's or something's victim, and power that blends into one body with the mass by proclaiming their common fate.

Aggression and victimism: something we see in the fierce and lamenting fundamentalism of the present day.

The perversion of the majority principle is measured first and foremost against the fate reserved for minorities. Let us consider Jews under Nazism as an extreme prototype. The minority's kinship, its genetic differentness, is emphasized, while as a group the minority is undifferentiated—any one Jew being worth another: it is a choice between hostility and indifference to their fate. This model does not inherently require that extermination take place, but as a model it may belong to our time horizon too, nor can it be ruled out when looking into the future of democracy: it is the model of the "two-thirds society," where the majority (two-thirds) of a people can democratically agree to keep all the political and material advantages for themselves, excluding the minority (one-third).

In times like ours, when the drive toward equality is weaker and societies are experiencing a greater and greater degree of social and ethnic differentiation, at a time when globalization is forcing cuts on us, this is a possible outlook. One wonders what stereotypes, what rationalizations will be used to justify the exclusion of a minority, barred from civil and maybe even human rights. Will it again be race? Why not? Or maybe income, unemployment, cultural identity, gender, or age (women and children are already the main focus of the reappearance of present-day slavery).

Racism was obsessed by "living space." It dealt with this issue by taking other people's space and their lives, reserving it all for themselves. Although we condemn it, this model can be traced throughout our history. Including and excluding others from physical, economic spaces or from access to rights has always been a problem, and the impetus for either negotiation or tremendous conflict. Nowadays, migrations from poor to rich countries are one of the shapes this has taken on.

With hindsight we can say that to this day the problem is defined as relative, and science, politics, and ethics have found other spaces and resources in the world to deal with it. How long will this be true? There are trends, such as increasing population, environmental pollution, and technical advances, that all appear to have unlimited, albeit not linear, growth in a constant environment, as constant as the radius of our planet.

The problem of living space may arise again, in absolute terms, and with it may also recur the conflict over which groups of human beings are worthy of living and which are not.

Techno-bureaucratic extermination may seem to be a rational solution to some, and in the event, Auschwitz will have been a realistic forerunner.

Auschwitz is a warning, and the transmission of its memory is the ethical act of those who bore witness.

The ethical act is not to forget such important things, not to bear false witness: truth as an effort of self-criticism, as a source of information and messages.

Ethics can be described as the responsibility to ask oneself questions, to raise them in others and address them. However, to answer them presumes a position of relative strength—be it physical, psychological, mental, or social: to be responsible to others one has to feel one's strength, the strength of the living over the dead, of those who can speak over those who cannot, of those who know over those who know not. Ethics can be described as the responsibility strength holds toward weakness, a weakness-encompassing strength, a strength that remembers its weakness to comprise it.

What is the place of memory in ethics? There is a passage in the Bible which highlights this question, in Leviticus 19:34, where it says, "But the stranger that dwelleth with you shall be unto you as one born among you, and thou shalt love him as thyself, for ye were strangers in the land of Egypt." That is, when you are living on a land of your own, and therefore in a position of strength, what will guide your understanding of those who are weak, and weak because they are not on land of their own? Your memory that you were a stranger in foreign land—and that this may happen again. In the time and in the place of your strength, you will remember your weakness, you will recognize your past and your possible future in the stranger. By remembering what happened to you and what the future may hold, you will recognize yourself in the other.

Quite rightly we praise memory as opposed to oblivion, but memory too can lead us astray. The memory of what has happened throughout the centuries—the burning of books and of human beings, forced exiles, requisitioning and pogroms—led many to believe that Nazism was but a worse edition of past heinous crimes: however, this was not so, Nazism was not just that. Many did not believe, did not perceive, the Final Solution—genocide—because there was no echo of it in their memories, no example. Hence the severe impact which delayed escape and resistance.

Memory is also a pre-judice (an *ex-ante* judgment) insofar as it binds us to what is known and may make it hard for us to perceive what is new. Memory helps us to foresee the foreseeable, and thus reassures us, but it can also hinder our perception of the unforeseen, and in this respect it can be misleading. Our faith in remembering what happened "so that it may never happen again" will not succeed in defeating our century's stupid and fierce bloodshedding faiths; it will do no more than reassure us unless it is also the memory of the unforeseeable, the awareness that history will never cease to surprise us, through good and through evil.

NOTES

1. "Like a small apple falling from a tree . . . squashing, covering, and emptying where in the soft soil the ants had carved their sweet shelters."
2. (Eng. tr. Primo Levi) *The Drowned and the Saved*, New York: Summit Books, 1988, p. 86.
3. (Eng. tr. Primo Levi) *If this is a Man–the Truce*, London: Vintage, 1996, p. 386.
4. Primo Levi, *The Drowned and the Saved*, p. 53.

The Approach to the Question of Good and Evil in the Writings of Hans Jonas and Hannah Arendt

Bernard Dupuy

During the years following World War II, when people realized the extent of the evil perpetrated by the Shoah and the questions it raised, this had little immediate effect on the thinking of philosophers or theologians. Universities resumed their prewar lecture series, and Martin Heidegger reclaimed his university chair without too much ado.

The issue of evil—in the perspective of the *excess* of evil and the modern *catastrophe* of world war—was certainly addressed with considerable insight. However, to some extent, the final Allied victory over the enemy forces at such a heavy cost obscured analysis of the unleashing of the evil, and people took their time over attempts at such reconstructions. Analysis of Nazism, whose wickedness was plain to all, could wait. People wanted to live again. Institutions and moral points of reference could be reconstructed for a world that had to reestablish the rule of law and justice. The free world paid tribute to its heroes, and moved on. However, the victims of the Shoah were in danger of being forgotten. There are procedures for canonizing saints, but collective sins and disasters are not objects of commemoration. There are no procedures—or at least no longer—of anathematization for condemning the perpetrators of evil. The initial cry of the voice of conscience was "Never again!" based on the belief that it was enough to ban any return to the past.

The country primarily concerned, Germany, defeated and in ruins, was bound to reflect on the resistible pressure of totalitarianism that it had experienced, on the evils that it had caused, and on the catastrophe to which it had led the way. In condemning the causes of the disaster, the German Protestant churches were particularly careful to state that they were jointly blameworthy for their lack of action and their silence, while at the same time condemning any recourse to the notion of collective guilt.[1]

When the World Council of Churches was founded at the Amsterdam Conference on "Man's Disorder and God's Plan" in 1946, Karl Barth, the main instigator of the Barmen Declaration along with Dietrich Bonhoeffer (who had since been executed), appealed to the message of the Scriptures in order to discern the signs of catastrophe foretold in the Bible. The churches were standing under the judgment of God. Then, under the influence of Jules Isaac and Jacques Maritain, the Seelisberg Conference publicly admitted historical Christian responsibility with respect to Jews, condemning the "teaching of contempt" and calling on the churches to rectify their teachings. It was only several years later, when the legal limitation on war crimes (twenty years) had expired, that the idea of imprescriptible crimes appeared. Until then, the testimony of Primo Levi, *If This Is a Man*, and Robert Antelme, *The Human Race*, published respectively in 1946 and 1947, had scarcely been noticed. They described the loss of traditional ethical standards in the concentration camps, although it was still hard to gauge the enormity of the questions raised. However, more radical questions now started to appear.

During the 1960s, the problem of radical evil—an age-old issue in Judaism and Christianity, introduced into philosophy by Kant after the Enlightenment,[2] and taken up again after World War I—moved to center stage. In a critical perspective and in apparent contrast with Karl Barth's confessional theology, Rudolf Bultmann argued that the original expression of faith formulated in early times has to be demythologized if it is to be extended and proclaimed to the modern world. (Indeed, he had argued this since his 1924 seminar at Marburg on the New Testament, which was attended by two Jewish students, Hans Jonas and Hannah Arendt.)[3] The hermeneutical question concerned the decision to believe (or not to believe), a question handed down from yesterday to today, and whether it could still be followed and accepted in new terms. When Hans Jonas and Hannah Arendt undertook their immense task of ethical reflection, they both followed this inspiration.[4] After World War II, awareness of the radical nature of the Shoah forced people to return to the sources of faith and to begin some serious reflection. The question was no longer that of adapting the revealed message to the world, nor that of morality or pastoral concern, but one going right back to the meaning of the biblical message.

Hannah Arendt gave powerful expression to the contradiction between historical evil and biblical faith. When she first heard about Auschwitz in 1945, she could not believe it. She immediately realized the shock-waves it would cause. Humanity did not seem to be capable, or guilty, of such an enormity. However, when the facts were confirmed six months later, she wrote:

> This is what really shook me to the core. Before that we used to say, "Okay, I know we've got enemies. That's the way things are. Surely it's normal for a people to have enemies?" but this was totally different. It was as if a void had opened up at our feet, because we had imagined that everything

else could somehow be sorted out—as so often happens in politics. Not this time, though. It should never have happened. And here I am not talking about the number of victims, but about the systematic production of corpses, etc.—I don't need to expand further on this subject. Auschwitz should not have happened. Something happened there that we still cannot really grasp.[5]

* * *

"Auschwitz could not, should not have happened." Here the moral conscience protests about reality in a way never seen before. Against any eudemonism, classical morality, optimistic redemption theology, Kantianism and neo-Kantianism, it has to be declared that evil is evil, and not a half-portion or the absence of goodness. Evil truly exists. There is no meaning to the suffering of innocent people. There is no possible reparation for the victims who did not come back and who left us no testimony of themselves. These victims perished, and suffered an offense which we ourselves did not witness. As Primo Levi wrote: "The final victims are our final witnesses." Seeking to condemn the various possible causes of evil in turn (totalitarianism, antisemitism, the work of the devil?), Hannah Arendt realized that she would have to situate her reflections not only within an historical or ideological perspective, but also within a "theological" one (to which she was very close, as Eric Voegelin pointed out), although she approached it "without being able to claim it."[6] If she felt obliged to give up the task of addressing the question of evil, this was less because of some refusal of religion than because she said she felt paralyzed "by the hollowness of the conceptual tools of western tradition when faced with this evil."[7] Here we come to the crux of the matter.

When Hannah Arendt's *The Human Condition* was published, Karl Jaspers—who had written several years earlier, "Everything that previously had value in the world has 'fallen to pieces'"—wrote to her: "Don't you think that YHWH has withdrawn from the horizon?" She replied, on March 4, 1952:

I do not think that any traditional religion, be it Jewish or Christian, could provide a foundation, wherever or however, for something as clearly political as laws. Evil has been revealed as more extreme than we had thought. Speaking objectively, modern crimes are not envisaged by the Ten Commandments.

It seems to us more than ever today, after the Shoah, that the question of evil in history and, in correlation, that of God's presence in history, as Emil

Fackenheim says,[8] has never been so acute. In the course of his exchanges with Rudolf Bultmann around 1961, Hans Jonas came up against the same issues. This was the time, remember, of Eichmann's trial, Hochhut's play *The Deputy*, and the opening of Vatican II. It was also the time of the rising but contested fame of Horkheimer and Heidegger. Hans Jonas began his reflections on the Shoah by introducing a new perspective. In his Ingersoll Lecture in 1961 he attributed the catastrophe of modern history to the loss of humanity and the disappearance of the sense of immortality. As he said:

> Since the Enlightenment, concern over individual reputation has taken the place of immortality of the person. Immortality as an objective belief, accepted as a fact down through the centuries and a constitutive element of the whole tradition of man's creation "in God's image," has become a metaphysical question without an answer in our century, and has been replaced by a product of vanity. People began to think that it was possibly an illusion.

For Hans Jonas, however, the alternative to which faith has been subjected in our times does not date from the period of the Enlightenment, but was already present in antiquity. Another approach to the problem of evil in creation and history had been provided by gnosticism, which, he argued, still retained its relevance: in gnostic thought, immortality, before being seen as a certainty, was understood as a test, one of life's challenges for each person. This aspect of human existence had been forgotten, and the Shoah showed that the absence of immortality was a radical evil. In losing the sense of living for others, modern humankind has lost the authentic meaning of life.[9]

* * *

In order to appreciate the innovation in the analyses advanced by Hans Jonas and Hannah Arendt, it is useful to recall the classical approach to the question of good and evil. It has to be shown that it has obstructed understanding of the forces of evil and, in a certain sense, prevented opposition to them. It is always assumed that evil is the *opposite* of good, that there is a *possibility of choosing* between the two, and that there is an incontrovertible *obligation* to choose the good.

The classical medieval position is as follows. It states that the possibility of evil is present in creation so that man might be free. And to counterbalance the danger of scandal in this affirmation of evil, which offends our innate longing for happiness, it immediately adds that evil is simply nothingness and

God does not see evil. Briefly, good is placed above evil—precisely what modern nihilism rejects—and providence is said to make sure that everything turns out for the best, and the precedence in creation of repentance over sin is claimed (the Jewish concept of the *teshuvah* willed by God before sin, and the Christian concept of the gift of freedom in order to oppose sin, which is not willed by God; these theses are thus common to Jews and Christians). This theology of evil was worked out within the context of a conception of providence. The theory of creation passed through secularism in the Enlightenment and lasted into Kantianism. Today it seems insufficient and unacceptable because evil has been shown to have the potential of breaking out with unprecedented fury, breaking the bounds of any morality. People have in fact been able to claim—and not without some apparent justification—that the modern confirmation of radical evil challenges the creation story, as well as biblical eschatology. The task of today's thinking is to take a fresh look at classical theology, and this is why Hans Jonas was able to argue that the question of good and evil was better grasped by gnostic myth than by any rational theology.[10]

For Hans Jonas, biblical eschatology as such is a challenge to reason. It must therefore be stated in general terms that a rational theology such as that of the Enlightenment era can never grasp it. However, this is even more true if we want to respond to the contemporary situation. Faith has been lived on the defensive since the Enlightenment, but Hans Jonas stated that the force of the habits of thought that have prevailed in reflections on faith, rather than faith itself, have set faith against itself. Since the Enlightenment, it has no longer been possible to appeal to the intervention of transcendent "powers," nor to mythological stories recounting the creation of the world or eschatology, nor to concepts of the coming or departure of the Messiah, nor to expectations of eschatology and redemption. The present challenge is thus that of knowing whether we should say that the medieval idea of providence is false and that the imagery in the Bible is now outmoded.

Although the question of the metaphors of biblical eschatology was raised before the Shoah, it took on a totally new dimension afterwards, becoming: "Can there still really be a divine intervention to save us?" The cry that rose from Auschwitz has become the primary question. It is no longer "Does God exist?" or even "Are there words with which we can talk about God?" or "Is it possible to name God?" but "Where was God when we called on Him?" It has taken the form of an accusation: "Why was God absent from Auschwitz?"—an *unanswered* cry from humanity to God. Further, for Christians this cry calls to mind Jesus' cry from the cross, repeating the words of the psalm, "My God, my God, why hast thou forsaken me?" The meaning of this verse is not the obvious psychological interpretation that Jesus felt despair. Rather, the cry condemns the false justice of the world. The one who utters it can appeal to nobody but God. He renounces the legion of angels, Simon Peter's sword and the approval of the powerful, and he condemns the irresponsibility of those who think they possess power but in reality "know not what they do." To accomplish this, this "righteous man" even had to stop appearing as a man who had himself assessed the realities of the world and could hope to find a court before which he could one day give an account of himself. He who wept over people's incomprehension, grieved over the loss of his friend Lazarus, and knew solitary agony, suffered from evil to an extent unknown to anyone else, or to the world. The words of the psalm show this: the righteous man is neglected by the chronicles of heroism and high moral thinking, and is counted "among sinners." As the Bible itself says, faced with such a death, there is place only for a "veiling of the face" because this death is counted as an impure death. And holiness is revealed in the scandal of this death. The words of the psalm give way to a silence, an absence. Is it possible that God does not answer when humankind calls on Him in distress? Even that must be admitted. The time of words is followed by that of silence. All post-Auschwitz thinking is affected by this enigma. What if the astonishing biblical affirmation of God's silence, repeated in the Old and then in the New Testament, means that God's silence is a kind of presence, as yet not perceived? What if it is an unutterable answer, an unshared answer that is not common to all people, a presence that can be clearly affirmed and recognized only by the victims?

It was Hannah Arendt who pointed out that in the face of the modern-day scandal of evil we ought first of all to find out how to think *after* Auschwitz (*or also* after Hiroshima). However, the next question was quite different, and sprang from the fact that Auschwitz (*and not* Hiroshima) is unthinkable. The question about Auschwitz is not whether we can think, write poems, or pray *after* Auschwitz (a question raised and popularized by Adorno, who had taken it on himself to claim that we cannot), but rather, and much more seriously: How could God have let Auschwitz *happen*? Is God a *weak* God? Or even: *What kind of God* could have let it happen? And this question has become our own, that of a whole era. It is no longer a question about history, politics, the moralization of war, moral philosophy, or metaphysics, for humanity and about humanity. It is no longer a question for the human sciences, and in fact suggests that they have lost their bearings. The present question of the *excess* of evil, which seems to invalidate any discourse about God, no longer bears on man's *capacity* to commit an (objective) evil, but on the fact of *inflicting* an evil on another, *on a subject*.[11] The Shoah makes a mockery of any idea of integrating evil into a prior all-encompassing vision of good. For its victims, the Shoah was not a test, or a punishment, or a testimony. Nothing of that kind. It wanted to kill in order to dominate. It simply sought to do harm. It did not kill only in order to suppress, but also in order to destroy the humanity in each prisoner. It annihilated the work of creation. It killed in order to do harm, and was an offense against *both man and God*. At the same time, as a question about humanity, and even before the question of sin can emerge, the Shoah raises a question about God, or, rather, coming from God—a question from humankind to God, or one that descends from God to humankind. When man claims that he is strong, God cannot cut him down to size except by showing Himself to be weak. This is a question put to religions—to Judaism or else to Christianity, and certainly to both. It is a question that, unlike those of yesterday that questioned or doubted revelation, can be answered only in revelation. It is a question that would silence our ancestor, the Enlightenment philosopher, a question whose place could be only in God, or to which only God Himself could give legitimacy and significance.

* * *

It must certainly be admitted that the question that rises from the human heart with regard to the Shoah is unanswerable, at least if it is asked on the basis of a banal, abstract question of God.[12] The conception of God in impersonal, dominatingly transcendent terms in order to avoid the danger of anthropomorphism means setting up an idea of a God who is immutable, distant, isolated, and all-powerful, but who ignores His creatures and is ultimately silent. According to Jonas, we have to abandon and reverse this bygone conception of God. We have to give up the rationalist idea of an immutable God, who is a stranger to evolution and who does not Himself evolve, as being totally contrary to the biblical manifestation of God. According to Jonas, the idea of God's revelation was better preserved in gnostic thought than in medieval rational thought. It is also found in Jewish thought, reappearing in the Kabbalah in the concept of God's withdrawal and self-contraction (*tsimtsum*) in the act of creation.[13] We must be able to stand in the presence of this living God, this immortal, strong, great God.

These questions link up with those of returning to biblical sources in the face of scholastic thought.[14] Hans Jonas's sources come from Jewish tradition, but are part of the same movement. However, while invoking the metaphor of God's withdrawal in His creation as found in the Lurianic Kabbalah, Jonas failed to recall that these date back to a much earlier time. The word *tsimtsum* has a midrashic origin and evokes God's fast (*tsom*), an idea that served to counterbalance and complement the cosmological and ethically neutral idea of emanation. For Jonas, if there has been a *tsimtsum* of God in history as in creation, we can understand His "absence" at the time of the Shoah. We would thus be able to think of a presence intentionally withheld and hidden. As was pointed out to him,[15] Jonas did not establish a link with God's *kenosis* as asserted in Christian theology and without which the incarnation could be nothing but a scandal or an absurdity of history.[16] Rather, he in fact returned to the notion of God found in great early theology.

On this basis, Jonas brought to the fore a God who Himself cares for His creation, even suffering over it, a God who is merciful and compassionate, a God "other than he who has reigned or been made to reign." He believed that we need have no fear in speaking of a God who is truly close. This would be the answer to the nihilism that showed its full extent in the Shoah. Such a different attitude responds—and can alone do so—to this nihilism, which constitutes the total destruction of any ethics, alienation of humankind, and rejection of God, and whose real name is Shoah; this approach is a call to responsibility in the sense of being for the other, God's call to humankind and even humankind's call to God. A sense of responsibility with respect to the whole of creation is the only possible response to the loss of the sense of immortality that Hans Jonas saw as the negative criterion of the modern age and the final lesson of the Shoah.

* * *

Hannah Arendt also meditated on the Shoah, but in more historical than metaphysical terms, often quoting René Char: "We are living without a testament." For her, what our era lacks is the notion of witness. In the modern world, where technology is used for the most inhuman ends, the witnesses have fallen silent. The Nazis even hoped to carry out their work right up to the last hour without witnesses. In such times, there was no more law, no more ethics. She asked: "What then is our law, when all ethics have vanished?" Paradoxically, ethics, an extreme ethics, found shelter among the victims. People could die an inhuman death, and even their death was taken from them, for they were forced to die nameless, scorned, and abandoned. She wrote: "No one will sing the Mass, no one will recite Kaddish. These dead leave no written testament behind them, and scarcely a name."[17] These unburied dead, these lost sheep of the house of Israel, experienced ultimate solitude. Their fate was to be left to themselves, abandoned and without pastors.

Here Hannah Arendt accused the powers that be, of all kinds. She held that the German Catholic Church had been more concerned over safeguarding its position and defending its rights than offering a word of comfort and defense to those being deported and persecuted: "In Germany, shepherds followed in the tracks of their flocks instead of leading them."[18] She also commented that Pope Pius XII had doubtless done all he could to denounce the deportations and to save individuals, but that his words had gone unheard. Whatever Hochhuth's confessional prejudices and his lack of sufficient historical data, he was right in repeating the cry of the victims, and the harsh fact remains: "They were abandoned by everyone, even the vicar of Christ."[19]

Hannah Arendt drew a bitter lesson from this terrible distress: true human goodness has no place in politics. It is no longer enough to rely on charity and solidarity: "We can learn from [the parable of the Great Inquisitor] that absolute goodness is hardly any less dangerous than absolute evil. . . and that it is beyond virtue."[20]

However, in her major work, which she initially titled *Amor Mundi*, but finally called *The Human Condition*, Hannah Arendt sought a way to emerge from this eclipse of goodness and this corruption of intentions. What then is man? What is the world? For her the world is not only the divine creation of heaven and earth. It is not to be identified with what preexisted our birth. It is not simply a framework for human action. The world is what the people who live in it and love it make of it. It is precisely because they are themselves newcomers and innovators in virtue of their birth that people act. Such was Arendt's faith in creation. "The world is our work and our concern. Before man, there was no one: every new-born being is the bearer of hope of a hitherto unknown word and action." This affirmation, which she had earlier found in St. Augustine and considered to be unprecedented, is absolutely biblical. It is in fact the point on which St. Augustine distanced himself from Neoplatonism, and the affirmation of a human freedom that is totally other. And it was right here that she found the ever-open doorway of forgiveness. As a corrective to the irreversibility of sin, she wrote, "human beings possess the faculty to forgive and, at the same time, in view of the unpredictability and uncertainty of the future, to promise, a supremely human faculty."[21] These words are the message, the witness, of Hannah Arendt's thought.

Act to make the world a possible place to live: this is the law that the Nazis ignored or denied. The prerequisite of wanting to share the world with others is to make it lose its character of possession for oneself and extraneousness for others. Those who build up the world are those who want every country to be everybody's country. This is the lesson that Hannah Arendt sought to draw from her reflections on the Eichmann trial, the final lesson in this passionately discussed, poorly received, but undoubtedly misunderstood book, which was never intended to pass judgment on the tragedy of the

Judenräte. She hoped that the judges would finally have dared say to Eichmann:

> . . .just as you supported and carried out a policy of not wanting to share the earth with the Jewish people and the people of a number of other nations— as though you and your superiors had any right to determine who should and who should not inhabit the world—we find that no one, that is, no member of the human race, can be expected to want to share the earth with you. This is the reason, and the only reason, you must hang.[22]

The Nazis did not want to hear this message, preferring the myth of a people superior to others to the message of fraternity.

When all is said and done, Hannah Arendt was very close to Hans Jonas in believing that "the black experience of grim times" should give rise to a call to responsibility. To those who feel their responsibility, it is given to love the world. For her, building up human community was the true way to define responsibility: it is a responsibility for others, "even including responsibility for acts that we ourselves have not committed." This is where she distinguished between the notions of responsibility and guilt, writing:

> While there can be only individual guilt, responsibility on the other hand is vicarious, always provided that we belong to a group or collectivity. Feeling oneself to be responsible is the price we pay for not living on our own but among other people, and for the fact that the faculty for action, which after all is the political faculty *par excellence*, can be fulfilled only within one of the many varied forms of human community.[23]

The faith proposed by Hannah Arendt for tomorrow's world is not, perhaps, faith in God, in the commonly held sense of the word as profession of faith—an area not hers to analyze or proclaim, or even make her own. However, what she was concerned over was what she called "faith in creation," faith in the intrinsic value of every human being inasmuch as he exists, inasmuch as he has been born. Each new arrival is capable of renewing the world. This was the meaning she gave particularly to the "good news" of the Christian feast of Christmas. She held that the meaning of this feast is to show "the potential salvation offered to humanity in the fact that humanity is constantly regenerating itself and will do so for evermore."[24] It was really "divine" news for her. She believed in the newness of the world and the renewal of humanity. True, she did not stress Israel's being chosen, exhibiting a certain modesty in this regard, as she explained in a letter to Gershom

Scholem,[25] for she did not want to exclude any other choice, whatever it might be. She saw choice as a moral imperative. However, it was here, in this extreme *imperative*, in the sense of responsibility for others, that she saw hope for humanity's future. And the responsible task, "the duty of acting, this miraculous and miracle-working faculty of being able to be present to the world," is the response to the threat that has been recognized and faced up to today, of the unleashing of evil in the world. As Hans Jonas observed, this was "one of her most precious ideas, and one she did not share without trembling."

NOTES

1. Stuttgart Declaration (October 18, 1945), text reprinted in Wilhelm Nicmöller, *Kampf und Zeugnis der bekennenden Kirche* (Bielefeld: L. Beohauf, 1948), p. 527.
2. Cf. Myriam Revault d'Allones, "Le courage de juger," in Hannah Arendt, *Juger: Sur la philosophie de Kant* (Paris: du Seuil, 1991), pp. 217–239.
3. Hans Jonas and Hannah Arendt both wrote studies of St. Augustine at the end of the seminar in which they analyzed the relationship between grace and politics, revealing orientations that would be seen in all their subsequent work.
4. Hans Jonas took gnostic thought and the hermeneutics of dogma as his starting point in investigating the possibility of faith. He explained his personal journey retrospectively in a 1976 article in memory of Rudolf Bultmann, "Im Kampf um die Möglichleit des Glaubens." Although Hannah Arendt was unwilling to address the Jewish Question in itself and for herself, she did wonder, "How should one do theology if one is Jewish?" See her reflections on this question in "Seule demeure la langue maternelle," televised interview with Günthur Gaus in *La tradition cachée* (1987; new ed., Paris: Bourgeois, 1993).
5. Arendt, "Seule demeure la langue maternelle," pp. 241–242.
6. Cf. Sylvie Courtine-Denamy, *Trois femmes dans des sombres temps: Édith Stein, Hannah Arendt, Simone Weil* (Paris: Albin Michel, 1997), p. 152.
7. Cf. Elisabeth Young Bruehl, *Hannah Arendt: For Love of the World* (New York: Yale University Press, 1982).
8. Cf. Emil Fackenheim, *La pensée de Dieu dans l'histoire*, preface by Bernard Dupuy (Paris: Verdier, 1976); reissued in paperback under the title *Penser la Shoah* (Paris: du Cerf, 1990).
9. Hans Jonas, *The Phenomenon of Life: Toward a Philosophical Biology* (New York: Harper & Row, 1963).
10. Hans Jonas, *The Gnostic Religion: The Message of the Alien God and the Beginnings of Christianity* (Gloucester, Mass.: Peter Smith, 1976).
11. It has recently been strongly stressed that the Bible's approach is far from an ontology that would situate evil within the being as *substance*; rather, it condemns evil as affecting man as *subject*. Human wickedness is tackled in the perspective of

people's particular fate, and henceforth human history, through the fate of a tiny people which condemns it, appears as the meta-empirical history of a struggle between
good and evil. Cf. Bernard Sichère, "Le dire juif du mal," in *Histoires du mal* (Paris:
Grasset, 1995), pp. 65–86.

12. See the 1962 correspondence between Hans Jonas and Rudolf Bultmann,
Zwischen Nichts und Ewigkeit. Zur Lehre vom Menschen (Göttingen: Vandenhoeck
und Ruprecht, 1963).

13. Hans Jonas, *Le concept de Dieu après Auschwitz: Une voix juive* (Paris: Payot,
Rivages-Poche, 1994).

14. Louis Bouyer had pointed out that for several centuries the words of the Lord's
Prayer, *Libera nos a Malo* ("Deliver us from the evil one") have customarily been
translated as "Deliver us from evil," which tends to make the reality of evil abstract.
See Louis Bouyer, "Le problème du mal dans le christianisme antique," *Dieu Vivant*
6:15–42.

15. Cf. Hans Jonas, *Entre le néant et l'éternité* (Paris: Belin, 1996). This refers to the
theology of the Patripassians, who believed that Jesus' body escaped suffering and
was exempted from the experience of death. They attributed the suffering on the cross
to the wishes of God the Father, thereby removing expiation from history.

16. Against the Patripassians, a certain Leontius of Byzantium stated that immortality, or rather incorruptibility (*aphtharsia*), could not be received as a word from heav-
en or a pure gift of God, if humanity has not been put to the test. He set a time of
"divine silence" at the heart of human history, a silence that presides over the ordeal
of martyrs and the release of bound souls from hell (1 Peter 3:19). In this interval,
Christ was "the support of those who are standing, and the righting of those who have
fallen." Leontius argued that at the end of his mission on earth, Christ had accomplished the extermination of the devil, the consignment of the Antichrist to nothingness, and the extinction of all prospects of punishment (*Patrologia Graeca*,
86:1248–1372).

17. "On ne prononcera jamais le kaddish" (June 19, 1942); translated and reprinted
in Hannah Arendt, *Auschwitz et Jérusalem* (Paris: Deux Temps Tierce, 1991), p. 40.

18. "*Le Vicaire*, un silence coupable?" (February 23, 1964); reprinted in *Auschwitz et
Jérusalem*, p. 228.

19. Ibid.

20. Hannah Arendt, *On Revolution* (New York: Viking, 1963).

21. Hannah Arendt, *The Human Condition* (Chicago: University of Chicago, 1958).

22. Hannah Arendt, *Eichmann in Jerusalem: A Report on the Banality of Evil* (New
York: Viking, 1964).

23. Hannah Arendt, "La responsibilité collective," published in *Ontologie et poli-
tique: Actes du Colloque Hannah Arendt (Paris 1988)* (Paris: Tierce, 1989); new ed.,
Pensée et polique (Paris: Payot, 1996), p. 177.

24. Arendt, *Human Condition*.

25. French translation in Gershom Scholem, *Fidélité et utopie: Essais sur le judaïsme
contemporain* (Paris: Calman-Lévy, 1978), pp. 222–228.

Auschwitz as Crucial Experiment:
The Lord's Suffering Servant in the Interpretation of André Neher and Emmanuel Levinas

Irene Kajon

The article is divided into three parts: the first discusses the question of the various meanings that can be given to the phrase "good and evil after Auschwitz"; the second is devoted to the reflection on ethicality carried out by André Neher and Emmanuel Levinas with reference to the figure of the Lord's Suffering Servant found in Isaiah; and the third focuses on the problems raised by this reflection.

REMEMBERING AUSCHWITZ AS A METHOD FOR REFLECTING ON THE HUMAN SPIRIT

I would start by ruling out two possible meanings of the formula "good and evil after Auschwitz." These would see it as inviting us to view Auschwitz (a) as a terrible event, in which the depth of desperation is certainly touched, but from which knowledge of good and evil can rise again, or (b) as an event that can be the source of a new morality among human beings. With regard to the former, it must be strongly reiterated that no redemption can ever flow from the unspeakable suffering of totally innocent men, women, and children; and with regard to the latter, that from very earliest times humanity has had knowledge of what good and evil are, however often it has failed to articulate this knowledge clearly or to act in conformity with it. I should like to quote Leo Strauss to help explain the reasons leading me to reject these two interpretations of the phrase under consideration. He writes as follows about the impossibility of drawing salvation from what is opaque:

> It is safer to try to understand the low in the light of the high than the high in the light of the low. In doing the latter one necessarily distorts the high, whereas in doing the former one does not deprive the low of the freedom to reveal itself fully as what it is.[1]

Thus he writes as follows about the universality of ethicality in human history:

> Such distinctions as those between courage and cowardice, justice and injustice, human kindness and selfishness, gentleness and cruelty, urbanity and rudeness, are intelligible and clear for all practical purposes, that is, in most cases, and they are of decisive importance in guiding our lives: this is a sufficient reason for considering the fundamental political questions in their light.[2]

However, a third meaning can be given to the expression in question, and this is the one I want to follow: Auschwitz is an event which, precisely because it is abnormal, can be seen as an experience capable of showing us essential aspects of the human spirit, and hence of bringing our knowledge of good and evil into sharper focus. As natural scientists can tell us, experiments do not distort the phenomena of which the law is being sought, but are, on the contrary, helpful in the effort to reach a more precise definition of this law. In the central chapter of *If This Is a Man*, which is entitled "The Drowned and the Saved," the chemist Primo Levi views Auschwitz as an experiment:

> . . . we can perhaps ask ourselves if it is necessary or good to retain any memory of this exceptional human state. To this question we feel that we have to reply in the affirmative. We are in fact convinced that no human experience is without meaning or unworthy of analysis, and that fundamental values, even if they are not positive, can be deduced from this particular world which we are describing. We would also like to consider that the Lager was pre-eminently a gigantic biological and social experiment. Thousands of individuals, differing in age, condition, origin, language, culture and customs, are enclosed within barbed wire: there they live a regular, controlled life which is identical for all and inadequate to all needs, and which is more rigorous than any experimenter could have set up to establish what is essential and what adventitious to the conduct of the human animal in the struggle for life.[3]

In his book Levi shows what is typical of human nature by recalling many significant episodes. Here I would simply draw attention to the sections where he describes acts of goodness (in other words, those performed without any return) and acts of justice (in other words, those giving each person his or her due) that took place first in the concentration camp proper and then during the period after the Germans left the camp and before the Russian army arrived.[4]

Levi uses simple, and hence very effective, language to describe the style of action of a human being who remains faithful to moral ideals and the corresponding affections.

Now if this is the meaning we assign to the phrase "good and evil after Auschwitz"—Auschwitz as an experience that brings out the forms of actions inspired by the notion of moral differences—then anyone intending to reflect on the question of ethicality in human beings cannot ignore the evidence of survivors, just as natural scientists are bound to pay close attention to a crucial experiment. It seems to me that listening to these witnesses represents the first step if contemporary ethics is to set out on the road leading to the actual thing to be determined.

THE INTERPRETATION OF THE LORD'S SUFFERING SERVANT IN NEHER AND LEVINAS

However, the main contemporary schools of ethics—from authors who construct a metaphysics of teleologically oriented Being, following in the footsteps of Aristotelianism or Thomism, to those who appeal to commandments expressed by a divine or human authority, those who appeal to the spontaneity of the subject who is himself capable of defining ethical values (through discursive reason, calculation of utility, intuition, a sentiment of sympathy, or simply an act of free will), and those who relate the moral sphere to sociology or biology or psychology[5]—have not taken the hard and troubling path indicated by the accounts of Holocaust survivors. Few thinkers have faced up to the need to discern a correspondence between what these accounts show and ethical reflection, but Neher and Levinas are among this small group, and in their writings the features of the actions of goodness and justice described by Levi as having taken place in a particular time and place become the features of ethical conduct, as proper to the human condition whatever its possible variations. However, in the books in which they bear Auschwitz particularly in mind as the background to their reflection, neither of them (and I shall return to this at the end of the present article) confines himself to the language that philosophical tradition, from Parmenides to German idealism, Husserl, and Heidegger, has developed to expound a theory of Being.[6] Rather, they make direct reference to the Hebrew Bible, drawing concepts from it, which they define partly with biblical and partly with philosophical terms, although the latter are used in a new context and hence with a different meaning from that assigned to them by philosophers. In order to highlight the specific features of the person who acts morally, they both refer to the Suffering Servant described in Isaiah.

The figure of the Lord's Suffering Servant has inspired a wide range of interpretations in both the Jewish and the Christian sphere. However, Neher and Levinas say that there is only one possible interpretation of this figure from the viewpoint of a biblical exegesis that seeks to take account of the philosophical problem of ethicality: the Suffering Servant represents the one called by a God who is far-off and incomprehensible, or close and capable of transforming the human heart, in order to manifest His glory through him; he is the one who, sick, weak, and lacking in any grace or beauty, suffers for humankind, not because this corresponds to his will, but because he is obliged to do so, albeit in freedom, and indeed acquiring freedom thereby, but who even so cannot give any sense to his suffering, setting it within a plan in which it is seen as a means to an end; he is the one who is first and foremost good, but whose action also makes justice possible on earth, a justice that requires weights and measures suited to what is to be weighed and measured; he is the one who walks in the shadows, but who trusts in the God who commands him not to fear the violence that the world could show him because of his nonviolent action; he is the one who in his life produces fruits that would appear to be lost to a superficial gaze, but that make peace possible even now, both with neighbor and those afar-off. In this interpretation of the Suffering Servant, both Neher and Levinas use the rabbinical concept of suffering for love as unjustified suffering borne for the sake of a neighbor because of a willingness to listen to the divine voice. Neher writes as follows in *The Exile of the Word*:

"sufferings from love," . . . is that absolute readiness of which only the passion of love can provide an example in human experience. The love whose incandescence is awaited in the fires of suffering is not that of man: the man of the first word, whom God seeks out, indicates, lays hold of ("I am the Lord *Thy God*"), the man who is always a second person, who is called upon, who is never alone in his self, whose solitude can be only a mirage and illusion, and who inevitably meets with his Seeker, in embrace or in injury, on the way or by the roadside, as a shepherd or as a wolf, as God or as Satan. The sufferings from love are those of the man who says "Yes" to this word, when it is no longer spoken but is heard across the silence.[7]

Willingness to listen to the Word then gives way, according to Neher, to the activity performed by human intelligence in history, although, as the root of all action, it can never be eliminated: "For the Jewish utopia, heteronomy can be located only behind, on Sinai or in Genesis. Ahead, however, man is alone in the terrifying ambivalence of his autonomy."[8]

Neher's statements here are echoed by those of Levinas in *Otherwise*

Than Being. For Levinas too, the only person who is an ethical subject is the one who is strong enough to pour himself out in favor of another in a "hemophiliac's hemorrhage." And it is only on the basis of such boundless gift of self on the part of the ethical subject that it then becomes possible, through the entrance of the "third" (a third who is, however—from the ideal, if not always the actual, viewpoint—already present in the contact between the "I" and the neighbor), to establish the order of justice, and along with it that of politics, institutions, knowledge, and technical and scientific civilization. For Levinas, the Suffering Servant is both the one who makes expiation for another—for he receives on his face, which is not phenomenon for him, the mark of a Name or of a Him who cannot be compared with any human "him," and who could thus be defined as "illeity"—and the one who acts so that each person should have his or her due, and so that the world of culture should be built up within time. The Lord's Suffering Servant does not utter any speech as a response to what is asked of him. However, the whole language in all its various articulations is derived from his silence, or from his only apparently rudimentary or faltering words—the act of offering himself, a simple yes, a short phrase that indicates his setting himself at service. The saying that says nothing is thus at the root of the saying that expresses a content, or rather of the "said" in dialogue, monologue, or writing. According to Levinas, the Suffering Servant does not live in the dimension of being, grasped by perception or consciousness, but above all in that of having to be. While remaining in being, he reaches the dimension of having to be, not through practical reason, but through the heart or pure affectivity. He in fact becomes free through the violence or the trauma that the Infinite, which can be determined only partially as having to be (for it contains more than the simple having to be that enters into contact with human existence), performs on him without mediation: the reason that is then awakened in him, as chosen, coincides first and foremost with mercy and then with justice; and the latter is the deepest source of the Logos, as faculty to reflect, reason, and speak. The Suffering Servant is the one who is animated by a spirit that comes to him from a dimension that, although different from that of finiteness, and superior and anterior to it, is present in the human being only when the latter does not abandon such finiteness. He is the one who has the other in himself, who is himself at the moment when the other grasps him as its hostage, and who henceforth, as member of society or humanity, acts for the other: the ethical relationship between the "I" and neighbor as against the far-off person, as distinct beings, can be opened up only on the basis of the conspiracy that challenges the logical law of identity, for in this conspiracy the "I" is "I" precisely when it is "not I" or, in other words, when it is obsessed or troubled by the other, precisely when it lives in the situation of being outside itself or of folly. For Levinas, this is the only way in which human beings can relate themselves to God, first to the Infinite who can never become image, enter the field of vision, or be the object of any subjectivity, however this may be understood—as consciousness or as capacity to divine or perceive—and then to an *Anarché* delineated by a thought aware of its insuperable limits. Thought is indeed linked indissolubly to a life lived in terms of its meaning, in the sphere of having to be approached not as a simple idea, but as present, however different from the manner of phenomena. Levinas writes as follows in *Otherwise Than Being*: "The exteriority of *illeity*, refractory to disclosure and manifestation, is a having-to-be in the face of another. In it there is announced not a *Sollen*, which is always asymptote, but glory."[9] Justice, of course, always entails the risk that the affect of goodness will be replaced by a reflection that sees people only from the viewpoint of their abstract equality, that addressing what is different from being will give rise to a knowledge directed solely to being, and that the nonphysical space set up by contact between human beings will give way to the space of representation or science. However, this risk cannot be completely avoided, except at the cost of mislaying the link between pure ethicality and the course of the world. The main thing for Levinas is to maintain the awareness that mercy, as an affect that is nonbiological or nonsociological but belongs to a pure sensitivity, has to remain the root of any human attitude to the world. The Lord's Suffering Servant is the model to which we have to look if we are not to lose this awareness: "This exposure without anything held back at the very spot where the trauma is produced, a cheek offered already to the smiter, is sincerity as saying, witnessing to the glory of the infinite."[10]

In their interpretation of the central chapters of the Book of Isaiah, Neher and Levinas thus analyze the forms in which ethicality is found. And what they describe turns out to correspond most closely—as could easily be shown by a comparison—to what Levi describes in his account of episodes in which, despite a very difficult situation, some people show themselves equal to what the term "humanity" signifies.

TWO OBJECTIONS TO NEHER'S AND LEVINAS'S REFLECTION ON GOOD AND EVIL, AND RELEVANT COUNTER-OBJECTIONS

Neher's and Levinas's reflection on ethics give rise to many questions, at least two of which must be faced because they appear to constitute a decisive criticism of this reflection.

The first objection can be expressed as follows: If in actual fact, as the two authors themselves maintain, absolute openness and availability to others always goes together with the movement of closing of subjectivity in itself, because of the need either for comparison between near and far in discussion and mediation, or for the activity to be performed in a world that still opposes the good, is it not inevitable that the sphere of ethics should be seen as suspended between goodness, as only indicated, and recognition of Others as an "I" like the "I" that performs this recognition, and the moral subject should thus be seen as suspended ambiguously between being fixed inasmuch as he gives of his own, even to the extent of giving himself, and constituting himself as person before any relationship with other persons? Is it not then a question of finding that in which the human consists in what is set ambiguously between ethics and ontology? Is goodness, which calls for the eclipse of self in favor of Others, not always set within society, in other words, in a sphere in which human beings are seen in relation with one another as distinct "I"'s? In empirical reality, are love and justice not inseparable, just as it is impossible to separate being referred to a "beyond" with respect to the visible being, and being assigned necessarily to the sphere of perception, representation, or awareness? Surely therefore we have to replace the extreme theory of ethicality proposed by Neher and Levinas, under which the immediate touching of the finite and the Infinite in love is the only thing that allows justice, and not only goodness, to manifest itself in the world. In this theory, on the one hand, the Infinite enters into the finite in a way that cannot do without appearance or manifestation, and, on the other, this appearance or manifestation of the Infinite in the finite does not entail the total pouring out or denial of self of the former in the latter. Would ethicality not then take the form of a co-presence, or balance—one that, of course, has to be precisely determined each time—between the demand to give and to forgive, and the demand to satisfy the requests put forward by each "I"? Surely this is the only way of escaping, on the one hand, from an ethics that places such stress on the subjection or subordination of the subject that it threatens to make it incapable of any action in history, and, on the other, from an ethics that confines itself to observing the need for a peaceful coexistence between individuals inasmuch as they are already given and formed.

The second possible objection to the ethics propounded by Neher and Levinas concerns its internal inconsistency and can be expressed as follows: When thought constructs a doctrine, how can it appeal to a fact that is prior to itself and entails its own negation—for this fact takes the shape of affectivity, however unnatural—without contradicting itself? Are those who use the weapons of philosophical reasoning not inevitably led to appeal to philosophical reasoning itself as their final point of reference? Is a theory that appeals to pure affect as a fundamental quality of human beings not bound to be led to destruction of the value of the theory itself, and thus forced to forgo presenting itself through the instruments of analysis and demonstration as used by reason? Can reason legitimately appeal to the heart not as a subjective sphere—and one that thus evades its grasp—but as a sphere on which to reflect and even to be taken as the basis of its very existence? And, if we accept that the heart finds its primary expression in the Hebrew Bible, is it permissible for philosophy to presuppose this text as the object of interpretation without giving up its claims to be a science? In this case, is thought not finally forced to make itself dependent on the dimensions of obscurity or of enigmatic or even incomprehensible words?

Both objections to the ethics of Neher and Levinas have indeed been raised.[11] However, it could be argued against the first that if goodness and justice, ethicality and knowledge, the subject who is absolutely humble and the subject who is active in the world, and the Infinite who is absolutely different from any phenomenon and the Infinite who becomes the object of representation and thought, are not initially distinct but always refer to one another in a single complex experience, is there not a danger that what constitutes particularly the whole psychic aspect of human beings will lose its specificity? Is there not a danger then, first, that goodness will become confused with self-affirmation in being, and second, that justice will become confused with self-eradication, so that, on the one hand, the relationship between the "I" and Others will be transformed into a special case of the relationship between distinct "I"s, and, on the other, the relationship between members of society will be transformed into an expansion or extension of the relationship between the "I" and Others? Is there not such a difference between goodness and justice, and between the sphere of having to be and that of being, that although it allows them to meet, it does not allow their mediation in a third term that would contain both in their stretching toward one another despite their diversity?

Some counter-objections can also be raised to the second objection. Does the heart or the Hebrew Bible not constitute the life that necessarily precedes philosophy, if the latter is seen not as a doctrine enclosing the All and based on itself, but as having its origin in the human being conceived as an integral whole? Does philosophy not depend, then, less on autonomous reason than on the fact that it consists of trust nourished in reason in place that is life itself, having moral experience in itself? Does philosophy not entail, then, a choice that allows other choices, all equally subjective, to exist alongside itself, while, vice versa, a philosophy that presupposes the universal reality of the ethical event—which, despite their insoluble and dramatic tension as opposites, entails affect and intelligence, living in contact with God and in the world, an attitude of listening and critical independence—appears to be the sole one capable of avoiding subjectivism? In this case, is not the present period of Jewish history, in which the memory of Auschwitz is strongly present as a crucial episode in human history, the first in which the Hebrew Bible can be put forward as an invitation to examine the ethical event as a presupposition for a philosophy that would otherwise become either an abstract speculation based solely on reason, or the expression of a solely personal state of mind? Insofar as Neher and Levinas focus on the notions of good and evil, they also offer a philosophy that intends to move beyond the philosophy of the past; and in this undertaking they use a special language that draws its inspiration both from Scripture and from philosophy, and that is at last extinguished in silence—the silence to which human beings are finally reduced when faced either with the victims of Auschwitz or with the unutterable Name.

NOTES

1. Leo Strauss, preface to Spinoza's *Critique of Religion* (New York: Schocken Books, 1965) 2.
2. Leo Strauss, "On Classical Political Philosophy" (1945), in *What Is Political Philosophy?* (Glencoe, Ill.: Free Press, 1959), p. 89.
3. Primo Levi, *Survival in Auschwitz* (New York: Touchstone, 1996), p. 87. (English translation first published under the title *If This Is a Man*.)
4. See the chapters entitled "The Canto of Ulysses," "The Events of the Summer," "Kraus," and "The Story of Ten Days."
5. For an analysis of the teachings of such authors, see E. Lecaldano, "Etica," in P. Rossi, ed., *La Filosofia* (Turin: Utet, 1995), 3.323–436.
6. For example, see André Neher, *The Exile of the Word: From the Silence of the Bible to the Silence of Auschwitz* (Philadelphia: Jewish Publication Society of America, 1981); and Emmanuel Levinas, *Otherwise Than Being; or, Beyond Essence* (The Hague: Martinus Nijloff Publishers, 1987).
7. Neher, *Exile of the Word*, p. 197.
8. Ibid., p. 190.
9. Levinas, *Otherwise Than Being*, p. 193, n. 35.
10. Ibid., p. 145.
11. See, for the first objection, M. M. Olivetti, *Analogia del soggetto* (Rome: Laterza, 1992); and for the second, J. Derrida, "Violence et métaphysique: Essai sur la pensée de Levinas," *Revue de Métaphysique et de Morale* 59 (1964): 322–354, 425–473.

PART IV
Within the Shoah

Remembrance and Responsibility:
Rescuers of Jews During the Shoah

Eva Fleischner

A word about my title. Remembrance looks back to the past, responsibility looks to the present and future, and asks, What can we learn from the past? What interests us here is not the past as past, but the light it sheds on the present and future.

In this paper I shall explore only one aspect of our remembrance of the Shoah: the rescuers of Jews, and what we can learn from them. "There are no longer any camps in Germany, or even . . . in Russia, although some still remain . . . elsewhere. We have a different battle to fight, and it is far from over. It is taking place in our memories of the past, in the judgments we bring to bear on it, and in the lessons we draw from it."[1] Some of these lessons can be learned from the rescuers.

Let me make a personal comment at the beginning of this paper. There is today a large and still growing body of literature on rescuers. I find in it much that is helpful. But what has influenced me most deeply is my personal encounter with some rescuers in France: women and men of every state in life, of every social background (although all of them were Roman Catholic; that was the nature of my research).[2] I dedicate this paper to them.

Although they differ greatly from one another, we can make some general comments about the rescuers.

Without exception, they see themselves as ordinary people, not as heroes or saints. They were not "bigger than life, but remained life-size in a time when most people were diminished by terror."[3] What they did appeared to them, under the circumstances, as the most normal thing to do. Perhaps the best-known example of this is Magda Trocmé, wife of André Trocmé, the Protestant pastor of Le Chambon-sur-Lignon. Thirty years after the event she described the first time she had helped a Jew in Le Chambon:

> It was already dark, a very cold winter night. Magda, working in her kitchen, heard a knock at the side door. A woman stood in the doorway. "She said she was a German Jew, coming from the north of France; that she was in danger, and that she had heard that in Le Chambon somebody could help.

Could she come into my house? I said, 'Naturally, come in, come in.' Lots
of snow. She had a thin pair of shoes, nothing else, that was all."[4]

I want to give two examples also from Frenchwomen I met. The first is
Germaine Ribière. When I asked her how it was that she was never arrested,
she answered:

> I think it was simply because I lived all this as the life of everyday. I did
> what had to be done, but I was not rash or careless. I did not take useless
> risks, I was aware of the consequences. We had a work to do. . . . There was
> nothing extraordinary about what I did, about the way I lived, during the war.
> I did what was required at the moment, you simply face life as it comes.
> Nothing extraordinary about it . . .[5]

The second is Marie-Rose Gineste (both women have been honored by
Yad Vashem). She wrote in her Mémoire many years later:

> I have probably forgotten some facts and events, never mind. What mat-
> ters is not to talk about them, but to have lived them, to have acted as I did
> during that period of underground struggle, during those four years which
> were a high point of my life. I believe I may say that during those years my
> actions were ordinary ones, actions of every day . . . [6]

I am not aware of a single instance in which a rescuer has come forward
on his or her own, to tell of what they did, or to ask for recognition. On the
contrary. Many have never spoken, or spoken only when sought out by some
researcher. They have shunned publicity; they feel uncomfortable with the
title "Righteous" (or "Just") "among the Nations." While no one ever refused
my request to meet with them I often encountered an initial reluctance or hesitation: "I don't have much to tell you, I really didn't do anything." Or, "I did
so little, given all there was to do." They wanted no memorials, no buildings
or plaques, named after them. And there were none, for many years.
Fortunately, for us and for the world, there was, and is, Jewish memory, the
remembrance and gratitude of those they had saved. There is Yad Vashem,
with its Avenue of the Just, its forest—growing vaster each year—of trees
planted in their honor, each tree bearing the name of a rescuer; its Department
of the Righteous, established in 1953 and maintained by the Israeli government, for the sole purpose of finding rescuers and honoring their memories.
    I had a moving experience of this Jewish memory not long ago, when I
spoke about French Catholic rescuers at the U.S. Holocaust Memorial

Museum in Washington. Part of my talk dealt with the failure, the silence, of the French hierarchy. I spoke of the few who did speak out, in the late summer of August 1942: of Archbishop Saliège of Toulouse and Bishop Théas of Montauban; of three other bishops who protested soon after. And I concluded by saying, "There were only five, five out of eighty." After my lecture a gentleman came up to me and said: "I must add an important footnote to what you said. You were too hard on the French bishops, there were more than five." And he proceeded to tell me how he himself had been saved, along with five hundred other Jewish children, thanks to a rescue operation quietly organized by Mgr. Paul Rémond, bishop of Nice. Little is known of this story so far, but I have no doubt that, thanks to M. Julien Engel's efforts, it will be told one of these days.

An important note concerning the French bishops should be added here. A few days after the closing, in Rome, of the symposium at which this paper was delivered, the bishops met at Drancy, a Paris suburb, and issued a lengthy statement of repentance for the failure of their church during the Shoah. The date chosen for this meeting, September 30, 1997, marked the anniversary of the first anti-Jewish legislation by the Vichy government, in 1940. The place was equally significant. During the Occupation some 75,000 Jews, both French and foreign-born, were brought to Drancy to await deportation to the east. Standing in front of a cattle car that has been placed in a park of the town as a memorial to this infamy, the bishops deplored the silence of the church and its long history of anti-Judaism. "Today we confess that this silence was an error. We implore God's forgiveness and ask the Jewish people to hear these words of repentance."[7]

To return to my main point: they saw themselves as ordinary women and men, doing simply what had to be done. Should we see them as they see themselves, as ordinary? Yes and no. Yes: If we make them into heroes they become distant from us, they have nothing in common with us; we admire them from afar precisely because they are better, more courageous, than we are. This absolves us too easily. For if, ever since the Shoah, we are left to wonder, in fear and trembling, if we would have been among the bystanders had we been there as non-Jews, we also may wonder, in hope, if we would have been among the rescuers. Or, more to the point, if we would be among them at another time and in another place. We must guard, then, against the temptation to see them as extraordinary.

And yet . . . They obviously were different in some way from the rest of "ordinary men" who stood by, or even assisted, often willingly, in the slaughter.[8] They were ordinary, and not ordinary.

Another characteristic. They were nonviolent, they refused to make war. They did not carry weapons (except "Weapons of the Spirit," the beautiful title of the film about Le Chambon by Pierre Sauvage). Most of them did not even know how to shoot. They refused to meet evil with evil. They refused to hate. Let me quote here from my interviews.

Germaine Ribière told me: "In the presence of hatred I feel an icy chill. . . . Hatred is not the world of God, it is the refusal of God."[9] And Marie-Rose Gineste wrote: "My commitment, my actions, were in no way motivated by hatred. I do not think I ever felt hate toward anyone."[10]

They refused to take up arms, to fight evil with evil. They did not stop the war, nor the murder of millions; they did not stop the genocide. What, then, did they achieve? They saved human lives, in some cases one single human life. If that seems a small, a humble achievement let us recall the saying of one of the ancient rabbis: "Whoever saves one human life, it is as though they saved the entire world." Human life was of supreme value to them. The lives of Jews most often, because Jews were the most exposed of all of Hitler's victims, but not exclusively of Jews.

And so they acted, when most people stood by. They did something, when most people did nothing. They did not try to save everyone, because they could not. But they saved someone, or some.

To save lives, to alleviate what suffering they could, was of more importance to many rescuers than were abstract ideas or ideology, such as resistance, or even religion. Magda Trocmé's daughter Nelly wrote of her mother: "Her dedication was not because of religion, it was because of people."[11] This was often true even of priests and religious. Two examples:

Daniel Pézeril was an auxiliary bishop of Paris about to retire when I met him in 1986; during the war he had been a young priest in a parish near the Sorbonne. He had helped many Jews. One of them, a scientist, wanted to thank the priest at the end of the war, along with his friends. After toasting Fr. Pézeril, the man asked, "What made you help us, Father?" The priest thought for a while, then answered that he had helped because the persecution of Jews violated every human right, it was an outrage. Then he added, "Also, because for me you are the chosen people."[12] His desire to help the persecuted comes before any religious motive. This is also true of Fr. Albert Gau, of Carcassonne. When I asked him why he had helped to save Jews, he answered, "Because they were hunted, they suffered so much."[13]

While the humanitarian motive was primary for many, some acted out of a deep, conscious Christian faith and love of Christ. My most striking example of such a person is Germaine Ribière. I want to read a few passages from an unpublished document, a journal she kept during the war; a simple black notebook with handwritten entries. She was living in Paris at the time, twenty-two years old, a student at the Sorbonne.[14] On May 14, 1941 she learned that 7,000 Jews in the Marais (the Jewish quarter of Paris) had been rounded up. "Most of them are said to be Polish Jews, and the poorest ones at that. Has the great dance begun in France? I ache for them in my whole being. I ache for my Jewish brothers and sisters. My God, give me strength."

May 27, 1941. . . . The tide is rising, rising. I am afraid that one of these days, when we wake up, it will be too late and we shall all have become Nazis. I am afraid, because people are asleep. Those who should keep watch are the ones who put others to sleep. We must speak the truth no matter what the cost. But who will do it? I know there are Christians who are willing to accept martyrdom if necessary; but they do not know what is happening. They wait for a voice, and the voice does not speak. We must pray that it will speak . . .

June 1941. I am in Paris for a few days [she had meanwhile moved to Lyon, headquarters of the Resistance]. . . . I have the impression that the earth is shaking, and I am shaking along with it. . . . Often I long to go away, all alone. But this would be running away. The world is our stage leading to God. We must not burn this stage, we must live it to the best of our ability.

March 24, 1942. Persecution of the Jews. Christ suffers in his body, and we Christians stand by and watch. I do not want to be a spectator. . . . Yesterday I visited Rabbi Deutsch [of Limoges]. I told him to make use of me in any way he can. I am willing to do anything for them, with the help of God. I cannot run away.

March 25, 1942. There is no way out. Humanity is the body of Christ. One part of that humanity is being tortured, those who are Jews. And we look on in silence as the crime is being perpetrated. We are the accomplices of evil, and we are at peace.

It is the body of Christ himself that is being tortured. We say that we believe in Christ, that we love him; yet we allow him to be despised. No, I cannot tolerate this silence, I cannot lie. I shall go all the way, with the help of God.

April 24, 1942. Since my last entry this immense history of the Jewish people continues. Man sinks each day more deeply into the swamp of sin.

The camps continue to run, the world of Satan heaves beneath our feet. But Christ will conquer in the end.

June 11, 1942. The problem of the Jews—no, the mystery of the Jews. The mystery of the human being. I try to confront all this. Always alone, in solitude, alone with Christ.

February 4, 1943. Every day the evil grows. Nazism tightens its grip, and Catholics are asleep. . . . We are told to bear witness to Christ. I am tired of this ridiculous prudence, of this fear of physical death!

What enabled her to see so clearly, and to act, when so many others were "asleep"? I posed this question to her, and she answered simply:

Christ. I come from a region of France [the Limousin] where there are vineyards. Jesus' parable of the vine and the branches was perfect for me. I knew what a vine is. Humanity is the body of Christ. I felt as if I were holding the vine and the branches in my hand. . . . How could I deny this relationship?

It was in this relationship that her deep sense of human solidarity was grounded. Solidarity with the Jewish people, but also with her fellow Catholics.

With the Jewish people: She feels their suffering as her own. "I ache for them in my whole being, I ache for my Jewish brothers and sisters" (May 14, 1941). "Persecution of the Jews. Christ suffers in his body" (May 14, 1941). "There is no way out. Humanity is the body of Christ. One part of that humanity is being tortured, those who are Jews" (March 25, 1942). "The problem of the Jews—No, the mystery of the Jews. The mystery of the human being" (June 11, 1942).

Her solidarity with her fellow Catholics is equally evident. She sees the failure of the church very clearly and suffers from it. But she never points the finger, she always says "we." "I am afraid that one of these days, when we wake up, it will be too late and we shall all have become Nazis" (May 27, 1941). The Jews are being tortured, "and we look on in silence. . . . We are accomplices of evil, and we are at peace" (March 25, 1942), etc. Many years later, reflecting on the war years, she tells of an instance when she was harassed by a French lieutenant for trying to help Jews. And she comments: "You see the kind of French people we were!" One might expect her to say "they" rather than "we." But she does not make the clear-cut distinction between collaborators and herself that one would expect. Her "we" is an expression of her deep sense of solidarity—in this case with the sins and failures of her own people, whether in her church or her country. She was wide awake, but the country was asleep, and this involved her also. "We say that we believe in Christ, that we love him, yet we allow him to be despised" (March 25, 1942). Just as the suffering of the Jews is, for her, part of the suffering of all humanity, of which she is a member, so too the sins of the bystanders and perpetrators are the sins of all, herself included.

And yet, she refuses to judge, to condemn, to hate. Instead, she weeps at the misery she sees all around her. "The human being is weak, miserable, sinful. And I am called to enter into this misery, into this sin."[15]

There is a remarkable consistency in the life of this woman. I mentioned earlier that the actions of the rescuers were often spontaneous gut reactions to a crisis. In Germaine's case I think they could have been foreseen, her whole life was of a piece. She often used the phrase "being faithful" in our conversations.

> I think I understood in those days that I could not be faithful. No matter what the cost. . . . When one has touched life at such a depth, when one has seen such destruction . . . Not to be faithful would be to lie to oneself. Inconsistency is not possible. . . . "Whoever says he/she loves God and does not love his/her brother or sister is a liar." We are miserable sinners, yes. But this fundamental refusal, No.[16]

A brief episode on the occasion of our first meeting further illustrates this consistency. We had arranged, at her suggestion, to meet for noon Mass and then have lunch together. We were walking to the restaurant, engrossed in conversation, when she suddenly interrupted herself. "I am worried about this little girl, I wonder if she has lost her mother." I had noticed, vaguely, a small girl in front of us, about two years old, but I had not really "seen" her. Germaine had seen, and worried. As it turned out, the mother was close by, walking ahead of the child. As I came to know her in the months that followed, and to learn of the extraordinary things she had done during the war, I realized how much of a piece she is. She is Germaine Ribière because she notices a little girl who may be lost and in need of her help, in the middle of Paris in 1985, just as the Jews needed her help during the war.[17]

I mentioned earlier that none of the rescuers ever sought rewards for what they had done. They sought no tangible rewards. But one reward was theirs. They were at peace with themselves, because they knew they had done the right thing; they had been true to their deepest selves. I found evidence of this in my interviews. I would often ask, "Would you do it again if you had to?" And without exception, the answer was always an immediate yes. Indeed, some spoke of those long-ago years as the best time in their lives, "one of the high points of my life" (Marie-Rose Gineste). For Germaine, not to have acted as she did would have been to lie, to deny her very being.

I am faced with a question at this point. Why they, and not the many others, the "ordinary" people? Research into the rescuers is giving us some insights into an answer.[18] Certain experiences seem to favor altruistic behavior, such as a happy and secure childhood, encounters with other social, cultural, or religious persons or groups, a habit of not conforming to the norm, etc. We need to learn more about what makes people good and merciful. And yet, in the final analysis, I am not sure that we really have a complete answer. Can we ever, with certainty, know ahead of time how we will respond? Perhaps in the case of a few (e.g., Germaine Ribière); but always?

André Stein writes that his encounter with rescuers has made it impossible for him any longer to believe that evil is absolute, a belief he had held all his life until then. " . . . if that is so, what is to prevent yesterday's bystander, or even perpetrator, from becoming tomorrow's rescuer?"[19] The question seemed shocking to me at first. But a story told by Viktor Frankl has helped me to take it seriously. It is a true story, it happened to him.[20]

The war had ended; Frankl had returned from Auschwitz and was once again practicing as a psychiatrist in Vienna. One day an Austrian diplomat came to see him as a patient; the man had shortly before returned from captivity in Moscow. As they talked, the diplomat asked Frankl whether by chance he had ever come across or heard of a certain Doctor X. Yes, Frankl answered, he had known him well.

> Dr. X had been a colleague of mine for many years before the war, we worked in the same psychiatric hospital. For me he was the epitome, the embodiment, of evil: an opportunist who would stop at nothing, who would step over dead bodies to get ahead. And indeed, my impression was borne out. After the Anschluss X was put in charge of the whole Nazi euthanasia program in Austria for the mentally ill. He used to drive into the countryside to ferret out some mentally sick person who was living quietly on a farm, and bring them back, straight to the gas chambers that had been set up for that purpose. A monster if ever there was one.
>
> At the end of the war he was arrested and placed in solitary confinement in Steinhof. . . . Suddenly, one day, he was gone. We all assumed that, as a former member of the SS, he had escaped to South America.

And now I discovered, from my patient, that X had ended up in a Russian prison. I asked him, "What kind of a man was he?" expecting the worst. The answer was totally unexpected. "An angel! You cannot imagine how good he was to all of us! He helped us in every way he could, medically; he comforted us. Never have I experienced such kindness and solidarity! He was an angel of mercy!"

"And I had been prepared," Frankl continues, "to deny this man all possibility of ever changing."

No one could have foreseen the extraordinary transformation that took place in this man. The example is extreme, yet it may point to the fact that we touch here the mystery of the human being, or what some of us call "grace."

What are some conclusions we can draw, some lessons we can learn, from studying the rescuers?

No matter how inspiring their stories, no matter how many there were, we are still left with the tragic fact that there were so few, far too few. Charlotte Delbo, survivor of Auschwitz, writes: "Looking at people I meet I wonder, Would he have helped me walk, that one? Would he have given me a little of his water? I study the faces of all the people I see. . . . Those about whom I know from the very first glance that they would have helped me walk are so few."[21] There were so few. We have no guarantee that there will be more the next time.

This means that we must not allow anyone, or any group, to be at the mercy of, to be dependent on, the goodwill of a few. We must create societies in which the human rights of all will be safeguarded by social, political, and legal structures that are just; societies in which no one will be a second-class citizen, at the mercy of the state.

At the same time, the rescuers tell us by their actions that it is possible not to cooperate with an evil system. "They become a guarantee, a pledge, for our humanity."[22] We need not look as far as the camps for acts of injustice, we are surrounded by them, daily. We are surrounded by apathy, including our own. We resign ourselves to wars, to massacres, to ethnic cleansing, to the ghettos of our inner cities, to the plight of refugees and immigrants. And the explanations we give for doing nothing are not really different from those given by the masses of ordinary men (and women) during the Shoah: "I didn't know," "I couldn't do anything," "It wouldn't make any difference," etc. Todorov says that "totalitarianism reveals what democracy leaves in the shadows—that at the end of the path of indifference and conformity lies the concentration camp."[23] The rescuers teach us that this is not inevitable, that we can walk another path. It is possible for us to expand our circle of care and concern beyond those who are by nature or blood close to us, beyond its usual limits; to live in solidarity with those we do not know, who thereby cease to be strangers to us. It has been said that in the 1930s and 1940s Jews had difficulty passing as non-Jews, not because of any facial characteristics or dress, but because of the look of deep sadness in their eyes. Can we learn to recognize that look, and allow ourselves to be moved by it?

A former rescuer, now an old woman, has said that "there is no good news about the Holocaust."[24] Indeed, the overwhelmingly dominant theme of the Shoah is not life but death—murder, brutality, inhumanity. To lose sight of this or be unwilling to confront it is to distort the terrible reality that was the Shoah. There was a time, immediately following the end of the war and the opening of the camps, when almost no one dared speak of Auschwitz. Little by little the world found the strength to confront the evil. Then there came a time when almost no one dared speak of goodness, out of a fear that to do so would trivialize or minimize the evil. Today we are perhaps better able to do justice to both the evil and the good. While there is no common measure or comparison between them, goodness was at work in humanity even in that dark time. We dare not speak of "good news" as we look back to that terrible world, nor of optimism. But, perhaps, as we remember the rescuers, we dare speak of hope.

NOTES

1. Tzvetan Todorov, *Facing the Extreme: Moral Life in the Concentration Camps* (New York: Henry Holt, 1996), p. 254.
2. This research was funded by a grant from the Vidal Sassoon International Center for the Study of Antisemitism, in Jerusalem.
3. Mary Jo Leddy, in the foreword to André Stein, *Quiet Heroes* (New York: New York University Press, 1988), p. 3.
4. In Philip Hallie, *Lest Innocent Blood Be Shed* (New York: San Francisco, London, 1979), p. 120.
5. Germaine Ribière, in Xavier de Montcols et al., eds., *Eglises et Chrétiens dans la IIe Guerre Mondiale. La Région Rhône-Alpes* (Lyon: Presses Universitaires, 1978), p. 205. Translation by the author.
6. Mémoire, unpublished.
7. See *Le Monde*, September 30, October 1 and 2, 1997; *New York Times*, Week in Review, October 19, 1997, pp. 1 and 4. For the full text, in English, of the statement, see *Origins* 27, no. 18 (October 16, 1997).

8. The reference is to Christopher Browning, *Ordinary Men* (New York: Harper Collins, 1992), and to Daniel Jonah Goldhagen, *Hitler's Willing Executioners: Ordinary Germans and the Holocaust* (New York: Alfred A. Knopf, 1996).

9. Conversation with Eva Fleischner, Paris, December 18, 1985.

10. Marie-Rose Gineste, Mémoire.

11. Hallie, *Lest Innocent Blood Be Shed*, p. 156.

12. Conversation with Eva Fleischner, Paris, August 28, 1986.

13. Conversation with Eva Fleischner, Carcassonne, November 4, 1985.

14. Some passages from this journal are quoted in my article "Can the Few Become the Many?" in *Remembering for the Future* I (New York: Pergamon Press, 1989), pp. 232–247.

15. Conversation with Eva Fleischner.

16. Conversation with Eva Fleischner.

17. This incident is mentioned in my "Can the Few Become the Many?" in *Remembering for the Future*, p. 237. For her work in rescuing Jews, Germaine Ribière was honored by Yad Vashem in March 1968. Many of those she saved were children. See my chapter "Germaine Ribière: I Will Not Be a Bystander!" in *Cries in the Night*, by Michael Phayer and Eva Fleischner (New York: Sheed & Ward, 1997).

18. See, among other works, Philip Friedman, *Their Brothers' Keepers*, 1957; Nechama Tec, *When Light Pierced the Darkness: Christian Rescue of Jews in Nazi-Occupied Poland*, 1986; Samuel Oliner and Pearl Oliner, *The Altruistic Personality: Rescuers of Jews in Nazi Europe*, 1988; André Stein, *Quiet Heroes*, 1988; Gay Block and Malka Drucker, *Rescuers: Portraits of Moral Courage in the Holocaust*, 1992; Mordecai Paldiel, *The Path of the Righteous*, 1993; Eva Fogelman, *Conscience & Courage. Rescuers of Jews during the Holocaust*, 1994; David P. Gushee, *The Righteous Gentiles of the Holocaust*, 1994.

19. Stein, *Quiet Heroes*, p. 310.

20. Lecture by Viktor E. Frankl in Voralberg, November 1987, "Zur Kritik der Kollektivschuldlüge."

21. Charlotte Delbo, *Auschwitz and After* (New Haven: Yale University Press, 1995), p. 254.

22. Leddy, in Stein, *Quiet Heroes*, p. 2.

23. Todorov, *Life in the Extreme*, p. 253.

24. Stein, *Quiet Heroes*, p. 85.

Courage after the Shoah:
Explorations of a Christian Virtue

Michael B. McGarry

Courage is hard to define. Not because we do not recognize it when we see it, but because it cannot be defined and delimited as a specific fact. . . . it is a way of living, which characterizes the whole man.

—Karl Rahner[1]

INTRODUCTION

At this conference exploring "Good and Evil After Auschwitz: Ethical Implications for Today," certainly for Christians after the Shoah the leading ethical implication is to make sure it never happens again.[2]

But there are other ethical implications, important but secondary to the first.

As we seek to understand the Shoah, troubling questions from this tragic event dramatically address us in Western Christendom. It has been said that, in the end, we will understand the Shoah not when we have understood the perpetrators or the victims, but only when we have understood the bystanders. And concerning the bystanders, we can be more precise: How did some bystanders step out from the sidelines to become resisters, helpers, and rescuers.[3]

In recent years, numerous studies have explored the psychological, sociological, and ethical dimensions of those—too few—Gentiles who rescued Jews and other groups threatened and targeted by the Nazis.[4] As we look back on this tragic moment in Christian history, we wish more Christians had been motivated by their faith, had resisted the Nazis' death-dealing efforts, had rescued Jews. But, as a matter of fact, the vast majority of Christians, for whatever reason, did not step forward to resist the Nazis or try to rescue their Jewish neighbors. In rescuer studies, which are both illuminating and frightening for the Christian ethicist, one finds that religious faith played a relatively small conscious role in the motivation of most rescuers who were interviewed and who reflected on their experience.[5] On one level, we can under-

215

stand why so few helped or rescued Jews: the risks were great and the punishments severe. In many countries resistance or offering assistance to Jews and other targeted peoples meant immediate death for oneself and one's family.

We who are Christians are puzzled and discouraged by these findings. So we wonder how, in Germany and neighboring countries, steeped in the Christian tradition, both Roman Catholic and Lutheran, it could have happened that the Jewish people were killed simply for being Jewish. The first answer is that Christians were "not Christian enough": they did not heed the call of their Master in loving their neighbor.[6] Not only, we observe, was Christian faith deficient in stopping the Nazi plague from overwhelming Europe, but many Christians seemed paralyzed or indifferent as they watched their Jewish neighbors herded onto trains for labor and death camps. But moments there were, in Nechama Tec's felicitous phrase, "when light pierced the darkness,"[7] when the too-few Christians stepped from the sidelines to resist the Nazis and to help and, in many cases, rescue Jews.

The factors that moved Christians to rescue behavior were complex; they were theological, economic, sociological, and psychological.

> Often Christians in good conscience decided that they should not (or could not) try to help Jews. Some wanted to help but believed they lacked sufficient opportunity and resources to do so. . . . Others felt profound sympathy for Jews but simply could not muster the courage to risk their own life on Jews' behalf. . . . the historical record indicates that many a Gentile offered help but then backed down when the risks became clearer, and others stood on the brink of rescue but finally turned away in fear of the consequences. Finally, many thoroughly decent people chose not to rescue, not because of a lack of courage but due to the moral conviction that their obligations to their own families and neighbors were primary.[8]

But among the many qualifications and distinctions which must be made, one word keeps surfacing to describe such rescue and helping behavior: "courage." In this "the century of the Shoah,"[9] what is the Christian to make of this? What role does, can faith play in urging Christians to be courageous? How can reflection on the Shoah help chart a way for Christians to value, and take on, courage?

After Auschwitz, one ethical implication, I believe, is that Christians must reflect on courage—the courage of the rescuer, of the few Christians we can retrieve with any pride and gratitude after the Shoah. In exploring courage, we ask what the rescuers possessed that other Christians did not that moved them to risk their lives for their Jewish brothers and sisters, and also how Christians today might learn from the rescuer experience in order to educate and form better Christians for the future, so that, should such horrible experiences arise for another generation, they will not be found wanting.

To explore courage as one Christian ethical implication of the Shoah, I propose the following: to review briefly one classical treatment of courage—that of Thomas Aquinas. Then I will offer a brief summary of rescuer behavior in the light of Thomas's treatment of the virtue of fortitude/courage, noting both what Thomas illuminates and what may be lacking. Then I will suggest, as the beginning of a "pedagogy of courage and compassion" for the post-Shoah Church, some biblical resources. Finally I will offer some practical suggestions for the Christian community that wishes to move itself and its children from being bystanders to being resisters, helpers, and rescuers.

DEVELOPMENT

But what exactly is the courage needed to step from being a bystander to being a resister, a rescuer? What moral strength did rescuers need to assist a neighbor, a stranger who knocked at the door in the middle of the night? How does one teach children to develop such courage, indeed, such holiness?

Virtue, Thomas, and Courage

Over the past few years, prompted in North America by Alasdair MacIntyre's influential *After Virtue*,[10] Christian ethicists have returned to virtue as a primary Christian ethical category.[11] As one contemporary proponent of the return to virtue ethics puts it,

> Virtue ethicists are different. We are not primarily interested in particular actions. We do not ask, is this action right? What are the circumstances around an action? Or, What are the consequences of an action? We are simply interested in persons.
>
> We believe that the real discussion of ethics is not the question what should I do, but who should I become? In fact, virtue ethicists expand that question into three key, related ones: Who am I? Who ought I to become? How am I to get there?[12]

Thus many ethicists, both Roman Catholic and Protestant, are reasserting the importance of virtue as a fruitful direction in place of a more "ethical decision-making" approach.[13] One of our questions—how were the rescuers different, what distinguishes them from nonrescuers—is the character, or virtue, question.

Almost all of these reconsiderations of virtue hearken back to Aristotle as they test, list, and order the virtues of the good person. Further, the writings of Thomas Aquinas, as the primary Christian translator of Aristotle, function as the reference point and distinctly Christian evaluation of the philosopher's work. Aquinas provides one classical consideration of courage which may help us examine the rescuers' quality of courage. It is therefore most appropriate to review, even if superficially, Thomas's treatment of courage. What are its dimensions? What are its distortions? And does the description of courage/fortitude found in Aquinas throw helpful light on the rescuers' reported experiences?

Thomas's treatment of fortitude, one of the four cardinal virtues upon which all other virtues hinge,[14] is found in Questions 123–140, Secunda Secundae of the *Summa Theologica*.[15] Building on Aristotle's consideration of virtue, as found in his *Nicomachean Ethics*, as a general definition, Thomas says that human virtue is "that which makes a man good, and renders his work good" (2ª2ᵃᵉ, Q 123. Resp). As a particular virtue, fortitude[16] is that virtue which "conforms man to reason" to act in the right way especially when human will is hindered to follow the rectitude of reason by "some difficulty that presents itself. In order to remove this obstacle, fortitude of the mind is requisite, whereby to resist the aforesaid difficulty, even as a man, by fortitude of body, overcomes and removes bodily obstacles."[17] That is, just as a man needs strength to lift and sustain a weighty object that stands between him and a particular goal, so does courage deliver strength to remove or overcome obstacles to achieve the good of reason. Thomas further insists that the goodness of the goal accomplished, not its difficulty, is the measure of courage.

Courage correctly guides the person between its excess, foolhardiness, on the one hand, and its deficiency, cowardice, on the other. This virtue may be exercised in a moment's surge of energy, as when a dire situation presents itself (e.g., rushing into a burning building to save a child) or over a long period of time (as someone who endures a lengthy illness with equanimity). As we shall see, both the instantaneous burst of courage and the patient and calculating endurance of courage were present in the rescuer.

Thomas then describes the parts of virtues allied to fortitude: magnanimity (lofty and noble generosity), magnificence ("great making"), patience (bearing pains calmly and without complaint), and perseverance (steadfastness). These strengthen the person to manifest courage when confronted by the threat of death.

Among the distinguishing personal traits of rescuers mentioned later in this paper is competence. Thomas notes that one distinguishing mark of courage is the requirement that, in addition to the inner disposition to take risks for the good, one must also develop and possess skills. "The cultivation of courage . . . unlike the cultivation of most inclinational virtues involves acquiring skills, abilities that aim to produce a product."[18]

Finally, fortitude is always related, positively, to hope and love. That is, one sets aside for the moment obstacles and fear to do the courageous act only in the hope that the goal (e.g., rescue of the threatened person) will be attained and the love toward the other that draws out, and warrants, the risk taking.

While hardly exhaustive, this brief outline offers us a classical schema for our consideration of the courage of those Gentiles who rescued Jews during the Shoah, and, by projection, how we might cull, from the theory and the experience, ways to impart this virtue to us and our children.

Portrait of the Rescuers

One would hardly expect the voice of the rescuer to echo the precise, theoretical language of St. Thomas Aquinas or even that of contemporary ethicists. So we must study the portrait of the rescuer, not only to test and stretch the abstract analysis, but also to provide a bridge between the theory and the practice. This bridge will help us devise, as best we can, educational strategies.[19]

We should remember from the outset that the voice of the rescuer falls prey to many limitations. Many rescuers never analyzed or evaluated their motives until a researcher, thirty or forty years later, approached them. Also, related to a vagueness about motives was the simple dimness of memory after a few decades as well as the unbridgeable distance between the urgency of the rescuing moment (e.g., the midnight knock at the door, the gathering of a neighbor's child into the attic without a moment's reflection, etc.) and retrospective reflections: Why did I do this? Nonetheless, with all their limitations, the studies of the rescuers are suggestive and helpful.

What did the rescuers of Jews during the Shoah look like? What traits, background, distinguishing characteristics did they bear?[20] To see the composite rescuer,[21] Gushee uses the categories of (1) family profile, (2) situational factors, (3) personality traits, and (4) religious motives.

1. What was the family background of the rescuer? Apparently a significant number of rescuers come from warm, nurturing families.

> Rescuers report that one parent . . . served as an articulately moral
> parental role model. . . . It was essential for parents to establish, articulate,
> and teach their values and to practice those values with or at least in the pres-
> ence of the child who would later become a rescuer.[22]

They benefited from parents who were strong role-models of caring and who taught them the importance of tolerance (not necessarily for the Jews in particular but for all human beings), inclusiveness, and the obligation to help people in need. Further, many rescuers had a significant encounter with suffering and death in their early childhood and saw their parents deal with it in an exemplary fashion.

2. In the experience of rescuing, a series of situational factors proved to be important. These included that rescuers had more friends, co-workers, and neighbors who were Jewish than nonrescuers; that there was a network or community of rescuers; and finally, that they were asked. Fully 67 percent of the rescuers were approached by someone for help, versus 25 percent of the nonrescuers (one must remember that Jews would be quite careful about whom they would ask). In addition to being asked, the rescuer had to have the means or the facilities to help. And finally, many were acquainted, either as neighbors or as fellows in the resistance, with the Jews whom they ended up helping.

3. Several personality traits distinguished rescuers from nonrescuers. To a great degree, rescuers displayed a certain adventurousness, a strong sense of personal responsibility, and a developed empathy for others' pain. Also to be counted were strong self-esteem, competence, self-confidence, and a willingness to stand up for one's beliefs. A number of rescuers reported that their own hatred of the Nazis, combined with their patriotism and a commitment to democratic pluralism, helped them muster the wherewithal to help Jews.

In their study, Sam and Pearl Oliner found that what characterized the rescuers were equity and care. With regard to equity, rescuers spoke of "what is right, what is fair"; with regard to motives of care, rescuers spoke of "connectedness, kindness, compassion" and the need to relieve another's suffering (e.g., "Any kind of suffering must be alleviated" or "When you see a need, you have to help"). This ethics of care applied to fully 76 percent of rescuers. Indeed, many rescuers spoke in terms of an instinctive, spontaneous impulse to alleviate suffering—with little reasoned reflection on what they were doing. What distinguished the rescuers from the nonrescuers was their early education in caring values—attending to the poor, the weak, those in need, and even to those beyond one's own group.

4. For Christians after the Shoah, most painful and puzzling perhaps is the

irrelevance of religious beliefs to the remembered motivation of most res-cuers. Nonetheless, in the research many rescuers reported that their religious beliefs did play a significant role in the move from being a bystander to being a rescuer. Among Christians who reported that their religion helped them, what resources influenced them most? (Again, one must be a bit cautious about making too much of a forty-year-old memory, but in the wake of the Shoah, we must explore every resource available to us.) Among those who reported the importance of religious motivation, David Gushee found six sig-nificant influences.[23]

First, many religiously motivated rescuers cited their strong sense of reli-gious kinship with the Jewish people. They recognized and valued that Jesus was a Jew and that the Old Testament was part of their Bible. Strong among such persons, then, were those whose religious practice included extensive Bible reading, especially of the Hebrew Scriptures. As one French Catholic put it:

> The religious education I had received had instilled in me respect for the Jewish people, and gratitude that they had given us the prophets, the Virgin Mary, Christ, and the apostles. Jews were for me people of the Covenant, of God's promises. Jesus, the Messiah, was a faithful son of the Law, which he had come to bring to perfection, not to abolish. I had never heard the Jews spoken of as Christ-killers; I had been taught that our sins crucified Jesus.[24]

Second, many religiously motivated rescuers remembered that they had once been on the receiving-end of religious persecution and marginalization. They knew what it meant to be discriminated against because of their mem-bership in a religious minority. These included many French Huguenots, Lithuanian and Ukrainian Baptists, and German Plymouth Brethren.

Third, many reported that they had simply perceived that their faith offered a critique of the government; they concluded that Christianity was incompatible with the Nazi ideology. Their efforts at rescue sprang from an abhorrence of Nazi brutality, godlessness, and racism.

Fourth, drawing from the Hebrew Scriptures in particular, many reli-giously motivated rescuers affirmed that every human life was precious in God's eyes and that all were equal. They remembered from the Book of Genesis that all humans were made in the image and likeness of God. and that "only God, who gave life, can take it away." From this conviction they refused to accept the Nazi dehumanization of the Jews. So the words of Genesis 4:8–10, "my brother's keeper," echoed in their minds when confronted with the rescuing opportunity.

Fifth, many Christian rescuers of Jews remembered and cited particular New Testament passages as prompting their courageous rescue of Jews. Most frequently mentioned were the Good Samaritan Parable (Luke 10:25–37), the Command to Love God and Neighbor (Matthew 22:34–40), the Last Judgment (Matthew 25:31–46), the Golden Rule (Matthew 7:12), and Galatians 3:27–28, "There is no longer Jew or Greek, there is no longer slave or free, there is no longer male and female; for all of you are one in Christ Jesus." (NRSV).[25]

Finally, many rescuers spoke of a way of perceiving their own relation to God and to others in what we would call their spirituality. When confronted with a particular situation, their practiced response was, "What is God calling me to do?" or "What would Jesus do in this situation?" Similarly some said, "I perceived that this was what God wanted me to do." Simple were their sentiments, but profound and courageous were the consequences.

While what Thomas would say about such a person is predictable, here a movement to a specific example, that of one family who rescued Jews, might advance our analysis.

One Example of Religiously Motivated Rescue

When I was a student at the Hebrew University in Jerusalem, I met Shula Bitran, who told me of her mother's rescue from the Nazis by two members of the Reformed Church. This was not unusual among Dutch "Righteous Gentiles." Members of the Dutch Reformed Church, Wop and Heltje Kooistra were lovingly devoted to reading the Bible. Wop in particular cherished the Hebrew Scriptures. "He read it all the time; he knew it like no other Christian I've known," Shula remembered. As members of the Dutch underground and frequently pursued by the Nazis, for three years Wop and Heltje hid Jews in their home, sometimes as many as ten at a time. More than a few times, Nazi searches endangered their family, almost uncovering their secret.

While such a story was all too rare, it was not unique. I asked Shula, therefore, "What gave Wop and Heltje Kooistra the courage to do something like this?" She answered without hesitation: "It was his faith; he was very religious. But it was a joint venture: it was his decision and her work." I pressed the question because there were many very religious people in Holland whose faith did not lead them to rescuing Jews. So I asked, "Was there anything in particular that gave them strength to do this?" She answered:

> I guess it was three things. First, from his reading of the Bible, he firm-
> ly believed that the Jews are the chosen people. In fact, he was a very strong

Zionist for the same reason. He believed there is the bond between the people and the land. Secondly for him, it was simply the Christian thing to do. They both shared very deep, humanistic values. Also, the Dutch people have a strong historical sense of freedom. They hated the Germans, particularly the Nazis, and he was a member of the underground. After the war, when everyone was liberated, Heltje Kooistra opened the door for all the Jews in the room, and told them, "Freedom!" The people in the village were quite surprised because none of them knew that all of them were in their house; the villagers were quite proud of them.[26]

Aristotle maintained that a person's true character is revealed in spontaneous action. This was certainly true of the Kooistras. They were not selfish, thoughtless people who, in an instant of conversion, performed a heroic deed. Rather, already beyond being bystanders through their involvement in the underground, the Kooistras had been conditioned—Thomas would say, habituated—in numerous ways to possess the wherewithal to say yes when the rescuing moment presented itself. Their Bible reading presented a world of moral concern that extended beyond their own kin. Or, it may be said conversely, their understanding of kin came to include others beyond their family as their brothers and sisters. The Hebrew Scriptures, studied and loved, which insist that God's covenantal love continues to be showered on the Jewish people, expanded their religious imagination. And their faith provided the necessary energy to do what Thomas prosaically says virtue does: it conforms one's actions to reason.

As an ethical implication for Christians after Auschwitz, we need to reflect on the dimensions and resources for courage revealed in the actions of rescuers. Therefore, using Thomas's categories, Gushee's summary of religiously motivating factors, and the example of the Kooistras, what was peculiarly courageous about their rescue actions? Shula Bitran claimed that Wop and Heltje Kooistra's faith gave them courage to do what they did. But what was it about their faith, without which they would not have done what they did? I suggest that Wop and Heltje's faith gave them four things that helped them to overcome their fear and engage in rescue: (1) a vision of the cosmos that corresponds to what Thomas calls reason, (2) emotional adrenaline or energy, both positive and negative, to act without much reflection, (3) a sense of inviolable personal integrity, and (4) a rationale for continued rescue, what Thomas refers to as courage expressed in perseverance and patience.

1. In his definition of courage, Thomas speaks of conforming one's action to reason despite, and over against, great obstacles. Reason, as the ability to see things as they are, entails certain action. As Albert Camus noted in *The*

Plague concerning the rescue of Jews in Le Chambon: "The essential thing was to save the greatest number of persons from dying . . . to fight the plague. There was nothing admirable about this attitude; it was merely logical."[27] The Kooistras' faith offered them a vision of seeing things the way they were. This vision enabled, indeed forced, them to see that the Jews were both their brothers and sisters and still the Chosen of God. While it is true that one does not need strictly religious faith to view others as one's siblings, authentic faith must include that belief. Shula Bitran testified that the Kooistras were steeped in deep humanistic values; where these values overlapped with their faith is difficult to tell.

The Book of Proverbs reminds us, "Without a vision, the people perish" (Proverbs 29:18). While the Kooistras had the divinely inspired biblical vision, they shunned naming their own actions as courageous (typical of almost all rescuers). They viewed the mystery of their actions from the inside rather than as we do, from the outside. And from that perspective, that vision, their actions were not noteworthy. They saw Jews as their own kin. That is, if Wop and Heltje had, in the middle of the night, taken in their own brothers and sisters who were desperately seeking asylum, we would admire them, but their actions would not be labeled strictly as courageous. Even more so, if their adult children had sought a hiding place with them, we would say that they had a natural obligation to take them in. It would not occur to us to label parents who hid their own children as courageous. Similarly, if parents closed the door on their children, we would say that they were terrible parents—they had a natural obligation to take them in. We would not call them cowards. So the Kooistras—and other rescuers—do not view their actions as courageous any more than we view parents who hide their own children as courageous. Their faith gave them a vision to see the Jews as their brothers and sisters, as kin worthy of the risks that rescue would entail.

When religiously motivated rescuers were questioned, many cited biblical passages. One frequently cited passage, the so-called Good Samaritan parable, raises the very issue of vision. In answer to the lawyer's question, "Who is my neighbor?" Jesus tells a story which stretches the listener's imagination. These passages—often parabolic—were powerful and persuasive in evoking identification with one character or other. Some rescuers said, "How could I have just walked by my neighbor?" Admittedly this interpretation of their own actions came many years after the event, but the rescuers recognized the inspiration for their behavior as perhaps present at the opportune moment.

So for the religiously motivated rescuer, first came a vision of Who is in my moral universe? or, more personally, Who is my kin? Who is my brother, my sister, my neighbor? To whom am I related? This sets up the first move in religiously motivated rescue behavior.

2. But a new vision, as religious faith could and did provide, is not enough. The movement from seeing to doing—from being a bystander to involving oneself—requires more than vision. Thomas asserts that fortitude is the moral ingredient that helps an agent overcome a presenting difficulty as adrenaline provides energy to help lift an otherwise imposing, even impossible, weight. What is the adrenaline, the push that says, "I must do this, I will do this"? It is emotion, indeed passion, which ignites the vision.

In his analysis of courage, Thomas considers only the emotions of fear and anger. Fear is the emotion that must be overcome for the sake of a greater good, and anger is, in some instances, the emotion that gives energy to the rational assessment to act. Thomas holds that courage is always about overcoming fear of opposition in general and fear of death in particular (see 2^a2^{ae} 123.3 & 4). While some rescuers spoke of fear, for themselves and those they loved, many seemed to have been quite oblivious to it. Few rescuers, including the Kooistras, spoke of their fear. But the emotion of anger—or, as in the Kooistra case, hatred of the Nazis—gave them the energy to begin to help. As one rescuer put it, "I was not courageous, I was furious."

3. Obviously, not every emotion serves courageous rescue. One must possess the right passion about the right things. There are two determinants of the rightness of passion: first, determining, Who is worthy of my taking risks? (the external object of my care), and second, determining, Who am I? What must I do? (the internal integrity of my character).

In various studies, rescuers and rescued spoke in terms of compassion and an ethic of care. Learning to be compassionate about the Jewish people required both passion and vision. These Wop and Heltje received through their Bible reading. Others needed only a category wider than the Jews—simply to identify a people in need—to initiate and sustain rescue behavior. (Indeed there were even the occasional antisemites who felt that simple moral duty required that they not cooperate in the Jews' extermination.) But when we ponder motivation which appeals to the religious person about why he or she should care for the Jew, we see that in recent years Christian churches have advanced a new way of speaking about Jews that is crucial to offering a new framework indicating for whom Christians must care.[28]

Another real, but usually unconscious, moving force among rescuers was their own character. Many felt that their own integrity was at risk if they did not act to help the Jews. When asked why they did what they did, some of them replied, "What else could I do?" Since we are, in so many ways, our actions, to ask "What else could I do?" was another way of saying, "Who else could I be?" This is tied to what some virtue ethicists mean when they underscore the importance of the question, "Who should I become?" (Conversely, if a rescuer's primary risk-taking was motivated by monetary gain, one would not say that such an entrepreneur had been courageous, although Jews who were harbored by such opportunists might still be grateful for a skilled, competent [albeit greedy] rescuer over a bumbling, inept, but well-intentioned rescuer. The former would certainly not deserve to be called courageous but might still be preferred to the incompetent rescuer.)

Most striking about so many Gentile rescuers was the almost universal denial of heroism: "I just did what anyone would do," or "What else could I do? She was knocking at my door." Or, as Shula Bitran said, "For him [Wop], it was simply the Christian thing to do."

> Many rescuers express profound discomfort when asked why they helped Jews. Some researchers have attributed this discomfort to personal modesty. . . . For many rescuers the question is almost unintelligible; one might just as well ask why the rescuer breathes. People were in need; it is obligatory to help people in need, regardless of the risk; so they helped people who needed help. What is there to understand?[29]

In this way, perhaps, courage is like the virtue of humility, which is lost once one thinks one possesses it. One may recognize humility in others but not in oneself. Can courage be such that to assert one's possession of it is thereby to forfeit it? Almost universally others refer to rescue actions as courageous, but few rescuers say that of themselves.

4. Finally, Thomas observes that perseverance ("the need to adhere to the good sought") and patience ("the need to overcome the sorrow brought by the inevitable loss of some goods") constitute two expressions of courage. For three years, the Kooistras hid Jews in their home. The momentary energy which they felt when they said "Welcome" to their first Jewish fugitive eventually gave way to three years of patient, clever, monotonous routine of finding food and covering traces of their actions. Eva Fogelman insightfully describes the patience of rescuer behavior in general:

> A rescuer's life was intricate and terrifying. A careless word, a forgotten detail, or one wrong move could lead to death. . . . At home the strains were often just as great. Overnight, relationships changed, as families adjusted to a new member being sheltered. The home atmosphere could become poisonous if one spouse did not support the other's rescuing efforts.

Comfortable routines were upset and new patterns had to be developed. . . .
A core confidence, a strong sense of self, and a supportive situation had
allowed bystanders to undertake rescue. But once the decision to help had
been reached and the rescue had begun, a different self—a rescuer self—
emerged, to do what had to be done and to keep rescuers from becoming
overwhelmed by new responsibilities and pressures.[30]

It was the "rescuer self" that displayed courage's two expressions of perseverance and patience.

To Ourselves and Our Children

And so, what are we Christians to do after Auschwitz—first for ourselves
and then for our children? For our children and we are not computers. It is not
a matter of simply mixing a number of ingredients to cause a certain effect.
But how can we teach ourselves and our children in such a way that we will
increase the likelihood of our and their stepping out, when the time comes,
from being a bystander to being a helper, a rescuer?

Robert Coles, in a recent consideration of moral intelligence in children,
remembers a conversation with a young boy. In it, the boy said:

> Courage is when you believe in something, you really do, so you go
> ahead and try to do what your beliefs tell you [to do], and if you are in dan-
> ger, that way—well, you're not thinking "I'm in danger." You're thinking,
> this is right, this is important, and I'm going to go ahead, and that is that.[31]

This simple yet perceptive description of courageous behavior was enact-
ed time and again during the Shoah's bleak years. The rescuer's courage was
needed in a thousand unique situations, yet the pattern of rescue seemed to be
quite consistent:

> Awareness of dehumanization sets the [rescue] process in motion when
> the condition is seen to warrant intervention. Personality and situation con-
> verge, to act or not to act, in response to the need to save a life. . . . The deci-
> sion to risk one's life happens quickly, coming from an inner core that auto-
> matically calculates the chances of success. Once rescue begins a new "res-
> cuer self" develops to take necessary actions and maintain secrets and a
> facade of normalcy. The stage, actors, and props may be different in each
> case, but the dynamics of the human response are always the same.[32]

The "entry points" for religiously inspired courage in this pattern come long before the rescuing moment. They are the thousand and one opportunities for education and character formation.

Already I have suggested that these religious contributions—vision; appropriate emotions of fear, anger, and compassion; and capacity for patient endurance—need to be further developed by Christian educators as one ethical implication of the Shoah for Christians.

David Gushee lists a number of worthwhile recommendations in answer to his trenchant question, "Is the Christian faith, as embodied and taught in Christian churches, up to the task of nurturing righteousness?" His recommendations are (slightly paraphrased):

1. Rediscovering character formation and its formation
2. Nurturing a spirituality that does justice
3. Rediscovering the constructive moral power of the Bible
4. Articulating a diverse vocabulary of neighbor-love
5. Identifying competent moral leadership.[33]

What in this essay I have emphasized are, in a way, amplifications of points 3 and 4 of Gushee's list. While it was not only Christian virtue that gave the wherewithal for Gentile rescue of Jews during the Shoah, what Christianity has to offer, I believe, is the vision and the appropriate emotion (rage, anger) and moral character. The Christian preacher and educator have these tools at their disposal if they already have them in their hearts (point 5). Courageous preaching requires courageous preachers. These were in short supply during the Shoah, and indeed people perished because they had not a vision.

CONCLUSION

We began this essay with Karl Rahner's observation that the virtue of courage is singularly hard to define. Thomas's classical description and definition underscored fortitude's dimensions and components. The distilled traits of those too-few Christians who moved from being bystanders to the courageous rescue of Jews during the Shoah found vivid expression in the experience of Wop and Heltje Kooistra of Holland. While the Christian religion played a disappointingly small role in most rescuers' motivation, we sought to highlight the specifically religious contribution to reported rescue behavior so that we might find some guidance for Christian preachers and educators so that at least one implication of ethics after the Shoah might be clear—how we might exploit the fortitude-encouraging dimensions of our faith. After the Shoah, then, we seek to offer a vision, to teach what to be passionate about (both the Jews and all who are beyond my kin), and, by the irreplaceable tool of example, to educate a new generation to an ethics of care, even as we have so dismally lived it these last few generations.

NOTES

1. Karl Rahner, *Meditations on Freedom and the Spirit* (London: Burns & Oates, 1977), p. 15.
2. See John T. Pawlikowski, "The Shoah: Its Challenges for Religious and Secular Ethics," in *Remembering for the Future*, ed. Yehuda Bauer, Alice L. Eckardt, et al. (Oxford: Pergamon Press, 1989), vol. 1, pp. 736–746.
3. Some recent studies have explored how some bystanders stepped out and became perpetrators. See Raul Hilberg, *Perpetrators, Victims, Bystanders: The Jewish Catastrophe, 1933–1945* (New York: HarperCollins, 1992); Daniel J. Goldhagen, *Hitler's Willing Executioners: Ordinary Germans and the Holocaust* (New York: Knopf, 1996); Christopher R. Browning, *Ordinary Men: Reserve Battalion 101 and the Final Solution in Poland* (New York: HarperCollins, 1992). Obviously this searching question will not be addressed here.
4. For the research and bibliography on the rescuers, see the excellent survey by David P. Gushee, *The Righteous Gentiles of the Holocaust: A Christian Interpretation* (Minneapolis: Fortress Press, 1994). See also Eva Fleischner, "Can the Few Become the Many? Some Catholics in France Who Saved Jews during the Holocaust," in *Remembering for the Future*, I:233–247. The pioneering work in this field is by Samuel P. Oliner and Pearl M. Oliner, *The Altruistic Personality: Rescuers of Jews in Nazi Europe* (New York: Free Press, 1988). See also Mordecai Paldiel, *The Path of the Righteous* (New York: Ktav, 1993); Douglas K. Huneke, *The Stones Will Cry Out: Pastoral Reflections on the Shoah* (Westport, Conn.: Greenwood Press, 1995); Eva Fogelman, *Conscience & Courage: Rescuers of Jews During the Holocaust* (New York: Doubleday, 1994); and many others.
5. Indeed, "most rescuers had not even considered the motives for their actions" before they were interviewed in the various studies. See Huneke, *Stones Will Cry Out*, p. 102.
6. In a previous work, I explored some of the theological beliefs that, while they did not cause the Shoah, created an atmosphere within which the Nazi ideology breathed freely and was not snuffed out. See my *Christology After Auschwitz* (New York: Paulist Press, 1977).
7. See Nechama Tec, *When Light Pierced the Darkness: Christian Rescue of Jews in Nazi-Occupied Poland* (New York: Oxford University Press, 1986).

8. Gushee, *Righteous Gentiles of the Holocaust*, p. 159.

9. Pope John Paul II, Address to the Jewish Community of Australia, November 26, 1986, in *Spiritual Pilgrimage: Texts on Jews and Judaism, 1979–1995*, ed. Eugene J. Fisher and Leon Klenicki (New York: Crossroad, 1995), p. 82.

10. Alasdair MacIntyre, *After Virtue: A Study in Moral Theory* (Notre Dame: University of Notre Dame Press, 1981).

11. The literature is large. See, among others, Lee Yearley, "Recent Work on Virtue," *Religious Studies Review* 16 (1990): 1–9; William Spohn, "The Return of Virtue Ethics," *Theological Studies* 53 (1992): 60–75; John W. Crossin, *What Are They Saying About Virtue?* (Mahwah, N.J.: Paulist Press, 1985); Stanley Hauerwas and Charles Pinches, *Christians Among the Virtues: Theological Conversations with Ancient and Modern Ethics* (Notre Dame: University of Notre Dame Press, 1997).

12. James Keenan, "Virtue Ethics," in *Christian Ethics*, ed. B. Hoose (New York: Geoffrey Chapman, 1997).

13. Benjamin W. Farley, *In Praise of Virtue: An Exploration of the Biblical Virtues in a Christian Context* (Grand Rapids: Eerdmans, 1995), p. 2, points out that not all Christian ethicists support this shift: "Some theologians caution that a renewed interest in virtue and moral character has the capacity to undo—at least for Protestants—the doctrine of salvation by grace through faith."

14. The other cardinal virtues are prudence, justice, and temperance. See James F. Keenan, "Proposing Cardinal Virtues," *Theological Studies* 56 (1995): 709–729.

15. St. Thomas Aquinas, *Summa Theologica* II, trans. by the English Dominican Province (New York: Benziger Bros., 1947). For a superb treatment of Thomas and courage, see Lee Yearley, *Mencius and Aquinas: Theories of Virtue and Conceptions of Courage* (Albany, N.Y.: SUNY Press, 1990).

16. While "fortitude" and "courage" are used in this paper interchangeably, one finds a consideration of "daring" sometimes closer to what we call courage, in the 1a2ae, Question 45. There "daring" bears the narrower definition of an excess of confidence.

17. 2a2ae, Q 123. Resp.

18. Yearley, *Mencius*, p. 117.

19. To extract the portrait of the rescuer, I depend primarily on references already given in n. 4.

20. In comparisons of the rescuer and the nonrescuer, the following factors proved not to be significant: age, gender, occupation, social class, politics, and religion. As Gushee (*Righteous Gentiles*, p. 100) puts it, "religion does not prove to be a significant predictor of rescue behavior." Sad to report, then, if a European Jew had desperately sought help from a Gentile during the Nazi period, he or she would have stood no greater chance for help if that person professed to be a Christian.

21. It should be noted that the profile does not describe the majority of rescuers; rather, it highlights those aspects of the self-reported characteristics of the rescuers that were statistically significantly higher for rescuers than nonrescuers.

22. Huneke, *Stones Will Cry Out*, p. 104.

23. Again, we avail ourselves of Gushee's work (pp. 119 ff.) which summarizes the standard studies of the rescuers.

24. Fleischner, "Can the Few Become the Many?" p. 239.

25. Douglas Huneke, "In the Presence of Burning Children: The Reformation of Christianity After the Shoah," in *Contemporary Christian Religious Responses to the Shoah*, ed. Steven L. Jacobs (Lanham, Md.: University Press of America, 1993), pp. 85–108, notes that "religiously-inspired non-conformity" found scriptural support and inspiration in St. Paul's admonition in Romans 12:2, "Be not conformed to this world, but be transformed to a completely new way of thinking so as to know what is the good and acceptable and perfect will of God."

26. Adapted from my "Emil Fackenheim and Christianity After the Holocaust," *American Journal of Theology and Philosophy* 9 (January–May 1988): 117–35, 129 f.

27. As quoted in Gushee, *Righteous Gentiles*, p. 162.

28. See Helga Croner, comp., *Stepping Stones to Further Jewish-Christian Relations: An Unabridged Collection of Christian Documents* (New York: Stimulus Books, 1977) and *More Stepping Stones to Jewish-Christian Relations: An Unabridged Collection of Christian Documents, 1975–1983* (New York: Paulist Press, 1985). See also the prophetic "Seelisberg: The Report of Commission 3" and "Bad Schwalbach: Proposals for Christians Religious Education," *SIDIC* 3, no. 2 (1970): 3–7.

29. Gushee, *Righteous Gentiles*, p. 161.

30. Fogelman, *Conscience & Courage*, p. 68.

31. Robert Coles, *The Moral Intelligence of Children* (New York: Random House, 1997), pp. 118 f.

32. Fogelman, *Conscience and Courage*, p. 314.

33. Gushee, *Righteous Gentiles*, pp. 167–74.

Aberrant Freedom and Impious Heroism:
Observations on Conscience and Suspension of Ethical Evaluation in the Auschwitz Case

Massimo Giuliani

> The possible meaning in the Lager of the words "good" and "evil," "just" and "unjust," let everybody judge . . .
>
> —Primo Levi, *If This Is a Man*[1]

THE PHILOSOPHICAL UNEASINESS WITH REGARD TO AUSCHWITZ

Philosophical and theological thought is uncomfortable, or, better, impatient, when faced with an ethical evaluation of the behavior—of both victims and persecutors—in concentration camps. We have to realize this, and seek the underlying reasons.

The state of uneasiness and impatience does not seem, in the first instance, to spring from the monstrosity or magnitude of what a moral conscience would in normal circumstances call evil, for the questions raised by Auschwitz are not new to theology or philosophy: How are we to envisage and represent evil? Can we speak of quality of and in evil? Is there, contrary to the Socratic view, a will to evil? What is the source of this will?

Uneasiness and impatience do not appear to be a result of the fact that Auschwitz radically undermines any boundary between good and evil, and that it is impossible to define ethical parameters in such extreme situations. In this perspective, Auschwitz can become a symbol of a state beyond good and evil, a kind of *experimentum regradationis*. However, in this case uneasiness would give way to an outright denial of any ethical discourse.

Nor do uneasiness and impatience seem to be a result simply of the refusal, albeit just and instinctive, to compare victims and persecutors, and more generally collective behavior and personal actions in a context of total physical and psychological coercion, in other words in the absence of freedom—for without freedom there can be no principle of responsibility or possibility of moral action.

The source of this philosophical uneasiness, if we can call it this, lies in the awareness that the very faculty of ethical evaluation is in the dock here. How are we to "judge judgment" when the reason behind the conception and organization of Auschwitz, and the reason called to express an ethical judgment on it, are in fact one and the same?

In the perverted reasoning of the Nazis and their collaborators, Auschwitz was the apotheosis of an asserted knowledge of good and evil, capable—partially thanks to the bureaucratic apparatus—of eliminating almost any margin of ethical doubt and autonomous judgment. The effect was that of the *a-nomia* found in those who see themselves as above any rule of law, or indeed as creators and sources of all legality, including other people's right to existence. This elimination of the persecutors' autonomy of self-awareness and conscience raises considerable problems for any investigation and ethical evaluation, and would seem to confine such evaluation to the sphere of the victims' behavior. However, we may legitimately wonder whether this can really be true, or whether it is not just one more wrong we do the victims.

Although for the Auschwitz persecutors it was *subjectively* the apotheosis of an asserted knowledge of good and evil, for the Auschwitz victims it was *objectively* the denial of any freedom of choice—not so much between good and evil, as between life and death. Even so, some choices of life were made in the Nazi concentration and extermination camps, albeit with mere fragments of freedom. The victims' choices are not only subject to moral judgment, but demand an ethical reflection, and on a deeper level constitute a parameter for such reflection.

We are not speaking here of forced actions dictated by the instinct for survival, but about acts performed and described as choices of conscience, or indeed as "requirements of conscience," either in the form of the statements of survivors or in the form found in Judaism of questions submitted for rabbinical responsa. Inasmuch as these mature acts of conscience represent fragments of freedom in extreme conditions, they force our disheartened thought to have recourse to the rhetorical tropes of oxymoron and paradox, perhaps the least unsuitable linguistic instruments for a reason split in or from itself to express the ethical conflict and self-contradiction of moral conscience, of which Auschwitz was cause, context, and consequence.

TWO EXTREME CASES OF CONSCIENCE AND RECOURSE TO OXYMORA

The evidence of survivors of the death camps, and even more the rabbinical responses to questions and problems that arose because of the Shoah (both during and after the event) today represent the main source for any philosophical, ethical, and theological reflection on this event, in other words for any reflection aware of the historical unity encompassing both the Shoah and the theological newness it entails. The rabbinic responsa entail examination of the whole body of halakhic literature, with a view to an application—and if necessary an expansion—of the Halakhah, and have thus for centuries been the ordinary means through which religious Jews have tackled the really extreme cases set them by history. According to tradition, the Halakhah is a vital part of the oral Torah, received and handed down by Moses together with the written Torah, which means that the same Sinaitic revelation is made explicit in the responsa, in other words takes on the force of law and gains historical relevance. The rabbinical responsa of the Shoah period thus show, first, the radical fidelity of Israel to the Torah and to tradition, even in apparently impossible conditions, and, second, the historical and dialogical structural dimension of written and oral revelation in Judaism. The questions that religious Jews asked their teachers, in the search for enlightenment on the possibility of right choices and behavior in line with the Halakhah during the period of Nazi persecution, are thus the "margins" that see the birth and development of the contradiction of an ethics without freedom, and of a judgment that must first and foremost judge itself.

Reflecting anew, on the basis of these presuppositions, on the responsa requested and given during the Shoah, and more generally on the extreme cases posed to the conscience and by the conscience at that time, is not only a way of offering justice to the victims—in other words to the main players, those actually faced with difficult and often "impossible" choices—but is also a way of helping to reconcile thought with its own limitations, both those on its capacity to encompass the evil committed by human beings against one another, and also those on ethical and theological judgment. It is indeed a way of accepting the limitations that the ethical defeat of Auschwitz has engraved in the history of humanity for ever.

The first case on which I want to reflect is a fairly well-known episode described by Judith Sternberg Newman, a nurse who survived Auschwitz.

> Two days after Christmas, a Jewish child was born on our block. How happy I was when I saw this tiny baby. It was a boy, and the mother had been told that he would be taken care of. Three hours later, I saw a small package wrapped in cheese cloth lying on a wooden bench. Suddenly it moved. A Jewish girl employed as a clerk came over, carrying a pan of cold water. She whispered to me "Hush! Quiet! Go away!" But I remained, for I could not understand what she had in mind. She picked up the little package—it was

the baby, of course—and it started to cry with a thin little voice. She took the infant and submerged its little body in the cold water. My heart beat wildly in agitation. I wanted to shout "Murderess!" but I had to keep quiet and could not tell anyone. The baby swallowed and gurgled, its little voice chittering like a small bird, until its breath became shorter and shorter. The woman held its head in the water. After about eight minutes the breathing stopped. The woman picked it up, wrapped it up again, and put it with the other corpses. Then she said to me, "We had to save the mother, otherwise she would have gone to the gas chamber." This girl had learned well from the SS and had become a murderess herself.[2]

This case is not codified as a question seeking an answer, but is "merely" an eyewitness account, tragic testimony about a choice made on the basis of an aberrant freedom, the only one possible at that moment. Indeed, the very word "choice" is quite inappropriate. As Lawrence Langer notes, "Convention vocabulary limps through a situation that allows no heroic response, no acceptable gesture of protest, no mode of action to permit *any* of the participants, including the absent mother, to retain a core of human dignity."[3] The account of the impotent witness describes such an extreme conflict of conscience that any ethical judgment is *almost* impossible—"almost," because Sternberg does express a judgment, and a severe one. However, the listener cannot give one in the same way, for how can we evaluate *a posteriori* a choice made in a situation in which the actors are placed beyond any *objective* evaluation of good and evil? It must be clearly said here that if a responsibility does exist, and if an ethical judgment must in any case be given, the responsibility for such a choice lies *wholly* and *only* with the Nazis (and not with the women who were the actor and witness of the infanticide). However, the author of this choice is then placed ethically beyond any judgment in a sphere of a-ethicality, which paradoxically places her alongside the oppressors' self-styled moral superiority. Does this mean that victim and persecutor are to be placed on the same level of non-judgability, albeit for *objectively* different "subjective reasons"? This is clearly unacceptable from the viewpoint of a common ethical conscience, because justice is not done to the persons and historical events. Perhaps our thinking has slipped here into a vicious and unacceptable circle in which aberrant freedom leads straight to impious justice. Although the choice made by the infanticide woman in Auschwitz was undeniably free, the fact that this freedom was free to choose only between two evils, *neither of which was less than the other*—the death of the newborn child and the death of both mother and child—means that we have to define this freedom as aberrant. Here we see the extreme-case nature of the Shoah, so that the only adjectivization available is an oxymoronic one, indicating the impossibility of our making any ethical judgment, or, if you prefer, the self-contradiction of any ethical judgment that leaves aside the physical and psychological conditions of the freedom that it seeks to judge.

The second case on which I propose to reflect is an even better example. Found in a collection of responsa, it is expressed in the form of a question asked of Rabbi Shimon Efrati of Bendery and Warsaw, in order to receive a halakhic solution. The question is whether a Jew hiding in a bunker in the ghetto escaping from the Nazis has to repent for having involuntarily suffocated a crying child in order to avert discovery and death for a group of hidden Jews.

> Whether or not it was permitted to place the pillow [over the baby's mouth] to save the rest of the people. If it was not permissible, even though [the death was inflicted] unintentionally, must this man agree to some form of repentance to atone for his sin?[4]

Here too, as in the other case, we are dealing with an infanticide committed to save another life, or rather a number of lives. Thus, Rabbi Efrati's responsum, which looks for varying opinions in the Talmud, focuses on the prohibition on sacrificing an innocent life for another innocent life, which was codified by Rambam (Maimonides). However, the questions on the lawfulness of an action or on expiation for an involuntary infanticide asked of a rabbi in order to receive a halakhic answer—of its very nature binding—set this second case, unlike the first, in a specifically religious context. Moreover, they are themselves religious questions, which demand and appeal to a religious judgment.

Apart from the complex halakhic answer (which obviously deserves careful analysis), reflection runs into some further problems here. The ethicality, in extreme cases and under certain conditions, of an act that is in itself unacceptable is not the only element involved, for there is also the theological question of whether such an act, which is in itself unacceptable, can be redeemed by a religious intention—through repentance and/or an act of expiation—and whether it can in any case be judged less evil by an authority external to the conscience of the performer, here a rabbinic authority. On this level, ethical judgment (even in the form of its suspension) and religious judgment (whether it absolves or not) can come into conflict, recalling the leap between the ethical and religious that Kierkegaard analyzed so effectively in *Fear and Trembling*. Although the question put to Rabbi Efrati of course lacks the *pathos* of the *akedat Yitzchak* (the binding of Isaac) related in Genesis 22, every child who died in the Shoah is the reverse image of Isaac. Regardless of our religious faith, any forced choice made in Auschwitz reminds us of the "free choice" of the just Abraham to bind Isaac on Mount Moriah. Kierkegaard called Abraham's choice a teleological suspension of morality, because the sacrifice of his son was an act of obedience, a gesture of faith in God. In Auschwitz, however, no Isaac was spared, and no ram replaced Isaac's descendants. Suspension of ethical judgment in the face of certain forced choices made by victims of the Shoah is thus radically different from suspension of morality in the face of the act of faith. The difference lies in the fact that to us today, both believers and nonbelievers, any teleological hypothesis for the Shoah event rings false, as both immoral and unacceptable, quite apart from the conception of God (or fate) that this *telos* presupposes.

Suspension of ethical judgment in the case of Auschwitz is simply the result of that aberrant freedom under which the victims were forced to choose not between life and death, as in the biblical text of Deuteronomy 30:15, and not between a good and an evil, but *between evils of which neither is the lesser*. Even supposing that, in the cases cited and many similar ones, the hoped-for result of the actions performed actually did take place, should we not still speak of an "unjust justification," an "impious heroism," or a "repugnant courage"? Further, what religious authority can claim to judge such an ethical conflict? Should not "religious reason" also accept the limitation of the suspension of judgment, giving up any teleological claim. On the other hand, would not such suspension of ethical judgment sound obscene precisely in the ears of the victims, since there is a danger that it will spread by osmosis to the various levels of the forced workers of the Shoah, the oblivious bureaucrats of industry and the German army, the many who, like Eichmann, were "only obeying orders"? Kierkegaard himself trembled at the thought of how narrow the line was between being the father of the faith and a tragic hero, or even a murderer.[5]

THE SHOAH, "STAR OF IRREDEMPTION" AND "BROKEN BRIDGE" OF THE RELIGIOUS CONSCIENCE

We have used these two cases of conscience in an attempt to explore the problem of ethical judgment during the Shoah from the viewpoint of the victims, and the implicit need for a suspension of this judgment, despite the risks involved in such a move. In the course of reflection, the use of frequent oxymora changed from a rhetorical device to a semantic dodging of issues, laden with ambivalent ethical and religious nuances (justice and irreligiousness always remain biblical concepts). Recourse to oxymora, to the language of paradox, to the metalogic of analogy, is necessary when what we want to express is beyond the capacity of language, transcending the ordinary sense of words and their normally accepted naming of things that are far from ordinary. The Shoah was not an ordinary case, and set against the backdrop of the history of Judaism (and also of Christianity) it eventually opens up a deep conflict within the heart of these religions of redemption. The Shoah transformed the idea of God and divine justice (for how can we deny that the questions of theodicy are always born anew from the ashes of themselves?) and obviously transformed the idea of human beings as the image of God. In other words, it also opened up a conflict within the heart of the "religion of man" that consists of trust in freedom and reason, and in that desire to pursue virtue and knowledge[6] whose compatibility with Auschwitz was the grief of Primo Levi's human and literary maturity.

The historical and theological fact that Auschwitz was a failed *aqeda* multiplied by six million forces us to a troubled— perhaps I should say troubling—relationship both with religion (or at least with any religion that proclaims the redemption of history) and with reason, in the name of which modernity has in fact opposed religion. For Judaism and Christianity—both religions of historical redemption, albeit with different slants—the Shoah is a real "star of irredemption"; it is a theological quasi-oxymoron to say that these religions are henceforth fated to live in the cone of black light thrown by the event; and that this shadow poses a radical challenge to their language of faith, if not hope, in redemption and salvation—obviously including the idea of and faith in the Messiah, whether already come or still expected. Irving Greenberg writes as follows:

> The Talmud says that the Messiah will be born on Tisha B'Av [the day on which the Jewish tradition mourns the tragedy of the Temple's destruction and all the catastrophes of the people of Israel]. A Talmud written in our time would state that the Messiah will be conceived on Yom Hashoah [the day on which the six million Jews murdered by the Nazis are remembered and honored].[7]

The special gift and strength of the religions of redemption is surely seen here: their capacity to transform an obstacle into an instrument of its own overcoming, to set the balm of conciliation on the deepest conflict, to see the potential seal of its recomposition in even the harshest breach. Even so, the Shoah does not seem to be an easily healable wound, or a breach that can be recomposed with a simple statement of intent. Moreover, trust in human freedom and reason is forced to suspend itself, to postpone at least for a moment its own religious yearning for redemption at all costs, and to leave the question of ethical judgment unanswered. And, as André Neher says, this amounts to leaving a break in the bridge of the questioning of conscience. This break speaks first and foremost of the human being's solitude in the face of the duty to save his fellow beings, because "man is inevitably set to work alone. . . . Man is alone with the fearful ambivalence of his autonomy, simultaneously the source of his strength and his weakness."[8] The evil inflicted and suffered in Auschwitz is grafted into the tragedy of this terribly ambiguous autonomy, and points—as Paolo De Benedetti recalls in his book *Quale Dio?* (or "Which God?"), taking up one of Paul Ricoeur's lessons—to "the mystery of fragility . . . [for] fragility is the very essence of the creature."[9] Auschwitz is thus the "star of irredemption" and the "broken bridge" of the contemporary religious conscience, which is suspended between modernity and tradition, between theology and humanism—where the fragility of being has become an irreparable historical break, and where the irreconcilability between religious and humanistic interpretations of the event is bound to jar much more than the conflict between *caesura* and *continuum* in the perspective of each individual religious tradition.

NOTES

1. English translation now republished as *Survival in Auschwitz* (New York: Touchstone, 1996), here p. 86.
2. Judith Sternberg Newman, *In the Hell of Auschwitz* (New York: Exposition Press, 1963), pp. 42–43. Quoted and commented on by Lawrence L. Langer, "The Dilemma of Choice in the Death Camps," now in John K. Roth and Michael Berenbaum, eds., *Holocaust: Religious and Philosophical Implications* (New York: Paragon House, 1989), p. 224.
3. Langer, "Dilemma of Choice in the Death Camps," p. 225.
4. Robert Kirschner, ed., *Rabbinic Responsa of the Holocaust Era* (New York: Schocken Books, 1985), pp. 65–87.
5. Søren Kierkegaard, *Fear and Trembling* (Garden City, N.Y.: Doubleday, 1954).
6. Cf. Levi, *Survival in Auschwitz*, quoting Dante's *Inferno*, xxvi, 118–120.
7. Irving Greenberg, *The Jewish Way: Living the Holidays* (New York: Touchstone Books, 1988), p. 367.
8. André Neher, *The Exile of the Word: From the Silence of the Bible to the Silence of Auschwitz* (Philadelphia: Jewish Publication Society, 1981), pp. 188, 190.
9. Paolo De Benedetti, *Quale Dio? Una domanda dalla storia* (Brescia: Morcelliana, 1996), p. 25.

Working Through Bereavement:
The Intersection of Memory and History

Some Reflections on an Interview with Marek Edelman, Second-in-Command of the Warsaw Ghetto Uprising

David Meghnagi

Only redeemed humanity has full possession of its past. . . . Only for redeemed humanity can every moment of the past be cited.

—Walter Benjamin

When one knows death so well, one has more responsibility for life.

—Marek Edelman

Let us try to imagine that we are part of a population that is decimated overnight; that in our city the population to which we belong is reduced to a few dozen people; that from one day to the next our closest and more distant relatives—our brothers and sisters and parents, our uncles, cousins, and grandparents—have been wiped out; and that after this there are not even any cemeteries where we can go to mourn them. Let us try to imagine this and more, and perhaps we shall be able to understand what the Nazi genocide really meant for those who suffered it—understand, from within, the significance of a trauma affecting the whole of European civilization, for the tragedy did not take place in some emotionally distant place, but in the heart of Europe. We shall be able to feel in our own flesh the violence contained in the words of those who call us to relativize in the name of some "higher view" of the historical process, saying that the time has come to forget.

After Auschwitz, nothing—art, poetry, philosophy, theology—can ever be the same again. It represented a break in the collective consciousness, which growing awareness has helped to extend in a slow and in many ways contradictory process, but one that was ineluctable in time and space. Think of Primo Levi's work: when he offered publishers the book that would later become a classic of concentration camp literature, he could find nobody willing to take it, so that it was printed at his own expense by a small publishing house, and another ten years would pass before the Italian company Einaudi thought better of its earlier rejection. Today we might maliciously wonder how educated and perceptive readers, who were self-proclaimed anti-fascists, could have opposed publication of *If This Is a Man*. However, the secondary reasons—the jealousy, personal envy, and pettiness that could have led them to pass a negative judgment on Primo Levi's book—fade into the background when weighed against events more interior to the human psyche and movements involving the life of society. The delay before Levi's work took its rightful place on the Italian cultural scene was part of a process, and reflected the collective working out of a bereavement that involved not only Jews, but culture as a whole. More years would have to pass before *The Garden of the Finzi-Continis* would appear, together with other important reflections and reexaminations of a painful aspect of our more recent history.

I thought I would offer two pieces by Marek Edelman, second-in-command of the Warsaw Ghetto Uprising, for your reflection. The first is a political report written immediately after the war, while the other appeared thirty years later and is the fruit of a long interview with Hanna Krall, a Polish Jewish writer, who was only a few years old at the time of the Holocaust. The gap between the two writings and their different internal rhythms reflect a mourning process whose burden cannot be borne solely by those who directly suffered the offense, because the trauma concerns not only these people, but the entire civilization to which we all belong.

Immediately after the liberation, Marek Edelman, the only leader to survive the revolt, felt the need to write a report for the central committee of his organization, the Bund.[1] The leading figures in the tragedy were almost all dead. Some of them would go down in history for deeds of great heroism, while most died anonymously. Some, like Emmanuel Ringelblum, the tireless archivist of the Ghetto, prevented a posthumous murder of memory. "Even the dead will not be safe from the enemy, if he wins," warns Benjamin, "and this enemy is still winning." Ringelblum's work is a source on which to draw in order to make sure that this enemy does not go on winning. Others, such as Mordechai Anielewicz, the young Zionist leftist leader of the Ghetto fighters, represented a Judaism risen again, phoenix-like, from the death camps. In Warsaw his street is in the heart of the new neighborhood where the Ghetto once stood. In Israel his statue, inspired by Michelangelo's *David*, watches over the new generations, saying that there will be no new Auschwitz. Others again, such as Itzchak Katzenelson, commemorated the destruction of a whole people in deeply moving verse. Edelman's work is a ritual act that preserves an appearance of normality in a world gone mad. He wrote his report as if there were still an organization and political interlocutors to whom to report, in the name of a movement that now existed only in memory. Polish Jewry had been wiped out. The leading figures in a unique season of suffering, sublimation, and extreme redemption were dead or were about to move to the newborn state of Israel or across the Atlantic. The few survivors were languishing in refugee camps waiting for exit visas.

Edelman's "report" is a lean, militant, vibrant text which makes the numbers speak, describing the stages in a collective realization that inevitably lagged behind the times set by a machine of destruction refined day by day. In a few pages the author throws the whole process into relief. The occupier's strategy had the clearly defined aim of pushing the Jewish population in a single direction, forcing it to live from hand to mouth without any plans for the morrow, dividing it, and making it play an unwitting role in its own destruction. The population of the Ghetto was forced to flow in from all directions, concentrating itself within a three-and-a-half-kilometer perimeter, and did not have time to realize the enemy's true intentions. In a few days people died by the hundreds and by the thousands. They were totally isolated from the world, the Polish resistance movement was only in its very early stages, and the German armed forces were victorious on all fronts. Terrified and panic-stricken, the people could not believe their eyes, hoping up to the very last that they would be saved, that they were leaving for work and not on their last journey. The circumstances prevented any attempt at organization, the people had no weapons, and any act of protest brought down the heaviest reprisals. The feeling of insecurity and danger was constant. People's best energies were used in the struggle against hunger, want, and typhoid. The core of the resistance was destroyed a full three times before it could obtain arms and go into action. In January 1942 a common ground for action was agreed, but another year would be needed before the plans became truly operational, finding a hearing among a population that had by now been reduced to a few tens of thousands from its previous half million.

Where the author would need to be a Sophocles or a Jeremiah to speak the unspeakable, he goes on talking as if a whole people still existed. Edelman escaped through the drainage system with a few other fighters when the whole Ghetto was razed to the ground and everything was on fire. He joined the Polish resistance, and he and the few who had survived fought in the front line for the defense of a city that had stood by in silence some months earlier as the Jews were wiped out. In a passage bordering on the surreal, he confines himself to a veiled criticism of his "Polish companions" for the isolation in which the Jewish fighters of the Ghetto were kept up to the very last. However, at the end he echoes the tones of a real Kaddish, recalling for all Abrasza Blum, the spiritual leader of the resistance movement; Jurek Blones,

a fearless commander, always in the front line; Mejlach Perlman, who knowingly chose death in the fire in order to help others; little David, who blocked
a tunnel with his body so that older companions and civilians could find
another hiding place; Sonja Davidowitz, who sent the others ahead because
she could no longer walk. Each one of these, with his or her name, represents
a whole world and stands for the many nameless fighters and civilians who,
in the heroism of daily life, kept alive the feeling of solidarity in a population
at the end of its strength and on its way to total destruction. "The site where
the Ghetto stood," notes Edelman on the last page, "has turned into an
expanse of ruins. . . . Those who were killed did their duty. . . . We who survived leave to you the charge of keeping their memory alive."[2]

Edelman would have to wait thirty-two years before returning to speak at
length of a wound still open, helped in this by a young writer who was a small
child at the time of the exterminations.[3] Hanna Krall escaped thanks to a
Polish family who kept her hidden throughout the war. She then took up the
task of mending the broken thread of dialogue between generations, finding a
place for a nameless pain, an unfillable vacuum that oppressed her no less
than those who had experienced those events in person. Saved by an act of
solidarity, she would be left to restore meaning to the absurd, mend a fracture
involving internal time and space, and give voice to new and old questions,
doubts, and uncertainties—to the torment of having stood by helplessly at the
deportation of 400,000 people, the unconscious burden of guilt that saps the
joy of living from within, and the grim depression and extreme humiliation
that survive time and can in some cases eventually lead to suicide.

Thirty years to go back and speak, to understand how and why, to remember and hand on the painful feeling that the same account would be impossible a second time. "It's precisely in places like this . . . that Wajda might shoot
his movie. Only Edelman says that he would not utter a single word before
Wajda's cameras, because he could tell it all only once. And he has told it."[4]

The dialogue between Edelman and Krall is lacerated and questioning,
full of doubt and internal conflict in a deeply changed world. Its silences seem
especially meaningful—things left out of the account in order to get past the
censor and avoid reprisals from a government that had not hesitated to
unleash a virulent antisemitic campaign in 1968 against the few Jews left in
the country. Similar demands seem to have led Hanna Krall and Edelman
himself to omit other issues that could have offended the sensibilities of the
opposition that was now forming around the Church.

The pain surrounding the interview is part of the process of working
through the bereavement, of a change in attitude that would change the face
of the country in a few years. Powerful social forces unimaginable at the time

of the interview were about to bring the historical and personal story of the author back to center-stage, and the interview was simply an omen of this. Until then Edelman had stayed on the sidelines of political life. An awkward witness to a past that does not pass, a silent prophet in a world hostile to Jews even if there were no more Jews in Poland, he had not played an active role again in any political or labor organization. He had sublimated his consuming anxiety and anguish in his profession as a doctor, meeting in every new patient one of the 400,000 he had seen wending their way through the Ghetto. Four years later, in 1981, he would be the Solidarity delegate for the city of Lodz. Young Poles who wanted to redeem their parents' world went to him to hear at first hand what extreme evil had made possible, what dangers were still lurking in a society where antisemitism was rife, regardless of whether there were any Jews left in the country.

Unlike Krall, whom he describes in friendly fashion as having a melo-dramatic side, Edelman does all he can to assume a world-weary stance. He paradoxically says that it no longer matters how many fighters were really enrolled in the Jewish Fighting Organization—220, as he says, or 500, as oth-ers claim. His detached tone when describing the isolation of the Jewish resis-tance in the face of the world changes when he speaks of the delay with which American Jews became aware of the true extent of the tragedy:

> There was a table with some twenty gentlemen sitting around it. Their faces expressed concentration and emotion: these were the presidents of the trade unions that during the war had given money for arms for the Ghetto. The chairman greets him and the discussion starts. What is the human mem-ory and is it proper to build monuments or maybe buildings—that sort of lit-erary dilemma. Edelman was being very careful not to just blab out some-thing improper, for instance, "And what importance does any of it have today?" He had no right to harm them in this way. "Be careful," he kept say-ing to himself, "careful, they have tears in their eyes. They gave money for arms. They went to President Roosevelt to ask him if they were true, all these stories about the Ghetto. You have to be good to them." (They must have gone to Roosevelt after one of the first reports prepared by "Waclaw." . . . the report was smuggled out by a messenger in his tooth, inside a filling, on microfilm, and reached the United States via London. But they'd had a hard time crediting it all . . . so they'd gone to their president to ask if these things could be taken seriously.) So he *was* good to them. He let them be moved and talk about human memory. But then, unintentionally, he hurt them so terribly: "Do you really think that it can be called an uprising.?"[5]

His relations with Jewish institutions were governed by a tangle of contradictory sentiments, in which anger at the outside world, which kept silent and looked on with indifference, shifts to the internal responsibilities of those who were unable to stand up to the Allied lies—a sign that on the deepest level the sentiment of disappointment is much more alive than he would wish people to believe from his public stance. In this light, the self-same criticism he makes of Anielewicz[6]—of having secretly harbored hopes of armed action on the part of the Home Army to open a breach into the Ghetto from outside, leaving aside any political and military aspects of the situation—can be seen as the secret admission of a painful sentiment of distrust toward the outside world.[7]

Edelman was brought up an orphan from an early age, and found his home in the Bund and his spiritual leader in Abrasza Blum. As the sole survivor of the leaders, he was unable to play a "heroic" role. He knew that a public hero is bound to cause resentment and incomprehension if he dares to be a man like others and to speak of friends with whom he shared the experience of struggle as normal beings. From the first moment—when he was called to report to the political parties that had gathered to hear him—he upset everyone by assuming attitudes contrary to their need for idealization, and describing events and telling anecdotes that ended up by irritating even those most sympathetic to him. When someone asked him how Mordechai Anielewicz became leader, he answered:

> He very much wanted to be a commander, so we chose him. He was a little childlike in this ambition, but he was a talented guy, well read, full of energy. Before the war he'd lived on Solec Street. His mother sold fish. When she had any left over, she would have him buy red paint and paint the gills so the fish would look fresh. He was constantly hungry. When he first came back to the Ghetto from Silesia and we gave him something to eat, he would shield the plate with his hand, so that nobody could take anything away from him.[8]

However, it must also be said that he is equally outspoken when describing episodes that put him in a poor light, for example when he was leaving the Ghetto and refused the request of some young prostitutes who had helped and fed him: "I said no. So you see. I only ask you one thing: don't make me explain today why I said no then."[9]

While Edelman is ambivalent toward Anielewicz, whom he criticizes for the decision to have recourse to collective suicide, he seems more sympathetic when it comes to his friend Jurek, who returned to the Ghetto to die with the others after escaping from the Gestapo, who had brutally tortured him. He emotionally remembers his companion Kellerman, who waited in vain for his return before hiding ("Right up till the last moment they must have been waiting for me, and I came too late");[10] Ania, who escaped from Pawiak Jail, but said that she would not accompany her companions out of the Ghetto because she could not leave her mother alone;[11] his friend Henoch Rus, who had not spoken to him for years, but thanked him at the time of the great round-up because his son, who had died at the beginning of the war after a blood transfusion, had died "at home, like a human being," thanks to Edelman.[12] He is compassionate with his luckier companions, and seems detached when he speaks of the president of the Judenrat, the Jewish Council set up by order of the German authorities, whom he criticizes for not having told the truth before killing himself: "This is the only thing we reproach him for."[13]

The lack of sympathy with which Edelman speaks of Anielewicz and the other Jewish resistance organizations indicates some unresolved conflicts. Recognition of the historical changes that took place after the tragedy also meant not losing a unique opportunity to recreate the conditions for an independent Jewish life; it meant recognizing that the birth of the Jewish homeland and its salvation were essential to avoid falling prey to a crushing despair and a never-ending mourning. It was not a case of giving up his own past ideas and the values on which they were based, but of going beyond them in his reflection in order to gain a deeper understanding of the unique nature of a tragedy. Each of the instruments produced by Judaism for its survival had its own rationality and validity. They were responses arising from a situation that, it was assumed, would remain within the limits of "normality" and "rationality." It was the world that turned out to be totally and unimaginably irrational, and Edelman himself reminds us of this in order to tell us that even questions asked in good faith can be like knives turning in the flesh, and that we have no right to ask an accounting of those who survived: "I had seen four hundred thousand people off at the Umschlagplatz. I myself, me, in person. They'd all passed by me while I stood there at the gate."[14]

Edelman stayed in Poland, disregarding those who wanted him to be a leader of Jews in the diaspora or to go to Israel as a representative of a new humanism that had risen from the ashes of Auschwitz. He chose to stay in the country that, after the liberation, had allowed a pogrom against the few survivors who were trying to return to their homes. He went on living as a "Bundist" even when his Bund no longer existed. He stayed on against the wishes of the Polish establishment, which did not forgive him, when he returned to active political life in Solidarity, for continuing to see his future as a Jew as not separate from that of the Polish national community, even when

Polish Jewry no longer existed, taking part in the Solidarity struggle, and suffering imprisonment in the weeks following the military coup d'etat. "To cel-
ebrate our anniversary here [in Warsaw] where social life is dominated
throughout by humiliation and coercion," he wrote in a letter explaining his
refusal to join the committee of honor for the celebrations of the fortieth
anniversary of the uprising, "would be to deny our fight."[15]

In the Ghetto Edelman represented the Bund, the organization that, more
than any other, had fought for the possibility of being both Jewish and Polish,
Jewish and Russian, Jewish socialist and citizen of one's particular state. The
watchword of the movement was "national and cultural autonomy." The revolutionary movement was unwilling to offer anything better to the only organization of "a people without a land," to the most oppressed of cultures, than
the prospect of a *cupio dissolvi* in the name of a palingenesis that existed only
in the imagination of those proposing it, and a utopia that later turned out to
be worse than the evils it intended righting, becoming the source of new kinds
of degeneration and corruption in the life and organization of society. The
model proposed by the Bund was ahead of its time, for the background
against which such a proposal would have had some possibility of success
was that of a united Europe, a framework of democracy and tolerance quite
the opposite of the nationalisms and totalitarianisms that would oppose one
another on the European stage after the collapse of the old Europe. To use the
words spoken by Gedali in Babel's *Red Cavalry*, "an International of good
folk" was needed[16]—a lowest common denominator among the various
European nations, which has only partially and slowly been acquired since the
war, finding a spur in the very immensity of the destruction wrought by the
two world wars. Nor is it a coincidence that the Bundist hypothesis has been
partially realized, though in completely different forms from those imagined
by its champions, and elsewhere—in the United States, far from the places for
which it was envisaged, but where the country's history makes it much more
difficult for a majority to support an illusory call to an uncontaminated national community.

The Bund was opposed by both Jewish and non-Jewish revolutionaries,
but regrettably responded in kind to those within the Jewish world who took
emigration to Palestine as a working hypothesis. "Seasick Zionists" for the
Bolshevik Plekhanov, the Bundists did not hesitate to turn the defamatory
accusations against them back on those who chose Zionism. Twin brothers,
Bundists and Zionists moved forward separately, uniting only when the focus
was no longer plans for life, but plans for a different death. Today the memory of this movement, which organized thousands of Eastern Europe's Jews,
restoring their offended sense of dignity, barely survives even in the Jewish

world, which at best sees it as the fruit of just one more illusion. Quite a number of people, reflecting bitterly on the present century's Jewish experience, wonder if it would not have been better to urge people to emigrate rather than to fight for human dignity in their own country. "If I'd urged the Jews of Europe to go to Palestine in the 1930s, instead of speaking out against Zionism," agonized Trotsky's biographer Isaac Deutscher just after the catastrophe, in an emotion-laden text, "I would perhaps have helped to save some of the lives that were later extinguished in Hitler's gas chambers."[17] Marek Edelman also considers the same agonizing question when he says, almost as if justifying himself to the last Jews who left the country after Gomulka's anti-semitic campaign:

> You see, before the war I was telling my fellow Jews that their place was here, in Poland. That we would build socialism here, and that they should stay here. So when they stayed, and the war then began, and everything that was to happen in this war to the Jews was beginning to happen—how was I supposed to leave?[18]

With the outbreak of war, the fate of European Jewry was tragically marked. If Jews were to escape, they had to flee across the Atlantic—a viable solution for only a privileged few after American restrictions were tightened up in the wake of the First World War. The State of Israel did not yet exist, and after the 1939 White Paper, the boatloads of immigrants who tried to land clandestinely on the coast of Palestine had to run the gauntlet of British coastal batteries, which did not hesitate to send the refugees back to where they had come from, in other words toward certain death in the camps.

The struggle and rebellion would spring not from the possibility of choice, but from desperation. People fought not for their lives, but for a different death against every hope and beyond the values by which they had lived for centuries: "We fought in order not to be butchered," says Edelman. In a situation like this there was no room even for drama, for drama and tragedy contain an element of choice and illusion denied those fighting in the Ghetto. The Jews who had taken up arms in a situation of extreme isolation and desperation were aware of the horrific truth that even if Hitler were to lose the war, he had certainly already won the most absurd battle—that against the Jewish people—for Polish Jewry had been wiped out. While human flesh was burning in the ovens, the Allies refused *for technical reasons* to bomb the railway lines along which a defenseless and terrified population was carried toward total destruction.

"Travelers going through Treblinka have observed that the trains don't stop at this station." Every day like that: Wilner brings information from the Ghetto, "Waclaw" writes the reports, radio operators transmit them to London, and the London radio—contrary to its practice heretofore—does not include any information about the matter in its programming.[19]

The only thing to do was to seek a different death—one that would "redeem" and be less "dishonoring" for those suffering it. Certain only apparently paradoxical statements scattered through the interview can be understood in this light. They echo as an obsessive call not to set up comparisons between those who died fighting and those who died in the gas chambers, and are an invitation to reflect on the absurd and to understand. For example:

After all, humanity had agreed that dying with arms was more beautiful than without arms.[20]

He screams that I probably consider the people who were surging into the train cars to have been worse than the ones who were fighting. Of course, I do, absolutely, everybody does, but it is stupid. . . . To die in a gas chamber is by no means worse than to die in battle. . . . It is infinitely more difficult than to go out shooting.[21]

The reader is invited to be more intelligent, to reflect in order to grasp the range of messages contained in the words. In this Edelman remains a child of the Jewish storytelling tradition: the rejection of any heroic claims hides the greatest of heroisms—that of daily life—which is the hardest to win and hold on to. "When one knows death so well, one has more responsibility for life."[22]

In the face of the tragedy that was about to befall Jerusalem, the prophet Jeremiah used the metaphor of Rachel to describe his state of mind. Rachel wept for her children, because they were no more, and she refused to be comforted, for those who had not come back would be missing forever. The prophet's dream ends on a note of hope: "Your children will come back." This experience was not given to those like Edelman who lived the experience of the Umschlagplatz. Even the prophets of doom would not have dared to imagine what his eyes saw. Those who lived that experience could no longer even draw on an archetype of the good mother. Elsewhere in the death camps, the silence and solitude were extreme. As Wiesel obsessively recalled, the silence was total: the silence of the city of the camps, the silence of the world, silence over victims and executioners, the absence of God and of His likeness in man.

As Levinas asks, "Who can describe the solitude of those who thought they were dying together with justice?" How can we speak of the innermost feelings and the torment of those who survived the catastrophe and were then driven mad by having pretended not to see their dying neighbor, or for having begged some extra hours or minutes, or for thanking heaven for having escaped a selection that always meant the worst for someone else? It was from the desire to make sure that the expected death did not take the form of the camps that the Ghetto fighters obtained a few pistols and some gasoline in order to fight an enemy who still seemed invincible. It was not for the sake of life that undernourished men forgotten by the world dared to face up with bare hands to an enemy who used airplanes and tanks to wipe out the last traces of life in the Ghetto. This is also one of the reasons why the Ghetto uprising has assumed the value of an exemplar—a model of the most extreme solitude, a metaphor of a human condition, and also the source of a new identity, as against old and new stereotypes, for those who had suffered the most extreme violence. The Ghetto uprising was the first armed civilian uprising in occupied Europe, a resistance that lasted three whole weeks—longer than the whole of Belgium and France had managed. It was the start of a change which would provide Jews with a basis for the new age of a Jew who does not let himself be sent off passively to the slaughter. The image of Israeli society with its army would then come to their aid, laying the foundations of a new identity and redemption to an experience that called for a high dose of clarity and historical awareness in order to avoid the accusation of having played a part in their destruction with their own behavior—as if in those circumstances the victims could have reacted in any other way. Thus they were exposed to the absurdity and the tragic mockery of having to seek examples of struggle and rebellion in order to justify themselves.

It would be a long time before this stereotype would start to crumble among Jews themselves, and people would learn to distinguish between human behavior in normal and extreme situations. And only recently have historians started to study the specifically Jewish contribution to the anti-Nazi resistance: as freedom fighters in the Spanish Civil War (a fifth of the 35,000 partisans, including some who came from Palestine); as sacrificial victims in occupied France at least until the Molotov-Ribbentrop pact was broken (who can forget the role of the Jewish tailors, abandoned to their fate?); as partisans in the Polish forests, in Bohemia, Hungary, and elsewhere, under false names because their enemies were also found in the very forces that were fighting Nazism; as soldiers in the Allied armies, in the Red Army, and in anti-Nazi espionage; and lastly as Jews in the Palestinian Jewish Brigade, which would later give birth to the Israeli Army. It is estimated that about one and a half million Jews fought against the Nazis. Wherever they could, Jews fought alongside their non-Jewish fellow citizens, with a higher percentage in Western countries.

We would end by setting the subjects of the Edelman interview alongside the work of some of the other writers who used reflection on their experiences in Nazi camps as a reference point in reconstructing their existence, the best-known of them being Primo Levi, Emanuel Levinas, and Bruno Bettelheim, each one different in background and temperament. The first was secular and progressive, the second was a philosopher with deep roots in the Jewish religious tradition, and the third was a socially committed psychotherapist with interests ranging over the most varied fields, but all three seem to agree with Edelman on one point: the absolute and boundless call to an ethics of an unlimited human solidarity. Each in his own way, and with his own conceptual and cultural frame of reference, stressed the impossibility of communicating the experience of the camps and also the dangers of becoming inured to evil. They apparently want to remind us in their own particular language that without ethics the very continuation of life is impossible. In the age that saw extermination become a bureaucratic plan, and hence a practice having no connection with the realm of sentiment, those who were reduced to the condition of *namelessness* laid claim to the most ancient and apparently most obvious truth, but certainly the easiest one to forget: the worth of the specific individual person. Gripped by deep anguish at the war's end, Edelman wandered from town to town and country to country, but wherever he went there was no longer anyone waiting for him. The world was celebrating victory. For him a whole world had been lost, and he lived with the feeling that there was still someone waiting for him, someone to be saved, still something he had to do somewhere. He gazed at the walls, the floors, and the deserted streets. He went home to bed, and stayed there for days, and then weeks, staring at the wall without speaking. His wife and his few remaining friends came to his aid, drawing pictures on the wall he was looking at. Delicate hands full of love in a shattered world now drew things for him: one day a stomach, another day a heart, then an aorta and other parts of the body. It took two years of this, with a constant succession of pictures being drawn on his "Western wall," before Edelman recovered the strength to return to his oldest aspirations.

The description of his work in the hospital, where he was employed as a heart specialist, is one of the most moving sections of his tale. Before every new patient, Edelman relived the anguish of the young Jew who was powerless in the face of the Nazis' brutality. In silence, like a speechless prophet, he would make sure that a patient's life was not seen as a number and that the everyday pettiness of the duty surgeon did not get the better of the duty to save a life.

When faced with a life to be saved, Edelman never spared himself, and when he could do nothing more, he still had the task of "assuring patients a comfortable death" and doing all he could to spare solitude and anguish for them. As he did in the Ghetto, he had to do something to preserve his own and others' feeling of integrity. In the Ghetto, he observes, everybody had to have something important to do, for activity was the only chance of survival.[23] "All this bustle might not have had any importance, because everybody was getting killed anyway, but at least one wasn't just waiting his turn idly."[24] However, this does not mean that people in the Ghetto did not love one another and were not bound to one another. Indeed, it was only by loving someone else and taking responsibility for that person that people could gamble on existence. In the Ghetto people ran to a rabbi to be united in marriage before deportation, and did not leave one another until the last round-up, in order to find a meaning to existence.[25] Having someone to protect was the condition for not giving up altogether. Contrary to what Edelman says, the whole existence of the hundreds of thousands of people trapped in the Ghetto was a life of choices concentrated in time and space. And his whole book, which states that in 1943 there was no room for choice because everything was already decided, shows the exact opposite. As Vidal Naquet observes in his preface to the French edition, Edelman's book "is a whole reflection on choices, today's choices and yesterday's choices": the choice of the patient who chooses to live or to let himself die; the choice of the doctor who gambles on life and does not see the patient simply as a number; the choice of nurses in the Ghetto who break an old man's leg so that he cannot be deported; the choice of Korczak, who does not desert the children in his orphanage even though he has a chance of escape; the choice of Paola Lifszyc, who follows her mother even though she has a chance of escape; the choice of Czerniakow to die alone without telling his brothers about what is at stake in that month of July 1942; the choice of Edelman not to commit suicide but to continue the struggle against the Nazis outside the Ghetto; the choice to be victim or slaughterer; the choice to take up life again afterwards in a shattered world. Three decades later, Edelman's memory still bears the image of Stasia as she welcomed him weeping because she thought he had been caught: while everybody else was fleeing, she had waited for him on the steps, with her beautiful "long, thick braids."[26] In the Ghetto Edelman had decided for 40,000,[27] for a different death. Now he could also decide for a single life, personally running the risk, because of the "little nuisances . . . of minor importance"[28] which had led to the last great exodus of the few Jews left in the country after the Nazi slaugh-

ter. In Poland in 1977 it was impossible to speak more explicitly of the viru-
lently antisemitic campaign of 1968, and of the inner solitude evoked by the
memory of the anonymous flowers that the Ghetto fighter had received on the
anniversary of the uprising each year, and that did not arrive in 1968 when he
had greatest inner need of them.[29] Disheartenment is represented by "an old
man with a white beard" whose broken voice chants laments "for six million
dead. Such a lonely old man, in a long black coat."[30] The contrast between the
grandiose monuments and the solitude of the survivors is seen in the description of an old man who cannot count more than seven people, which is not
enough to recite the prayer of the dead, the Kaddish.[31]

Edelman chooses the image of a palm tree to represent the connection
between what he did in the Ghetto to save people and his present activity as a
doctor. Just as earlier the wall symbolized the progress from nameless pain to
life, now it is the palm tree, another archetypical Jewish symbol. Under a
palm, like a palm, Edelman, the new Job, can continue his struggle in order
"to arrive before God":

> In the clinic where I later worked, there was a big, tall palm tree there
> in the hall. I would stand underneath that palm tree sometimes—and I'd look
> out over the rooms where my patients were lying. This was a long time ago,
> when we didn't yet have today's medications or operations or devices avail-
> able, and the majority of the people in those rooms were in effect simply
> condemned to death. My assignment was to save as many as possible—and
> I realized, that day under the palm, that actually it was the same assignment
> as I'd had there, at the Umschlagplatz. There, too, I would stand at the gate
> and pull out individuals from the throngs of those condemned to die.[32]

"When you've had to see all those people off on the trains," observes
Edelman to himself, "later on you can have some things to settle with Him."[33]

> So you never know who's outsmarted whom. Sometimes you are happy
> that you've succeeded, you have checked everything thoroughly and you
> know that nothing bad should happen anymore, and then Stefan, Marysia's
> brother, dies because he was overwhelmed with happiness.[34]

Thoughts come thick and fast, the past overlays the present, and when the
tension of an operation on a patient eases, the joy over what you have managed to do also evaporates.

You finally realize the proportion; one to four hundred thousand. 1:400,000. It is simply ludicrous. But—and here Edelman concludes by paraphrasing a talmudic maxim—every life is a full one hundred percent for each individual, so that perhaps it makes some sense after all.[35]

NOTES

1. Marek Edelman, *The Ghetto Fights: Warsaw, 1941–45* (London: Bookmarks, 1990).
2. Ibid., p. 77.
3. H. Krall (1977), *Shielding the Flame (an Intimate Conversation with Dr. Marek Edelman, Last Surviving Leader of the Warsaw Ghetto Uprising)* (New York: Henry Holt, 1986).
4. Ibid., p. 81.
5. Ibid., pp. 11–12.
6. "He had a lot of youthful verve and enthusiasm, only he had never before seen an 'action.' He hadn't seen the people being loaded into wagons at the Umschlagplatz. And such a thing—when you see four hundred thousand people being sent off to the gas chambers—can break a person. We did not meet on April 19th. I saw him the day after. He was already a different man. Celina told me: 'You know, it happened to him yesterday. He was just sitting and muttering: "We're all going to die. . . . ' " He managed to get roused up again only once after that. We got a message from the Home Army to wait in the northern part of the Ghetto. . . . He must have thought that some reinforcements were being sent. We kept trying to dissuade him. 'Let it go, the area there is completely dead, we won't get through.' You know what? I think that all along he had actually convinced himself of the possibility of some sort of victory. Obviously, he never spoke about it before. On the contrary. 'We are going to die,' he would yell, 'there is no way out, we'll die for our honor, for history. . . .' All the sorts of things one says in such cases. But today I think that all the time he maintained some kind of childlike hope." Ibid., pp. 4–5.
7. The same observation be made about the public position he assumed in his "emotional" response to the young German soldier who wrote to him saying, "We are both victims of that terrible war." Ibid., p. 11.
8. Ibid., p. 4.
9. Ibid., p. 41.
10. Ibid., p. 64.
11. Ibid., p. 66.
12. Ibid., p. 63. The child had died after a blood transfusion for which Edelman had offered his help. After his son's death, Rus had never spoken to Edelman again.
13. Ibid., p. 9.

14. Ibid., p. 39.

15. Ibid., p. 122.

16. Isaak Babel, *Red Cavalry*, pp. 38–40.

17. Isaac Deutscher, "The Spiritual Climate of Israel" (1954), in *The Non-Jewish Jew and Other Essays* (London: Oxford University Press, 1968), p. 128.

18. Krall, *Shielding the Flame*, p. 39.

19. Ibid., p. 95.

20. Ibid., p. 10. A few pages earlier the same view is seen in such reflections as: "People have always thought that shooting is the highest form of heroism" (p. 3).

21. Ibid., pp. 36–37.

22. Ibid., p. 33.

23. Ibid., pp. 42–43.

24. Ibid., p. 43.

25. Ibid., p. 115.

26. Ibid., p. 68.

27. Ibid., p. 81.

28. Ibid., p. 102.

29. Ibid., pp. 39–40.

30. Ibid., p. 74.

31. Ibid., p. 79.

32. Ibid., p. 85.

33. Ibid., p. 86.

34. Ibid., p. 116.

35. Ibid., p. 117.

Spirit and Flesh:
Toward a Post-Shoah, Post-Modern Incarnational Ethic

James Bernauer

When Pope John-Paul II visited Germany in June of 1996, he gave a talk in Paderborn in which he praised several people who, "faced with the totalitarian dictatorships, courageously and fearlessly witnessed to the truth of the Gospel."[1] Among the seven he named was Helmut James von Moltke, who was executed by the Nazis for his resistance activities and for his vision of a postwar German democracy. On August 23, 1940, von Moltke wrote this to his wife: "N[ational] S[ocialism] has once more taught us reverence for what is below us, i.e., material things, blood, ancestry, our bodies."[2] I must confess that initially I was shocked by the statement, and my remarks are an effort to do justice to this good man's judgment and to the difficult truth which he is asserting, namely, how Nazism successfully exploited a strong religious alienation from the body and, thus, Christianity's estrangement from its own incarnational tradition. At the end of the war, Karl Jaspers differentiated German guilt according to various levels: political, criminal, moral, and metaphysical.[3] I would like to argue that there is a fifth level of ethical-spiritual responsibility which explores how our most foundational religious images, concepts, and practices for intimate and public lives may contain seeds of hate and violence that could come to flourish almost automatically in certain cultural crises. But that is to race ahead.

How was it possible for National Socialism to be so successful in capturing the minds and hearts of so many Christians either as committed believers or as tolerant bystanders? The Nazi period forces all of us to ask this question, to confront our dangerous ethical selves: How adequately or inadequately do we fashion ourselves, or are we fashioned, intellectually, ethically, spiritually, to appreciate or refuse certain types of moral appeal? These practices of the self define how an individual comes to feel that a matter warrants moral concern and what steps one is obligated to take in response to that moral signal. Certainly it is the case that National Socialism appropriated a ready-made set of national virtues—honesty, diligence, cleanliness, dependability, obedience to authority, mistrust of excess.[4] Still, if we are to understand why these

257

virtues came to be so characteristic, and why people were so prepared to tolerate evil, we must interrogate the dynamics of the spiritual formation passed down by German culture.

To speak of spiritual life at this time might seem to miss the mark when one remembers the brutal reality of Nazi deeds. What has to be faced, though, is that the beginning of the Hitler regime coincided with a passionate desire among many Germans for a spiritual renewal, indeed for a politics of spirit which National Socialism attempted to define. At this distance it is difficult to appreciate how promising a year 1933 was expected to be. In fact, Paul Tillich at the time accused perhaps the most prominent of his theological colleagues (Emanuel Hirsch) of associating the year so closely with 33, the traditional date of Jesus's death and resurrection, that the year of Hitler's coming to power was given the "meaning of an event in the history of salvation."[5] What has to be acknowledged is that there was an intense atmosphere of spiritual transformation that year. Philosophers and theologians felt as though a special invitation had been extended to their talents.

If I had time, I would like to look in detail at how this spiritual moment was perceived. For now, let me just say that many philosophers and theologians regarded it as a moment of crisis, and I would claim that the most important element of the crisis was how one was to relate to oneself, how one might affirm oneself as worthwhile. But to speak of spirit in the context of a culture which still possessed deep roots in Christianity was also to discuss flesh; cravings for spirit inevitably connect to a discourse of sin, sensuality, and sexuality. If spirit expressed vitality and creative force, flesh possessed many satanic features, assaulting reason and proclaiming human weakness.[6] This dualistic reading of the spirit-flesh struggle as soul versus body or sexuality is certainly inadequate to Paul's theology, and yet, as we know, it has often characterized Christian discussions of sexual matters both in the past and the present.[7] Here we may have, though, the source of Christianity's own greatest weakness in its encounter with Nazism, for much pathology seemed to flourish in modern religious culture's charting of sexuality. It is the charting with which I am concerned, not the sexual morality that may be put forward as a response to it. Certainly many of the Church's statements since Vatican II have delineated a much more positive appreciation of the sexual realm than had been the case. And I do want to emphasize this: I am not accusing a code of morality but rather the ethical-spiritual foundations of the very self who finds suitable a type of morality or its overthrow. Having selected sexuality as a privileged route to moral status, the Churches did not create a very sophisticated palette of insight into it. The broodings of moral theology were too frequently isolated from the traditions of Christian spiritual theology.[8] I will not repeat for you the series of Christian statements from this period which denounced the social permissiveness of co-education, and its supposed lack of concern for the lust in children and adolescents; nor those which denounced the immodesty intrinsic to public swimming pools; nor the many warnings about the dangers of nudity and male friendships. This determination to exorcise eroticism all too often encouraged a fierce self-hatred. While Christian moral formation was inadequate, in my judgment, to the sexual domain, the Church's anxiety about it did not come from nowhere and did reflect an awareness that for a century there had been a new sexual challenge in German culture. The religious sponsorship of, or at least association with, most major social events in a person's life at that time, as well as practices such as confession, allowed the Church to hear the effect upon an individual's intimate life of large cultural forces.[9] Historians and philosophers have indicated the many different factors which thrust sexual change into the center of moral crisis: the Napoleonic period's relaxation of legal constraints enlarged the menu of sexual desire and practice; the secularization of society reduced the authority of priests and their traditions as well as encouraged a disassociation between morality and religion; industrialization placed new stresses upon the family; the very organization of society was taking life and its functions as objects of scrutiny and control.[10] The Church, however, tended to see in a certain relaxation of sexual moral codes a decline of faith, and thus an historical intimacy between Christian existence and the spirit-flesh struggle was reconfirmed and strengthened, now with modern sexuality as its unchallenged center. The pivotal role which Christian moral formation conferred upon disciplining sexuality as a result of this had two major consequences.

First, it exposed Christians to a Nazism that could be thought of as either ethically allied with Christianity or as a liberation from religion's inadequacy to the richness of human life. National Socialism found the religious preoccupation with sexuality in moral formation to be helpful in a variety of ways: it sustained the emphasis on those secondary virtues which made people so compliant; it habituated people to an atmosphere of omnipresent sinfulness which seemed to grow with every step beyond childhood; it educated people into a moral pessimism about themselves and what they might be able to achieve; and this issued in what the Jesuit Alfred Delp, who was later to be executed by the Nazis, described as a paralysis of the inner self.[11] While it has been frequently acknowledged that an absence of German self-confidence was a precondition for Hitler's successful career, the focus of responsibility has normally been given to economic factors; the moral-spiritual dimensions should not be ignored.[12] It is this religious subversion of self-confidence which lies behind the primacy given to obedience as a virtue, and an extraordinary insensitivity to the demands of conscience. Many religious and moral practices established a profound alienation from one's self and one's desires. And this self-alienation was also a mode of alienation from the public space: the model for dealing with moral difficulty was set by sexuality—avoidance of danger and cultivation of a tranquil interiority. Often this trained people into a permanent submissiveness or stimulated an intense yearning to get beyond the sexual guilt of Christianity, a state which Nazism held out as one of its promises.

Nazism, in effect, put forward the bold project of overcoming the dualisms fostered by religion: body versus soul, flesh versus spirit.[13] National Socialism spoke to—and did not just flatter—the German tradition of and pride in inwardness, the *Innerlichkeit* which advocated a strenuous self-cultivation.[14] But the Nazi revolution bound together this celebration of inwardness, of the German spirit, with a profound affirmation of one's historical moment, of one's own German body, social and personal. It was to be praised for its health, its beauty, its utility, and, most of all, as the temple for the transmission of biological life. The extent of its sexual ethics could be put forward as what is most distinctive of Aryan ideology.[15]

Its ethics was a strategy of sabotage against alternative relations to sexuality. It made a foe of the sexual libertinism of the Weimar Republic and of the Soviet Union. The sexual laxity which had been identified in the past with that ancient enemy, the French, now was tied to Communism's relaxation of legal restraints.[16] After it had replaced the Weimar Republic, the Third Reich mounted a widespread campaign of sexual purification: denunciations of pornography, homosexuality, and any eroticism not governed by the desire for procreation, for these would eclipse the central status which sexuality had on the "battlefield of life."[17] This crusade against eroticism was terribly attractive to German Christians—and, I might add, made Hitler appear as a force for moral renewal to Christians in the United States as well.[18] Catholic anxiety about Communism included its perceived sexual license and hostility to family values. Thus, on the eve of the Second World War and the Holocaust, Germany was blanketed with a campaign for decency. But National Socialism was far more cunning than most expected. The campaign for decency was by no means an acceptance of Christian codes. National Socialism constructed a post-Christian erotic. While Church leaders were regularly denouncing the dangers of immodesty, Nazi culture was celebrating the beauty of the nude body and the benefits of exhibiting it—from galleries of art to the joyful gatherings of youth. The Nazis were very successful in portraying Church views as hopelessly prudish, the Church's sexual teaching as unrelentingly hostile to the joys of sexual life, and in encouraging young people to look elsewhere for a wise understanding of their erotic desires.[19] One might have hoped that the long pondering about sexual activities would confer upon Christians a particular sophistication in grasping some of the subtle tones in Nazism's sexual propaganda. I have found few signs of such proficiency.[20] It is as if the long stress on the natural law had made them deaf to the changing sounds of historically contingent evil. Indeed, there seems a special blindness, a general failure to recognize how demonic the unrelenting stress on eroticism's demonic force could also be.

The inadequacy of this moral formation had a second face. In that endless searching after the reasons why the Jews were so victimized by the Nazis, why so many collaborated in their murder, and especially why so many stood aside and failed to do what could have been done, I propose that the issue of sexuality gives an essential answer. Before the Jews were murdered, before they were turned away from as not being one's concern, the Jew had already been defined as spiritless, on the one hand, and sexually possessed, erotically charged, on the other. In contrast to that special German inwardness which I mentioned earlier, the Jew was portrayed not only as empty of spirit but as an enemy of it. German philosophers worried about what was called a *Verjudung* of *deutschen Geistesleben*, a "Jewification" of German spiritual life.[21] The Jewish intellectual was both a materialist and a pharisaic rationalist in comparison with German depth thinking. Deprived of spirit, the Jew was defined in Nazi propaganda as essentially carnal, as excessively sexual, indeed as boundlessly erotic, whose conduct was not under the control of the moral conscience.[22] Lust robbed the Jews of reason and, thus, reduced them to an animal level, a status which would soon come to be reflected in Nazi torture.

Some roots of the Nazi portrayal are in Christianity.[23] I am not able here to trace these roots, but I do wish to note the inadequacy of a frequently appearing model in which Christian anti-Judaism and modern antisemitism are placed on a chronological calendar where the former is superseded by the latter. In fact they coexisted in the Nazi period and blended in ways that have yet to be adequately mapped. Nevertheless, with that said, the extreme victimization of the Jews by the Nazis comes from the position into which they were placed on the erotic field of modern sexuality.[24] That field need not be isolated, however, from religious discourses and practices. This sexual depiction was not static but functioned dynamically within an ethical field defined as a life-and-death struggle (*ein Kampf auf Leben und Tod*) taking place between the healthy life force of Aryan blood and the disease-laden Semitic death substance.[25] This final element in modern sexual culture may certainly be described as racist, but it also relates to the Christian sexual discourse in at least one specific way. This life-and-death struggle paradigm shows the legacy of that spirit-flesh struggle in which all sexual sin was grave or mortal, that is, condemning the sinner's soul to the death of eternal damnation.

It was in their customary portrayal of Jews as an erotic flood that the Nazis spoke to Christian anxieties about the sexual climate of their culture. Jews were sexually dangerous, their printing companies even blamed for producing far too suggestive pictures of the saints which were displayed in German homes.[26] If we look for the reasons why so few people were troubled about standing on the sidelines, why so many failed to get involved with the victimized Jew, practically or even emotionally, I would claim that this is certainly a major source of that moral indifference. For the Germans, who were proud of that spiritual inwardness which was the legacy of their culture, and who were humiliated by the sexual war which was waged in their bodies, the carnal Jew represented a contamination, the destruction of the spiritual sense and the eruption of the uncontrollable erotic body. It was to meet one's end as a moral and religious being. In the light of the predominant Christian style of moral formation, one could have predicted that, even while protests were mounted on behalf of the crippled and the insane, the Jews would be abandoned. At best.

Goebbels, Hitler's propaganda minister, claimed that the Third Reich had changed people inwardly, that it had given people the opportunity to escape the bourgeois epoch and embrace a new ethic of "heroism, masculinity, readiness for sacrifice, discipline."[27] He is only half-right. Certainly, the Nazi movement was successful in absorbing common secondary virtues, which, at times, were even defended by Christians as particularly appropriate to the religious sensibility.[28] But these virtues were appealing to people and were developed by them because they were eminently suitable for a struggle with one's flesh, that other self which had to subdued. This campaign's instrumentalization and depersonalization of sexuality was a principal source of that doubling process which some have argued is the key to appreciating how average citizens could function with a good conscience while contributing to mass murder.[29] The split self accounts for how, in the midst of administering the death camps, SS soldiers could be praised for their decency, their loyalty, their truthfulness. Despite the destruction of millions, Himmler could assure his men that "our inward being, our soul, our character has not suffered injury from it."[30] This is why the Nazis made a sharp distinction between authorized and illegitimate killings.[31] As strange as it may seem, Hitler's biographer, Joachim Fest, seems justified when he asserts that National Socialism exercised its greatest appeal among those who had a craving for morality. On the other hand, I do want to stress this: Goebbels was half-right. One of Nazism's genuine novelties is that it fashioned from a traditional morality of secondary

virtues and of sexual asceticism an ethic which evoked from the German people an extraordinary willingness to discipline themselves and, in millions of
cases, sacrifice themselves physically. While frequently exploiting the religion's divided self, Nazism created a post-Christian ethic by establishing the
opportunity for an intense choice of one's self, in the here and now, an eroticism of one's self in time. There is a major shift in Western experience here.
Within cultures shaped by Christianity, one's sense of worth was through self-
denial and surrender to the vocation one was given by Providence. Who one
was to become in that state free from time and flesh regulated one's com-
merce with oneself and others. Nazi eroticism was tied to the affirmation of
who one is biologically, to the embrace of one's body and, through that, one's
people. The model of virginity yields to that of breeding. I would claim that
their relationship is not one of strict opposition, as, for example, Levinas
maintains when he contrasts a materialistic bondage to a biological past to a
religious spiritual freedom from that bodily burden.[32] On the level of ethical
formation, the struggle of spirit with flesh was no less a bondage and, indeed,
was prelude to Nazism's own enslavement.

CONCLUSION

Just as a study of our age's culture could not be performed without a treatment of psychoanalysis, I would argue that twentieth-century history becomes
unintelligible when abstracted from the erotic field. Needless to say, I do not
hold that it is reducible to that domain. We have looked at an ethical practice
in which National Socialism forged a regime of erotic danger and sexual pleasure and a manner of relating to sexual life which was less indebted to biology than it was to an inherited sphere of spirituality, the struggle of spirit with
flesh. Within that field, Nazism presented itself as achieving erotic pleasure
by overcoming dualisms: a Christian alienation of the soul from the body, and
a Jewish alienation of the carnal from the spiritual. An ethics that is really
after Auschwitz must take into account this history by establishing a spiritu-
al-moral formation for Christians which does justice to their faith's affirmation of the worth of the human body and which integrates the teaching about
sexuality with the Church's discourse on human dignity. Major steps have
already been taken in this direction by many Church statements and practices.
To give one very concrete example of a positive practice from my local situation, I would point to the search in Jesuit colleges over the last twenty years
for a more adequate mode of integrating the pursuit of intellectual excellence
and the quest for ethical maturity. It could be argued that recent emphasis on
faith and justice as the organizing principle of a Jesuit style of education

addresses the double failure of religious and academic cultures. It shifts moral formation from a model in which sex in the drama of flesh versus spirit is privileged as the central seismographic sign of healthy ethical life to the task of integrating the human needs of the historical moment with a personal self-appropriation stressing one's capabilities for meeting those needs and one's personal dignity as sexually embodied. It also unmasks the supposed political-moral neutrality of an academic culture which does not seem to possess the ethical insights and solidarities by which to be critical of its knowledge formations. And perhaps the most important step toward the development of these resources has already been taken by those Jesuit schools which stress as an integral component of their education an engagement and solidarity with communities which are traditionally victimized by our society's most powerful institutions.

NOTES

1. Pope John-Paul II, "Linking Evangelization and Ecumenism" (June 22, 1996), in *Origins: CNS Documentary Service* 26, no. 9 (August 1, 1996): 139.
2. Helmut James von Moltke, *Letters to Freya, 1939–1945*, ed. and trans. by Beate Ruhm von Oppen (New York: Knopf, 1990).
3. Karl Jaspers, *The Question of German Guilt* (New York: Dial Press, 1947).
4. See Carl Amery, *Capitulation* (New York: Herder & Herder, 1967), pp. 29–34.
5. P. Tillich, "Open Letter to Emanuel Hirsch" (October 1, 1934), in *The Thought of Paul Tillich*, ed. J. L. Adams, W. Pauck, and R. Shinn (New York: Harper & Row, 1985), p. 364.
6. The anxiety about consideration of the sexual and erotic dimensions of fascism has several faces. A very major reason for evading serious investigation of the sexual dimension in the period of National Socialism is the extraordinary success of Hannah Arendt's depiction of Adolf Eichmann and her thesis on the banality of evil, namely, the view that Nazi crimes were executed as a result of a certain "thoughtlessness." To understand him, there is no need to explore his emotional and affective life. Let me say outright that I stand in awe of Hannah Arendt's philosophical achievement, and I admire much in *Eichmann in Jerusalem* (New York: Viking, 1963). At the same time, I have become suspicious about the grounds and effect of her portrayal's popularity. Recall for a moment Bruno Bettelheim's uneasiness with the success of the book, play, and film of Anne Frank's diary. He wrote: "I believe that the world-wide acclaim given her story cannot be explained unless we recognize in it our wish to forget the gas chambers, and our effort to do so by glorifying the ability to retreat into an extremely private, gentle, sensitive world, and there to cling as much as possible to what have been one's usual daily attitudes and activities, although surrounded by a

maelstrom apt to engulf one at any moment" ("The Ignored Lesson of Anne Frank," in *Surviving and Other Essays* [New York: Vintage, 1979], p. 247). Has Hannah Arendt's Eichmann turned us away from a scrutiny of our passions, especially our erotic ones, by leaving the more consoling message that it is our reluctance to think which will lead us into disaster? I believe it has, but she bears only partial responsibility for that. We know from her consideration of the later trials of those who worked at Auschwitz that she had begun to recognize something else beside the banality of evil. To quote her: "The chief human factor in Auschwitz was sadism, and sadism is basically sexual." She goes on to say that the "smiling reminiscences of the defendants . . . and their unusually high spirits throughout . . . reflects the sweet remembrance of great sexual pleasure, as well as indicating blatant insolence" (Introduction to *Auschwitz: A Report on the Proceedings Against Robert Karl Ludwig Mulka and Others Before the Court at Frankfurt* [New York: Praeger, 1966], pp. xxvii–xxviii).

7. For discussion of this theme, see Peter Brown, *The Body and Society: Men, Women, and Sexual Renunciation in Early Christianity* (New York: Columbia University Press, 1988), esp. pp. 47–49, 86, 296–297, 348–349, 376–377.

8. See John Mahoney, *The Making of Moral Theology: A Study of the Roman Catholic Tradition* (Oxford: Clarendon Press, 1987), pp. 28–29, 45. Also see Michael Langer, *Katholische Sexualpädagogik im 20. Jahrhundert: Zur Geschichte eines religionspädagogischen Problems* (Munich: Kösel, 1986), p. 127.

9. See Edward Shorter, "Towards a History of *La Vie Intime*: The Evidence of Cultural Criticism in Nineteenth-Century Bavaria," in *The Emergence of Leisure*, ed. Michael Marrus (New York: Harper Torchbooks, 1974), pp. 38–68.

10. See Michael Phayer, *Sexual Liberation and Religion in Nineteenth Century Europe* (Totowa, N.J.: Rowman & Littlefield, 1977); Michel Foucault, *A History of Sexuality*, vol. 1: *An Introduction* (New York: Pantheon, 1978); and Roy Pascal, *From Naturalism to Expressionism: German Literature and Society, 1880–1918* (New York: Basic Books, 1973), esp. pp. 198–228.

11. Alfred Delp, *The Prison Meditations of Father Delp* (New York: Macmillan, 1963), pp. 118, 146–147.

12. Waldemar Gurian, "The Sources of Hitler's Power," *Review of Politics* 4, no. 4 (October 1942): 391.

13. See on this the new study by George Mosse, *The Image of Man: The Creation of Modern Masculinity* (New York: Oxford University Press, 1996).

14. On this topic, see W. H. Bruford, *The German Tradition of Self-Cultivation: "Bildung" from Humboldt to Thomas Mann* (Cambridge: Cambridge University Press, 1975).

15. See Ferdinand Hoffmann, *Sittliche Entartung und Geburtenschwund* (Munich: J. F. Lehmanns Verlag, 1938), p. 51, and W. Hermannsen and R. Blome, *Warum hat man uns das nicht früher gesagt? Ein Bekenntnis deutscher Jugend zu geschlechtlicher Sauberkeit* (Munich: J. F. Lehmanns Verlag, 1940). These are respectively the fourth and fourteenth volumes in the important series directed at German youth and edited by Heinz Müller: *Politische Biologie: Schriften für naturgesetzliche Politik und*

Wissenschaft (1936–1940). For a general text on Nazi sexual ethics, see Friedrich Siebert, *Volkstum und Geschlechtlichkeit* (Munich and Berlin: J. F. Lehmanns Verlag, 1938).

16. See Laura Engelstein, *The Keys to Happiness: Sex and the Search for Modernity in Fin-de-Siècle Russia* (Ithaca, N.Y.: Cornell University Press, 1992).

17. Hans Peter Bleuel, *Sex and Society in Nazi Germany* (Philadelphia: J.B. Lippincott, 1973), p. 57.

18. See Frederick Ira Murphy, "The American Christian Press and Pre-War Hitler's Germany, 1933–1939" (Ph.D. diss., University of Florida, 1970).

19. Wilhelm Arp, *Das Bildungsideal der Ehre* (Munich: Deutscher Volksverlag, 1939); Langer, *Katholische Sexualpädagogik im 20. Jahrhundert*, p. 115. For examples of Nazi denunciations, see *The Persecution of the Catholic Church in the Third Reich: Facts and Documents Translated from the German* (London: Burns Oates, 1940), pp. 440, 464, 472–475. The anonymous editor of this collection was a German Jesuit residing in Rome, Walter Mariaux.

20. It could be argued that an exception would be the resistance shown by German Catholic women, motivated by ideals of virginity, to Nazi efforts to reduce women to the level of mere breeders of children. I cannot develop this issue here, but see Michael Phayer's *Protestant and Catholic Women in Nazi Germany* (Detroit: Wayne State University Press, 1990).

21. As an example, see Martin Heidegger's October 2, 1929 letter to Victor Schwoerer, included in Leaman, *Heidegger im Kontext*, pp. 111–112. It is also an expression which Hitler used frequently. For example, see *Mein Kampf* (Boston: Houghton Mifflin, 1971), p. 247. Also see the fine discussion by Steven Ascheim, "'The Jew Within': The Myth of 'Judaization' in Germany," in *The Jewish Response to German Culture: From the Enlightenment to the Second World War*, ed. Jehuda Reinharz and Walter Schatzberg (Hanover, N.H.: University Press of New England, 1985), pp. 212–241.

22. For a Jewish defense against these charges, see Chajim Bloch's *Blut und Eros im jüdischen Schrifttum und Leben: Von Eisenmenger über Rohling zu Bischoff* (Vienna: Sensen-Verlag, 1935). On the charges, see Sander Gilman, *The Jew's Body* (New York: Routledge, 1991), p. 258.

23. For example, see Heiko Oberman, *The Roots of Anti-Semitism in the Age of the Renaissance and Reformation* (Philadelphia: Fortress Press, 1984).

24. My treatment of modern sexuality follows the categories developed in Michel Foucault's *The History of Sexuality*, vol. 1: *An Introduction*. I analyze this history in my *Michel Foucault's Force of Flight: Toward an Ethics for Thought* (Atlantic Highlands: Humanities Press, 1990), pp. 121–184. Following him, I want to identify the elements of that modern field. First, there is the body: the Nazis opposed their view of a trained, classically beautiful body to the Jewish body, weakened by deviant genitalia and unrestrained sexual appetite. Second, regarding children, there was the juxtaposition of an idealized German innocence with the Jewish invention of a childhood sexuality that was believed to reflect both an actual sexual precocity and talmu-

dic allowance for intergenerational sex. *Der Stürmer*, Streicher's newspaper, utilized medieval tales of Jewish ritual slaughter of Christian children in accounts which stressed acts of torture and the sexual satisfaction they implied. In addition, he emphasized cases of child molestation which involved Jews. Third, in contrast to the image of the German mother, who delighted in offspring and their care, and who felt threatened by the sexual advances of Jewish men, especially medical doctors, there was the Jewish woman, who was inclined to neurosis, attracted to prostitution, and craving emancipation from the home. The Nuremberg Laws prohibited sexual relations between Aryan and Jew in part to prevent contamination by syphilis, which was identified with Jews. Fourth, Jews harbored all sorts of sexual perversions, especially homosexuality. These perversions stand behind the Jewish invention of psychoanalysis and sexology. For the Nazis, the Jewish menace was a constructed sexual experience, hidden but omnipresent, camouflaging in other innocuous symptoms the secret causality perverting Aryan life. For extensive examinations of these themes, see George Mosse, *Nationalism and Sexuality: Respectability and Abnormal Sexuality in Modern Europe* (New York: Howard Fertig, 1985), and the extraordinary series of works by Sander Gilman, especially *Sexuality: An Illustrated History* (New York: John Wiley, 1989); *Jewish Self-Hatred: Anti-Semitism and the Hidden Language of the Jews* (Baltimore: Johns Hopkins University Press, 1986); *The Jew's Body: Freud, Race and Gender* (Princeton: Princeton University Press, 1993). Also see Klemens Felden, "Die Übernahme des antisemitischen Stereotyps als soziale Norm durch die bürgerliche Gesellschaft Deutschlands (1875–1900)," a 1963 doctoral dissertation at Ruprecht Karl-University in Heidelberg. Also Allen Edwardes, *Erotica Judaica: A Sexual History of the Jews* (New York: Julian Press, 1967), pp. 106, 180; Friedrich Koch's *Sexualpädagogik und politische Erziehung* (Munich: List Verlag, 1975) and *Sexuelle Denunziation: Die Sexualität in der politischen Auseinandersetzung* (Frankfurt: Syndikat, 1986), pp. 83–86; Dennis Showalter, *Little Man, What Now? "Der Stürmer" in the Weimar Republic* (Hamden, Conn.: Archon, 1982), pp. 189, 198. See Otto Hauser, *Rassebilder* (Braunschweig: Georg Westermann, 1925); Guida Diehl, *Die deutsche Frau und der Nationalsozialismus* (Eisenach: Neulandverlag, 1933); Bruno Blau, "The Jew as Sexual Criminal," *Jewish Social Studies* 13, no. 4 (October 1951): 321–324; Erich Goldhagen, "Nazi Sexual Demonology," *Midstream*, May 1981, pp. 7–15; Gunther Runkel, *Sexualität und Ideologien* (Weinheim and Basel: Beltz Verlag, 1979), esp. pp. 122–127. Also Herwig Hartner, *Erotik und Rasse: Eine Untersuchung über gesellschaftliche, sittliche und geschlechtliche Fragen mit Textillustrationen* (Munich: Deutscher Volksverlag, 1925); Barbara Hyams, "Weininger and Nazi Ideology," in *Jews and Gender: Responses to Otto Weininger*, ed. Nancy Harrowitz and Barbara Hyams (Philadelphia: Temple University Press, 1995), p. 166.

25. Werner Dittrich, *Erziehung zum Judengegner: Hinweise zur Behandlung der Judenfrage im rassenpolitischen Unterricht* (Munich: Deutscher Volksverlag, 1937); Barbara Hyams and Nancy Harrowitz, "A Critical Introduction to the History of Weininger Reception," *Jews and Gender: Responses to Otto Weininger*, p. 4; and Jay

Geller, "Blood Sin: Syphilis and the Construction of Jewish Identity," *Faultline* 1 (1992): 21–48.

26. Langer, *Katholische Sexualpädagogik im 20, Jahrhundert*, p. 20.

27. Speech given to Nazi Party members on June 16, 1933. Cited in James Wilkinson, *The Intellectual Resistance in Europe* (Cambridge: Harvard University Press, 1981), p. 112.

28. Jakob Nötges, *Nationalsozialismus und Katholizismus* (Cologne: Gilde Verlag, 1931), esp. pp. 170–196.

29. See Robert Jay Lifton, *The Nazi Doctors: Medical Killing and the Psychology of Genocide* (New York: Basic Books, 1986), pp. 418–429.

30. Himmler's October 4, 1943 speech in *Trial of the Major War Criminals Before the International Military Tribunal*, vol. 29 (Nuremberg, 1948), p. 145.

31. See Raul Hilberg, *The Destruction of the European Jews*, vol. 3 (New York: Holmes & Meier, 1985), pp. 1012–1029.

32. See Emmanuel Levinas, "Reflections on the Philosophy of Hitlerism," (originally published in 1934), *Critical Inquiry* 17, no. 1 (Autumn 1990): 62–71.

PART V
Proposals

Good and Evil After Auschwitz in Papal Teaching

Remi Hoeckman

AUSCHWITZ HAS OPENED THE EYES OF MANY

In his introduction to *Pope John Paul II on Jews and Judaism, 1979–1986*, Eugene J. Fisher mentions that in assessing the major events of the year 1986 in the Diocese of Rome, the Pope singled out his visit to "our elder brothers in the faith of Abraham," in their Rome Synagogue, as his most significant action of the year.[1] "It will be remembered," he predicted, "for centuries and millenniums in the history of this city and this Church. I thank Divine Providence because the task was given to me."

Pope John Paul II took the implementation of the Second Vatican Council's Declaration *Nostra Aetate* (n. 4) as his task. His meeting with the Jewish community of Rome, which, in his own words, was meant to be at one and the same time "a reality and a symbol," was an act that brought to a close, both really and symbolically, "a long period which" (and I am using his words again, as I will do throughout this paper) "we must not tire of reflecting upon in order to draw from it the appropriate lessons."[2]

The period which the Pope had in mind was "the long history of anti-semitism which culminated in the Shoah,"[3] "the genocide decreed against the Jewish people during the last war, which led to the *holocaust* of millions of innocent victims,"[4] "whose sacrifice . . . has not been fruitless."[5] Why? Because "the terrible persecutions suffered by the Jews in different periods of history have finally opened the eyes of many," he told the delegates to a meeting of representatives of Episcopal Conferences and other experts in Catholic-Jewish relations on March 6, 1982, in the Vatican. But it was, most of all, what he called the "dehumanizing outrages" of Auschwitz that had opened our eyes, and it is the Catholic Church's sincere wish, expressed in postconciliar Church documents, as well as in papal teaching—"through myself," as the Pope has put it[6]—that by keeping the memory of it alive, it may open the eyes of all and everyone, everywhere, in order *"to ensure that evil does not prevail over good"* again.[7] This is basically—and allow me to put it this way—the "good" that has come out of the "horrendous experience" of that "heinous evil"[8] which Auschwitz was and continues to symbolize today. Of course, the name Auschwitz—and the names of all the other death camps which detonate the memory of the cruelties perpetrated by the Nazis against millions of people, Jewish and non-Jewish—do have a unique significance for the "people whose sons and daughters were intended for total extermination,"[9] "for the simple reason of being Jewish."[10] The Pope would agree, I am sure, with the formulation of Elie Wiesel: "Not every victim of the Holocaust was a Jew, but every Jew was a victim."[11]

A WARNING CALL TO ALL OF HUMANITY

I would like to specify that the goal and content of the Nazi victimization scheme of which we are talking (and my root argument goes beyond the debate about Jewish and non-Jewish victimization under the regime of the Nazi criminals, and how they relate) was both the physical destruction of *peoples* (the Jewish people, the Gypsies, the Poles) and the annihilation of *persons*, the total destruction of their humanity, personhood, and dignity, the destruction of the very *imago Dei* in them. Pope John Paul II has called this "horror" the "triumph of evil,"[12] the condemnation of which (and the reflection on which) runs as a "saving warning" through his teaching.[13] In fact, the Pope understands that it is not *his* voice which is this saving warning, but rather that it is the *Jewish witness* to the Shoah that is a saving warning for Christians and for all humanity, for all the powers of this world, for every system and every individual, "a witness and a silent cry before the eyes of the Church, of all peoples and of all nations," a continuation in the contemporary world of the prophetic mission itself. The Church, in turn, is therefore not only committed to listen to this uniquely Jewish proclamation, but to unite its voice to that of the Jewish people in their continuing "particular vocation," one may say, to be a light to the nations. "The Pope raises his voice of warning in your name," Pope John Paul II told the Jewish leaders in Warsaw.[14] Eugene Fisher has summarized it like this:

The order of the Pope's theological reflection on the Shoah is important. As he stated in his letter to Archbishop John L. May (August 8, 1987), an "authentic" approach first grapples with the "specific," and therefore specifically Jewish reality of the event. Only then, and with this continually in mind, he seems to be saying to us, can one begin to seek out its more "universal" meaning.

In Miami, the Pope spoke of the "mystery of the suffering of Israel's children," and he calls on Christians to learn from the "acute insights" of

"Jewish thinkers" on the human condition, and to develop in dialogue with Jews "common educational programs which . . . will teach future generations about the Holocaust so that never again will such a horror be possible. Never again!" (September 11, 1987). From "the suffering and martyrdom of the Jewish people," understood within the context of their "constant progression in faith and obedience to the loving call of God" over the centuries, then, our remembrance of the Shoah may lead to "even deeper hope, a warning call to all of humanity that may serve to save us all" (July 24, 1988, Vienna), a prophetic "prick of conscience" that may tell us "what message our century [can] convey to the next" (Mauthausen, June 24, 1988).[15]

Similarly, in his June 5, 1990 address to those preparing the Special Assembly for Europe of the Synod of Bishops, John Paul II commented that:

the Second World War . . . with its immense cruelty, a cruelty that reached its most brutal expression in the organized extermination of the Jews . . . revealed to the European the other side of a civilization that he was inclined to consider superior to all others. . . . Perhaps in no other war in history has man been so thoroughly trampled on in his dignity and fundamental rights. An echo of the humiliation and even desperation caused by such an experience could be heard in the question often repeated after the war: *How can we go on living after Auschwitz?*[16]

This fundamental question, which formulates accurately the theme of this Symposium, has given direction to the Holy Father's thinking in vital areas. As he told the Jewish community in Mainz, Germany, on November 17, 1980 (early in his pontificate):

The innocent victims in Germany and elsewhere, the families destroyed or dispersed, the cultural values or art treasures destroyed forever, are a tragic proof of where discrimination and contempt of human dignity can lead, especially if they are animated by perverse theories on a presumed difference in the value of races or on the division of people into persons of "high worth," "worthy of living," and persons who are "worthless," "unworthy of living." Before God all human beings are of the same value and importance.

GOING TO THE ROOTS OF EVIL

With regard to these facts of evil, the Pope wishes to identify their causes in order to let the historical truth play its rightful role in the process of shaping the future: "To single out and denounce such facts and stand together against them is a noble act and a proof of our mutual brotherly commitment," he told the executive committee of the International Council of Christians and Jews (ICCJ) on July 6, 1984, in the Vatican, "but it is necessary to go to the roots of such evil," and he emphasized the role of education in this regard. Indeed, all this "would not be enough if it were not coupled with a deep change in our heart, a real spiritual conversion," because "the ultimate source of violence is the corruption of the human heart," he said to the Young Leadership Section of the ICCJ whom he received in the Vatican on July 2, 1993. But I shall return to this point later.

Receiving a delegation of the participants in a theological Catholic-Jewish colloquium which was taking place at my university (the Pontifical University of Saint Thomas Aquinas in Rome—the Angelicum) on April 19, 1985, and referring to "the catastrophe which so cruelly decimated the Jewish people, before and during the war, especially in the death camps," the Pope identified the main cause of that "triumph of evil" as follows: "It is [the] absence of faith in God and, as a consequence, of love and respect for our fellow men and women which can easily bring about such disasters." The Pope has done so repeatedly; for example, in his above-mentioned letter to Archbishop John L. May: "Reflection upon the Shoah shows us to what terrible consequences the lack of faith in God and a contempt for man created in his image can lead," he wrote. On another occasion he proposed a response: "Let us pray together that it will never happen again, and that whatever we do to get to know each other better, to collaborate with one another and to bear witness to the One God and to his will, as expressed in the Decalogue, will help make people still more aware of the abyss which mankind can fall into when we do not acknowledge other people as brothers and sisters, sons and daughters, of the same heavenly Father."[17]

In fact, "in our days [too] one can have the sad impression of an absence of God and his will from the private and public lives of men and women. When we reflect on such a situation [i.e., 'the present secularist context'] and its tragic consequences for mankind, deprived of its roots in God and therefore of its moral orientation, one can only be grateful to the Lord because we believe in him, as Jews and Christians, and we both can say, in the words of Deuteronomy: 'Hear, O Israel, the Lord our God is one God' (Deuteronomy 6:4)."

The "terrible consequences [for humankind] which can arise from a denial of God [and] a contempt for man"[18] which John Paul II has in mind, can be clustered as follows: antisemitism ("a sin against God and humanity") and its ugly manifestations; racial hatred and genocide; the creation of a culture of death; the violation and even denial of human rights and of the "rights of God";[19] the destruction of human dignity and the sanctity of life; the construction of "an insane ideology which [can] set in motion an entire system of contempt and hatred against other human beings," "crushing them to pieces,"[20] "sending them to death camps";[21] "murderous madness directed against [people] whose 'crime is to be different'";[22] "a new paganism: the deification of the nation."[23] In fact, all these can be summarized as "crimes against God and humanity,"[24] "crimes against man and humanity."[25]

In his Encyclical Letter *Centesimus Annus* (1991) Pope John Paul II wrote about these crimes in terms of "the consequences of a basic error" which consists in "an understanding of human freedom which detaches it from obedience to the truth, and consequently from the duty to respect the rights of others. The essence of freedom then," he affirms, "becomes self-love carried to the point of contempt for God and neighbor, a self-love that leads to an unbridled affirmation of self-interest and which refuses to be limited by any demand of justice." The Pope then looks at the "extreme consequences" that such an error had in the tragic series of wars that ravaged Europe and the world between 1914 and 1945:

> Without the terrible burden of hatred and resentment which had built up as a result of so many injustices both on the international level and within individual states, such cruel wars would not have been possible, in which great nations invested their energies and in which there was no hesitation to violate the most sacred human rights, with the extermination of entire peoples and social groups being planned and carried out. Here we recall the Jewish people in particular, whose terrible fate has become a symbol of the aberration of which man is capable when he turns against God.

And he makes an appeal: "May the memory of those terrible events guide the actions of everyone, particularly the leaders of nations in our own time, when other forms of injustice are fueling new hatred and when new ideologies which exalt violence are appearing on the horizon."[26]

IT IS NOT ENOUGH TO REMEMBER

We need to remember. We want to remember, but, he told hundreds of Christians and Jews, including a number of survivors of Auschwitz, gathered together at a concert given in the Vatican on April 7, 1994 in commemoration of the Shoah, "it is not enough that we remember, for in our own day . . . there are many new manifestations of the antisemitism, xenophobia, and racial hatred which were the seeds of those unspeakable crimes. Humanity cannot permit all that to happen again." And he concluded by affirming forcefully:

> We have a commitment, the only one perhaps that can give meaning to every tear shed by man because of man. . . . We have seen with our own eyes, we were and are witnesses of violence and hatred which are kindled in the world all too often and consume it. We have seen and we see peace derided, brotherhood mocked, harmony ignored, mercy scorned. . . .
>
> This is our commitment. We would risk causing the victims of the most atrocious deaths to die again if we do not have an ardent desire for justice, if we do not commit ourselves, each according to his own capacities, to ensure that evil does not prevail over good as it did for millions of the children of the Jewish nation.
>
> We must therefore redouble our efforts to free man from the specter of racism, exclusion, alienation, slavery, and xenophobia; to uproot these evils which are creeping into society and undermining the foundations of peaceful human co-existence. Evil always appears in new forms; it has many facets and its flattery is multiple. It is our task to unmask its dangerous power and neutralize it with God's help.[27]

John Paul II chose the same theme for the address which he delivered to the diplomatic corps on January 15, 1994:

> Having for too many years experienced a division imposed by reductive ideologies, the world should not now be experiencing a season of exclusions: on the contrary, now should be the season of coming together and of solidarity. . . . Glancing at the world today, we can only state with deep regret that too many human beings are still their brothers' victims. But we cannot resign ourselves to this. . . . Let us act in such a way that humanity will more and more resemble a genuine family in which each individual knows he is listened to, appreciated, and loved, in which each is ready to sacrifice self for the benefit of the other and no one hesitates to help the weaker one. . . . Each one of us is invited to the boldness of brotherhood.

COLLABORATION FOR THE GOOD OF ALL HUMANITY

Each one of us. Or, in the words of Rabbi Abraham Heschel, "none of us can do it alone. Both of us [Jews and Christians] must realize that in our age anti-Semitism is anti-Christianity and that anti-Christianity is anti-Semitism."[28]

"Christians and Jews *together* have a great deal to offer to a world struggling to distinguish good from evil, a world called by the Creator to defend
and protect life but so vulnerable to voices which propagate values that only
bring death and destruction."[29] Thus, "as Christians and Jews, following the
example of the faith of Abraham, we are called to be a blessing for the world
(cf. Genesis 12:2 ff.). This is the common task awaiting us. It is therefore necessary for us, Christians and Jews, to be first a blessing to one another. This
will effectively occur if we are united in the face of the evils which are still
threatening: indifference and prejudice, as well as displays of antisemitism."[30]
And in his letter of April 9, 1993, to the Carmelite nuns at Oswiecim, John
Paul II wrote: "How the future will grow from this most painful past largely
depends on whether, on the threshold of Oswiecim, 'the love which is greater
than death' will stand watch."

Listening to these words today, after centuries of suspicion and enmity in
Jewish-Christian relations, we can only be grateful for this change, which the
Jewish scholar Geoffrey Wigoder described as follows at a meeting of the
International Catholic-Jewish Liaison Committee in Jerusalem in 1994: "One
of the great advances in our relationship since World War II is that the
Catholic Church, instead of being part of the problem, has become part of the
answer, and this has gained special momentum during the pontificate of John
Paul II, who has shown himself highly sensitive on this subject."

In an audience with Jewish leaders on February 15, 1985, the Pope gave
expression in the following terms to the new spirit which the Vatican II
Declaration *Nostra Aetate* has created in Jewish-Christian relations:

> Where there was ignorance and therefore prejudice and stereotypes,
> there is now growing mutual knowledge, appreciation, and respect. There is,
> above all, love between us, that kind of love, I mean, which is for both of us
> a fundamental injunction of our religious traditions and which the New
> Testament has received from the Old (cf. Mark 12:28–34, Leviticus 19:18).

And on another occasion he put it like this:

> The origin of our "common spiritual heritage" (cf. *Nostra Aetate*, 4),
> therefore, is to be found in the faith of Abraham, Isaac, and Jacob. Within
> this common heritage we may include veneration of the Holy Scriptures,
> confession of the One Living God (cf. Exodus 20:3, 23, Deuteronomy 6:4),
> love of neighbor (cf. Leviticus 19:18), and a prophetic witness to justice and
> peace. We likewise live in confident expectation of the coming of God's
> kingdom, and we pray that God's will be done on earth as it is in heaven. As

a result, we can effectively work together in promoting the dignity of every human person and in safeguarding human rights, especially religious freedom. We must also be united in combating all forms of racial, ethnic, or religious discrimination and hatred, including antisemitism. I am pleased to note the significant level of cooperation that has been achieved in these areas over the past quarter-century, and it is my hope that these efforts will continue and increase.[31]

I would like to point out that the Pope does insist on the need and possibility of Jewish-Christian collaboration on the basis of what *Nostra Aetate* described as "the spiritual patrimony common to Christians and Jews," which he explained during his pastoral visit to Brazil on October 15, 1991: "Adoring the one true God, in fact, we discover our common spiritual root, which is the consciousness of the brotherhood of all people. This awareness is truly the closest bond which unites Christians and Jewish people." "It is ultimately on such a basis that it will be possible to establish—as we know is happily already the case—a close collaboration toward which our common heritage directs us, in service of man and his vast spiritual and material needs," he told a group of Catholic and Jewish leaders on March 6, 1982. "Through different but finally convergent ways we will be able to reach . . . this true brotherhood in reconciliation and respect, and to contribute to a full implementation of God's plan in history." In fact, addressing what he called "the problem of morality," the Pope spoke to the Jewish community of Rome on April 13, 1986, about "the great field of individual and social ethics." "We are all aware of how acute the crisis is on this point in the age in which we are living," he said. "In a society which is often lost in agnosticism and individualism, and which is suffering the bitter consequences of selfishness and violence, Jews and Christians are the trustees and witnesses of an ethic marked by the Ten Commandments, in the observance of which man finds his truth and freedom. To promote a common reflection and collaboration on this point is one of the great duties of the hour." Indeed he told the diplomatic corps on January 13, 1997: "What the international community perhaps lacks most of all is not written conventions or forums for self-expression . . . but a *moral law and the courage to abide by it.*"

Another basis for the Pope's continuous appeal to Jewish-Christian collaboration "in favor of all humanity where the image of God shines through in every man, woman, and child, especially in the destitute and those in need,"[32] is found in his profound belief in "the fundamental dignity and the goodness that dwell within every human being."[33] He has reflected on this in several speeches, for example after the Vatican concert commemorating the

Shoah: "[In spite of the evil existing in the world] man is inclined to justice," he said. "He is the only created being capable of conceiving it. To save man does not only mean not to kill him, not to mutilate him, not to torture him. It also means satisfying the hunger and thirst for justice that is within him"; "[the] longing for peace is deeply rooted in human nature";[34] "the world is waiting for a world of peace."[35]

HOPE AND PROMISE

On the morning of June 24, 1988, John Paul II welcomed leaders of the Jewish community in Austria to the Apostolic Nunciature in Vienna. The reflections and sentiments which he shared with them that morning, and which he also expressed later in the day during his visit to the former World War II concentration camp at Mauthausen, are significant. He spoke of the experience of his and the Church's "deep and mysterious union in love and faith with the Jewish people," affirming his conviction that "no historical event, however painful it may be, can be so powerful that it could contradict this reality which belongs to God's plan for our salvation and fraternal reconciliation." He spoke about faith and love, especially of the Jewish people's "journey in faith and obedience in response to the loving call of God." He also spoke of hope. "You and we are still burdened by the memory of the Shoah," he said, but "out of those cruel sufferings can grow . . . deeper hope. . . . To remember the Shoah means to hope and to see to it that there will never be a repetition of it." "Speak, you who have suffered and lost your lives; you have the right to do so. We have the duty to listen to your testimony."[36] "This is our commitment,"[37] he promised; "be sure of this: you are not alone in bearing the pain of this memory; we pray and watch with you, under the gaze of God, the holy and just one, rich in mercy and pardon.[38]

On the other hand, the Pope also invites us, Christians and Jews, to "try to perceive, salvage, and renew the *good* things that occurred in our mutual relations . . . over the centuries."[39] In his mind, this is part of "righting the wrongs,"[40] and I am thinking here of his lifelong friendship with Jerzy Kluger, subject of the book entitled *Letter to a Jewish Friend*, authored by Gianfranco Svidercoschi,[41] as I am sure he did as well when he said to a delegation from the Anti-Defamation League that he received at Castel Gandolfo on September 19, 1994: "Friendship stands against exclusion and makes people stand together in the face of threat."

Is this not a good that can come out of Auschwitz? Is this not the meaning of the call to be a blessing for the world and therefore of the call of Jews and Christians to be first a blessing to one another? It is something in which the Holy Father profoundly believes. His whole life, his whole ministry, bear witness to it. At the same time he is deeply convinced of the need to *educate* ourselves, to *educate* our young generations in this spirit, providing them with moral guidance, lest our hopes be in vain and our promises empty. We need to learn how to create space for one another, space that is needed for engaging fearlessly on a journey of a mutual and, when possible, common exploration of one another's traditions and history, perceptions and expectations, and above all of the image and likeness of God in one another, for it is from this discovery that moral responsibility can grow, the responsibility which we have for the other not accidentally but essentially, a responsibility which underlies our identity. We cannot give a truthful answer to God's question "Where are you?" without answering the other question which God is asking us as well: "Where is your brother?" (cf. Genesis 3:9, 4:9). The truthful response to these questions, especially after Auschwitz, where ethics failed, could indeed be the most profound ethical response to the Holocaust.[42]

NOTES

1. This book, edited by Eugene J. Fisher and Leon Klenicki, and published in 1987 (Washington, D.C.: USCC), together with a later publication entitled *Pope John Paul II, Spiritual Pilgrimage: Texts on Jews and Judaism, 1979–1995* (New York: Crossroad, 1995), edited by the same authors, contains most of the Pope's addresses and writings quoted in this paper. The *Osservatore Romano* and the Information Service of the Pontifical Council for Promoting Christian Unity are other sources. In some places, translations have been adjusted for more inclusive language.
2. See his address in the Synagogue of Rome on April 13, 1986.
3. See his address on the occasion of a concert held in the Vatican on April 7, 1994 to commemorate the Shoah.
4. Address in the Synagogue of Rome.
5. See his address to the representatives of the Jewish community in France on May 31, 1980 (in Paris). The Pope, paying homage to the Jewish victims of the Nazis in France, specified what he meant by these words: "It was from there that there really began, thanks to the courage and decision of some pioneers, including Jules Isaac, the movement that has led us to the present dialogue and collaboration, inspired and promoted by the declaration *Nostra Aetate* of the Second Vatican Council."
6. Address in the Synagogue of Rome. Cf. his address to Jewish leaders in Miami on September 11, 1987.
7. Address given after the concert on April 7, 1994.
8. Ibid.

9. Homily delivered at Auschwitz on June 7, 1979; repeated on several occasions afterwards.

10. Address given before the concert on April 7, 1994. In the above-mentioned address to Jewish leaders in Miami, he said: "Considering history in light of the principles of faith in God, we must also reflect on the catastrophic event of the Shoah, that ruthless and inhuman attempt to exterminate the Jewish people in Europe, an attempt that resulted in millions of victims—including women and children, the elderly and the sick—exterminated only because they were Jews."

11. Cf. Fisher, *Pope John Paul II on Jews and Judaism*, p. 15.

12. At the Sunday Angelus of January 29, 1995.

13. Cf. his address to Jewish leaders in Warsaw on June 14, 1987.

14. On June 14, 1987. Cf. his letter of August 8, 1987 to Archbishop John L. May, then president of the National Conference of Catholic Bishops in the United States; his address to Jewish leaders in Miami; and Eugene J. Fisher's commentary on the texts compiled by the Anti-Defamation League in the volume *Pope John Paul II, Spiritual Pilgrimage*, p. xxxix.

15. Ibid.

16. Ibid., p. xxx (emphasis added).

17. Address to the participants in the Angelicum Colloquium.

18. Address to members of the Jewish Central Council at Cologne on May 1, 1987, and his letter to Archbishop John L. May.

19. Address to Jewish leaders in Miami.

20. Words spoken at the Mauthausen concentration camp on June 24, 1988. Rabbi Mordecai Waxman, in his address to the Holy Father in Miami, called the "triumph of evil," the Shoah, "triumph of an ideology of nationalism and racism, the suppression of human conscience, and the deification of the state—concepts that are profoundly anti-Christian as well as anti-Jewish." John Paul II has on various occasions quoted his predecessor, Pope Pius XI, who wrote in his Encyclical Letter *Mit Brennender Sorge* (1937): "He who takes race, or the people or the State, or the form of government, the bearers of the power of the state, or other fundamental elements of human society . . . and makes them the ultimate norm of all, even religious values, and deifies them with an idolatrous worship, perverts and falsifies the order of things created and commanded by God."

21. Address to the Jewish community in Vienna on June 24, 1988.

22. Cf. the Pope's message to the Polish Bishops' Conference on the occasion of the fiftieth anniversary of the outbreak of World War II, August 26, 1989. Cf. also his homily during a Mass in Wloclawek on June 7, 1991: "In fact, it was in this century that the philosophy was created in whose name a man could kill another man because he is different, because he is of a certain ethnic group, because he is Jewish, because he is a Gypsy, because he is Polish. A discrimination of masters against slaves."

23. Address to the diplomatic corps on January 15, 1994.

24. In a reflection preceding the prayer of the *Regina Coeli* on April 18, 1993, in which John Paul II recalled the fiftieth anniversary of the Warsaw Ghetto Uprising.

Cf. also his address given during the general audience of October 28, 1992: "In the face of the recurrent episodes of xenophobia, racial tension, and extreme fanatical nationalism, I feel it is my duty to emphasize that every form of racism is a sin against God and humanity, since every human person bears the stamp of the divine image." Cf. also a speech given during his pastoral visit to Hungary on August 18 and an address to the British Council for Christians and Jews on November 16, 1990.
25. *Centesimus Annus*, n. 17.
26. Ibid.
27. Cf. *L'Osservatore Romano*, no. 15, April 13, 1994. And on Sunday, January 29, 1995, before praying the Angelus, the Pope remembered the fiftieth anniversary of the liberation of the prisoners of Auschwitz. Referring to that time which he called "one of the darkest and most tragic moments in history," he commented on the Holocaust: "It was a darkening of reason, conscience, and the heart. Recalling the triumph of evil cannot fail to fill us with deep sorrow, in fraternal solidarity with all who bear the indelible scars of those tragedies. Unfortunately, however, our days continue to be marked by great violence. God forbid that tomorrow we will have to weep over other Auschwitzes of our time. Let us pray and work that this may not happen. Never again antisemitism! Never again the arrogance of nationalism! Never again genocide! May the third millennium usher in a season of peace and mutual respect among peoples."
28. A. J. Heschel, "No Religion Is an Island," *Union Theological Seminary Quarterly* 21, no. 2 (January 1966): 1.
29. The Pope's address before the concert in commemoration of the Shoah.
30. Message to the Polish people on April 6, 1993, on the occasion of the fiftieth anniversary of the Warsaw Ghetto Uprising.
31. Address to representatives of the American Jewish Committee on March 16, 1990. The Pope had expressed the same thought during his visit to the Synagogue of Rome: "It must be said . . . that the ways opened for our collaboration, in the light of our common heritage drawn from the Law and the Prophets, are various and important. We wish to recall, first of all, a collaboration in favor of man, his life from conception until natural death, his dignity, his freedom, his rights, his self-development in a society which is not hostile but friendly and favorable, where justice reigns and where, in this nation, on the various continents and throughout the world, it is peace that rules, the *shalom* hoped for by the lawmakers, prophets, and wise men of Israel."
32. Address to representatives of the American Jewish Committee on February 15, 1985.
33. His Apostolic Letter on the fiftieth anniversary of the outbreak of World War II, August 26, 1989.
34. Message for the twenty-fifth annual World Day of Prayer for Peace, January 1, 1992.
35. Address to participants in an interreligious meeting sponsored by the Sant'Egidio community, April 30, 1991.
36. Meditation at Mauthausen.
37. Address after the concert in commemoration of the Shoah.

38. At the prayer of the *Regina Coeli* on April 18, 1993.
39. Address to the Jewish community during his pastoral visit to Poland, June 9, 1991.
40. Ibid.
41. New York: Crossroad, 1994.
42. The fact that John Paul II, in *Crossing the Threshold of Hope*, singled out the great Jewish thinker Emmanuel Levinas is significant. Cf. Robert Eaglestone, *Philosopher to the Pope*, in *The Tablet* 6 (April 13, 1996): 472.

The Banality of Good and Evil:
Antisocial Behavior, Prosocial Behavior, and Jewish Religious Teaching

David R. Blumenthal

THE PROBLEM

As we approach the end of the century and try to bring some perspective to its most traumatic event, the holocaust,[1] the task before us seems overwhelming.[2] Can one really bring some perspective to such an event? Is the very attempt to do so a banalization of the lives of those who died, or survived?[3] For theologians, two questions cry out for answers. First, where was God? Put more fully, how can we, as religious people, reconcile our belief in the continuous presence of God in the life of the Jewish people with our conviction that the holocaust was not punishment for our sins? Or more simply, how did God, as depicted in our holy traditions, permit the holocaust to happen? I have ventured an answer, not accepted by many people, in *Facing the Abusing God: A Theology of Protest*,[4] but this is not the place to rehearse those arguments.

The second question is, where was humanity? Here, the issue is not the cruelty and sadism of the holocaust, for, although cruelty and sadism were certainly present—indeed they were systematically cultivated into a "culture of cruelty"[5]—they were not peculiar to the holocaust. Nor is the question one of numbers, for there have been other mass murders and even genocides in which larger numbers of people have been killed.[6] The issue in the holocaust is also not one of state policy, although that certainly set off the holocaust from previous forms of genocide.[7] The real horror of the holocaust lies in the compliance of the masses with the final solution. The key question about humanity, then, is: why did so many tens of millions of people go along with the holocaust? Put differently, how did the nazi regime persuade the overwhelming masses of Europe to remain bystanders? to accept passively, if not actively, the extermination of the Jews? Terror was certainly a factor, but it is not a sufficient answer.

An equally puzzling question is posed by those who rescued Jews: why did they rescue? Or, put more clearly, how did the rescuers manage to resist the persuasion of the nazi regime such that they defied it? If obedience characterized the masses, what describes the resisters and rescuers?

The answer to the question "where was humanity?" lies in careful historical study of the period of the holocaust.[8] However, extremely useful data can also be found in the field of social psychology. Indeed, much is known about human compliance and resistance in social situations. A series of social-psychological experiments in compliance, known loosely as the obedience experiments, were conducted and the results widely discussed.[9] And a series of experiments in prosocial action, known loosely as the altruism experiments, were also conducted, and their results are rather widely known too.[10] To answer the question "where was humanity?" then, one must study the obedience experiments, the altruism experiments, as well as the historical literature on perpetrators and rescuers during the holocaust.[11] Such a full social-psychological and historical study has not yet been undertaken, yet we must do so if we are to answer the basic question of human responsibility.

The question "where was humanity?" poses a particularly serious problem for educators and theologians, for it raises the issue: Where did moral and religious education flounder? Why did moral and religious education fail to create more resistance to evil and encourage more doing of good? Why did the teaching of good and evil in organized societal and religious institutions fail to prevent the holocaust? If there are answers to the question of human compliance and resistance in social psychology and history, then it is the responsibility of educators and theologians to bring these insights back into the church, the synagogue, the mosque, and the school, and to modify what one teaches and how one teaches it so as to increase resistance to evil and to encourage the doing of good. Put differently, educators and theologians must recognize the failure of earlier theologies and teachings, and must draw wisdom from the study of humankind through history and social psychology in order to improve society's ability to cultivate resistance to evil and to do good.

Thus, answering the question "where was humanity?" implies two tasks: first, a descriptive-analytic task rooted in history and social psychology, and then, a normative-prescriptive task intended to better humankind's ability to teach resistance to evil and to cultivate doing of good.

ON ANTISOCIAL BEHAVIOR

The data on antisocial behavior show that several factors enable an overwhelming percentage of ordinary, good people to commit acts that they know are wrong.

First, *insertion into a social hierarchy in which legitimate authority does, or tolerates, evil facilitates the doing of evil.* In the Milgram experiments, subjects were instructed to administer electric shocks of increasing intensity to other human beings in order to help them learn a set of associated words. Subjects routinely showed signs of nervousness when the other person manifested pain and discomfort, but subjects also routinely followed the instructions of the experimenter and continued administering shocks well into the painful, and even into the lethal, range. The conclusion drawn from these experiments was that it was insertion of the subject into a social hierarchy which enabled the legitimate authority (the experimenter) to demand the doing of an act which the subject knew was wrong; that is, that the demand of a legitimate authority within a social hierarchy was sufficient to allow, even to compel, the subject to do precisely the act he or she knew was wrong. Similarly, during the period of the extermination of Polish Jewry, ordinary conscripts in German police battalions were instructed to round up and kill Jews. Such persons routinely showed signs of nervousness when first asked to kill wantonly but also routinely followed the instructions of their superiors and continued to round up and kill Jews. Again, insertion of the subject into a social hierarchy in which the legitimate authority (the commander) demanded an act the subject knew was wrong was sufficient to allow, even to compel, the subject to do precisely the act he knew was wrong.

Corollary: *The ability of legitimate authority to rationalize wrong action for the subject also facilitates the doing of evil.* In justifying wrongdoing, legitimate authority grants intellectual-moral permission to the subject to commit a wrongful act. In the Milgram experiments, authority rationalized the need for administering electric shocks by appealing to the need for scientific knowledge: science required that the experiment go on. In the German police battalions, authority rationalized the rounding up and killing of Jews by appealing to the need to obey orders, to military discipline, and to antisemitic and racist teaching.

Corollary: *Salience to the authority also facilitates the doing of evil.* In the Milgram experiments, the closer the proximity of the subject to the authority (experimenter), the greater the degree of obedience. And, conversely, the greater the distance between subject and authority, the less the degree of obedience.

Put more broadly: *The ability of legitimate authority to appeal to rules, to define roles in the hierarchy, and to evoke the values of discipline, duty, and unquestioning loyalty facilitates the doing of evil.*[12]

These social processes by which authority acts—insertion of the subject into a social hierarchy; rule, role, and value definition; rationalization; and salience—enable individuals to commit wrongful acts while believing that they are actually doing something good. In urging these rules, roles, and values upon persons, legitimate authorities within social hierarchies persuade individuals that compliance—even with demands for wrongful acts—is a good; that is, that to be obedient is, indeed, to be good. Perpetrators in such a hierarchy commit wrongful acts in the full belief that they are being good; that is, that they are following the rules, filling the roles, and embodying the values of legitimate authority. Subjects in the Milgram experiment, while they admitted feeling uncomfortable, nonetheless did not have the feeling of having done wrong. Soldiers in the German police battalions did not feel guilty. Hannah Arendt observed that Eichmann did not feel any remorse at having organized the extermination of vast numbers of Jews. Rather, he clearly felt he had been a good person and an obedient soldier.[13] Milgram called this the "agentic shift." Arendt coined the phrase "banality of evil" to describe the nonpathological nature of this evil that disguises itself as obedient goodness. And Kelman and Hamilton used the phrase "Crimes of Obedience" to describe wrongdoing which appears as an act of goodness.

Second, *a teaching of exclusivism facilitates the doing of evil.* A society that teaches the alienness of the other, fear of the stranger, and the existence of a dichotomy between "us" and "them" prepares the individual to commit wrongful acts. This is done by undermining the humanity of the other, by limiting the possibility of empathy for the victim, and by reducing salience to the victim. A society that uses the language of exclusiveness and xenophobia, and that, in the family and social environment, cultivates punitive norms for the outsider facilitates the doing of evil. Such a society sets linguistic and behavioral norms that are antisocial. In the Riceville experiment, the categorization of blue-eyed and brown-eyed children differentiated the one from the other and set the one, and then the other, in a lower social place. In the German police battalions, the categorization of Jews as subhumans and Germans as superhumans, embodied in the contrast in power between armed uniformed men and unarmed civilians, set the Jews apart and made action against them easier. The dehumanization of Jews in the concentration camps into numbers and the "excremental assault"[14] practiced on them made it easier to see them as nonhuman and hence to act to kill them. Indeed, all racism, sexism, and antisemitism work on a teaching of the alienness and inferiority of the other.

Third, *the normal social processes of modeling, identification, peer support, and incremental learning facilitate evil.* Seeing one's superiors committing or encouraging wrongful acts allows modeling and identification to influence individual persons to do, or tolerate, wrongful acts. Seeing one's peers committing or tolerating evil makes it easier to do the same. And, as the proverb says, practice makes perfect. The first wrongful act may be difficult, but the tenth is no longer hard to execute. Incremental learning facilitates the doing of evil. These processes enable a society to create a "normocentric"[15] thrust for those who partake of it; that is, these processes allow a society to set the norms of accepted action for members of the society. In a society that tolerates and teaches evil, the normocentric thrust facilitates evil. All this is quite clear from the social-psychological experiments, as well as from the historical data on the holocaust.

Fourth, none of the subjects in the social-psychological experiments manifested any psychological pathology. As a matter of fact, pathological types were usually screened from the samples before the experiment was begun. Similarly, the men tried in Nuremberg, Eichmann, and the soldiers of the German police battalions did not manifest any pathological symptoms. All were "normal," ordinary persons. It is, however, the case that *discipline in childhood, when it is erratic and/or excessive, inculcates obedience to authority.* If a child is disciplined erratically, it will adapt by being as obedient as possible in order to avoid erratic punishment. Similarly, a child who is disciplined excessively will adapt by being as obedient as possible in order to avoid being excessively punished. The complement is also true: If a child is prohibited from making age-appropriate decisions, it will not develop the requisite empowerment and self-esteem. Alice Miller, in analyzing child-rearing manuals from pre-nazi and nazi Germany, concluded that erratic and excessive discipline was a common phenomenon in Central European culture.[16] She even remarks that Hitler's screaming, which Americans see as comical because of Charlie Chaplin's parody thereof, was precisely the kind of erratic and excessive discipline to which Germans had become accustomed through the kind of child-rearing advocated in their manuals and practiced by many parents.[17]

ON PROSOCIAL BEHAVIOR

The data on resistance and prosocial action are equally clear.[18]

First, *insertion into a social hierarchy in which legitimate authority does, or tolerates, good facilitates the doing of good.* Put more broadly: *The ability of legitimate authority to appeal to rules, to define roles in the hierarchy, and to evoke the values of caring, justice, and inclusiveness facilitates the doing of good.* In the Milgram experiments, when a second authority figure (experimenter) was present who legitimated stopping the shocks or who allowed the subject to choose the shock level, resistance increased dramatically, with subjects following the authority who sanctioned the doing of good. In the Staub experiments, when a legitimate authority gave permission to leave the room to help a suspected victim in an adjacent room, subjects left to help, whereas when the same authority forbade leaving the room, subjects did not leave to help. Similarly, among those who rescued Jews during the war, fully 67 percent did so only after they had been asked by someone, usually a legitimate authority, to do so. And, when categorized by motivation, over half (52 percent) of the rescuers indicated they had rescued for "normocentric" reasons; that is, because caring behavior was the moral norm set by the intimate authorities in their environment. Furthermore, research with businesses, schools, and other institutions that encourage prosocial action indicates that, where authority demands, or sanctions, the values of caring, acts of goodness will flourish. The weight of authority, then, permits or sanctions the doing of good. Corollary: *The force of authority is reinforced by its ability to explain and rationalize why the doing of good is demanded, necessary, or just plain good.* Corollary: *Salience to authority that demands, or authorizes, the doing of good facilitates the doing of good.*

Second, *a teaching of inclusiveness and caring facilitates the doing of good.* A society that teaches the common humanness of the other, that stresses the value of caring, and that emphasizes compassion and responsibility prepares the individual for the doing of acts of goodness. This is true because stressing the humanity of the other increases salience to the victim. A society that uses the language of empathy and responsibility, and that cultivates norms of caring in the family and social environments facilitates the doing of good. Such a society sets linguistic and behavioral norms that are prosocial. Persons who came from close and large families and/or who had previous contact with Jews were more likely to be rescuers. Fully 37 percent of those who rescued indicated that they had been motivated by empathy for the victims. Further, many of the rescuers continued caring work with displaced persons, the elderly, the sick, and the homeless. The study of the parable of the Good Samaritan may have generated a greater rate of caring response to a victim.[19] Research with businesses, schools, and other institutions that encourage prosocial action indicates that inculcation of the values of caring produces acts of goodness. Further, salience to the victim facilitates the doing of good and caring acts.

Third, *the normal social processes of modeling, identification, peer support, and incremental learning facilitate the doing of good.* Seeing one's elders doing and sustaining acts of goodness allows modeling and identification to influence one to do likewise. Seeing one's peers doing acts of caring makes it easier to do the same. In the Milgram experiments, when a planted subject resisted, the true subject went along, and in the Staub experiments, when a planted subject helped, the true subject also helped. The availability of a network for rescuers made rescue much easier. Research with businesses, schools, and other institutions that encourage prosocial action indicates that where the values of caring are modeled, acts of goodness are done. Further, as the proverb says, practice makes perfect. The first act of caring may seem awkward, but by the tenth such act, doing good seems normal. Incremental learning facilitates the doing of good. These processes enable a society to create a normocentric thrust for those who partake of it; that is, these processes allow a society to set the norms of accepted action for members of the society. In a society that tolerates and teaches good, the normocentric thrust facilitates good. All this is quite clear from the historical as well as the social-psychological evidence.

Fourth, *discipline in childhood, when it is reasoned and proportionate, inculcates caring attitudes.* This is the main conclusion of the study of rescuers: that if a child is disciplined in a way that makes the punishment fit the crime, and if punishment is explained and comprehended, the child will acknowledge the elementary justice of the discipline. Furthermore and more important, if the "punishment" does not fit the "crime" and the child can appeal and discuss the punishment, the child will learn that authority is reasonable. Such a child will acquire a sense of self-competency and will be willing to challenge other authority when the occasion arises. The complement is also true: If a child is encouraged to make age-appropriate decisions, it will develop the requisite empowerment and self-esteem.[20]

A UNIFIED FIELD THEORY

The incidence of obedience/resistance varies with the amount of stress applied externally. In the standard Milgram experiments, 65–85 percent of the subjects conformed, while 15–35 percent resisted. This is close to a 60 percent indifference rate and a 40 percent helping rate among the Princeton experiment subjects, and a 50–75 percent nonhelping rate and 25–50 percent helping rate among the subjects in the Staub experiments. As might be expected, among the German police battalions, where pressure was greater, 80–90 percent conformed, while 10–20 percent resisted, and among rescuers, where pressure was at its greatest, the number of resisters was very small. It seems to me, then, that the antisocial-prosocial parameter (sometimes inaccurately called the obedience-resistance parameter) constitutes a continuum which yields a dynamic range of results. This continuum, it further seems to me, is better than a set of discrete categories which yield static unrelated results.

Within the discipline of social psychology, experimental studies of obedience and of altruism are not usually done together. Nor is analysis of these complementary phenomena usually undertaken as a whole.[21] Bringing both sets of data and analysis together broadens the perspective on human behavior. Similarly, within the discipline of history, systematic social-psychological questions are not often asked. Adding the historical to the social-psychological data and analysis also broadens the analytic field. A full, expanded effort would combine two disciplines—social psychology and history—that deal with the same phenomena and generate a very broad view of human motivation and action.

Social-psychological research in the areas of both obedience and altruism, taken together with historical evidence from the holocaust and other moments in history, yields, in my opinion, a unified field theory of good and evil human behavior. In this unified field theory, the social-psychological factors that facilitate evil, facilitate good, and vice-versa, as follows: Insertion into a social hierarchy in which legitimate authority appeals to rules, roles, and values facilitates both the doing of good and the doing of evil. The ability of legitimate authority to rationalize as well as to create salience to the authority or to the victim facilitates the doing of both evil and good. The capacity of a society to set linguistic and behavioral norms also facilitates both the doing of good and the doing of evil. The socialization processes of modeling, identification, peer support, and incremental learning which set the normocentric thrust of a society work for good and for evil. Finally, childhood disciplinary patterns, ranging from erratic and excessive forms of physical and sexual abuse across the full spectrum to reasoned and proportionate forms of caring punishment, facilitate the doing of good as well as of evil. Until now, research in one area or discipline has proceeded without the benefit of insights accumulated in another. Systematic research now needs to be done to confirm, or deny, this unified field theory hypothesis.

ANTISOCIAL BEHAVIOR, PROSOCIAL BEHAVIOR, AND JEWISH RELIGIOUS TEACHING

All the evidence—social-psychological as well as historical— indicates that religious affiliation and praxis is not a determining factor in antisocial or prosocial behavior. Religion did not help or hinder subjects in the Milgram, Staub, or other experiments in any systematic way. Nor was it a factor in any systematic way among the German soldiers of the police battalions or among the rescuers. Rather, the role of religion is episodic. Some use it to justify anti-social behavior, and some use it to justify prosocial behavior; there is no over-all consistent pattern.   In view of this, we, as theologians, religious educa-tors, and morally sensitive human beings, need to move from the descriptive-analytic task to the normative-prescriptive task; that is, we need to move from analyzing the factors that facilitate the doing of good and evil to prescribing norms that will discourage evil and encourage good.[22] We need to ask, what ought religious authorities and institutions do to cultivate prosocial attitudes and behaviors, and to discourage antisocial attitudes and behaviors? This, it seems to me, is the normative answer to the question "where was humanity?" It is the prescriptive implication of the description and analysis. Setting proso-cial moral norms is also the answer to the question "where will humanity be the next time a major social crisis occurs?"

There are four steps that Jewish religious authorities must take to assume their responsibilities in the area of moral education.[23]

First, *Jewish religious authorities must admit the failure of much of their previous efforts to discourage antisocial attitudes and behaviors, and to encourage prosocial attitudes and behaviors.* As noted, the results of social-psychological and historical research indicate this to be true, but it does not seem to have penetrated fully into the minds of religious educators. To put it most simply: If religious moral education works, why do we not see more prosocial action among religious persons?

Second, *Jewish religious authorities must identify and actively teach prosocial texts and traditions.* For the Tanakh, this would include the stories of Shifra and Pu'ah, the midwives who resisted Pharaoh's genocidal decrees; Rahab, the prostitute who resisted the Jericho secret police to hide the spies; Nathan, the prophet who confronted King David forcefully on his adultery with Bathsheba and the murder of her husband; Saul's officers who refused to kill the priests of Nob who had sheltered David; Abraham, who argued with God about the justice of destroying the cities of Sodom and Gomorrah; Moses, who consistently defended the people of Israel against God's unjust threats; and the author of Psalm 44, who protested vehemently against God's desertion of God's people in time of war. For rabbinic Judaism, the literature of prosocial texts and traditions would include the norms for proper court pro-cedure and judicial protest; the laws commanding that one reprove someone behaving improperly and rescue someone in trouble; the uses and limits of military disobedience and nonviolence; and the doctrines of doing good deeds, going beyond the demands of the law, honoring God's creatures, and martyrdom.

Third, *Jewish religious authorities must identify and actively inculcate prosocial value-concepts.*[24] The term "value-concept" has both intellectual content that can be analyzed and normative value that sets moral expectations. All societies have value-concepts. In contemporary American English, the following are a few of the many value-concepts which inform our moral discourse: justice, fairness, kindness, caring, goodness, cruelty, evil, rectitude, mercy, etc. In rabbinic tradition, there are many value-concepts which inform traditional Jewish moral discourse: *tselem* (image, imitatio Dei); *brit* (covenant), which implies *talmud Torah* (study of Torah); *mitsva* (commandedness); *tsedek* (justice), which implies *lifnei 'iver* ("you shall not put a stumbling block before the blind"), *ve-'asita ha-tov veha-yashar* (you shall do what is right and proper), and *patur mi-dinei adam ve-hayyav be-dinei shamayim* ("exempt in a human court but not in heaven"); *tsedaka* (righteousness, charity); *middat hasidut* (the standard of the pious/caring/nonviolence), which derives from *hesed* (loyalty, grace, caring) and implies *gemilut hasadim* (doing good deeds); *lifnim mi-shurat ha-din* ("beyond the line of the law"); *shalom* (peace) and *mipne darkhei shalom* (for the sake of social peace); *tikkun 'olam* (repairing/restoring the world); *yetser ha-ra'* and *yetser tov* (the impulses to evil and to good); and *pikuah nefesh* (saving a life). There are many more.

Fourth, *Jewish religious authorities must recognize that it is not only what one teaches but how it is taught that makes the difference.* It is not only the content of the teaching but the social-psychological context in which it is taught that makes the real difference between successful and unsuccessful moral education. To make this point clear and to demonstrate how it can be done with the Jewish sources, I make the following seven strong recommendations for teaching prosocial values in a Jewish context:

1. *Establish a means by which authority can be challenged.* Use an ombudsperson and/or a whistle-blowing mechanism to create a legitimate way to challenge authority. Also, use a care team whose task it is to oversee and aid institutions to develop and maintain caring relationships with those for whom one is responsible. This would embody such value-concepts as *hokhe'ah tokhi'ah* and *talmud Torah*.

2. *Teach the following five prosocial skills:*

a. *Perspective taking and empathy.* This enables one to understand how the other feels, to appreciate the affective dimension of the other's situation. Ask, "What do you think he or she feels?" Ask, "What does she or he feel even if she or he cannot express it?" Ask, "How angry, happy, ashamed, proud ... is he or she?" Ask, "What would you feel in that person's place?" Ask, "What is empathy? What is sympathy?" Everyone is capable of perspective-taking, and everyone will need to be the object of perspective-taking by others in the course of life. Being able to empathize is an important prosocial skill. This would embody such value-concepts as *middat hasidut* and *kevod ha-beriyot*.

b. *Identifying and coding one's own feelings.* Our feelings are basic to who we are; they are the ground for much of our being and the agency for much of our action. We need to know our own feelings. Ask, "What did you feel when you saw . . . ?" Ask, "Can you recall feeling ashamed, guilty, joyous, powerful, hurt, nurturing, modest, immodest, content?" Ask, "What is the difference between anger and rage? Have you ever felt either? What was it like?" Ask, "How do you feel when someone threatens you, challenges you publicly, praises you in front of others?" Almost everyone has experienced every one of these emotional states at one time or another. Being able to label them and to recognize them is an important prosocial skill. This would embody such value-concepts as *yetser ha-ra', yetser tov,* and *tov lev.*

c. *Identifying authorities, hierarchies, norms, roles, and social processes.* Everyone exists within a series of social hierarchies. Everyone is subordinate to someone else and superior to yet others. Every situation is replete with norms, roles, and social expectations. Ask, "What is the social hierarchy in this situation?" Ask, "To whom are you subordinate? To whom are you superior?" Ask, "Is there more than one authority at work here? more than one set of subordinates?" Ask, "Upon what is the legitimacy of the authority based? Do you agree with that authority and its legitimacy?" Ask, "What would you have to do to break the rule, the norm? What would you have to do to challenge the authority?" Ask, "Are you, as an authority, acting in a responsible way, within the limits of your legitimacy? And, if not, how do you as an authority challenge your own authority and reshape it?" Knowing one's place in various hierarchies and, hence, imagining how one might challenge that hierarchy is a major prosocial skill—and it can be learned.

d. *Externalizing repressed prosocial impulses.* Doing good, as Batson has shown and as rabbinic tradition teaches, is a basic part of being human. All people want to do good to others, even if the motivation is sometimes egoistic. Yet many people hesitate to do good. Ask, "If you could do good and not have to . . . , what would you do?" Ask, "Quick! What does your impulse to do good tell you to do?" Ask, "What would be the really good thing to do here?" Ask, "What act of caring have you done today?" Ask, "What can you do that would be really kind?" Ask, "Whom do you know who is a really good person? What does she or he do? How do you know he or she is good?" Realizing that one does know good when one sees it, recognizing good impulses in oneself and realizing that the impediments to doing good are not as formidable as they seem, is an important prosocial skill. This would embody such value-concepts as *gemilut hasadim*.

e. *Conflict management*. Conflict does not need to be overcome or eliminated. Quite the contrary, conflict is a natural part of life. It does, however, need to be managed so that human relationships do not deteriorate into resentment, hatred, and violence. Teach the skills of mediation. Instruct people in the art of finding superordinate goals. Ask, "What is at stake behind the surface issues for each party?" Ask, "What are the common goals of these people?" Ask, "Why should these persons cooperate with one another?" Ask, "If these people cannot be reconciled, what kind of relationship can they have? If they cannot live in harmony, what intermediate relationship could they have?" This would embody such value-concepts as *shalom*.

3. *Model prosocial attitudes and behaviors*. Do them yourself, hire staff who have a record of prosocial action, use prosocial attitudes and behaviors as part of the evaluation and promotion process, and acknowledge prosocial heroes and heroines.

4. *Implement prosocial action*. Undertake specific projects, establish personal contact with the disadvantaged, create a feedback mechanism, and provide a full-time person to develop prosocial programming.

5. *Teach the value-concepts of prosocial action*.

a. *Use the language of justice and caring*. Discuss the terms pity, compassion, concern, affection, love, care, cherish, nourish, protect, understanding, empathy, kindness, mercy, sympathy, attachment, devotion, heart, feeling, respect, awareness, recognition, intimacy, attention, warmth, and consideration. And the complements: pain, sorrow, grief, worry, anxiety, distress, suffering, trouble, sensitiveness, stress, intimidate, persecute, threaten, and terror. And the terms justice, fairness, law, integrity, virtue, uprightness, rectitude, equity, impartiality, righteousness, morality, and ethics. This would embody such value-concepts as *lifne 'iver, lo tisna'*, and *lifnim mishurat hadin*.

b. *Teach the specific value-concepts of prosocial action*. Inclusiveness, extensivity, ingroup-outgroup, globalism, goodness, kindness, justice, caring, morality, critical thinking, protest, resistance, bonding, conflict management and resolution, win-win, humanness, and humanity. Talk about inclusive language. The way we phrase what we want to say forms who we are and who we become.

c. *Teach critical thinking and the nature of social processes*. Teach about social hierarchies, authority, obedience, disobedience, resistance, protest, heteronomy and autonomy, norms, rules, values, and orientations. Not only the skills, but the conceptual and axiological background to social processes must be taught. Teach critical thinking: How does one identify a lie? What is propaganda? Who is manipulating whom? Whose power is at stake here?

d. *Develop syllabi and a curriculum of instruction in prosocial action.*

6. *Develop networks.* They must be broad, make everyone stakeholders, and involve legitimate authority.

7. *Be intentional about what you are doing.* Do all this knowingly, conscious of what you are doing and why. This would embody such value-concepts as *mitsva, tselem,* and *kavvana.*

The question that is our legacy from the holocaust, "where was humanity?" and in particular, "where were the passive masses of humanity?" will haunt us well into the next century. Indeed, this question may well become the premier question that the twentieth century commits to human history. Description and analysis of the data pertaining to this question from the disciplines of history and social psychology can allow us to achieve some intellectual clarity in answering it. And prescribing and setting norms which discourage evil and encourage good may allow us to achieve some moral control over human history.

NOTES

1. As a matter of theological and moral principle, I do not capitalize words like "holocaust," "final solution," etc. I certainly never capitalize "nazi."

2. The material in this article is a précis of my forthcoming book, tentatively entitled *The Banality of Good and Evil: A Social-Psychological and Theological Reflection* [published as *The Banality of Good and Evil: Moral Lessons from the Shoah and Jewish Tradition* (Washington, D.C.: Georgetown University Press, 1999).].

3. For other issues on this theme, see D. Blumenthal, "The Holocaust and Hiroshima: Icons of Our Century," forthcoming.

4. Westminster, Pa.: John Knox, 1993.

5. F. Katz, *Ordinary People and Extraordinary Evil* (Albany: State University of New York Press, 1993).

6. S. Katz, "The 'Unique' Intentionality of the Holocaust," in *Post-Holocaust Dialogues,* ed. S. Katz, (New York, New York University Press: 1985), pP. 287-317. Now, see idem, *The Holocaust in Historical Context* (New York: Oxford University Press: 1994).

7. Ibid.

8. On the perpetrators, see, for example, C. Browning, *Ordinary Men: Reserve Police Battalion 101 and the Final Solution in Poland* (New York: Harper Collins, 1992). On the rescuers, see, for example, S. Oliner and P. Oliner, *The Altruistic Personality* (New York: Free Press: 1988), reviewed by me in *Critical Review of Books in Religion* 3 (1990): 409–411.

9. See, for example, S. Milgram, *Obedience to Authority: An Experimental View* (New York: Harper & Row: 1974), also available as a film; and "In the Eye of the Storm" and later in "A Class Divided"; the latter appeared as a book by W. Peters, *A Class Divided Then and Now* (New Haven: Yale University Press: 1987). The latter is known as the Riceville Experiment because it first took place in the town of that name.

10. See, for example, E. Staub, "Helping a Distressed Person," L. Berkowitz, *Advances in Experimental Social Psychology,* (New York: Academic Press: 1974), 7:293–341; J. M. Darley and C. D. Batson, "From Jerusalem to Jericho: A Study of Situational and Dispositional Variables in Helping Behavior," *Journal of Personality and Social Psychology* 27, no. 1 (1973): 100–108, known as the Princeton Experiment; C. D. Batson, *The Altruism Question* (Hillsdale, N.J.: Lawrence Erlbaum Associates, 1991); and P. Oliner and S. Oliner, *Toward a Caring Society: Ideas into Action* (Westport, Conn.: Praeger, 1995). The last is a study of prosocial practices in business, educational, and other social institutions.

11. One should also include other historical data fields, such as Vietnam and African-American slavery.

12. The typology is that of H. C. Kelman and V. L. Hamilton, *Crimes of Obedience* (New Haven: Yale University Press, 1989).

13. H. Arendt, *Eichmann in Jerusalem: A Report on the Banality of Evil* (New York: Viking Press, 1963).

14. T. des Pres, *The Survivor: An Anatomy of Life in the Death Camps* (Oxford: Oxford University Press, 1976).

15. The term is derived from Oliner and Oliner, *Altruistic Personality,* cited above.

16. A. Miller, *For Your Own Good* (New York: Farrar, Straus, & Giroux, 1983).

17. It is to be regretted that the subjects in the social-psychological experiments conducted in America were not questioned about discipline during their childhood years. If Miller is right, those who conformed most would be the ones who came from backgrounds where childhood discipline was more erratic and/or excessive.

18. Prosocial action is action which is good in the sense that at least one human being, other than the subject, benefits from it. An act is prosocial regardless of the intent of the subject. It need not be self-sacrificial or even entail high risk. Altruistic action carries the connotation of purely unselfish action; that is, of action that does good but which is also motivated by good intentions. An altruistic act does not necessarily have to be self-sacrificial; it usually is understood as entailing some risk. Resistance is prosocial action that, in order to accomplish its task, must resist the demands of a legitimate authority. It can be selfishly or unselfishly motivated, need not be self-sac-

rificial, and usually entails risk. Clearly, not all prosocial action is resistance to a social norm or hierarchical authority, while most but not all resistance is prosocial action. (Resistance exercised for its own sake with no prosocial intent would be psychologically valid but ethically questionable.) See above, n. 10, for a list of sources on resistance and prosocial action.

19. Darley and Batson recorded a 40 percent rate of caring for a victim, even though, as they point out, one would have expected the rate to be higher after study of the text of the Good Samaritan and, presumptively, among students for the ministry. This is slightly higher than Milgram's 15–35 percent resistance rate and much better than the German police battalion rate of 10–20 percent resistance.

20. It is to be regretted that the social-psychological experiments on altruism and prosocial behavior did not control for the history of childhood discipline.

21. For a preliminary attempt, see E. Staub, *The Roots of Evil: The Origins of Genocide and Other Group Violence* (Cambridge: Cambridge University Press, 1989).

22. Unfortunately, in American English, the word "norm" has two meanings which here must never be confused. The first indicates that which is in fact done, that which is normal. The second indicates that which ought to be done, that which is morally desirable. Norms in the sense of standard behavior are descriptive and are deduced from data, but norms in the sense of oughts critique standard practice and are prescriptive and consciously articulated and taught by legitimate authorities as moral and ethical desiderata of human behavior.

23. While I approach this from the perspective of Jewish religion, it goes without saying that the same issue poses itself to other religious traditions and to the secular-humanist tradition of Western culture as well. For all, description and analysis are not enough; prescribing and setting norms are necessary. The steps outlined below are valid for other religious and secular traditions.

24. The term comes from M. Kadushin, *The Rabbinic Mind* (New York: Jewish Theological Seminary, 1952).

PART VI
By Way of Conclusion

After Auschwitz, Ethics a Prime Responsibility

Jean Halpérin

I am fully aware of the difficulty of my task. Being the last but one to take the floor, much of what I had wanted to say has already been admirably covered by previous speakers.

Some of the papers that have been read would have called for reactions on my part, but the constraints of time prevent me from doing so in any detail.

My first duty, however, is an easy one to perform. It is to express our heartfelt gratitude to our friends from SIDIC, to the Pontifical Gregorian University, and to the Università di Roma Tor Vergata for having made this remarkable symposium possible.

Having said this, the topic of this symposium and the subject of the paper that I myself have chosen to read command great care and, above all, the language of truth, barring any form of complacency—at the risk of sounding provocative. We are also, as a matter of course, forbidden to indulge in sweeping generalizations or mere wishful thinking.

Many of us realize that it may not be possible to fully grasp, understand, or explain the accumulation of dreadful events and deeds that have left their imprint on world history since the fateful years 1933 to 1945. This, however, surely, does not exonerate us from the duty to try and draw lessons from what happened and from the way in which it was, generally speaking, allowed to happen.

Beyond the causes of the evil that marked these events, one fact at least appears to leave no doubt whatsoever: the results and consequences could certainly have been curtailed had there been less indifference in the face of evil or, for that matter, a greater awareness on the part of groups or individuals. With a sharper sense of responsibility and a stronger ethical commitment, the scope of the disaster would have been reduced.

I would even go one step further and submit that resistance to evil from the very start could have had the effect of avoiding or stopping the catastrophe altogether. This sentence may sound trivial or innocuous. In fact, it conveys an essential message, the importance of which has lost nothing as decades pass by. The apathy of practically all governments and the deafening silence of the civilized world, including the churches and other groups or institutions, such as the League of Nations or the International Red Cross among others, with only very rare exceptions, are of major significance for the past as well as for the future. The subject would have warranted a special paper at this symposium. It is indeed an area that raises a host of agonizing questions illustrating the impact of the deficit—or failure—of ethics at that time.

I must confess that I was stunned to hear one of our colleagues using the phrase "nazi ethics." Listening to him, I thought that we would have to radically revise our vocabulary. Words have a meaning, and we must not allow them to be perverted.

There is an appallingly long list of initiatives, deeds, statements, or gestures that did not take place and which could or would have changed the course of events.

Abstention in the face of evil must under any circumstances be regarded as becoming part of evil itself and an encouragement thereof.

There is also a long list of wrong actions that had the gravest consequences. To give only one example (mentioned already by F. B. Dupuy and by Dr. Etienne Lepicard), it should be recognized that the signing, in May 1933, of the Concordat between the Holy See and the German government had the immediate result of making the German nazis *salonfähig* in the eyes of the world and of public opinion. Some of the reasons which led to that fateful decision are well known: for instance, to obtain freedom of action for Catholic associations or institutions. This illustrates the danger of wrong speculation and false perceptions of the short-term self-interest of the Church.

Much could be said also with regard to the inadequacies of the Barmen Declaration.

Hence, another important lesson to be drawn emphatically from the past: not only must evil be at all times effectively opposed, but also one should never compromise with evil, or accept any concessions, even for the sake of what may appear as short-term gains.

Furthermore, there is no possible justification for any relativization of evil. For instance, the churches were certainly wrong to behave the way they did vis-à-vis nazi Germany even if it was out of fear of the communist threat supposed to be a worse evil. The wrongs of others cannot be used as an excuse.

This, then, is a first and compelling lesson to be drawn from the way in which the Shoah was allowed to reach such a climax. We have been taught by history, in no uncertain terms, that this kind of evil cannot and must not be equated with a natural disaster defying human action.

It is worth noting that when the United Nations Charter was drafted at the San Francisco Conference in the spring of 1945, it was found necessary no less than eight times to explicitly emphasize concern for the respect of human rights and fundamental freedoms. This was done almost to the day when such ominous places as Auschwitz, Treblinka, Maidanek, Belzec, Sobibor, Buchenwald, Dachau, Ravensbrück, Mauthausen, Bergen-Belsen, Theresienstadt, Stutthof, and others were liberated.

One would wish to read this as implying a solemn commitment on behalf of the peoples of the United Nations to do away, once and for all, with the neglect with which human rights and the dignity of human beings had been treated until then.

I must, however, for the sake of truth, point out the fact that Article 2, paragraph 7 of the Charter still, at the same time, protected member states against interference in what is called domestic affairs, including violations of human rights.

This raises some awkward questions with regard to the implementation of human rights, even bearing in mind the adoption of the Universal Declaration by the General Assembly of the United Nations as early as December 10, 1948.

Almost fifty years after that event, which, at the time, had been rightly perceived as momentous, we must admit that the inventory of violations of human rights and fundamental freedoms all over the world far exceeds such progress as has been recorded. Not only did it take no less than sixteen years for the mechanisms of implementation, i.e., the Covenants, to be adopted, but even they have demonstrated much impotence.

Indeed, we may wish to send from here a message of encouragement and expectation to the newly appointed U.N. High Commissioner on Human Rights, Mary Robinson, who is embarking on such a difficult and vital task. She should know that our sincere prayers accompany her for the success of her mission.

More genuine and effective steps are required at all levels to put an end to the widespread resistance to any further real implementation system.

In other words, important as sound principles may be, it is even more essential to see to it that ethical commandments are effectively practiced and observed.

The present state of affairs in too many parts of the world clearly shows that much remains to be done if ethics is to be given the full weight of responsibility toward the self and the other.

Looking at, and pondering on, the state of the world everywhere today, one cannot escape the anguished feeling that we still have a long way to go until the awareness of good and evil—after Auschwitz—will have become a reality. It is therefore our duty to create such awareness.

Listening to younger colleagues here, we felt gratified to realize that they are fully committed to actively participate in the process of awareness.

A major contribution to this specific topic can be found in a study recently published in the journal *Esprit* (July 1997) by an Italian diplomat and political scientist, Roberto Toscano, under the title: "Guerre, violence civile et éthique: La diplomatie à la lumière de Levinas." It is not surprising that the author has found as the main point of conceptual reference the works of Emmanuel Levinas, who is the thinker par excellence of otherness and of infinite and total responsibility.

To quote R. Toscano (op. cit., p. 154), "The appearance (the 'epiphany,' to use his term) of the face of the other is for Levinas the starting point for ethics insofar as it functions as an inescapable call to responsibility."

Those familiar with the thought of Emmanuel Levinas know how much of it is rooted in the spiritual heritage and the true sources of his wisdom.

It is rewarding to feel how acutely the thoughts of our teachers André Neher, Emmanuel Levinas, Uriel Tal, and Primo Levi, of blessed memory, have been with us during this week.

Useful food for thought is also provided in the proceedings of a symposium which took place at the Catholic University of Milan under the title "Educare dopo Auschwitz" (1995) with the participation, among others, of Cardinal Martini and F. Jean Dujardin.

There is another issue, raised here on the very first day, which we must try and face squarely. To put it briefly, it can be formulated as follows: is there a way to explain how and why the Shoah took place in the middle of European Christian civilization?

A number of factors seem to have had a devastating effect. Among them, the age-old "teaching of contempt," which can be traced down to the Second Vatican Council; the lack of memory about which Prof. J. B. Metz had so much to say when he referred to the need for an anamnestic culture, in conformity with Deuteronomy 4:9[1]; the danger of thinking in terms of vicariousness which tends to exonerate the individual of his or her own and total responsibility. Again, we are taught by our Scriptures and by our own experience that we must not escape our personal responsibility by relying on others, not even on the All-Other.[2]

We should not forget that the commandment "Thou shalt love thy neighbor as thyself" (Leviticus 19:18) is preceded in Leviticus 19 (16–17) by:

"Thou shalt not go up and down as a talebearer among thy people; neither shalt thou stand aside when mischief befalls thy neighbor, I am the Lord. Thou shalt not hate thy brother in thy heart; thou shalt certainly rebuke thy neighbor, and not suffer sin on his account."

Hence, the categorical imperative of overcoming the temptation of indifference when good and evil are at stake. Elie Wiesel has rightly emphasized time and again that the greatest sin of all is indifference.

It is as if we were made to understand, in the light of our experience, the full meaning of Deuteronomy 30:15 and 19: "See, I have set before thee this day life and good, and death and evil. . . Therefore, choose life." I am grateful to Cardinal Cassidy and to Dr. Lepicard for having already so forcefully made this point earlier in our symposium.

On the side of good, the righteous among the nations teach us a lesson that we are not allowed to belittle or to underestimate. They confirm in their own way what is said in the Mishnah Avot (4:2) by Ben-Azai: "A good deed leads to another good deed, and a sin leads to a further sin."

It was important hearing from Rev. Michael McGarry and Prof. Eva Fleischner about the basic difference between bystanders and rescuers.

In this connection, I would like to commend to your attention a thought-provoking article recently published in the Swiss monthly *Orientierung* (61, 1997) by Carl Holenstein under the title "Von der Mühsal, die richtigen Fragen zu stellen." It points to the true dimensions of human responsibility and to the unending duty to fully face it under any set of circumstances. It also illustrates the damage caused by the silent majority condoning evil. To that extent it allows a more meaningful and sharper reading of the widely criticized and discussed book by Daniel Goldhagen, *Hitler's Willing Executioners*.[3]

The Catholic journal *Concilium* published an excellent issue in 1984 containing some significant papers, but under a general heading that could be misinterpreted. The heading reads: "Judaism After Auschwitz: A Radical Question," as if that "radical question" were not also and no less of direct and grave concern to Christianity and to the churches as well.

Incidentally, this error in perspective, to put it mildly, can also be traced in paragraph 25 of the "Notes of 1985 on the correct way to present the Jews and Judaism in preaching and catechesis in the Roman Catholic Church," published by the Holy See Commission for Religious Relations with the Jews,[4] mentioned here already on the first morning.

There is, finally, another fundamental lesson to be drawn from the past, and particularly from the years 1933–1945. The time has certainly at last come to recognize again that it is a dangerous fallacy to maintain that politics can be separated from ethics, or, to put it differently, that politics and ethics belong to two intrinsically different realms. The tradition to which I belong teaches me that ethics must be made an integral part of politics, difficult as it may seem to be.

If the spiritual forces—wherever they are—do not have the courage to constantly teach ethics and to see to it that they are actually respected, who will?

They should, therefore—after Auschwitz—take the lead, individually and jointly, to elaborate and launch, with the vision and the sense of responsibility required, an ambitious program of action which would echo and put into effect in our time the teachings of the prophets.

Memory—of what has happened in our days—and awareness must lead us together to *a way of being and acting*, in order to better respond to our joint calling and vocation as human beings.

On the threshold of the Jewish New Year, I hope and pray that we and all humankind will be blessed by true shalom.

NOTES

1. "Only take heed to thyself and keep thy soul diligently, lest you forget the things which thy eyes have seen, and lest they depart from thy heart all the days of thy life; and teach them to thy children and thy children's children."
2. Cf. *Die Kirchen und die Juden. Versuch einer Bilanz* (Gerlingen: Lambert Schneider, 1997), particularly Erich Zenger, "*Nostra Aetate.* Der notwendinge Streit um die Anerkennung des Judentums in der katholischen Kirche," pp. 49–82. Also, Michel Remaud, *Israël serviteur de Dieu*, 2nd ed. (Jerusalem: Centre Ratisbonne, 1997).
3. See also Pierre Bouretz, "Daniel Goldhagen, la Shoah et l'Allemagne: Les piliers ont-ils vraiment tremblé?" *Les Temps modernes*, no. 592 (February–March 1997).
4. I am referring in particular to the following sentence in the document: "Catechesis should . . . help in understanding the meaning *for the Jews* [emphasis added] of the extermination during the years 1939–1945, and its consequences."

Victims' Voices:
Texts Selected and Introduced by

Joseph Sievers

Many of the victims of Nazism, Jews as well as others, had no chance to leave any written record. Among those who managed to set down their thoughts in letters, diaries, and other writings, some included reflections about the time "after Hitler." Of testimonies of this kind that have survived, only a few examples are presented here, without any pretense that they are representative in their points of view. One could have cited the writings of Rabbi Kalonymus Shapira, the rebbe of the Warsaw Ghetto, of Alfred Delp, S.J., or of Edith Stein. The list of well-known and less-known authors, Jews and non-Jews, could be very long.[1] Here are offered selections from the writings of three persons of very different backgrounds. What unites them is the fact that they show a very high sense of responsibility for the future, a future that they did not live to see.

MOSHE FLINKER

Moshe Flinker was an Orthodox Jewish youth who wrote his diary, in Hebrew, in Brussels, where his family had taken refuge.[2] He was born in The Hague, Netherlands, on October 9, 1926.

December 8 [1942], Night

Shortly after we came to Brussels and found an apartment, my mother began to question my father about my future. I was spending my days idly. At times I read Hebrew, but mother considered that this would lead nowhere. The first times she expressed her views, I laughed and even father paid little attention to them. I wondered how she could worry about a happy future at a time when we were faced with the problem of life or death. My father gave her a similar answer whenever she broached the subject to him.

During the last few days when my mother raised the question of my future, my reaction was again one of laughter, but when I was alone, I too began to ponder this matter. What indeed is to become of me? It is obvious that the present situation will not last for ever—perhaps another year or

two—but what will happen then? One day I will have to earn my own liv-
ing. At first I wanted to drive such thoughts away but they kept coming back.
So I started thinking seriously about the problem. After much deliberation,
I've decided to become . . . a statesman. Not any sort of statesman, but a
Jewish statesman in the Land of Israel. Even though it would take a miracle
to free us now, the rest of my idea—living in our land—isn't so far-fetched.
Then perhaps, the rest of the world might slightly change its attitude towards
us. The relations between other nations may also alter a bit. But our people
are so exile-minded that many generations would have to pass before we
became a free people physically and mentally (the latter is the main thing).
That is why we will need leaders to guide us on the road to true spiritual
freedom.[3]

December 18, Morning

As far as my study of Arabic is concerned, I am not learning it simply
because I like it or anything like that. I have begun—and hope I may finish—
to study this language because a large part of the inhabitants of the land of
Israel and the surrounding countries speak it. And, in view of my plans, I see
that I will need this language more than any that I studied in school. It is
obvious that we shall have to live in peace with our brothers, the sons of
Ishmael, who are also Abraham's descendants. I am sure that the terrible
riots in the Land of Israel before the war were incited by Germany and Italy;
such terrifying outbreaks must not recur. I think that, had the Jewish leaders
learned Arabic and so have been able to speak with the Arab leaders, that
violence would not have occurred. And therefore I am trying very hard to
learn the language.[4]

May 19, 1943

I have written several times about a question which has been bothering
me for some time; namely, what I will be when I am on my own, which I
imagine will be in about five or six years. I thought at one time that I had
answered this question, and that I would be a statesman, a Jewish statesman,
and in that way work for my people and my God. I then thought that this was
a very good solution because, as we see from current events, and learn from
the example of the leaders of the various countries, most statesmen did not
reach their present positions of eminence by lengthy study nor by originali-

ty of ideas or anything of that kind; rather, they were impelled firstly by a strong will to govern, and secondly by various other, relatively unimportant reasons. This made me think that my present situation would be inducive to my becoming a statesman because for that profession one need not study night and day, but rather one requires a strong character and a heart of steel. So when, together with these qualities, I would obtain knowledge in various other areas, then everything would be perfect.

When I first got this idea and wrote it in my diary, I tried to do all I could to bring it about. Everything I did and thought was, as far as possible, related to this aim. But after some time had passed I saw, and what is more important I felt, that it was all worthless. Really, what can I do? I am in touch with no one. At most to further this object, I studied a lot of Arabic. But as the war grew more and more terrible, I came to feel that if results of lasting value were to come out of it, that is, if we attain the redemption for which our people has been waiting and hoping for two thousand years, then these cannot occur through diplomacy or other deceit or by the grace of the great powers. In that case, there is no longer any value to the Arabic I am studying, and my activities in this direction would appear to be useless. Thus nearly all the positive content to my life is shown to be pointless, and I am left with almost nothing. My great complaint is against this terrible emptiness. I now understand that ideas and thoughts are worthless if one cannot convert them into action. My inner vacuum, moreover, is giving rise to all kinds of thoughts, which are expressing themselves in strange desires. For in life one cannot be neutral, neither positive nor negative; if one has nothing positive, then all sorts of negative tendencies appear unhindered. So now all day long I do nothing but search for some positive content for my life, so as not to be entirely lost. In every single thing I hope to find a meaning which will fill me and satisfy me, but it is as if I heard a voice inside me always saying: "You are deceiving yourself if you think this is of value for you; it can at best fill only part of your spiritual void." This has been my situation for quite some time; I am lost and seek in vain, for meaning, for control, for purpose.

But so far I have found nothing. In my prayers I ask that the Lord take pity on me and bestow on me His lovingkindness and that His holy spirit fill me that I might live again. I also ask of the Lord that He have mercy on His downtrodden and degraded people, deprived of all rights, except for the right to be mocked and the right to be murdered. O Lord, have mercy upon Thy people, pity them, pity them! And have mercy on Thy servant also, for I wish only to worship Thee, my Lord. Have pity!?[5]

No Date

When I speak of vengeance, I do not wish you to understand by this that every Jew who can bear a sword should arise and attack a German, to avenge the blood of our brothers and sisters and their endless pain. No, my beloved brothers, when one speaks of vengeance of this sort, it is always accompanied by a prayer to the Lord that He should execute our vengeance. For in our desire to avenge what is to be avenged we should have to rise all over the world, for there exists no people and no land that has not caused us bitter and hard troubles.

No, my brothers, I want you to observe only the positive side of vengeance. Our revenge, for our sufferings today and for the sufferings of our long exile, which we have been bearing for more than two thousand years, will be the building of our country and the settling there of our people—the return of our beloved people to their homeland. That will be the greatest revenge that could ever happen. For this vengeance we ask the help of our Lord, the Lord of Israel, Who has protected us from annihilation throughout our long exile. He will surely save us and settle us anew in our homeland, our holy land, the Land of Israel.

My Lord! Cause my will to follow Thy will![6]

No Date

I am sitting facing the sun. Soon it will set; it is nearing the horizon. It is as red as blood, as if it were a bleeding wound. From where does it get so much blood? For days there has been a red sun, but this is not hard to understand. Is it not sufficient to weep, in these days of anguish? Suffering stares at me as on every side and in every direction, and still further troubles appear before your eyes. Here a man and woman, both over seventy, are taken away. There you meet a Jew who has been hiding and has no money to live, and elsewhere you meet a Jew whose fortune has gone because he invested it in dollars, which for some unknown reason have become worthless. Trouble never ends. . . . And every time I meet a child of my people I ask myself: "Moshe, what are you doing for him?" I feel responsible for every single pain.[7]

On April 7, 1944, the Eve of Passover, Moshe and his entire family were arrested and deported to Auschwitz. He and his parents perished there, but his five sisters and a younger brother managed to survive.

ETTY HILLESUM

Esther Hillesum was born in Middelburg, Netherlands, on January 15, 1914. Her father, a classics teacher in a high school, was descended from a Dutch Jewish family. Her mother, Rebecca Bernstein, was of Russian origin. Etty, as Esther was usually called, grew up in a rather assimilated Jewish environment. She got a law degree, but also studied and taught Russian. In March of 1941, at age twenty-seven, she began to write a diary. She continued to write even in the transit camp of Westerbork. On her last journey, which took her from Westerbork to Auschwitz, she carried part of her diaries with her.[8] According to a Red Cross report, she died in the extermination camp on November 30, 1943.

Monday Morning, October 20 [1941]

Sometimes I want to flee with everything I possess into a few words, seek refuge in them. But there are still no words to shelter me. That is the real problem. I am in search of a haven, yet I must first build it for myself, stone by stone. Everyone seeks a home, a refuge. And I am always in search of a few words.

Sometimes I feel that every word spoken and every gesture made merely serve to exacerbate misunderstandings. Then what I would really like is to escape into a great silence and impose that silence on everyone else.[9]

October 21, After Dinner

It is a slow and painful process, this striving after true inner freedom. Growing more and more certain that there is no help or assurance or refuge in others. That the others are just as uncertain and weak and helpless as you are. You are always thrown back on to your own resources. There is nothing else. The rest is make-believe. But that fact has to be recognized over and over again. Especially since you are a woman. For woman always longs to lose herself in another. But that too is a fiction, albeit a beautiful one. There is no matching of lives. At least not for me. Perhaps for a few moments. But do those moments justify a lifetime together? Can those few moments cement a shared existence? All they can do is give you a little strength. And perhaps a little happiness. God knows, being alone is hard. For the world is inhospitable. In the past I used to dream of giving (my heart) to one person. But it was not to be. And when you reach such painful truths at the age of twenty-seven, you sometimes feel quite desperate and lonely and *anxious*, although independent and proud at the same time. I have confidence in myself, and I shall manage by myself. The only measure you have is yourself. And the only responsibility you can shoulder in life is responsibility for yourself. But you must do it with all your strength.[10]

[June 20, 1942]

I believe in God and I believe in man, and I say so without embarrassment. Life is hard, but that is no bad thing. If one starts by taking one's own importance seriously, the rest follows. It is not morbid individualism to work on oneself. True peace will come only when every individual finds peace within himself; when we have all vanquished and transformed our hatred for our fellow human beings of whatever race—even into love one day, although perhaps that is asking too much. It is, however, the only solution. I am a happy person, and I hold life dear indeed in this year of Our Lord 1942, the umpteenth year of the war.[11]

August 24, 1943 [Part of a letter from the Westerbork concentration camp to friends in Amsterdam]

There was a moment when I felt in all seriousness that after this night, it would be a sin ever to laugh again. But then I reminded myself that some of those who had gone away had been laughing, even if only a handful of them this time. . . . There will be some who will laugh now and then in Poland, too, though not many from this transport, I think.

When I think of the faces of that squad of armed green-uniformed guards—my God, those faces! I looked at them, each in turn, from behind the safety of a window, and I have never been so frightened of anything in my life as I was of those faces. I have run into trouble with the word that is the leitmotif of my life: "And God created man after His likeness" [Genesis 1:27]. That passage spent a difficult morning with me.

I have told you often enough that no words and images are adequate to describe nights like these. But still I must try to convey something of it to you. One always has the feeling here of being the ears and eyes of a piece of Jewish history, but there is also the need sometimes to be a still, small voice. We must keep one another in touch with everything that happens in the various outposts of this world, each one contributing his own little piece of stone to the great mosaic that will take shape once the war is over.[12]

DIETRICH BONHOEFFER

There is no need to introduce Dietrich Bonhoeffer. A brilliant theologian, active in the Confessing Church, he was connected with various groups of the resistance against Nazism. On April 5, 1943, he was arrested. He was executed in a concentration camp in Flossenbürg, Bavaria, less than one month before the end of the war, on April 9, 1945. The collection of his works is very extensive and will fill sixteen volumes in the critical edition now under way. This is not the place to cover the breadth of his writings or to comment on them. Instead, what is presented here are some fragments of his proposal for a new Christian ethics. He began this project in 1940 and continued to work on it even during his imprisonment.

Rarely perhaps has any generation shown so little interest as ours does in any kind of theoretical or systematic ethics. The academic question of a system of ethics seems to be, of all questions, the most superfluous. The reason for this is not to be sought in any supposed ethical indifference on the part of our period. On the contrary, it arises from the fact that our period, more than any earlier period in the history of the West, is oppressed by a superabounding reality of concrete ethical problems.[13]

One is distressed by the failure of *reasonable* people to perceive either the depths of evil or the depths of the holy. With the best of intentions they believe that a little reason will suffice them to clamp together the parting timbers of the building. They are so blind that in their desire to see justice done to both sides they are crushed between the two clashing forces and end by achieving nothing. Bitterly disappointed at the unreasonableness of the world, they see that their efforts must remain fruitless and they withdraw resignedly from the scene or yield unresistingly to the stronger party.

Still more distressing is the utter failure of all ethical *fanaticism*. The fanatic believes that he can oppose the power of evil with the purity of his will and of his principle. But since it is part of the nature of fanaticism that it loses sight of the totality of evil and rushes like a bull at the red cloth instead of at the man who holds it, the fanatic inevitably ends by tiring and admitting defeat. He aims wide of the mark. Even if his fanaticism serves the high cause of truth or justice, he will sooner or later become entangled with nonessentials and petty details and fall into the snare set by his more skilful opponent.

The man with a *conscience* fights a lonely battle against the overwhelming forces of inescapable situations that demand decisions. But he is torn apart by the extent of the conflicts in which he has to make his choice with no other aid or counsel than that which his own innermost conscience can furnish. Evil comes upon him in countless respectable and seductive disguises so that his conscience becomes timid and unsure of itself, till in the end he is satisfied if instead of a clear conscience he has a salved one, and lies to his own conscience in order to avoid despair. A man whose only support is his conscience can never understand that a bad conscience may be healthier and stronger than a conscience which is deceived.

It looks as though the way out from the confusing multiplicity of possible decisions is the *path of duty*. What is commanded is seized upon as being surest. Responsibility for the command rests upon the man who gives it and not upon him who executes it. But in this confinement within the limit of duty there can never come the bold stroke of the deed that is done on one's own free responsibility, the only kind of deed that can strike at the heart of evil and overcome it. The man of duty will end by having to fulfill his obligation even to the devil.

But if someone sets out to fight his battles in the world in his own absolute *freedom*, if he values the necessary deed more highly than the spotlessness of his own conscience and reputation, if he is prepared to sacrifice a fruitless principle to a fruitful compromise, or for that matter the fruitless wisdom of the *via media* to a fruitful radicalism, then let him beware lest precisely his supposed freedom may ultimately prove his undoing. He will easily consent to the bad, knowing full well that it is bad, in order to ward off what is worse, and in doing this he will no longer be able to see that precisely the worse which he is trying to avoid may still be the better. This is one of the underlying themes of tragedy.

Some who seek to avoid taking a stand publicly find a place of refuge in a *private virtuousness*. Such a man does not steal. He does not commit murder. He does not commit adultery. Within the limits of his powers he does good. But in his voluntary renunciation of publicity he knows how to remain punctiliously within the permitted bounds that preserve him from involvement in conflict. He must be blind and deaf to the wrongs that surround him. It is only at the price of an act of self-deception that he can safeguard his private blamelessness against contamination through responsible action in the world. Whatever he may do, that which he omits to do will give him no peace.[14]

Who would wish to pour scorn on such failures and frustrations as these? Reason, moral fanaticism, conscience, duty, free responsibility, and silent virtue, these are the achievements and attitudes of a noble humanity. It is the best of men who go under in this way, with all that they can do or be. Here is the immortal figure of Don Quixote, the knight of the doleful countenance, who takes a barber's bowl for a helmet and a miserable hack for a charger, and who rides into endless battles for the love of a lady who does not exist. . . . It is a mean-spirited man who can read of what befell Don Quixote and not be stirred to sympathy.

Yet our business now is to replace our rusty swords with sharp ones. A man can hold his own here only if he can combine simplicity with wisdom. But what is simplicity? What is wisdom? And how are the two to be combined? To be simple is to fix one's eye solely on the simple truth of God at a time when all ideas are being confused, distorted, and turned upside-down. It is to be single-hearted and not a man of two souls, an *anêr dipsychos* (James 1:8). Because the simple man knows God, because God is his, he clings to the commandments, the judgments, and the mercies that come from God's mouth every day afresh. Not fettered by principles, but bound by love for God, he has been set free from the problems and conflicts of ethical decision. They no longer oppress him. He belongs simply and solely to God and to the will of God. It is precisely because he looks only to God, without any sidelong glance at the world, that he is able to look at the reality of the world freely and without prejudice. And that is how simplicity becomes wisdom. The wise man is the one who sees reality as it is, and who sees into the depths of things. That is why only that man is wise who sees reality in God.[15]

To look in freedom at God and at reality, which rests solely upon Him, this is to combine simplicity with wisdom. There is no true simplicity without wisdom, and there is no wisdom without simplicity. This may sound very theoretical, and it is theoretical until it becomes clear at what point this attitude has its basis in reality so that it can itself become real.[16]

NOTES

1. For an analysis and partial English edition of the work of Rabbi Kalonymus K. Shapira, see Nehemia Polen, *The Holy Fire: The Teachings of Rabbi Kalonymus Kalman Shapira, the Rebbe of the Warsaw Ghetto* (Northvale, N.J.: Jason Aronson, 1994; paperback ed., 1998). A more general study of Jewish religious responses to the Shoah has been undertaken by Eliezer Schweid, *Ben Hurban Le'yeshua* (Tel Aviv: Hakibbutz Hame'uhad, 1994). Further bibliography (including references to system-

atic bibliographies by the author), will be found in Gershon Greenberg, "Consoling Truth: Eliezer Schweid's *Ben Hurban Le'yeshua*: A Review Essay," *Modern Judaism* 17 (1997): 243–258.

2. His diary notebooks were found by his surviving sisters after their return from Auschwitz. The first Hebrew edition was published, on the recommendation of Nobel laureate Shmuel Y. Agnon, in 1958. The following excerpts are based on the English edition, *Young Moshe's Diary: The Spiritual Torment of a Jewish Boy in Nazi Europe*, ed. Shaul Esh (Jerusalem: Yad Vashem, 1965).

3. *Young Moshe's Diary*, pp. 35–36.

4. Ibid., p. 47.

5. Ibid., pp. 87–89.

6. Ibid., pp. 117–118.

7. Ibid., p. 122.

8. These diaries have been lost forever. The only ones to survive, left by Etty with a friend in Amsterdam, cover the period from March 9, 1941 to October 1942. The Dutch original was published in part in 1981. The following excerpts are based on the English edition, introd. by J. G. Gaarlandt, trans. Arnold J. Pomerans *Etty Hillesum: An Interrupted Life & Letters from Westerbork* New York: Henry Holt and Comp., 1996. A critical edition of all the extant writings of Etty Hillesum has been prepared under the editorship of Klaas A. D. Smelik, *Etty: De nagelaten geschriften van Etty Hillesum 1941–1943* (Amsterdam: Uitgeverij Balans, 1986; 3rd rev. ed., 1991).

9. *Etty: A Diary*, p. 55.

10. Ibid., pp. 55–56.

11. Ibid., p. 145.

12. Ibid., p. 340; translation slightly altered.

13. Dietrich Bonhoeffer, *Ethics* (New York: Macmillan, 1965), p. 64.

14. Ibid., pp. 65–67.

15. Ibid., pp. 67–68.

16. Ibid., p. 69.

Biographical Information

DR. DIRK ANSORGE – Born in Gelsenkirchen (Germany), Dr. Ansorge pursued his course of study in philosophy and Catholic theology at Bochum, Jerusalem, Strasbourg, and Tübingen. He completed his doctoral work with a thesis on John Scotus Erigena which was awarded the 1993 "Karl-Rahner-Preis für theologische Forschung." Since 1993 he has been a lecturer in systematic and biblical theology at the Catholic Academy of the Diocese of Essen (Germany).

PROF. EMILIO BACCARINI – Born near Rome, he received his doctorate in philosophy from the University of Rome "La Sapienza" with a thesis on the phenomenology of Husserl. After completing various studies on the themes of phenomenology and subjectivity, Prof. Baccarini turned to the thought of Levinas and other exponents of contemporary Judaism. He teaches at the University of Rome "Tor Vergata" and at the Pontifical Lateran University. He is the director of the international journal *SIDIC* (Service International de Documentation Judéo-Chrétienne).

RABBI JACK BEMPORAD – He is the director of the Center for Interreligious Understanding. A native of Italy, Rabbi Bemporad came to the United States at the age of six. After graduating from Tulane University and from Hebrew Union College, he was ordained a rabbi in 1959. He has served as Chairman of the Interreligious Affairs Committee of the Synagogue Council of America and in this and other capacities has been active in Jewish-Christian dialogue. He has lectured at various universities in the United States and abroad.

PROF. JAMES BERNAUER, S.J. – Born in New York City, he studied philosophy and theology in the United States with research stints in Paris and Tübingen. He is a member of the Department of Philosophy at Boston College (Chestnut Hill, Massachusetts). Fr. Bernauer is currently working on a study of the moral-spiritual formation among German Christians in the years preceding the rise of National Socialism.

PROF. DAVID R. BLUMENTHAL –The Jay and Leslie Cohen Professor of Judaic Studies at Emory University in Atlanta, Georgia. A graduate of The University of Pennsylvania, The Jewish Theological Seminary of America, and Columbia University, Prof. Blumenthal also studied in Jerusalem and Paris. He has written widely in diverse areas of Judaic Studies: medieval Judaism, Jewish spirituality and mysticism, the relationship of Jewish studies to the university, Holocaust studies, and, his current interest, contemporary Jewish theology.

RABBI BENEDETTO CARUCCI VITERBI – Born in Rome, he earned a degree in literature from that city's "La Sapienza" University in 1986 and a Rabbinic degree from the "Collegio Rabbinico Italiano" in 1992. He teaches Biblical Exegesis and Rabbinic Literature in a program of the "Collegio Rabbinico Italiano" and Jewish Liturgy at the Liturgical Institute of the "Pontificio Ateneo S. Anselmo." He also serves as director of Jewish Studies for the school system of the Jewish community of Rome.

CARDINAL EDWARD I. CASSIDY – Born in Sydney, Australia, where he completed his studies prior to priestly ordination, Cardinal Cassidy is a graduate of the Pontifical Ecclesiastical Academy of Rome. As a member of the diplomatic service of the Holy See for more than thirty years, he served in a variety of posts in India, Ireland, El Salvador, Argentina, China, Bangladesh, South Africa, and Holland. Created a Cardinal by Pope John Paul II in 1991, he serves as President of the Pontifical Council for Promoting Christian Unity and of the Commission for Religious Relations with the Jews.

PROF. GIANFRANCO DALMASSO – teaches philosophy at the University of Rome "Tor Vergata." He has done research on contemporary French thinkers and in this context has been instrumental in bringing Jacques Derrida to the attention of the Italian public. His recent interests have been devoted to the question of the structure of rationality in its relation to ethics.

PROF. BERNARD G. M. DUPUY – A Dominican priest from Paris, Fr. Dupuy taught for many years on the Dominican theology faculty at Saulchoir and later at the Institut Catholique in Paris. Since 1967 he has been the Director of the *Istina* Center of Studies and of the periodical *Istina*. A member of various national and international organizations dedicated to Jewish-Christian relations and to the ecumenical dialogue, he has published several theological works in the field.

PROF. EMIL L. FACKENHEIM – Born in Germany, where he was ordained a rabbi in 1939, he was held for three months in the Sachsenhausen concentration camp. He reached Canada by way of Aberdeen, Scotland. After earning his doctorate in philosophy from the University of Toronto in 1945, he was a professor of philosophy there from 1948 until his retirement in 1983. Since that time he has taught as Visiting Professor at The Hebrew University in Jerusalem. For his notable contributions to philosophy and Judaism, Professor Fackenheim has received many awards, including five honorary doctorates. His current principal interest is the relationship between the Holocaust and the State of Israel, and of both to a future Judaism.

PROF. EVA FLEISCHNER – Born in Vienna, she completed her studies in the United States and Paris. A Catholic theologian, she was Professor of Religion at Montclair State University from 1972 to 1991. Since her retirement, she has continued to teach at various American colleges and is currently a lecturer at Marquette University. Professor Fleischner has been involved with the study and teaching of the *Shoah* since the late 1960s.

PROF. MAUREENA P. FRITZ, N.D.S. – Born in Melfort, Saskatchewan (Canada) and a member of the Congregation of Our Lady of Sion, she completed her graduate studies in the United States and Canada and later did post-doctoral work in Jerusalem. In 1990 she became a Full Professor at the University of St. Michael's College in Toronto where she remains on the faculty as a Professor Emerita. From 1986 until 1996 she served as faculty member and Executive Director of the English Language Sector of the Ratisbonne Institute in Jerusalem. She currently serves as President of the Bat Kol Institute in Jerusalem.

DR. MASSIMO GIULIANI – Born in Varese, Italy, he earned his degree in philosophy at the Catholic University of Milan. He entered the field of journalism in 1988 and, in 1993, moved to Israel where he undertook further studies at the Ratisbonne Center and received a Ph.D. at the Hebrew University. He participates frequently in meetings and conferences on Jewish-Christian relations both in the U.S. and abroad.

PROF. PETER J. HAAS – An ordained rabbi with a degree from Hebrew Union College, Professor Haas earned a doctorate in Religious Studies from Brown University. His 1988 work, *Morality after Auschwitz*, was listed as an outstanding book by *Choice*. He is presently on the faculty of Case Western Reserve University.

PROF. JEAN HALPÉRIN – Born in France, where he studied at the Sorbonne and the University of Lyons, he completed his studies at the University of Zurich. He is Professor Emeritus of Economic and Social History at the University of Zurich and currently teaches courses on Jewish thought at the University of Fribourg. A member of numerous organizations dedicated to Jewish-Christian dialogue, he is also the President of the Center of Jewish Studies at the University of Geneva.

DR. REMI E. HOECKMAN, O.P. – Born in Belgium and a member of the Dominican Order, Fr. Hoeckman studied in Louvain, Fribourg, and Geneva. He earned his Doctorate in Sacred Theology from Fribourg University where he specialized in Ecumenical Studies. He is a former Professor at the Theological Faculty of the Pontifical University of St. Thomas Aquinas in Rome. Since 1993 he has served as the Secretary of the Holy See's Commission for Religious Relations with the Jews.

PROF. IRENE KAJON – Born in Rome, she graduated in philosophy from the University of Rome "La Sapienza." Since 1981, Professor Kajon has held a research position in the Faculty of Letters and Philosophy of that university. She currently teaches the history of Jewish philosophy there. She has also taught for two year at the "Universidad Nacional Autonoma de Mexico." She has published widely on German and Italian Jewish thought of the 1800s and the relationship between Judaism and German philosophy in general.

DR. ETIENNE LEPICARD – Born in Grenoble (France), he earned a degree in medicine in Paris in 1986. He moved to Israel where, since 1990, he has been an assistant in the Medical History Division of The Hebrew University and the Hadassah Medical School of Ein Karem (Jerusalem). He is completing a doctoral dissertation in History, Philosophy, and Sociology of Sciences at The Hebrew University. His research is particularly concerned with problems relating to medical ethics.

DR. STEFANO LEVI DELLA TORRE – Born in Turin, he graduated from the Polytechnic Institute of Milan with a degree in architecture. He now works as a painter and teacher of design in that city. While in the 60s and 70s he was very active in the student movement, since the 80s he has turned to the study of Judaism under the influence of Haim Baharier. He was a member of the editorial board of the journal *Rassegna Mensile di Israel* and has published various articles of an exegetical, historical, and political nature in the field of Jewish Studies.

MICHAEL B. MCGARRY, C.S.P. – After studies in the United States, Canada, and Jerusalem, he was ordained a priest in 1975 and has held academic and pastoral posts at various institutions. From 19°˂ ˈ1993 he was the Rector of St. Paul's College in Washington, D. C. Fr. McGarry is a member of numerous ecumenical and Jewish-Christian organizations. He has recently been appointed Rector of the Tantur Ecumenical Center in Jerusalem.

PROF. DAVID MEGHNAGI – He is professor of clinical psychology at the Third University of Rome and is a member of the Italian Psychoanalytic Society and the Italian Society of Psychology of Religion. He has promoted and helped organize various meetings and congresses relating to psychoanalysis and Judaism. He currently coordinates a Research Unit on the Sociology of Judaism. He is a member of the editorial board of the review *Rassegna Mensile di Israel* and has published widely in this and other periodicals.

PROF. JOHANN BAPTIST METZ – Born in Auerbach (Germany), he did his early studies at Bamberg, Innsbruck, and Munich. Ordained a priest in 1954, he was professor of Fundamental Theology at the University of Münster from 1963 to 1993. Now a Professor Emeritus, he has continued teaching at the University of Vienna. As a member of numerous scholarly and ecumenical organizations, Fr. Metz has collaborated frequently on the publication of scholarly collections and periodicals. Until 1994 he was the Director of the Dogmatic Section for the international journal *Concilium*.

PROF. JOHN T. PAWLIKOWSKI, O.S.M. – A Servite priest, Fr. Pawlikowski is Professor of Social Ethics at Catholic Theological Union of Chicago. He has been a member of the Holocaust Memorial Council since 1980 and serves on several committees related to ecumenical affairs and Jewish-Christian relations. He has been a member of delegations, representing the Archdiocese of Chicago and the Holy See, in various dialogues and encounters designed to foster relations between Jews and Palestinians.

PROF. DIDIER POLLEFEYT – He teaches the theology of Jewish-Christian relations in the Faculty of Theology at the Catholic University of Louvain (Belgium). He also offers Religious Studies courses in the Faculties of Economics and of Arts. He does research on the *Shoah* and its theological and ethical implications in the Department of Moral Theology and has published extensively in this area.

PROF. ARMANDO RIGOBELLO – Born in Badia Polesine, Italy, he was Professor of Moral Philosophy at the University of Perugia and at the University of Rome "La Sapienza." Since 1982, he has taught moral philosophy at the University of Rome "Tor Vergata." From 1989 to 1992 he was president of the Italian Philosophical Society. His numerous publications have been devoted especially to the problems of the philosophy of Kant and the problem of transcendence.

PROF. JOSEPH SIEVERS – Born in Germany, he has studied at the University of Vienna and holds a Ph.D. in Ancient History/Jewish Studies from Columbia University. He has taught at Queens College, CUNY, and at Seton Hall University. Since 1991 he teaches history and literature of the Second Temple period at the Pontifical Biblical Institute in Rome. He is a member of the editorial board of *SIDIC* and of the *Journal for the Study of Judaism in the Persian, Hellenistic and Roman Period.*

Index